BECAUSE WE CAN CHANGE THE WORLD

Second Edition

This book is lovingly dedicated to Tyler Murray (1982–1996) and to everyone who fights to make sure that all children are surrounded by communities of support and caring.

BECAUSE WE CAN CHANGE THE WORLD

A PRACTICAL GUIDE TO BUILDING COOPERATIVE, INCLUSIVE CLASSROOM COMMUNITIES

Second Edition

Mara Sapon-Shevin

CORWIN
A SAGE Company

This book was previously published by: Pearson Education, Inc.

For information:

Corwin
A SAGE Company
2455 Teller Road
Thousand Oaks, California 91320
www.corwin.com

SAGE Ltd.
1 Oliver's Yard
55 City Road
London EC1Y 1SP
United Kingdom

SAGE Pvt. Ltd.
B 1/I 1 Mohan Cooperative Industrial Area
Mathura Road, New Delhi 110 044
India

SAGE Asia-Pacific Pte. Ltd.
33 Pekin Street #02-01
Far East Square
Singapore 048763

Printed in the United States of America

Library of Congress Cataloging-in-Publication Data

Sapon-Shevin, Mara.
Because we can change the world : a practical guide to building cooperative, inclusive classroom communities / Mara Sapon-Shevin. — 2nd ed.
    p. cm.
Includes bibliographical references and index.
ISBN 978-1-4129-7838-5 (pbk.)

    1. Classroom management—United States. 2. Classroom environment—United States. 3. Cooperation—Study and teaching—United States. I. Title.

LB3013.S26 2010   2010009466
373.1102—dc22

This book is printed on acid-free paper.

12   13   14   10   9   8   7   6   5   4   3   2

Acquisitions Editor:	Dan Alpert
Associate Editor:	Megan Bedell
Editorial Assistant:	Sarah Bartlett
Production Editor:	Veronica Stapleton
Copy Editors:	Codi Bowman and Adam Dunham
Typesetter:	C&M Digitals (P) Ltd.
Proofreader:	Wendy Jo Dymond
Indexer:	Molly Hall
Cover Designer:	Michael Dubowe

Contents

Because We Can Change the World: A Practical Guide to Building Cooperative, Inclusive Classroom Communities, Second Edition, http://www.corwin.com/changetheworld

Preface

"Metal mouth." "Faggot." "Retard." "Fatso." "We don't want you in our group."
"You're not my friend." "I hate kids like you."

Many people's memories of school include rejection, isolation, teasing, and exclusion. When you think about school, maybe you remember the groups you weren't permitted to join; the child who was "different" and teased unmercifully; or the private snickers and the not-so-private jokes about children who were poor, didn't have the "right" clothes, came from atypical families, or whose academic skills either lagged behind or were far ahead. For many children, schools are places of isolation and loneliness. Many children report that school is meant for other kids, that they "don't belong." Is this what schools have to be like? Are there other possibilities? Can we hold a different vision of classrooms? Of schools? Of the world?

When I wrote the first edition of this book, I was concerned about the many students for whom school wasn't a safe place but rather a site of struggle and rejection. I was concerned that an increasing focus on academics made many teachers feel that they didn't have the time, support, or skills to work on issues of classroom climate and peer interactions. The need to create different schools—compassionate, caring, and responsive ones—seemed essential then. Now, 10 years later, the world is different, and—for many children—it is not any better. The task now seems even more urgent.

Bullying and cyber-bullying have reached epidemic proportions. The level of violence in schools includes not only the day-to-day acts of aggression but also multiple school shootings that have left students and teachers dead and wounded and entire communities devastated and confused.

International events include the destruction of the World Trade Center on September 11, 2001, which left many people scared and increasing numbers of citizens endangered by racial and religious prejudice and fear. As I write this, wars are raging in several countries at once, and the United States is sharply divided about the road to peace. Growing economic and social challenges have left many people homeless, jobless, and impoverished, creating even bigger gaps between the haves and the have-nots.

Our schools are more diverse than ever, with students of color now representing nearly 50% of the school-age population. And yet, schools are more segregated than ever, with more than 70% of black students now attending predominantly minority schools and white students remaining the most segregated in their school settings. Although this growing diversity presents opportunities for great learning, it can also occasion prejudice and discrimination, making the need for anti-racist and anti-oppressive education even more critical.

The good news is that it is increasingly recognized that building a strong, cohesive classroom community is the foundation of a successful classroom. All students must feel

safe, respected, and valued to learn new skills. Fear, discomfort, and anxiety are fundamentally incompatible with the learning process and make teaching and learning difficult. Successful classrooms are those in which students feel supported in their learning,
willing to take risks, and challenged to become fully human with one another and open
to new possibilities.

The increasing heterogeneity of classrooms—through the movement to fully include
students with disabilities and other efforts to desegregate classrooms previously divided
by race, gender, or ethnicity—makes the need for classroom communities even more
salient. If we are to have classrooms that not only include students who are diverse in
many ways but also make them welcome, appreciated, and valued members of the classroom environment, we will have to set community building as a high priority.

And our vision need not end with the classroom. Within classroom communities, we
can help students acquire the attitudes and skills they will need to move beyond the borders of the classroom and school and into the broader community. It is often said that
schools are designed to "prepare students to function well in society." Although this is
certainly true, it is equally accurate that the students we teach today will shape the society
they (and we) live in tomorrow. The experiences that teachers structure for students can
enable them to act boldly in the world, taking individual and collective responsibility for
making things different and better. When we teach, we change our students, the world,
and ourselves.

Although most teachers receive instruction in how to teach reading, math, social studies, and science, there is often little preparation for understanding and shaping the social
climate of the classroom: what do I do when kids fight? What if some students have no
friends, and others seem isolated? Should children have to work with others if they don't
want to? What should I do about racial name calling?

Teachers often don't feel well prepared to deal with broader issues either: How can
I help students to feel powerful (instead of hopeless) in the face of racism, poverty, and
violence? How can I deal with challenging, even controversial, issues in ways that are
responsible and responsive? Can I help my students to envision and enact other possibilities in the face of unemployment, abuse, and intolerance?

This book is dedicated to teachers who are trying to make a difference in the lives
of their students and to teachers who want to make their classrooms warm, nurturing
environments for learning and who are looking for help and support in that endeavor.
Often, books for teachers can be characterized either as books of educational theory or
as how-to books. This book blends theory into practice in a way that helps teachers to
think more clearly about their practice and then to modify their practice in accord with
their best thinking.

It has been said that there is nothing more practical than good theory. It is also true
that we can learn theory from good practice. In trying new ideas, exploring challenging
directions, and implementing varying practices in our classrooms, we can begin to look
at and think about our students differently. Changing our practice can help to illuminate
our values and our beliefs about children, learning, schools, and society. As we change
concrete aspects of our classroom practice, we can move from the specific to the more
general, find connections among the things we do, seek congruence and harmony
between our beliefs and our day-to-day actions, and realize that everything we as teachers do can be linked to broader concepts and principles.

The response to the first edition of this book was overwhelmingly positive. Teachers,
administrators, and other school personnel appreciated the combination of research and
specific activities. Readers recognized my goal of combining a strong foundational basis

to school change with specific suggestions about "what to do now!" One reviewer wrote that the book "enchantingly blended theory and practice in a way that was extremely accessible" (Applebaum, 1999). Another reviewer described the book as "filled with gentleness and grace yet solidly based on research and practical information" (Review, 2000). The book has been used by teachers engaged in professional development as well as by undergraduate and graduate students working on teaching degrees and advanced credentials, including courses as diverse as classroom management, strategies of teaching, introduction to education, and language arts methods.

This book explores the many facets of community building and social change, and it provides practical strategies and ideas for creating and maintaining classrooms that support and nurture diversity and help students learn to act powerfully. The activities described are ones that can be implemented in a wide variety of classrooms with a minimum of materials or preparation. These are not quick-fix ideas; the activities presented here are seen as entry points into a deeper exploration of the components of classroom community; and they encourage teachers to build, modify, and expand based on their classrooms and experiences. My hope is that the combination of principles of community building coupled with descriptions of specific activities to implement in the classroom will give you, as a teacher, immediate access to new ways of thinking and behaving in your classroom.

This book is designed to be applicable to teachers who work with students from preschool through middle school; the ideas and activities are not limited to general-education or special-education classrooms but encourage cross-pollination and the development of inclusive, heterogeneous classrooms. The book focuses on all kinds of diversity: racial, ethnic, family, ability/disability, gender, and class; and, it combines principles—expressed without jargon—and guidelines with direct classroom applications.

The book begins with an elaboration of a *courage, inclusion, value, integrity, cooperation,* and *safety* (CIVICS) curriculum for schools, which is seen as a set of organizing values for creating caring, inclusive classrooms.

Subsequent chapters deal with various aspects of building community: Schools as Communities (Chapter 2), Sharing Ourselves With Others (Chapter 3), Knowing Others Well (Chapter 4), Places Where We All Belong (Chapter 5), Setting Goals and Giving and Getting Support (Chapter 6), Working Together to Learn (Chapter 7), and Speaking Truth and Acting Powerfully (Chapter 8).

Each chapter begins with stories—examples of classrooms or situations in which a particular aspect of community is present or absent. What, for example, does a classroom look like where children are provided opportunities to know others well? What does a class look like when those opportunities are not presented?

Following these examples, a brief vision statement is presented. What would it look like to have a classroom in which cooperation and connection are encouraged, for example? This vision goes beyond the stories that begin the chapter and includes illustrations concerning pedagogy, curriculum, and social relationships.

The vision statement is followed by an analysis of the challenges of impediments to this vision, including a brief exploration of situations, beliefs, myths, and practices, which have interfered with full implementation. For example, how have our experiences around competition and the ways in which classrooms are often structured kept us from seeing cooperation as a viable option or implementing cooperative structures?

New to this edition is a section titled Reframing Our Work, in Chapters 2 through 8, which provides an opportunity for readers to reflect on and analyze their experiences relative to each topic and how their classroom and schools measure up—a way of asking,

"How are we doing in this area?" This section can be used as a discussion guide to encourage reflective practice and can serve as a needs assessment, pointing the way toward next steps and goal setting.

The major section of each chapter consists of suggestions and examples for classroom practice related to the vision statement. Included in each chapter are specific community-building strategies or activities, cooperative games that support the concepts, songs related to the theme (music accessible through the book's Web site, http://www .corwin.com/changetheworld), children's literature titles that explore the area with suggestions for using such books, and ways of linking this vision to the ongoing curriculum in the class.

This book is written with great appreciation for classroom teachers everywhere who are nurturing the human beings in their care while holding to a strong vision of a just world. The title of this book *Because We Can Change the World* (and the book itself) constitutes a response to all those who assail teachers with the often despairing, sometimes disparaging, question, "Why would you want to be a teacher anyway?" This book is for teachers who know clearly that what they do in their classrooms makes the world a better place and for those teachers who need to be re-encouraged in their original vision. My belief is that teachers can and do make a difference in the lives of their students and deserve tremendous support for that task. I hope this book will continue to be part of that support.

Acknowledgments

Writing acknolwedgments for a book about community building, cooperation, social justice, and inclusion provides the opportunity to reflect on all the people who are part of my world now and part of my vision of yet a better world. There are so many people whose friendship and support give me glimpses of what the world is and can be if we recognize and embrace our interconnectedness. My vision has been crafted in community, and I am immensely grateful to those whose lives and commitments shape my own.

The Syracuse Community Choir, directed by Karen Mihalyi, is a singing group based on the principles of inclusion and cooperation. The choir's gift to the community and to me is its demonstration that all people can sing and have a right to be included; my own place in the choir is a constant reminder of what it means to be fully known and fully welcomed by a diverse group of people.

The People's Music Network for Songs of Freedom and Struggle and the Children's Music Network are two groups that also evidence the ways in which people can work and sing together to make the world more just. The lessons I have learned about supporting people of diverse abilities and creating a climate of welcome and acceptance inform all the work that I do.

My friends at the Syracuse Peace Council and Syracuse Cultural Workers never give up on making the world a better place, thus allowing me to remain hopeful and involved as well.

My Danskinetics (now Yoga Dance) community, led brilliantly by Megha Nancy Buttenheim, and my NIA community, tenderly nurtured by Pam LeBlanc, both provide me with places to move, grow, flow, and get my "ya-ya's" out.

I am particularly appreciative of the dedicated musicians and composers whose music enriches my book. Without their notes, my words would have no melody, and so I thank Bob Blue, Sarah Pirtle, Ruth Pelham, Phil and Hannah Hoose, Robin Smith, Susan Salidor, Joanne Hammil, Carol Johnson, Jan Nigro, Jenny and David Heitler-Klevans (and Ari and Jason), Nancy Schimmel, Bonnie Lockhart, Pam Donkin, Sally Rogers, Mayer Shevin, and Minnie O'Leary.

Two important members of my musical community have passed away between editions, and their important voices carry on through their legacies. Bob Blue, whose song "Courage" has become my trademark, never gave up on people and always thought that better things were possible. I miss him dearly and think of him constantly. Tom Hunter's piece "Mrs. Squires" provides a glimpse of a man who was warm and wise and consistently willing to take a stand.

All of the teachers mentioned in the text have provided hands-on, in-person examples of what it means to operationalize principles of community in the classroom. Without the stories these teachers have shared, my text would be far less rich and certainly less useful. In particular, I owe incredible gratitude to the four teachers with whom I have worked on a study of inclusion based on Vivian Paley's *You Can't Say You Can't Play*. Anne Dobbelaere, Kathy Goodman, Mary Mastin, and Cathleen Corrigan are teachers par excellence. Stepping into their classrooms, I was always reminded of why I wanted to be a teacher in the first place, and a part of me wishes I were small again so that I could join their class meetings and circle times as a recipient of their loving care. Sadly, Cathleen Corrigan passed away shortly before this book was completed. Her legacy of caring and concern remains forever with us, and her funeral, at which an entire community testified to the power and extent of her influence, was the final gift she left us.

Cathi Allen, Debbie Quick, Jose Cadillo, Diane Knott, Melissa McElroy-Elve, Sid Morrison, Jo Marie Vespi, Carolyn Messina-Yauchzy, Mary Schiltz, Lori Keevil, Barbara Sklolnick Rothenberg, Pam Johnson, Leslie Alexander, Midge Regier, and Lois Eddy all provided wonderful examples of caring, thoughtful teaching that are cited throughout the book. I also thank Tom Hunter and Jeff Tate, whose words of wisdom grace my text.

I owe great appreciation to the many students who have endured my passionate commitment to community building and full inclusion singing. The ways in which they have taken to heart my endless repetitions of "time spent building community is never wasted time" have provided me with insights, hope, and many new possibilities. My students at the University of North Dakota and Syracuse University have good-naturedly sung and played as we have built community, sharing their many gifts with the class. Particular appreciation is due to the students in my Strategies of Teaching class and the teachers in my Cooperative Classrooms, Inclusive Communities course, who have helped make community building an important part of all that we do together.

Much of the material in this book is drawn from my experiences teaching my class titled "Cooperative Classrooms, Inclusive Communities" and my course "Creating Safe and Peaceful Schools." Twice I have had the privilege of co-teaching with Sarah Pirtle, and she has enriched my thinking, my teaching, and my life through her commitment to justice and her generous heart.

Kim Rombach and Gayle Szuba, two superb teachers, both read early versions of this manuscript and provided helpful suggestions and much-needed support. Their confidence in me and this project sustained me during times of self-doubt.

Since the publication of the first edition of this book, hundreds of teachers have written to thank me for my work and tell me how they are using my book in their classrooms. I owe them all my deep appreciation; in many ways, I am only the chronicler of other people's work. I am lucky to hear about those who are so committed to children and education and all I can say is "keep those wonderful stories coming my way!"

Many other colleagues and friends have helped me to think about the meaning and practice of community building. I am extremely grateful to Leslie Alexander, Lee Bell, Nancy Schniedewind, Anna Snyder, Beth Blue Swadener, Lucille Zeph, Ellen Davidson, Linda Davern, Janet Duncan, Barbara Ayres, Mary Fisher, Debbie Staub, Barb Streibel, Lauri Pepe Bousquet, Alfie Kohn, David Johnson, Loydene Berg, Danelle Keith, Tim McConnell, Richard Villa, Spencer Kagan, Jay Klein, Marsha Forest, Jack Pearpoint, Bill Bigelow, Joseph Shedd, Bob Peterson, Joan Dalton, Bill Eyman, Ellen Barnes, Mimi Bloch, Robin Smith, Michael Dowd, Mark Ginsburg, Bill Ayers, Ann Monroe-Baillargeon, Celia Oyler, Paula Kluth, Suzanne SooHoo, Nick Meier, Melodie Hougard, Maureen Curtin, Sue Barter, Fiona Foley, Sharon Ryan, Ann and Johnny Baker, Mignon Lee-Warden, Belinda Epstein-Frish, Diane Swords, Peter Swords, Andy Mager, Cheri Caparelli, Steve Reiter, Annegret Schubert, Carrie Jefferson Smith, Kathy Hinchman, Jill Christian-Lynch, Rachel Brown, and Victoria Kohl for thoughtful challenges and compassionate support.

Naming this book was truly a community project. I spent many hours with friends trying to choose a title. Several hiking trips, many long car rides, and even a few canoe trips were spent brainstorming, considering, and rejecting ideas ranging from the boring to the silly. The final title—which I hope reflects the importance of teaching—was the product of many minds and hearts. Particular appreciation to Fran Maiuri, Jana Maiuri, Sarah Pirtle, Alfie Kohn, Bill Ayers, and Mayer Shevin for their active participation in the naming project.

Mayer Shevin, played several important roles in this book. He transcribed and notated all of the music for the first edition of the book and endured my seemingly endless corrections until it was "just right." His skills as a musician and a community builder are evident in the work he has done here.

My daughers Dalia Sapon-Shevin and Leora Sapon-Shevin are a critical part of all I do and all I know. Dalia uses her life to nurture others through art and food, and she is a consistent model of what it means to really "see" people and not treat them as invisible. Leora's gifts for healing and teaching are inspirational in their depth and breadth. Her tender heart makes me a better person.

Nancy Schimmel sings me soothing lullabies in times of need and knows how to make me laugh. Kari Klassen has looked out for me lovingly as I dived with sharks and ran from monkeys; she is always on my side. Emmi Schubert Reiter goes on waterslides with me and discusses and models risk taking and courage. Eli Marco Mager shows me what youthful passion (for basketball, bowling, Egypt, fire fighting, and the American Revolution) looks like.

Peppy (who doesn't know he is a Chihuahua) sat next to me as I wrote and edited and provided me with steady support and company. His nonjudgmental attitude toward my writing was helpful at difficult moments, and although I know he would like his name on the cover, this will have to suffice.

And my deepest appreciation to Karen. She has my back, my paw, and my heart, and she is fiercely in my corner at all times. Thank you for helping me learn to breathe into my life.

About the Author

Mara Sapon-Shevin is Professor of Inclusive Education in the Teaching and Leadership Department of the School of Education at Syracuse University. She teaches in the university's Inclusive Elementary and Special Education Teacher Education Program that prepares teachers for inclusive, heterogeneous classrooms. She frequently consults with districts that are attempting to move toward more-inclusive schools and to respond more positively to student diversity, providing workshops and support for teachers, students, parents, and administrators.

Mara presents frequently on inclusive education, cooperative learning, social justice education, differentiated instruction, friendship, community building, school reform, and teaching for diversity. She works with other educators and community members to design workshops and learning experiences to help participants build relationships across ethnic and racial groups and collaborate for friendship and peaceful coexistence. Mara can often be found leading conference groups in community building, singing, and dancing.

The author of over 150 books, book chapters, and articles, Mara is also the coauthor of a seven-session curriculum titled *Endracism/Endinjustice: Challenging Oppression, Building Allies* (with C.J. Smith, available from Syracuse University, 2004) designed for high school and college students. She is the coproducer of a DVD titled *And Nobody Said Anything: Uncomfortable Conversations About Diversity* (with R. Breyer, Syracuse University, 2005) that explores critical teaching incidents on social justice for faculty in colleges and universities.

Active in the community, Mara sings with the Syracuse Community Choir and is involved in the Children's Music Network. Her most recent book is *Widening the Circle: The Power of Inclusive Classrooms* (Beacon Press, 2007). Her other passions include dancing, quilting, scuba diving, and chocolate—some of which she tries to do at the same time!

Introduction

We often hear people say that we live in challenging times. Although this is true, there have no doubt been many periods in history when this was also said—and been equally true. It is hard to imagine anyone, particularly someone involved in the world of education, teaching, and children, who would say, "We live in easy, effortless times."

However, there are indeed some particular challenges that make education and teaching today difficult, and that also means that we have the potential to make a huge impact on the children we teach and the world they will create.

What we do in schools matters not only while students are there but also for the rest of their (and our) lives as well. Teaching matters. When I was struggling with a title for the first edition of this book, I tried to come up with a phrase that captured the enormity of the task of teaching and the importance of envisioning and working toward a collaborative vision. I sat around restaurant tables with friends and would say, "No one leaves the table until we have a title." But, invariably, with paper placemats scrawled with ideas, we would eventually go home, and the title remained elusive. We tried out many possibilities: "Many Stones Can Form an Arch" (rejected because it sounded like a book about architecture); "Many Voices, One Song" (did it sound too much like a music book?); "Together We Can Move Mountains" (powerful but too vague); "The Ocean Refuses No River" (evocative but fuzzy).

Finally, the title came to me: *Because We Can Change the World.* I was so thrilled—it felt just right, a title that evoked the fact that what we do in schools makes a difference in the wider world as well!

A disturbing conversation ensued with an editor, however. He called to say that the editorial board didn't understand the title. I was puzzled—it seemed quite clear to me. "Isn't the book about schools?" he asked. "Yes, of course," I responded. "Then shouldn't the book be called *Because We Can Change the Schools*?"

I explained then, and have repeatedly since that moment, that our work is important because it is by changing the *schools*—the education, learning, messages, beliefs, and understandings of our students—that we change the *world*. Having a wonderful year in kindergarten is obviously better than having a painful year there. And having a great sixth-grade class where students are kind and supportive is a fantastic goal for students at that age. But the bigger questions are "How does the schooling experience we provide for students when they are young shape the adults they will become?" "What kinds of human beings are we creating?" and "How will our choices and actions *now* help to form the people who will both inherit and create the world?"

What are some of the particular challenges we face now as we struggle to create schools that are welcoming and inclusive of all students? What gets in our way both individually and collectively as we try to envision classrooms, schools, and communities in which people are kind, caring, interdependent, and proactively engaged in working for social justice? How can we support one another in creating schools that model the best of what people can be with and for one another rather than re-creating societal flaws within our classrooms?

Because each challenge can also help us to articulate more clearly what we really want, it helps to look honestly and directly at what is hard.

VIOLENCE AND ILL TREATMENT ALL AROUND

The National Survey of Children's Exposure to Violence conducted in 2009 (Finkelhor, Turner, Ormrod, & Kracke, 2009) found that children are exposed to violence every day in their homes, schools, and communities. The study claims that more than 60% of the children surveyed were exposed to violence within the past year, either directly or indirectly. The researchers looked at different forms of violence, including assaults, bullying, sexual victimization, child maltreatment by an adult, and witnessed and indirect victimization.

Experienced teachers are painfully aware of how this violence is both reflected in their schools and affects children and community members. And many other forms of interpersonal violence are also reflected in our classrooms. A third-grade teacher decided to model her classroom-management program on the television show *Survivor*. Students were seated in rows, and at the end of each week, one student was voted off each row and had to sit in a special section of the room where they were denied recess privileges and other treats. What did students learn from this strategy—about who they are, who others are, and how they should treat classmates?

If our students watch television, what models do they have of people treating one another kindly and with compassion? Situation comedies are full of racial, sexual, and ethnic epithets and teasing, bullying, put-downs, and just plain meanness. I asked a group of college students whether they could recall a television show in which, for example, siblings treated each other lovingly; an excellent discussion ensued, and there were occasional memories of older siblings being supportive of younger ones, but most of the examples were of competition, rivalry, and ill treatment. I asked the group, "What would it be like to have a show in which one child came home from school upset and the other children rallied around him offering support, suggestions, and encouragement?" "It would be boring," they said. "Who would watch it?"

It must also be confusing to children to be told, "Use your words and not your fists," and "Violence isn't the solution," but then to watch endless hours of violence on television: wars, invasions, crime reports, and movies that glorify fighting and killing. How can they make sense of what they are learning, particularly when those messages seem to conflict?

Educator Linda Lantieri (1995), cofounder of the Resolving Conflict Creatively Program and coauthor of *Waging Peace in Our Schools*, describes the horrible events that took place at her alma mater, Thomas Jefferson High School in New York City:

> The students at Thomas Jefferson High School went home after the shootings that left one student dead and a teacher wounded, and a few nights later on their televisions they saw "Saturday Night Live" portray the scenes at their school in a comedy skit. For the producers of the program, there were no tears, funerals, or images of kids crying in teachers' arms. Yet most adults are confused and appalled when they see young people commit violent acts with no apparent remorse. (pp. 386–387)

Although the challenge is there, our classrooms provide us with opportunities to model, teach, and support different ways of interacting. In one teacher's classroom I visited, students shared each morning how they were feeling, giving both a number from 1 to 10 and a descriptor, "excellent," "sad," or "a little worried." I asked students what they did when they heard a classmate report a low number or an unhappy feeling. "We check in with them later in the day," they responded. "We ask if there's anything we can do to help." This protocol and its subsequent interactions didn't just happen; it was the result of a staff decision to change the social climate of the school and to do so on a daily basis.

All across the world, I have seen children be kind to one another. A first grader gently cradles the head of a classmate with cerebral palsy so that he can hear the story and see the pictures during rug time. Middle school students undertake a campaign to eliminate the phrase "that's so gay" from their school when they see how much pain it is causing. A sixth-grade boy gently rubs another boy's back after a lesson on peer massage and the benefits of touch during periods of stress and anger.

It is not hopeless, but it does take consistent effort and focus.

DROWNING IN TESTING

Challenges also come from within the educational field. We live in an era of high-stakes testing, increasingly narrowed and prescribed curricula, and the conflation of *accountability* with testing and of *high quality* with standardization. Many teachers feel that they are prevented from teaching how they know best, in ways that are responsive to the children in their classrooms. High-stakes testing makes culturally relevant teaching difficult because it doesn't take into account the particularities of different classrooms. A focus on academic achievement gets enacted in some schools as needing to push aside attention to the social-emotional climate of the schools, to how children treat one another, and to how they feel at school.

A teacher approaches me in tears; there had been repeated racial incidents on her school's playground, and she felt an urgent need to engage students in discussion and action related to creating safe schools and accepting communities. But when she brought this imperative to the school administrators, she was reminded that the statewide standardized tests were coming up soon and that there simply wasn't time to address these issues with students. She was told that she must concentrate exclusively on academic achievement so that the school would look good on the tests and not risk funding cuts or negative publicity. Her attempts to explain the relationship between students' sense of safety and belonging and achievement scores were dismissed as interesting but not compelling.

The diversity of students in today's schools and the ways in which poverty, racism, and violence creep—and sometimes stomp—into our classrooms presents a host of challenges for teachers. How do we create classroom climates that embody equity, social justice, inclusion, and diversity while still achieving high academic standards? How do we maintain our focus on democratic, child-centered education in the face of a system that tells us that test scores are all that matter and that there isn't enough time to pursue what are often labeled *soft* or secondary educational goals, such as classroom community or a commitment to ending racism and other oppressions?

A commitment to equity—to create the conditions that allow all children to experience success—does not mean that we create homogenizing classrooms that minimize or negate differences and simply deliver the same curriculum and pedagogy to every child in the name of *fairness*. *Fair* and *equitable* are not synonymous. Rather, working for equity requires more sophisticated teaching and differentiation strategies: we must teach in ways that are culturally relevant to each of the children in our classrooms; we must be able to provide the supports that each child requires to be successful and provide that support within a cohesive community rather than segregating and isolating individual students. And we must critically examine the societal inequities that make equitable schooling challenging. How equitable is it, for example, to fund schools according to property taxes, which results in some schools being rich in resources and others not having even basic supplies? How equitable is it that some children come to school hungry, cold, without having slept, and wearing inadequate clothing? Equitable schooling will require changes in how we "do" schooling at many levels: personal, institutional, and societal.

To some, making a commitment to social justice means that we must add a whole new program to an already overcrowded curriculum. In reality, however, there are *teachable moments* for social justice *everywhere,* and a teacher who is primed and committed to noticing and responding to such moments can infuse values about belonging, right treatment, and justice throughout the day. Consider, for example, what teaching opportunities are provided by the following situations:

- A fifth-grade boy draws swastikas on the paper of the only Jewish girl in the class.
- As they do their seatwork, students are pulling up the sides of their eyes to look Asian and chanting a rhyme about Japanese and Chinese people.
- A sixth grader is slammed against the locker in the hallway and told he is a "stupid little faggot" and he better watch where he walks.

All of these are real incidents, and no doubt, teachers can think of many more within their classrooms and schools. The challenge is to respond to these in productive, educative ways that help all of us move toward a more inclusive and diverse society rather than letting them go by, either because we don't notice them or because we feel inadequate to respond or too rushed to prioritize such efforts.

We need not choose between academic achievement and a positive school climate as though these were incompatible or antagonistic goals. Teacher Ellen Davidson teaches high-level mathematics by using problems and examples that are multicultural and linked to social justice issues (Schniedewind & Davidson, 2006); Bob Peterson (Au, Bigelow, & Karp, 2007; Bigelow & Peterson, 2002) involves his elementary school students in understanding how government works by encouraging them to learn about and immerse themselves in local political issues. A middle school teacher teaches letter writing by having students write to public officials about an issue of concern, learning to use their voices and their writing to make a difference.

Academic achievement and a strong community are both highly compatible and mutually interdependent. It is impossible for most students to achieve academically if they do not feel safe, supported, welcomed, and accepted. And it is hard to imagine that we could consider someone well educated if he or she couldn't interact comfortably with a wide range of people, resolve conflicts, and use his or her skills to analyze, understand, and engage with complex social and global issues. A strong classroom community is the foundation on which all of our work must rest.

The complexity of creating classrooms and schools that enable students to make a difference in the world cannot be denied. Teachers need incredible support for what they do. Perhaps teaching has never been harder than it is now. But this also means that good teaching, caring and loving classrooms, and inclusive and diverse schools have never been more important to our future.

1

CIVICS

An Agenda for Our Schools

What does it mean for a school or a classroom to be a community? What are the characteristics that define community, and what are the values that might be central organizing forces in those communities? And perhaps most significantly, why does it matter whether schools look like and feel like communities?

There is a growing recognition of the importance of developing respect for human dignity, for teaching students to be active participants—both in their education and in the community—and for beginning this important work at a young age. Creating classroom communities where students feel accepted and feel like they belong is not just about a feel-good curriculum. Rather, there are clear correlations between students' sense of belonging and their academic and social achievement.

In a review of the research on "Students' Need for Belonging in the School Community," Osterman (2000) found that the experience of belongingness is critical in an educational setting and that students' experience of acceptance influences multiple dimensions of their behavior and achievement in school. She also cautions that some schools adopt organizational practices that not only neglect but may actually undermine students' experiences of membership in a supportive community.

A study by Battistich, Schaps, and Wilson (2004), who are associated with the Child Development Project (CDP), found that students who had been part of their comprehensive elementary school intervention designed to reduce risk and increase resilience performed far better when they reached middle school. Students who had been part of the CDP were more engaged in and committed to school, were more prosocial, and engaged in fewer problem behaviors than comparison students during middle school. They also had higher academic performance.

Social studies education has come to mean not only teaching history and geography but also teaching about social justice in the broader context and interpersonal behavior at a direct level. In her book *Social Studies for Social Justice*, Rahima Wade (2007) argues that

Starting in kindergarten we must educate youth to care about humanity and to begin to understand the immensity of the challenges that will face them as adults. We must embark upon teaching them the skills and knowledge that will ultimately enable them not only to live productive and empowered lives but also to work alongside like-minded others for the betterment of those who suffer from oppression and other inequities. (pp. 1–2)

Educators are realizing that we need not dichotomize or choose between *teaching skills* and *teaching students to be caring and responsible human beings*. We need not sacrifice reading to teach sharing or abandon math goals in favor of teaching mutual support and help. Rather, the classroom community can be structured so that students learn reading *through* sharing and work on math goals *with* teacher and peer support.

And the growing focus on culturally relevant pedagogy and multicultural education also makes it clear that our sense of community must be expansive, inclusive rather than exclusive. We must teach our students to be members of multiple communities, fluent at moving between communities, and knowledgeable about a wide range of people and cultures.

I would like to revive an old word, a word that has fallen into disuse and ill repair. The word is *civics*. What is civics? Civics can be defined as those skills, attitudes, and beliefs needed to be a member of a community. Civics was a course that many people in previous generations took—it was a course about learning to become a useful citizen. Few schools offer courses in civics these days; for some, the word civics may even have negative connotations—as indoctrination into unquestioning obedience or mindless parroting of official rules and regulations. For many, the phrase "citizenship education" is equally narrow and limiting, implying that becoming a U.S. citizen, for example, means embracing particular values of Christianity or the dominant culture in ways that diminish or even destroy the histories and cultures of other groups. But what if we saw our task as preparing world citizens?

I would like to propose here that we adopt a new kind of civics curriculum, a civics curriculum that would help us to shape classrooms, schools, and a society that values community. Learning to be a part of that community is an essential, perhaps *the* essential, goal we should set for our students and ourselves.

In an article titled "Educating Global Citizens in a Diverse World," James Banks (2003a) argues that

Cultural, ethnic, racial, language, and religious diversity exist in most nations in the world. One of the challenges to diverse democratic nation-states is to provide opportunities for different groups to maintain aspects of their community cultures while at the same time building a nation in which these groups are structurally included and to which they feel allegiance. A delicate balance of diversity and unity should be an essential goal of democratic nation-states and of teaching and learning in a democratic society. (para. 1)

Banks (2003a) sees the goal as achieving a balance between unity and diversity and refuses to see these two objectives as antagonistic or incompatible. He feels strongly that

Because of growing ethnic, cultural, racial, language and religious diversity throughout the world, citizenship education needs to be changed in substantial ways to prepare students to function effectively in the 21st century. Citizens in this century need the knowledge, attitudes, and skills required to function in their cultural communities and beyond their cultural borders. . . . Students also need to acquire the knowledge and skills required to become effective citizens in the global community. (para. 4)

Because my focus is on teaching children to be part of community at many levels—the classroom, the school, the neighborhood, the nation, and the world—my civics curriculum looks different from previous civics courses that emphasized laws, governmental structures, and regulations. This civics curriculum is founded on six values that could inform our teaching, our curriculum, and our interactions with others. These values might run through the entire school community and beyond, guiding the behaviors of students, parents, teachers, and administrators. Each value is as important for the adults in a school as it is for the students; it is hard, for example, to ask students to be courageous if they do not see that behavior modeled by adults. It is not enough to make schools safe for students to learn if we cannot also make schools safe places for teachers to learn, to grow, to take risks, and to challenge themselves. The proliferation of programs on character education shows the growing recognition that teachers (and parents) teach values all the time by everything they do, regardless of their awareness of that agenda. Our goal is not to be value neutral. The relevant discussion is not about whether to teach values but which values to teach, how thoughtful we are about what we are teaching, and how these values should be selected and operationalized.

Within this new civics curriculum, civics can be represented as follows:

C ourage

I nclusion

V alue

I ntegrity

C ooperation

S afety

What would each of these principles look like if it were used as an organizing principle for our teaching and classroom communities?

COURAGE

Courage is one of those "soft" words we don't use much in education. To state that courage should be one of the defining values of our educational system is to push hard against a system that is more comfortable talking about accountability, effectiveness, and quality management systems. But if we are going to change our schools so that they serve *all* children within respectful, nurturing communities, then courage is what it will take.

A song by folksinger Linda Allen (2001) says, "Courage is the letting go of things familiar." Courage is what it takes when we leave behind something we know well and embrace (even tentatively) something unknown or frightening. Courage is what we need when we decide to do things differently. Perhaps we have always done ability grouping, but now, decide to leave it behind and embrace more heterogeneous ways of grouping students. Perhaps we have always segregated students with significant behavioral and learning challenges, and now, we decide to work toward more inclusive, integrated models of education. These changes required preparation, training, and support—yes—but they also require courage. Courage is recognizing that things familiar are not necessarily things that are right or inevitable. We mustn't mistake what is comfortable with what is possible.

An Australian teacher, Rosemary Williams (personal communication, 1995), describes what she does as "bungee teaching." She explains, "First you take the training, then you check the ropes, then you assemble your support team on the ground—but at some point, you have to jump." You can't wait to feel fully ready or prepared because you never will. We might identify our commitment to changing the ways schools respond to diverse learners as "bungee inclusion." We must, of course, make a plan, prepare ourselves, and gather information and resources. But at some point, we must decide that we will go ahead and do it, even though we don't feel ready, even though we are scared, insecure, and being asked to do something we have never done before.

What gets in the way of our acting courageously? The first obstacle is often fear. We are all scared of the unknown, of looking bad, and of failure or humiliation. Many of us have felt punished in the past for taking risks, making it difficult to break out of our molds and do things differently.

But there is much at stake. When we act in solidarity with others to change patterns of exclusion and isolation, we take a strong stand that goes far beyond our schools. The song "Courage" by Bob Blue (1990) makes this point eloquently.

Courage

A small thing once happened at school that brought up a question for me

And somehow it forced me to see the price that I pay to be cool

Diane is a girl that I know; she's strange like she doesn't belong

I don't mean to say that it's wrong, we don't like to be with her though

And so when we all made a plan, to have a big party at Sue's

Most kids at our school got the news, but no one invited Diane

The thing about Taft Junior High is secrets don't last very long

I acted like nothing was wrong when I saw Diane start to cry

I know you may think that I'm cruel, it doesn't make me very proud

I just went along with the crowd, it's sad, but you have to in school

You can't pick the friends you prefer, you fit in as well as you can

I couldn't be friends with Diane, or soon they would treat me like her

In one class at Taft Junior High we study what people have done

With gas chambers, bombers and guns in Auschwitz, Japan and My Lai

I don't understand all I learn; sometimes I just sit there and cry

The whole world stood idly by to watch as the innocent burned

Like robots obeying some rule, atrocities done by the mob

All innocents doing their job, and what was it for, was it cool?

The world was aware of this hell, but how many cried out in shame?

What heroes and who was to blame, a story that no one dared tell

I promise to do what I can to not let it happen again

To care for all women and men; I'll start by inviting Diane

Lyrics available at www.matchups.com/blue/courage.html

Many people can relate to this song because they were Diane, are the parent of Diane, have taught Diane, or remember the Diane from their school days. At an early childhood conference, I shared this song with a large audience. After my presentation, a woman approached me and said, "I just want you to know—I was Diane." And she burst into tears. The woman, now in her 40s, described how she had grown up rural and poor and had gone to school in clothes that did not meet the standards of her classmates. Her teacher, in an attempt to create community, had sat the children in a circle. But no one wanted to sit next to this "raggedy, country girl," and so the teacher had placed her in the center. This woman's pain, more than 30 years later, was still real and tangible. The hurts of rejection and of being left out, teased, or humiliated— unfortunately—are familiar to many people.

But there is another pain as well; the pain experienced by those of us who saw Diane, who saw another child rejected and teased, and didn't know what to do. This is the same pain we experience when we see a homeless person in the street or witness some other travesty of justice or fair play—the sense that something is wrong here, that something should be done, and, often, that we don't know what that something is. When we see another person rejected, isolated, or turned away, we can recognize that a blow to any member of the community is, in a way, a blow to the entire community. If we are a solid unit, a cohesive group, then we cannot tolerate mistreatment of any individual.

The song also allows us to see that it is within schools that most children first experience grouping, labeling, and the valuing and devaluing of individuals. It is in school that we learn who is of worth and value and who is beneath contempt. It is in school that we learn how to befriend and how to turn away. And those lessons, once learned, have tremendous implications for all aspects of our lives. But there is also good news: it is within schools that we can teach children to act in solidarity; we can teach children to have the courage to step away from the crowd or challenge the bullies if that crowd is hurting someone; we can allow children opportunities to take risks and to act courageously. It is within schools that we can teach children to have the courage to make a difference.

INCLUSION

What does *inclusion* mean? Inclusion means we all belong. Inclusion means not having to fight for a chance to be part of a classroom or school community. Inclusion means that all children are accepted. Although the concept of "all children" should be fairly self-evident, it is still difficult for many to grasp. "But, of course, you don't mean a child like Matthew?" someone will ask. Although children will require different levels of support and resources, the concept of inclusion means all children—all children, not just those who are clean or who have agreeable parents or who come to school ready to learn. *All* means all. Or to paraphrase a country-and-western song, "What part of all don't you understand?" (Perry & Smith, 1992).

Inclusion can be distinguished from earlier terms such as *mainstreaming* or *integration* by understanding what it means that there is a "presumption of inclusion." In other words, you don't have to earn your right to be included or struggle to maintain it. It is up to the teachers and administrators involved to make inclusion a viable possibility, not the responsibility of the children to prove that they are entitled to be educated with their peers.

What gets in the way of our acting inclusively? Unfortunately, many of us have been systematically taught patterns of exclusion, and some of us have even come to accept exclusion as inevitable or undesirable. Growing up, many of us were told that there simply wasn't enough time, success, room, or love for everyone and that some people had to be excluded. Those messages, once internalized, can be difficult to counteract (Sapon-Shevin, 2007).

The dangers of embracing a philosophy of exclusion go beyond the day-to-day hurts of not being invited to birthday parties or chosen from the team. In their most extreme forms, a philosophy of exclusion leads to the destruction of our communities.

An experience I had with exclusion was illuminating. In the summer of 1993, the Nazi Party announced that they would hold a march and rally near Syracuse, where I live. They announced that they had scheduled their march for Yom Kippur (the most sacred of Jewish holidays) and that the march would go from the Auburn town hall to Harriet Tubman Square (a landmark to the famous African-American abolitionist). For weeks, a small group of us met, trying to discern the appropriate response to such a demonstration of hatred and prejudice. There were some that favored doing nothing, arguing that the best way to discourage such behavior was to have it met by silence and lack of attention. But unfortunately, media attention had already created a situation in which the chances of nothing happening were small. It seemed inevitable that the event would be well attended (if only by onlookers) and that there would be considerable press and media coverage. The decision, finally, was to assemble a group, as a "visible presence" (as we called ourselves) and to hold signs that said, simply, "No." Another group of people appointed themselves peacekeepers and committed to maintaining the peace and keeping things from becoming violent. The period of planning for the march was a tense time for me. I was upset by the fact that there were Nazis marching, and as a Jewish woman, I felt particularly vulnerable and frightened. But my feelings were stirred even further by the fact that my then-14-year-old daughter, Dalia, wanted to be part of the demonstration. Part of me, as a parent, was proud that I had raised a child who was willing to take a stand, a child who went to 30 hours of meetings as well as 10 hours of nonviolence training over two weekends. And another part of me, of course, was terrified, frightened that I was somehow agreeing to let my precious child be somewhere she could get badly hurt. I wrestled with this through many sleepless nights and was only somewhat reassured by the many people who made personal pledges to look after her and keep her safe throughout the march.

But my biggest lesson came from my younger daughter Leora. Leora, at 11, was not coming to the march. We had decided that she would spend the day with Robin Smith, a friend of the family, attending synagogue with her in the morning. Because Leora worries a lot about the people she loves, we hadn't shared every detail of the march with her. Riding in the car two days before the march, I said to Leora, "I just want to tell you what's happening on Saturday: Papa, Dalia, and I are going to go to Auburn to march, and you are going to spend the day with Robin." Leora immediately began to cry. "Why are you crying?" I asked. "Because I'm scared," she responded. "What are you scared of?" I pushed. "I'm scared you'll get hurt," she replied.

I reassured her, as well as I could, that we were committed to nonviolence, that we would take every precaution, and that we would leave if the march became violent or difficult. Leora began to cry again. "Now what?" I asked. She looked at me plaintively. "Why are they doing this?" I took a deep breath. My experience has always been that when children ask a question, they want a real answer. They don't want research or statistics or an article to read; they want an immediate, simple answer. "Well," I ventured to say, "I think they are confused people who think that only white people should live and that anyone who is black or Jewish or gay or lesbian or disabled or an immigrant should-n't be allowed to live." She looked at me, paused for a moment, and then, shaking her head, offered, "Picky, aren't they!"

Leora's characterization of race hatred and a politics of violence and exclusion as "picky" is both laughable and yet completely on-target. When and where did those folks learn who was "in" and who was "out," who was acceptable and who was unacceptable? What were the school experiences of the young Nazis, and what did they learn? What are the risks of failing to teach children an inclusive response to difference?

Schools can become the places where we teach children to be inclusive, teach them to embrace differences as typical and acceptable, and encourage them to reach across categories and lines and labels to form friendships and strong relationships. Whatever lessons we teach young people, whether in kindergarten or third grade, shape their understandings beyond the walls of school.

Jowonio School in Syracuse, New York, recently celebrated its 40th anniversary. Jowonio (an Onondagan word that means "to set free") was the first school in the country to systematically include children who were labeled as "autistic" within regular classrooms with "typical" children. The administrators, teachers, parents, and students at Jowonio are solidly supportive of inclusive communities and of the importance of many kinds of children learning to play and work together. At the event organized to celebrate Jowonio's 25th anniversary, I offered this poem as a celebration of the gifts that Jowonio has given to the community and as my appreciation of the meaning of inclusive schooling.

What the Children of Jowonio Know

The children of Jowonio know—not because they have been told—but because they have lived it

That there is always room for everyone—in the circle and at snack time and on the playground—and even if they have to wiggle a little to get another body in and even if they have to find a new way to do it, they can figure it out—and so it might be reasonable to assume that there's enough room for everyone in the world

The children of Jowonio know—not because they have been told—but because they have lived it

That children come in an dazzling assortment of sizes, colors and shapes, big and little and all shades of brown and beige and pink, and some walk and some use wheelchairs but everyone gets around and that same is boring—and so it might be reasonable to assume that everyone in the world could be accepted for who they are

The children of Jowonio know—not because they have been told—but because they have lived it

That there are people who talk with their mouths and people who talk with their hands and people who talk by pointing and people who tell us all we need to know with their bodies if we only listen well—and so it might be reasonable to assume that all the people of the world could learn to talk to and listen to each other

The children of Jowonio know—not because they have been told—but because they have lived it

That we don't send people away because they're different or even because they're difficult, and that all people need support and that if people are hurting, we take the time to notice, and that words can build bridges and hugs can heal—and so it might be reasonable to assume that all the people on the planet could reach out to each other and heal the wounds and make a world fit for us all

VALUE

The third central organizing characteristic of our communities can be defined as value. What would it mean to not only believe but also act on the belief that all people are of value and everyone counts? What would it take to organize our schools so that we could really value every individual, for himself, without reference to the value of other individuals?

Two of the biggest obstacles to this kind of valuing are our predisposition to devalue people and our systematic instruction in ranking people according to set criterion. Many of us were raised with sometimes explicit and sometimes very subtle messages about who was good and who wasn't. From outright racist, homophobic, or anti-Semitic statements such as "You can't trust a Jew," or "Faggots are dangerous," or "Blacks aren't as good as whites," to more subtle messages about who we should or shouldn't play with, invite to our parties, or interact with, many of us were kept from seeing the value in all human beings.

At the same time, many of us were not allowed to value ourselves fully either. Ironically, when a four-year-old is thrilled with the picture she has drawn, pointing out the details of color and shading, we label that child as having "good self-esteem," but when a 44-year-old is pleased with what she has accomplished, we label that pride as "arrogance," "showing off," "snobbishness," or being "full of oneself." And if it is hard to be pleased with ourselves, our accomplishments, and our triumphs, it becomes increasingly hard to appreciate others. A child who has been told he or she is no good, lazy, and stupid is unlikely to be able to reach out to another child with warmth and acceptance.

Often, comparison with others also keeps us from taking pride in who we are. No matter how accomplished I am at something, someone has achieved more. I am thrilled with how I've decorated my new house, but surely there are people with nicer homes; I am now able to run 2 miles without stopping, but there are people (younger and older than I am) who run 10 miles a day effortlessly. We find ourselves making constant comparisons: "Well, I have a better job, but she has a better car; I have a bigger house, but her children are doing better." Constant devaluing and ranking and constantly looking at how we compare to others keeps any of us from feeling really pleased or accepting of ourselves or of others.

Unfortunately, our schools are structured so that we often focus most of our attention on what children cannot do, on their weaknesses or areas of need. This keeps us from seeing the whole child and narrows our lens of appreciation. A mother once told me about her daughter, who I'll call Jackie. Jackie was adopted as a young person and experienced a difficult early life. Now, at 10, reading was still elusive for her. But Jackie's gift was gymnastics. She excelled on the balance beam, did graceful backflips, and flowed on the parallel bars. This was where Jackie was affirmed and experienced a sense of success and belonging. The school, however, concerned about Jackie's failure to progress in reading, suggested to her mother that Jackie should quit gymnastics so she would have more time to work on her reading. Luckily for Jackie, her mother was a strong advocate for her child and gently told the well-meaning teachers that it made no sense to deprive Jackie of the one thing that made her feel good about herself to work on her weakness. And somewhat predictably, after several years during which Jackie felt better and better about herself as a person and a learner, she was better able to profit from reading instruction and learned to read. If her life had come to revolve around the one thing she was not good at, one wonders what might have happened, not only for her reading but also for her self-esteem and sense of herself as a valued and valuable human being.

How can we create classrooms where children learn to value and appreciate one another? At a recent workshop, I asked participants to bring in and share with a small group an object that was important to them. People brought and shared a variety of things: a shell, an old photograph, a childhood book, a stuffed animal, a plaque. I then asked each person to talk about one of the other people in their group, telling others not what that person had shared but what they had *learned about that person* from what they had shared. People's responses were profound: "I learned that relationships are very important to Sharon—she cares deeply about her friends"; "I learned that Steve loves nature and that he really notices the beauty around him." And perhaps most touchingly, this about a woman whose outward reserve could have been mistaken (without this exercise) for standoffishness or aloofness, "I learned that there's more to Mary than meets the eye. She really has a deep, spiritual side to her." Many people were quite moved during the sharing experience. The joy of being seen so clearly and so fully by relative strangers was overwhelmingly affirming.

My daughter Dalia invented a Thanksgiving ritual that we participate in each year. She gives each person enough little slips of paper for every other person at the table and asks them to write one thing they like or appreciate about each person. Little people who cannot write are encouraged to draw or dictate their messages. All the slips are put in a box, and the box is then passed around the table. Each person takes a turn drawing out a slip of paper and reading it: "I like Sharon's warmth and the way she reaches out to people." "I like the way Iman cares about his work and is committed to making a difference." "I like the way Lucy giggles when something is funny and makes everyone else giggle too." The slip of paper is then given to the person it is about.

This is a challenging task for some people because in addition to appreciating and valuing people you know very well (siblings, relatives), you must also notice things to appreciate about relative strangers who you may have only met hours before. It is also hard for some people to receive their appreciations—societal messages about not feeling good about oneself can make it difficult to say, "Yes, I do have a great sense of humor. Thanks for noticing." And yet I have never seen anyone who did not take these little slips of paper home, tucked in a purse or a shirt pocket. Many people have reported, years later, that they still have the slips pasted on their mirrors or on their desks.

We need to give all people multiple chances to show themselves fully and be seen by others. And we must give many opportunities for people to see others, notice things about them, and appreciate them. Rather than belittling people for craving approval, we can realize that all people want, need, and deserve appreciation, and we can help students and teachers find appropriate and systematic ways of receiving and giving such appreciation.

INTEGRITY

The second *I* in *civics* stands for integrity. Integrity means wholeness. What would it be like to be able to claim (or reclaim) all parts of yourself? What would our lives be like if there were no lies or secrets about who we really are, if we were able to show ourselves fully, knowing that we would be accepted in our complexity, acceptable even with our seeming contradictions and inevitable inadequacies?

One way of looking at this issue centers on how schools respond to differences. Are differences seen as something to be avoided, ignored, worked around, and minimized? Or as characteristics to be understood, valued, appreciated, supported, and celebrated?

When my daughter Dalia was almost three years old, my childcare situation fell apart suddenly, and I embarked on a quest to find a new day-care center. I visited one center that I really liked. The teachers seemed warm and supportive, and then, at the end of my visit, I sat down with the director. "There's something I haven't mentioned," I said. "Dalia is a vegetarian." "Oh, dear," exclaimed the director, "I don't think we could handle that. I mean we've never had a child like that before. That would mean explaining it to the kids, and their parents and the staff would have to make special accommodations, and I just don't think we could deal with that." Our interview ended rather abruptly. It was clear to me that this was not the place for my daughter. If this was how the director reacted, I could only imagine what discomfort and fear she would communicate to her staff and they to the students. How could my daughter be in such a setting and be comfortable with who she was?

So I went to the last day-care center on my list of possibilities, nervous now about the outcome of my search. This day-care center was lovely: tiny chairs and toilets, lots of parental involvement, and a strong commitment to diversity and inclusion. At the end of my visit, I nervously initiated the same conversation about Dalia and her eating requirements. "Oh, that's no problem," said this director. "We have Mohammed, who doesn't eat pork; and we have Rachel, who keeps kosher; and we have Justin, who is lactose intolerant. We just make it all part of our teaching curriculum with the children."

And so they did. Dalia's vegetarianism was well accepted and well understood by her classmates. She came home one day and told me, "Today, I explained to my friends why I don't eat Jell-O because gelatin is an animal product, and they didn't know that." And Dalia learned about other religions, other dietary requirements and customs, and about respecting differences. The children were not only accepting of one another, but also they were knowledgeable. It was not uncommon to hear children say, "Justin—you can't eat the yogurt because it's a dairy product, but we have some bananas you could eat," or to hear them brainstorming inclusive snacks: what could they make that all of them could eat?

The children, following the wonderful model of their teachers, evidenced not just acceptance of diversity but understanding and celebration. There are those who say that our goal should be teaching children to tolerate differences. Certainly, tolerance is better than hatred, prejudice, and active rejection. But I would like us to set our goals higher than tolerance. After all, how many of us want our friends to simply tolerate us? Don't we want enjoyment, appreciation, and depth of understanding?

Tom Hunter (n.d.), a children's songwriter, writes movingly about a teacher who saw and accepted him fully: Mrs. Squires (see Box 1.1).

BOX 1.1   MRS. SQUIRES

I don't remember a lot about third grade, but I do remember Mrs. Squires, and what I remember are not her lesson plans or unit themes. Nor do I have any recollection of her knowledge of Piaget, or whether she used math manipulatives. What I do remember are moments, and one in particular about two weeks after school started when she asked me to stay after school. I remember being afraid, because staying after school was supposed to mean you were in trouble. Right away, she said, "You're not in any trouble; I just want to talk with you."

To understand what followed, you need to know that I stuttered a lot when I was a child. I used to say, "stuttered badly," until someone helped me to realize I was good at it—better than any other kid in my class. That was small comfort at the time, but I did like the idea—I never stuttered badly; I stuttered a lot, and well.

In our empty classroom that day after school, Mrs. Squires told me, "I know people have ended sentences for you when you've had trouble talking, and I know teachers have said you didn't have to read out loud. In this class, I have a message for you—I will not end sentences for you, and you're going to have to read out loud when it comes your turn." She paused, and then said, "And we'll get through it together."

I don't remember any heavy drama in that moment. No lights flashed. No angel choirs sang— at least none I heard. What I do remember is the feeling that something significant had just happened. For one thing, she had wanted to talk with me alone like that. But there was something more too, some sense that I was learning something new and important.

When it came to my stuttering, every other grown-up I knew had tried to fix me, to make it all better. In a way, of course, that made sense—stuttering is not fun for the stutterer or the listener. It's natural enough to want to decrease the frustrations, understandable that people believe attempts to "make it all better" are kind and helpful. Mrs. Squires had a different message. Rather than "We'll make it all better," she said, "We're in this together."

The conversation that day after school wasn't long. I'm not sure I said anything, but I did get the message. It wasn't a verbal thing, really, though I do remember the words. It was an experience, something like being able to relax a little, maybe like a deep breath. It was a moment when someone paid attention to what was important to me, in a way that others hadn't.

The experience of having the realities of my life noticed deepened through that year with Mrs. Squires. I remember that when someone giggled during one of my longer speech blocks, she said there was no room in her classroom for that. I remember a couple of times when she found me at recess to tell me she was fascinated by what I was doing with my mouth. She never did end sentences for me. I did have to read out loud when it came my turn. And she was always there, sometimes walking across the room to stand quietly beside me when I had trouble reading or talking.

I don't know when it happened, really. It probably wasn't on any particular day I could identify, or at any particular time. But gradually, I became aware that Mrs. Squires stuttered, too. She wasn't as good at it as I was, but she did stutter. She'd pause at odd times to get a word out. Sometimes her mouth would twitch noticeably, or she'd briefly bounce on one sound or another until she said the word. I don't remember it as a big deal. It was just the way she talked, and it's probably why she was so interested in me. We shared something, a world of speech and sounds and fears that most people don't know about. She knew me in ways others didn't.

Not long ago, I was talking with a teacher friend of mine about how rare and difficult it is for teachers (and adults in general) to celebrate their own talents, to acknowledge what they are good at. She mentioned being good at singing, knitting, cooking, and telling stories. Then she said, "I think I'd also have to say I'm good at sadness." When I looked confused, she said she'd known a lot of sadness as a little girl, and more as a young woman. She had worked hard at coming to terms with it, and now, as a teacher, she's aware of how well she connects with children who themselves know sadness. She's good at it. Right away, I thought of children who need her as their teacher—children (in growing numbers) who know sadness well and simply need someone to share it with them.

(Continued)

(Continued)

I believe we all have our own versions of what that teacher said, experiences that make us good at something or other. I'm probably not as good at sadness as she is, nor am I as good at stuttering as I once was. I am good at creating situations in which people are listened to, situations in which children get to stutter out what's in them, or sit there and wonder for a long time, or have feelings and observations that they simply want acknowledged. I love it when we can get through it together. It's in my bones, carried with me from those moments when some one connected with me and what I knew.

Mrs. Squires connected well, and I'll always be grateful. But she's not the only one. It's what any teacher does when he or she understands the human interaction at the heart of good teaching. The lesson plans fade. The latest programs to raise test scores come and go. This "effective strategy" gives way to that one. What lasts are moments of connection. I believe we carry those moments with us forever, sometimes in fuzzy pieces of memory, sometimes in clear and detailed ones. Moments of connection make us feel we belong. Moments of connection open us up to learning.

I'm glad I got to see Mrs. Squires again, and to thank her. She smiled as she listened to me remember her from thirty-nine years ago. "I don't remember all of that," she said, "but I do remember some of it. We shared something pretty special." She stuttered a little as she said it.

How can we create schools in which the Mrs. Squires of the world flourish so that children can be accepted, loved, and taught for who they are?

COOPERATION

What would it be like if our classrooms and our teaching were based around a principle of cooperation, people working together to achieve a common goal, supporting and helping one another along the way? Unfortunately, few of us experienced schools or learning as a cooperative enterprise. More likely, we either worked in isolation from one another or were pitted against one another in competitive situations such as spelling bees, tracked reading groups, and so on. Because of our personal histories, we often think of competition as inevitable or even desirable.

Consider the following scenario, so familiar to many of us. The game is Musical Chairs. An adult is leading a group of children in the game. They are instructed to walk around the chairs to the music and then, when the music stops, to get in the chair nearest to them. The child who is left without a chair is out of the game and must go sit on the sidelines.

The children do as they are told. They move around the chairs to the music, eyeing the chairs and one another with nervous suspicion. When the music stops, they scramble for the chairs, knocking one another over and shoving others out of the way. One child who gets a chair yells to another child, who is approaching, "I was here first." Two children try to sit on the same chair, and the stronger child pushes the weaker child onto the floor.

One of the children who is pushed out of a chair and eliminated from the game goes over to the corner and starts to cry. A well-meaning adult approaches the child and says, "Come on, now it's just a game. You're not being a very good sport." When the game is over, one child is victorious—the last child left with a chair. All the other children have been eliminated. The adult leader smiles and asks the students, "Now wasn't that fun? Would you like to play again?"

What did we learn from playing this game? We learned that there aren't enough chairs to go around. We learned that pushing and shoving in the name of winning was acceptable behavior. We learned that it's all right to shove a child who is smaller, weaker, or who doesn't understand the game to win. We learned that other people are what stand in the way of our winning or being successful. And we learned that only some of us are smart, are capable, are good, are winners.

It is clear how this kind of competition is destructive to community. Our classmates become—not our allies and our support—but our enemies who must be conquered for us to be victorious.

But we could play, instead, Cooperative Musical Chairs. In this version of the game, children walk around the chairs to the music, and although there are fewer chairs than children, the goal is phrased, "Everyone must be on a chair for the group to win." So what happens? Children share chairs; they giggle; they sit on laps; they problem solve. "Someone hold on to LaDonna; she's falling off Michael's chair." "Quick, grab Eli; he can fit in over here." The goal is not to exclude, but to figure out, as a group, how everyone can be accommodated and included. As the number of chairs is reduced, the challenge increases, and children usually engage in extensive problem solving and negotiation to figure things out, certainly a higher-level cognitive skill than pushing classmates off chairs!

But competition isn't the only obstacle to our envisioning cooperation as our normative goal structure. Strong patterns of isolation and an unquestioned stress on *individual achievement* also make cooperation seem elusive or unrealistic as a goal. Often, when we accomplished something as a child—a Lego construction, a puzzle, a drawing—and brought our creation to an adult for comment and approval, there were two comments. First, "Oh, how nice," then followed swiftly by, "And did you do it all by yourself?" The message is clear: things accomplished alone are of higher value and more deserving of praise and appreciation than things accomplished in collaboration or cooperation with others. Teachers who discourage students from helping one another ("I want to know what you can do, not what your neighbor can do") and who see students erecting boundaries around their desks with textbooks are seeing some of the unfortunate but inevitable results of a focus on individualism and competition.

Structuring our schools and our classrooms cooperatively would mean looking closely at not just how we teach but also what we teach as well. Do we encourage students to find out about peaceful, collaborative responses to conflict, or do we study only the battles and the wars and ignore the peace in between? Do we actively teach students the skills they need to work together: listening, sharing materials, negotiating conflict, asking questions, and encouraging one another's participation and involvement?

Teachers are similarly affected by the goal structures set by administrators and other instructional leaders. Are teachers encouraged to share their ideas and materials, or are there prizes for the best teacher of the year, thus discouraging collaboration and interaction? Are teachers provided with opportunities to meet, talk, share, problem solve, and support one another? Are forms of teaching that entail cooperation—team teaching, cross-age groupings—encouraged and supported? The current focus on competitive merit pay for teachers and the publication of each school's test scores hardly encourage collaboration and mutual support.

Embracing cooperation as a guiding principle would mean believing the poster that says, "None of us is as smart as all of us" and enacting that belief in all aspects of our curriculum, pedagogy, and school organizational structures.

SAFETY

Safety is the last characteristic of our school communities. Many kinds of safety are required for children to learn. At the most basic level, there is physical safety. Children (and teachers) must be confident that they will not be hit, hurt, or physically abused in any way. In many schools, ensuring that basic kind of safety is a serious challenge. But physical safety is not enough. Safety also means emotional safety—the safety to be yourself, to be vulnerable, to ask for help, and to be warmly supported. It is physiologically impossible for people to learn when they are afraid. When you are standing on the ski slope, terrified that you will die, it is difficult to listen to and integrate instruction. And if you are terrified of failure or humiliation, you can't learn either.

When my daughter Dalia was in the seventh grade, just months after having started at a new school, she came home one day and announced, "Today at school, I learned to tell time." I was very surprised by her announcement. "But Dalia," I began, "you've known how to tell time since first grade!" "No," Dalia explained, "I never really understood it—didn't you ever realize that's why I have a digital watch? I've really been faking it for all these years." As the story unfolded, it seemed that Dalia had told several of her close friends at lunch that she didn't know how to tell time. Rather than responding with scorn or derision, they simply showed her how. Several things about this story are remarkable. First, they met her revelation with positiveness rather than scorn. Second, they then went on to teach her how. And perhaps important from a different angle, how easily people can learn when they are not expending their energy trying to cover up or get by, afraid that someone will find out about their weakness or deficiency.

Unfortunately, most of us do not feel safe enough to let others in on the places and ways in which we are struggling. In some school settings, it is impossible for the teachers themselves to ask for help and support without being stigmatized and scorned. Several years ago, a local first-grade teacher, Marie, was fired after her first year of teaching. The teachers' union became involved, and there was considerable community interest because firing was unusual in this district. When the full story was shared, one of the points made against this teacher was that four times during the year she had gone to the principal in tears.

Going to the principal in tears is not unusual for first-year teachers or for many other far more senior-level teachers, nor is struggling with your first teaching assignment. This young teacher felt overwhelmed by trying to implement a multilevel, multiple intelligence curriculum in her classroom as a first-year teacher. All such cases, of course, are complex; to fully assess the situation, we would want to know more about Marie's overall performance in the classroom and about her success with students. Certainly, students are entitled to be taught by thoughtful, stable, and effective teachers. But new teachers are also works in progress requiring nurturance and support. The principal's reaction could have taken many forms: "Why don't I take Mrs. Lopez's class for an afternoon—she does a lot of differentiated instruction—and she can come spend time with you," or "Why don't I take your class, and you can spend time in hers," or "Why don't I send you to this differentiated instruction conference that's coming up," or "Maybe we should set up a teacher study group on Wednesday morning before school—we can have coffee and doughnuts and talk about multilevel teaching." Any of these responses would have been helpful, supportive, and might have helped Marie to become a better teacher. But instead, the principal's response was to document Marie's fears and to make careful note of her feelings of inadequacy and lack of adequate preparation.

This is an example of a teacher not having the safety she needed to ask for help. In this case, she actually did ask for the help she needed, but the consequences of showing her vulnerability and needs were devastating. Teachers and students alike need the safety to take risks, the safety to show their vulnerability and the safety to grow. Without this kind of safety, teachers become narrow and defensive of their current practice, and students focus their energy on staying safe and looking good rather than on taking on new projects and stretching themselves.

Courage, inclusion, value, integrity, cooperation, and safety are all essential components of a healthy classroom community in which all students and their teachers can grow in an atmosphere of support and mutual help. The values identified in this chapter are important for teachers as well as for students. The challenge now is to operationalize these values in ways that seem doable—to take a characteristic and translate it into specific practices and procedures for the classroom. We do not want to reduce these values to the word of the week shared in an assembly or over the loudspeaker each month but not represented in any concrete way in classroom practices. Only by translating theory into practice can we reap the benefits of our desire and commitment to creating cooperative, inclusive classrooms.

2

Schools as Communities

Joshua, a first grader, has just been diagnosed with cancer. His teachers talk honestly with the other first graders throughout Joshua's treatment program, and the students write to him when he is in the hospital. The teachers organize a phone call system so that someone touches base, albeit briefly, with Joshua every day. When the radiation and chemotherapy he is receiving cause his hair to fall out, Joshua comes to school with a baseball cap. His classmates are understanding. Some days he is too weak to participate fully in classroom activities; classmates take turns sitting in the reading area with him looking at books. Joshua is encouraged to share his experiences and his fears openly with his classmates, and occasionally, the teacher or a student has cries; there are always tissues available.

Kyle is a sixth-grader in his neighborhood elementary school. Although Kyle has Down syndrome, he participates and learns fulltime in a regular classroom with support services. One day, after Kyle has gone through the lunch line with his tray, he approaches a table of students and asks to sit with them. They snicker and turn away. He approaches another table and is told to "scram" by one of the students there. He finally joins another table and deposits his tray. He realizes he has forgotten to get a straw and goes back to the lunch line to get one. When he returns, his tray has been moved to an empty table.

The first anecdote illustrates a strong, warm, and nurturing classroom community, a place in which Joshua is fully accepted, nurtured, and loved. His classroom is a place in which his strengths and his difficulties are shared with others who support him. The second anecdote evidences a lack of community—a situation in which there is no such acceptance, a place where differences are not valued or accepted but become the source of humiliation, ridicule, and rejection.

THE VISION

What makes a school or a classroom a community? Why does forming community matter? How can we create schools and classrooms that feel safe and nurturing? Think back on a time when you experienced a genuine sense of community. Maybe it was a play you were in during high school. With a group of other students, you rehearsed, worked on the set, struggled through setbacks and disasters, made jokes and laughed, and then, finally, put on the play, delighting in a shared triumph with new and old friends.

Maybe you remember a political campaign you worked on with others, going door to door, passing out leaflets, and attending meetings and strategy sessions. As you worked, you talked and got to know the others in the group. Sometimes, you had heated debates and argued, but often, you laughed and shared your ideas and your hopes for the future. You grew closer to the people you worked with and treasured the sense of connection you felt with them.

Or maybe you remember a camping trip with your church group or girl scouts or your family. You remember setting up the tents in the rain; everyone was crabby and wet. Building a fire together and cooking dinner, hanging the food in the tree away from the bears, and then telling ghost stories around the campfire—you remember it all. You remember how pleased you all were when the tent stayed up during the storm and how good the food tasted that you prepared and shared together. Closeness. Connection.

There are many kinds of communities. Some are intentional (when a group of people decide to work, live, or play together), and some occur by chance (four people end up spending hours cleaning up the school basement after a flood). Some communities last a long time; some are short-term or transient; each can be powerful. Feelings of connectedness, belonging, being a part of something larger than yourself—that's what community is all about.

What are the characteristics of a community, and what do these look like in schools?

Security

A nurturing community is a place where it is safe to be yourself. Think of the friends with whom you are the most relaxed—the ones who know you well and still like you—the ones to whom you can say anything and be heard. A safe, secure community allows for growth and exploration. In a safe community, it is possible to take risks, show people who you really are, ask for help and support, and delight in accomplishments. In a safe classroom, a child can share that he doesn't understand the math and know that his admission will be met with help and support rather than scorn and humiliation. In a safe classroom, a student can proudly show what she has accomplished, confident that classmates will be delighted, proud, and full of praise and admiration rather than envy or indifference.

Open Communication

In a cohesive community, there is open communication. People share freely what is happening, what they need, and what they worry about. In safe, accepting communities, people's individual differences and different needs are openly acknowledged, "Caitlin's eyes are that shape because she is from Korea." "Aryeh doesn't share other children's lunches because he keeps kosher and only eats certain foods." "Daniel uses a communication board to 'talk' because that's the easiest way for him to tell us what he's thinking." If there is a problem on the playground, students know that they will be able to talk about what happened. If a student is upset about something, there are ways to communicate that to the teacher and to classmates. Students and teacher alike know that it is all right to talk about anything of concern and problems are not swept under the rug. All forms of communication—oral, written, artistic, and nonverbal—are encouraged. Because *all* students in the classroom have a right to be safe, of course, if any particular student's behavior causes others to feel unsafe, this must be addressed as a community as well.

Mutual Liking

In supportive classroom communities, students are encouraged to know and like their classmates. Multiple opportunities are provided for students to connect with one another—partners for chores, peer reading, and group murals—and students are given many chances and strategies for learning to see and say nice things about classmates. When students share their stories, the teacher asks, "Let's hear three different people tell us what they liked about Jaquon's story." When a student is sad, the teacher asks volunteers to support that child. Students are not forced to be friends, but the entire classroom is structured so that students learn to see and appreciate their classmates well.

Shared Goals or Objectives

Cooperative communities are those in which students work together to reach a shared goal or objective. The whole class creates a mural for the hallway; students write, direct, and act in a class play that includes the effort and participation of each student. Children are encouraged to help one another with schoolwork as well as personal problems. The teacher sets class challenges: "If we can all get the floor picked up in the next five minutes, we'll have time for a chapter in the mystery I'm reading to you," or "We're having some problems figuring out the transportation for the field trip. Let's come up with some ideas about how we can make sure everyone has a ride and gets there on time." Students don't work *against* one another but *with* one another. Comparative evaluation is strenuously avoided, as are public displays of class status, such as star charts and achievement races. Students see their classmates as friends, allies, and coworkers rather than as competitors or enemies. There is a strong sense of *our class*, *our project*, *our story*, and *our goals*.

Connectedness and Trust

In well-developed communities, people feel they are a part of the whole. They know that they are needed, valued members of the group. They know they will be missed if they are not there. They know that others are depending on them to put forth their best effort. Trusting others in your classroom community means telling classmates the truth: "I'm having a bad day because I'm worried about my parents getting a divorce," or "I really don't understand how to conjugate verbs, and I'm frustrated." Trust also means asking others for help and support: "Could you eat with me today because I'm worried about that girl who's been calling me names at lunch?" or "Can you teach me how to play soccer so I can play with you guys during recess?" And trust and connectedness mean sharing the good things—knowing that your classmates will be thrilled that you finally passed the math test or excited that you're going to get to see your father this weekend.

Community matters not just because it feels good now. Community is important not just as a place where we feel connected and supported but as a solid base from which we move out into the world. Being a member of a community can help us understand that *together* we are better; *together* we are stronger. A song by Bev Grant says, "Together we can move mountains, alone we can't move at all" (Grant, B., 1974). Learning to be an effective community member in a classroom is a stepping-stone to being a productive member of other communities and other struggles. Students who say, "I've noticed a problem. I'm going to see if I can get some other people to help me think about what to do," can become citizens who say, "What can we do about the anti-Arab sentiment in our community?" or "We're organizing a recycling campaign to save the environment."

The focus of this book is primarily on creating classroom communities that will help *students* to feel safe and nurtured and become powerful and engaged, but it is also about what *teachers* need and deserve. It is very hard to ask teachers to create inclusive, support-ive, and cooperative classroom communities when they themselves do not feel valued and supported. Teachers who feel that they are "all alone" in their school, without allies or support, often find it difficult to sustain efforts to create classroom community. Every characteristic of community identified as important for students is equally important for teachers: safety, acknowledgment, mutual respect, and open communication. There is no better model for students than to see teachers supporting one another and helping one another. How powerful it is to hear one's teacher say, "I was really wrestling with some-thing, but I had a good talk with Mr. Dominguez down the hall, and he really helped me." Teachers and students can become part of a mutual support system that enriches multi-ple communities.

It is possible, of course, for people to form communities to exclude others or to work toward antidemocratic ends; forming community is not enough—we must always ask, "Community toward what end?" What can we hope to achieve by work-ing together in solidarity with others? This book is titled *Because We Can Change the World* because it addresses the ways in which what teachers do in their classrooms has an impact far beyond the purview of third grade or kindergarten. By giving students examples of other ways the world can work than they might have experienced before, teachers can actively affect the world students will envision and create. Students who have experienced extensive personal and structural violence in their lives can gain experiences with other ways to solve problem and support one another. Students whose experiences with diversity have been limited or negative can be taught new ways of thinking about and interacting with people who look, act, or sound different than they do. Safe, nurturing communities can be oases in a world seemingly over-come with violence and racism, but they can also be examples, proving grounds, and models of possibility and hope.

CHALLENGES TO THE VISION

If forming a community that evidences the characteristics described previously is so desirable, why is it so hard? If we can articulate the vision, what stands in the way?

Schools and society are structured in ways that make community formation difficult. Examining these barriers can help us understand the breadth of the task before us and can give us some new ways of addressing these impediments.

One of the characteristics of our society is diversity. People vary along hundreds of dimensions (size, age, skin color, religion, and so on). That diversity could be and should be enriching and exciting. Few of us would want to live in a world in which all people were identical. But unfortunately, two common societal responses to that diversity can be identified, each of which is a major barrier to the development of safe, nurturing communities. The first barrier is that of exclusion. Certain people (or certain groups) are not allowed to participate fully. Whether we are describing residential areas that do not welcome people of diverse races, clubs that do not include both sexes, or schools that do not welcome children with differences in physical appearance or cognitive skills, the message is the same: you can't come in, you aren't welcome here, and you don't fit.

The movement to include all children fully in typical classrooms (rather than place some children in more segregated settings) is an effort to redress some of the forms that exclusion has taken in schools. Policies and practices designed to promote racial integration stem from the same desire to create school communities that embrace diversity, welcome it, and celebrate it. As Johnetta Cole (2005) has said, "We are for difference: for respecting difference, for allowing difference, for encouraging difference, until difference no longer makes a difference" (para. 4)

Many of us, however, grew up with exclusion as part of our school experience. We were forced to accept the premise that not all people could work together or play together or learn together; many of us grew up with little experience with people who we perceived as different from ourselves. What toll did that exclusion take?

We never got a chance to know and feel safe with a wide range of people. Whether the people we were kept separate from were the elderly, Mexican Americans, children with disabilities, or the "opposite" sex, we were denied opportunities to know and enjoy large numbers of people.

We were taught to fear difference. Our isolation from people who were different often kept us from learning about other groups: What do people from Korea eat? Why do Jews have that little scroll on their door? Why does that man use his hands to talk instead of his voice? We were not well informed about difference, so it became something to fear. Often, if we asked a question about why someone was different, we were shushed, yelled at, or made to feel stupid. And that fear kept us from getting closer to people and learning about them. Isolation. Fear. Isolation. Fear. A vicious circle.

Our understanding of democracy and citizenship became distorted. Lack of interaction with a wide range of people and exposure to situations in which people of color, for example, or students with disabilities were systematically excluded was confusing in the face of what we were learning about democracy in America and the importance of each individual. How could we recite "with liberty and justice for all" and watch people of color excluded from full participation? If all people were equal, why are only certain students allowed to go to the special enrichment program?

We feared for our safety in the community. If we saw, for example, that a child who didn't speak English well had to leave our class (or was never a member of it and had to receive his instruction elsewhere), what message did we get about the value of difference? If a child in our class who was having a hard time emotionally and displaying distressed and distressing behaviors was removed to another school, what sense did we make of our secure place in the classroom?

Jeff Tate (n.d.), a parent from Texas, expressed it well in the kindergarten story in Box 2.1.

BOX 2.1   VOICE FROM THE KINDERGARTEN TABLE

I was sitting there, ya know, right where I always sit next to Eve and Josh and George Sapito (he has hair all the way down his back ya know). We all sit together at the same big table, all of us together.

Stefen sat at our table for a while. I mean he was with us ... all of us—Me, Eva, Josh, George Sapito (with the long hair) and, uh, Stefen, who was a cool spitter. We was always together. Our kindergarten table.

But ya know what? One day Stefen wasn't there anymore. He was just gone. I asked Mrs. Gillooly, "Where's my friend Stefen? Is he sick?"

"Yeah, where is he?" asked Eva and Josh and George Sapito (with the long hair down his back).

"Well," said Mrs. Gillooly, "Stefen does not belong here. He is too different and needs special help. He needs his own classroom with others who need help. Others like him."

"Oh," I said, "aren't we going to have a going away party for Stefen like we did for Marsha Materinski when she moved to San Francisco?"

"No," said Mrs. Gillooly.

"Will I be different soon and have to go to this special place?"

"I don't think so," said Mrs. Gillolly.

Ya know, I thought about all this stuff, and I guess my friend Stefen must of done some real bad stuff to go to this special place. Maybe he went there 'cause he didn't drink his milk last week at lunch. Yep. I bet that's it!

I told him to drink it. I told him to!

I told Eva and Josh and George about the milk. They said, "Yes, it must have been the milk that Stefen did not drink that made him go away to a special place."

We always drink our milk now.

And so far, me and Eva and Josh and George (with the long hair down his back) are still at our kindergarten table all the time.

I will always drink my milk, always. I promise.

The message about difference was alarming: children who are different are removed. What if they knew about me? What if they knew that my father is an alcoholic or that I have strange dreams at night or that I don't really understand the math at all? Would they remove me? How secure is my place in this classroom community? In this school? In this world?

It is difficult to form a community when children experience the exclusion of others or fear for their removal. It is difficult to ask for help if needing help will be perceived as a weakness and lead to exclusion. It is difficult to take the risks necessary for learning and personal growth in an atmosphere of fear. In fact, fear and learning are completely incompatible. Students must feel completely secure about their continuing place in their classroom community for them to relax, take risks, learn, and connect with others.

But including all students in a single setting is not sufficient for community development. In many schools and classrooms, another practice, so pervasive that it is difficult to examine, acts as a strong barrier to community. In many situations, the learning environment is structured competitively, and students are required to compete for what appear to be limited rewards or praise. Alfie Kohn (1986) has said that asking us to look critically at competition is like asking a fish to describe water—it has always been there, always surrounded us, and we tend to take its existence for granted, seem to believe that it is inevitable that people will interact in a framework of competition.

In the previous chapter, the game of Musical Chairs was identified as a powerful example of the ways in which children are often pitted against one another in classroom environments, are taught that to succeed they must be first, strongest, and best. But the damaging lessons of such experiences go beyond rewarding competition and aggressive behavior. What does this kind of competition and exclusion teach us about differences? What happens to the child, in Musical Chairs, who is slower, shorter, smaller, doesn't speak English, has cerebral palsy and moves with difficulty, or doesn't realize you are playing? That child is eliminated. Out of the game—usually first. What is the message? Differences are bad. Differences are a liability. People with differences will be excluded. And, perhaps worse, it's all right to use people's differences against them to win. Although we would never encourage a student to push a child with cerebral palsy, the game makes this acceptable behavior. And what about Marcos, who doesn't speak English well and was unfamiliar with the game? We need not explain it to him or help him in any way. His difference made him easy to eliminate.

In the cooperative version of the game, Cooperative Musical Chairs, children are also aware of one another's differences, but in a completely different way. If we know that Marcos doesn't speak English well, then we must figure out how to explain it to him and include him in the game. If Karen's cerebral palsy makes her move more awkwardly or tentatively, then we may have to offer physical support and encouragement for her to participate. We find out about one another's differences, not to *use them against others* but to help them. In a competitive situation, we find out people's weak spots so we can take advantage of them. In a cooperative structure, we find out about people's weaknesses and struggles so that we can support them better. If we want to create inclusive, safe communities in which all children feel valued and supported, then competition is a major barrier. What toll has a long history of competition taken on our abilities to be closely connected to others?

We view ourselves as never good enough or smart enough or worthy enough. Someone has always accomplished more or sooner, and we are taught to measure our success against others. I am finally able to run two miles and should be rejoicing in my improvement; instead, I am fixated on the people who run farther or faster. I am not able to feel fully proud of my accomplishment.

Our sense of safety is diminished. My junior high French teacher who sat students by their rank in class established an atmosphere in which every other student's success was a threat to my status; every other student's failure was in my best interest. I continually looked over my shoulder to see whether anyone was doing better than I was, always worried about my standing. The setting was hardly conducive to a sense of safety and connection! Actually, the atmosphere was not even conducive to my learning French with joy and ease.

We are discouraged from taking risks in our learning and growth. Because competitive environments are often linked to public shame and humiliation (being the first eliminated in the spelling bee, being last chosen for the softball team), we become much more cautious in what we will undertake. Sometimes we believe that if we can't be the best at something, there is little reason to do it. How many kindergartners who start out loving to draw are still drawing and painting in sixth grade? Most have been convinced that there are some kids who are good at art and that art is for people who are talented. Many have stopped trying. Think of the areas in which you have taken yourself out of the running: "I used to like to skate, but I was never very good at it," or "The music teacher told me to just move my lips in chorus because I was spoiling it for everyone else." There are many areas of participation and learning that have been lost to us because of the fear of failure—failure in a competitive system in which we weren't as good as someone else.

We learn to see others as obstacles to our success. As was obvious in the game of Musical Chairs, competition encourages us to see other people as in our way. Rather than seeing you as someone who could help me learn or could support me through my difficulties, you are what stands between me and the prize. The teacher announces that the first child to read 10 books will receive a prize. If I am a good reader and feel I have a chance at this prize, then the other good readers become my competition. No longer do we recommend books to one another or share favorite passages with one another; instead, we eye one another suspiciously and try to pace ourselves according to what others are doing. If a poorer reader, a slower reader, asks for our help, we are reluctant to take the time to give it because helping someone else might keep us from winning. Our classmates become enemies in the race for the prize; community is damaged.

We are encouraged to win at any cost. A competitive agenda makes winning the ultimate goal. We begin to focus not on learning, changing, or supporting others but on being the one to win. Cheating is endemic in competitive classrooms; if the goal is to read 10 books, I'll read the shortest easiest ones I can find. Or I'll read just the ends of the books or enough to report on but no more. I won't pick the long book I am really interested in if that will keep me from winning. Our personal commitment to learning is damaged and our relationships with others are distorted as well.

It becomes harder for us to see other people fully and to be supportive of their efforts. Because competition pits people against one another, we see people through the narrow lens of the particular area of the competition; I don't notice all the things you're good at, only whether you're a better or worse speller than I am—will I beat you, or will you beat me? I may not notice that you are a wonderful artist at all if that is not what we are competing in. And if we are competing in art and only one painting will be chosen for the display case, it becomes much less likely that I will take the time or have the inclination to notice and admire what you have drawn. Competition reduces people to narrow definitions and rankings, making it harder to see people as complex, multifaceted, and multitalented individuals.

If exclusion and competition are two of the major impediments to forming and maintaining inclusive, cooperative classroom communities, how can we structure our classrooms to promote caring, connection, trust, and safety?

REFRAMING OUR WORK

Even the most capable, dedicated teacher cannot make community happen overnight. Building communities takes time, patience, effort, skill, and dedication. And every community is different; the same strategy that worked wonderfully last year may crash and fail this time. Every group of students is unique, with individual challenges, strengths, obstacles, and joys. But teachers can notice what is happening in their classrooms and can ask themselves about each action, "How will this decision (about grading, about curriculum, about grouping) affect the sense of community in this classroom?" Teachers can become as intentional about community building as they are about their math curriculum or science unit.

The following questions are not meant as an evaluation but as a way of noticing and thinking about ourselves and our experiences, the current temperature of the classroom climate, and the bigger picture. If the answer to any of these questions is "I don't know," then further attention is needed—go out and look, ask, and investigate. If the answer to the question is not one that pleases you, ask, "How can I address this issue with my students? What could I do to create the conditions for students to respond differently to their classmates?"

Beginning With Ourselves

- When you were growing up, did school feel like a safe and welcoming place to be?
- What do you remember about how teachers and other adults treated you in school?
- Did you feel that you belonged in school?
- How well did you know your classmates, and how well did they know you?
- If you could go back and create a school that would have been perfect for you, what would it be like?

Looking at Our Classrooms and Schools

- **Will kids work with other kids?**

Could I, at this point, pair up any two students and have them work well together? Are there some students with whom no one will work? Do some students have only one friend or workmate? How willing are my students to interact with students who are different from them in some way (sex, race, ability, socioeconomic level, religion)?

- **When children need help, what do they do?**

When students are struggling with work, is there a way for them to get help without scorn or derision? Do students routinely ask other students for help? When a child needs help, does he or she say, "I'm stupid—I don't get it," or "Would someone please show me why the apostrophe goes after the *s*?" When children have done badly on a test or an assignment, do they rip up the paper or hide it, or do they turn to someone for help and support?

- **When children have an accomplishment, how do others respond?**

When it becomes public that a student has accomplished something—learned the multiplication table, drawn a wonderful picture, figured out how to wire the flashlight—what do other students say? Do they say, "Good for you, that's great," or "Big deal, I learned how to do that last week"? Are students able to appreciate that one child's accomplishment may be significant for him or her even though they themselves have already achieved mastery?

- **How would the children talk about or describe their classroom? Do the students feel ownership of their classroom?**

What kind of language would students use when talking about their room? Their classmates? What they're learning? Would they say, "We're learning . . ." or "In our class, we have this system or this program . . ."? If a visitor came to the room to be shown around, what would students identify as the significant aspects of the room or the class?

- **When a conflict arises in the classroom, what happens?**

When two children are having a disagreement or a fight, what happens? Do they always turn to the teacher for arbitration? Do they ever turn to other students or peers for help in mediation or conflict resolution? How do classmates react when two students are involved in a struggle? Do they stand around and cheer, or do they take active steps to help restore peace and a mutually acceptable solution? Is there any system of conflict resolution in place in the classroom, or do students think that the rules are unpredictable, unfairly enforced, or arbitrarily imposed?

- **Are there places/ways for students to bring up issues that are of concern? For the teacher to bring up issues of concern?**

Are students free to raise questions or concerns about the class: "We would like to discuss the way learning centers are being assigned," or "Could we make some changes in the homework policy to account for after-school sports?" If teachers have a concern, can they bring it up with the students: "I've been concerned about the name-calling I've been hearing in the halls, and I would like some ideas about what we could do about it." Who holds the power in the classroom, and how is authority and decision making shared? What are students learning about themselves as decision makers, thinkers, change agents, and learners?

These questions are only the beginning. Teachers can look around their classrooms and ask, for any particular activity or practice, "Does this bring students closer together or push them farther apart?" An awareness of this question and the importance of taking a stand for community are critical as we attempt to form classrooms that are nurturing and supportive.

Many teachers have found that, although they are extremely busy and don't feel they can take on one more thing, time spent building community is *never wasted time*. The benefits of classroom community—a sense of connectedness, trust, interresponsibility, and safety to take risks—are important in and of themselves. But establishing a strong classroom community also lays the groundwork for powerful academic growth, enabling teachers to work on students' reading, writing, and math skills in a classroom environment that supports students' acceptance of multilevel teaching, accommodations, and diversity.

What's the Big Picture?

There is a strong relationship between what students experience in school and the kinds of human beings they will become. School is where children learn some of their first and most important lessons about who they are and how they are connected to others. Thinking about these questions may help us make these connections and realize the importance of the work we do in schools:

- How do the lessons our students learn in school become life lessons, and what life lessons do we want them to learn?
- What would the world be like if all people saw themselves as full members of a global community?
- What experiences can we provide for students to help them become confident, skilled, and caring people?

HOW TO BEGIN

Perhaps it is the beginning of the school year, and you are trying to establish a positive class climate. Or maybe, it is midyear, and you have decided that your classroom community needs work. The following are some suggestions for things to do in the classroom. Think of each activity not as recipe but as an outline. Take from it what makes sense, modify it, and make it your own. Adapt. Modify. Be creative. Take the principle or the seed of the activity and make it fit your students and your classroom.

The activities in this book are all designed to promote active, experiential learning for students (and teachers). This kind of teaching may be challenging for those whose educational histories (as learners or teachers) included primarily large-group, teacher-talk instruction. Current research on teaching, however, supports the importance of involving students fully in the learning process, engaging as many of their modalities or intelligences as possible. As children move, sing, talk, and play, they are learning—often in ways that will stay with them far longer than a textbook lesson. If the activities described here are different from what you usually do, I would encourage you to move slowly and thoughtfully, at your pace (just as you would support students in learning something new). Perhaps you can find a colleague who would like to try some of these activities also and then compare notes. Maybe you and another teacher could combine your classes to try a cooperative game or activity together or to share a singing experience. Do as much or as little as feels comfortable to you, but push yourself and your students beyond the familiar as well. Students (and their parents) who are unfamiliar with more experiential ways of teaching may also wonder why you're singing or playing in school—what a wonderful opportunity to share with your student and their parents your beliefs about how children learn best and the importance of active, constructivist learning. Better yet, invite them into the classroom and let them experience some of the activities you are doing with their children. Enjoy!

A Brief Note on the Folk Process

The ways in which folk songs (songs of the people) are passed down from generation to generation and spread from group to group—often with changes in the tune or the words—is known as the *folk process.* Because folk music is typically transmitted informally (sung around the piano, shared at rallies and marches, passed—literally—by word of mouth), it is often difficult to definitely identify the author or composer of a specific piece. It is common to hear a performer introduce a song by saying, "I learned this song from Pete Seeger, who learned this song from a folk singer in North Carolina, who learned it from the coal miners in West Viriginia who sang it during their union strike." It is considered important, in the folk music community, to honor the legacy of a song and to name, as far as possible, the origins or source of the original melody or lyrics. Many of the ideas, games, and activities in this book have benefited from this same folk process, having been passed from workshop leader to teacher to professor to parent and on and on and back again. Wherever possible, I have tried to identify where I learned or read about the activity, but no doubt, some will see an activity here and say, "Oh, I learned that from so-and-so," or "I thought that was my idea!" Some of the ideas contained here I learned from students whose names I do not remember, others are ones that I have developed myself (or so I think) or have modified based on other examples or experiences. In truth, good ideas are hard to copyright precisely because their validity and instant applicability lead others to take ownership (in the positive sense of the word) and claim them as their own. So I thank all the teachers and students, named and unknown, who have shared ideas directly and indirectly for this project and encourage all readers to make their ideas theirs and share them widely as well.

ACTIVITIES

How can teachers build a sense of community—a class that is not just a group of people but a cohesive community with a shared identity?

Class Name or Theme

Instead of being just "Room 3" or "Mrs. Lansing's fifth grade," let students decide on a class name or theme. Kathy Goodman, a second-grade teacher at Ed Smith Elementary School, calls her classroom "The Helping Hands Classroom." The outside door has a wreath made up of the handprints (cut out of construction paper) of each class member. The class talks about what it means to give one another a *helping hand*, and there are frequent references throughout the day to "remember, we're the helping hands classroom."

Older students might elect a more mature label for their class. When I ask students to pick a name, I set only three rules: (1) everyone in the group must agree to the name, (2) the name cannot be a put-down of self or others—no "jerks" or "terminators"—and (3) the name cannot be competitively oriented—not "The Best Third Grade" or "The Losers." The process itself can be a powerful learning experience for students, as they discuss the power of language, images, and associations. Coming to a shared agreement requires that students listen well to one another and respect others' feelings.

Community Bulletin Boards

Rather than having bulletin boards that are teacher made or that display the work of only the five top students, create a classwide mural or bulletin board to which all students contribute, modeling that everyone is needed and can be a part of the project. One teacher created an underwater scene, and all students made things to go in the picture: fish, scuba divers, seaweed, treasure chests, and so on. All contributions were accepted and valued, and the diversity of colors, creations, and contributions made an exciting display.

Another way to create a classroom community display is for each student to contribute a self-portrait to a collage-like wall. Depending on the age and skill level of the students, these might be actual self-portraits (faces and bodies), or they might be written self-portraits—statements about who I am and what I care about. Students can also draw their personal coat of arms divided as follows.

Something I care about	Something I'm good at
Something I want to learn	Something about me people like

These can then all be joined into a solid block or pattern.

Class Meetings

Class meeting time, an opportunity for students to gather to talk and share, is a strategy that will appear frequently in this book. Regardless of the topic, providing a safe, respectful place for conversation and communication is always important. Some teachers set one or more regular weekly meeting times, often in a special place (on the rug—with desks cleared away from the middle of the room). Setting rules for the class meeting is very important. Some basic rules you might want to consider include the following.

Only one person talks at a time. It can be helpful to use a talking stick (or any object) that the speaker holds while speaking. When the speaker has finished talking and has passed the stick to the next person, this represents the end of his or her turn.

Everyone else listens. Respectful listening is very important. With very young children, you might want to discuss what this looks like (eye contact, quiet, and the like). Unless there is an agreed on way for people to indicate their support or agreement (silent hand waving, for example), it is expected that listeners will not interrupt, interject, or comment.

Everyone keeps confidentiality. This is a critical rule and requires extensive clarification. Students need to know that what they say in the circle will remain in the circle. Safety for group members requires that students feel free to say what they want or need to without fear that others will refer to it later. This rule will probably need to be revisited throughout the year, but it is a crucial aspect of creating a safe community. Although we tend to think about confidentiality as an issue only for older students or adults, even young children need to know that what they say will not be used against them. If Ben tells the class that he still wets the bed, he might be devastated to have that spoken about again or elsewhere unless he initiates it himself.

No put-downs of self or others. Refraining from making unkind or negative remarks about others can be framed fairly clearly for students—we don't say anything nasty or mean about other people in this class or about what they have shared. No "That's dumb," or "You're weird." Some teachers implement an "ouch" policy—if anyone says something that hurts someone's feeling, the hurt student says, "Ouch"—the student who said something can then be asked to rethink or possibly apologize for their statement. It is also possible to implement an "oops" rule—when a student or teacher says something that comes out wrong, (something we can all relate to), he can say, "Oops," immediately. This serves as a way of acknowledging publicly, "I didn't mean it to sound like that," or "That didn't come out the way I wanted it to." This is another important learning opportunity for both the speaker and the listeners. Breaking the habit of putting ourselves down can be hard. Teachers should model making positive statements about themselves and help students to stop engrained patterns of, for example, beginning statements with "I'm probably wrong about this," or "You're all going to think this is stupid," or "I know this is really dumb, but . . ." Teachers and class members can gently remind the student that there is a no put-down rule and can encourage the student to reframe their statement without putting themselves down. This is another important rule for building a safe community.

The teacher can set regular times for class meetings, and/or meetings can also be student-initiated (see Box 2.2). It is important to remember that class meetings are not a quick fix and that it takes time and multiple opportunities for students and teachers to learn to use class meeting time well, trusting one another and the process. The organization Responsive Classroom has an excellent Web site (http://www.responsiveclassroom.org/newsletter/search.html# Meeting) with many articles about how to make morning meetings meaningful for students. Teachers discuss how they sometimes have sharing on a specific theme, how they encourage a high level of discussion and questioning, and how they use morning meetings to talk about upsetting topics like war and death.

BOX 2.2

In Cathi Allen's third-grade class in Bountiful, Utah, there are frequent class meetings. Cathi says that the safety net to this process is the early establishment of agreed on rules that foster appreciation, mutual respect, attentive listening, and the honoring of confidentiality and the right to pass. Through brainstorming what a classroom looks, feels, and sounds like where one can feel safe and learn, the students quickly agree that the adopting of four or five simple classroom guide

(Continued)

(Continued)

lines that encourage the honoring of one another will facilitate that environment conducive to safety and learning. These guidelines then become a central focus of the community circle from Day 1 and throughout the year.

At a class meeting several weeks into the year, the impromptu topic is honoring the agreement at recess. As is customary, morning recess has just ended, and the students are finding a place in the circle as they enter the room. There seems to be a heated discussion going on among several of the students and a few have sad faces as they enter.

Mrs. Allen, sensing a need to bring the discussion to the group, throws out the following question to the circle: "Now that everyone has settled in, how are we doing with honoring our class rules outside of the classroom?" Several hands shoot into the air. Michael begins the discussion by stating that others make fun of him because he's not very good at soccer. He loves to play soccer, but isn't sure it's worth being taunted. As the discussion continues around the circle, some feel they're honoring the rules while others express the belief that they're *trying* hard even though they sometimes forget. A few let Michael know they're sorry others have made him feel bad and want him to know he can join them, where he'll be honored.

Then it's Nathan's turn. "Recess makes me sad because I don't have anyone to play with." Although the students have been actively honoring each speaker by listening carefully, an added sense of silence descends on the group. Nathan, who always honors others and treats them with respect and caring, has just touched their hearts. Nathan is quiet and shy; no one has noticed that often he was alone.

Spontaneous suggestions pour forth—some active solutions on the part of other students— "You can play with me. I'll save you a swing." "Me and my friends love to have anybody play. You can play with us. The more, the better!" Other suggestions are proactive on Nathan's part—"Sit by me at lunch, and we can go out together." "Hey, give me a wave when you see me outside, and I'll come get you to play." "Write down what you like to do, give it to me, and we'll make plans." All are spontaneously from the heart of students who have grown to honor and care about one another.

Cathleen Corrigan, a fourth-grade teacher, had a clipboard on the wall in her room. Whenever a student had an issue he would like discussed at class meeting, he wrote it on the clipboard. The student did not need to put his name next to the item if he didn't want to. This allowed students to generate the agenda for the meeting and still have the safety of not identifying with the problem. Students raised issues such as teasing on the playground, pencils being stolen, cliques, and other concerns. Sometimes, by the time the meeting occurred, students would report, "Oh, that's been taken care of." Knowing that their concerns would be taken seriously and that there was a forum for discussion was extremely important to having students own their classroom and feel powerful about creating a supportive community.

When teacher Debbie Quick taught fourth grade, she had daily class meetings with her fourth graders. They could bring up items directly or anonymously by writing them on a paper and depositing them in a box. She sometimes planted an issue that needed to be talked about. At one point, students were upset about a child (who has a disability) who was staring at them. Debbie put it in the box and, with the child's permission, discussed the staring. Kids found out that the girl was just trying to initiate friendship interactions, and then they brainstormed how to connect with her. She ended up with many friends.

GAMES

Why play games? Games are a traditional way of providing children with fun and represent activities generally chosen for their appeal to children. Games have general acceptance as a standard part of childhood programming. But games can also be examined as ways of structuring the environment for a brief period according to very specific rules. In most competitively structured games, it is not uncommon for the game to structure taunting or teasing (King of the Castle), grabbing or snatching in scarcity situations (Musical Chairs or Steal the Bacon), monopolizing or excluding other children (Keep Away), hitting or hurting others (Dodge Ball), or tricking others to eliminate them (Simon Says). By thoughtfully selecting cooperative games, teachers can provide students with opportunities to treat one another in prosocial, desirable ways (touching one another nicely, saying nice things to one another, or working actively to include all participants).

Cooperative Musical Chairs (Orlick, 1978)

The object of the game is to keep everyone in the game even though chairs are systematically removed. Start with one less chair than there are children. Play music and instruct the children to walk around the chairs, and when the music stops, everyone must be in a chair for the *group* to win. Sharing chairs, lap sitting, problem solving, and group support are all encouraged. After eight children have successfully shared seven chairs, one chair is removed so that eight children must now share six chairs. Continue removing chairs until all children are perched, snuggled, heaped, and combined on one or two chairs. Instead of chairs, you can use carpet squares or pieces of construction paper on the floor.

Musical Laps (Harrison, 1976)

This is another cooperative version of Musical Chairs. The whole group forms a circle all facing in one direction, close together, each with hands on the waist of the person ahead (looks like a closed train). When the music starts, everyone begins to walk forward. When the music stops, everyone sits down on the lap of the child behind them. If the whole group succeeds in sitting in laps without *anyone* falling to the floor, the *group* wins. If anyone falls down, gravity wins, and the group is encouraged to problem solve, strategize, and try again. This game typically doesn't work the first time through. Players are generally standing too far apart so that gaps develop and players don't each have a lap. The leader should resist the (strong) temptation to make the game work the first time. Rather, the players should all discuss the following: (1) What do you think happened this time? (2) What could we do differently next time to make it work?

After players have come up with a plan, they try again. When the group is finally successful, it is possible for everyone to extend their arms out to the side, and the whole group cheers. It is acceptable problem solving to place students carefully in the circle (i.e., so that a 150-pound student is not sitting on an 85-pound student).

Because staying up and supported is a group goal, arranging and rearranging for success becomes part of the learning from the game.

Extending Our Thinking

Both these games are alternatives to traditional music chairs in which pushing, shoving, and grabbing lead to success. In both games, there is a goal: keeping the circle together in laps or fitting everyone onto chairs. The obstacle is the task itself—how can all the people involved figure out how to overcome the obstacle? The obstacle is *not* other people. Musical laps can help students explore the importance of group problem solving. The game rarely works the first time—gravity usually wins. Even young children playing this game have been observed engaging in elaborate problem solving and hypothesis testing: "Let's each give each other a squeeze before we sit down." "Let's switch Karen and Jason so that Jason ends up sitting on Diante and not on Michelle." When the group finally succeeds, there is general rejoicing. An additional positive feature of this game is the fact that when the group collapses (usually with laughter and giggling), it cannot be identified as "Billy's fault"; because many children fall, it is usually clear that it is a problem for the whole group to solve.

People to People

Students stand with a partner. The leader (which can be a student) calls out, "Knee to knee." Both children must touch their knees together. "Elbow to elbow." "Thumb to thumb." "Foot to foot." After several calls, students move to another partner. Students can also form two circles—an inner circle and an outer circle—and when the caller says, "People to people," they shake hands with the person across from them and then move onto the next person (each person moving one step to the right). After several calls of "people to people," each followed by a handshake, the caller can name a body part or an article of clothing that must be touched ("Shoe to shoe," or "Shin to shin").

Touch Blue (Harrison, 1976)

Children stand in a group, and the leader calls out, "Touch blue," or "Touch watch," or "Touch nose." Each child must touch that object or color on another child. To complicate the game and further entangle the children, the instructions can be cumulative, "While still touching blue, now touch nose, and with your elbow, touch yellow." Children can take turns being the caller.

SONGS

Why sing? Singing together can be a wonderful way to build community. Unfortunately, many of us were told that we weren't singers and that only those with lovely voices and perfect pitch should sing. Singing with your class can be a perfect way to help students (and you) experience risk taking in a safe environment. Singing together is a highly cooperative activity, encouraging all children to have a voice and participate, creating a sound that no one person could make alone. Songs build community, producing a sense of harmony and unity. Songs with parts, such as rounds, teach coordination of effort and serve as a model for work in cooperative small groups or community meetings. It has been said that words speak to our minds but music to our hearts. Making a lovely sound together creates an experience to be cherished.

Song leader Nick Page (1995) offers the following reasons why "singing should be central to education and to life" (p. 141):

- Singing is our birthright. We are given ears and brains with which to listen and voices with which to make sounds. We are born into a universe in which harmony exists in all things. To sing and to make harmony is to become fully human (p. 142).
- Everyone who can hear can sing in tune. Openly solving children's out-of-tune singing problems shows that our problems can be solved—that we all have strengths and weaknesses, but with the work and support of others, most problems can be solved. Too many problems or differences are kept secret and hidden in the closet. Children get the wrong message when failure is seen as acceptable. Children see the correct message when they see teachers solving the problems of students in supportive ways. It gives every child the sense of confidence that if he or she has a problem, it too can be solved—the problem doesn't have to be treated as a hidden wound (pp. 142–143).
- Celebrating the diversity of music is essential for students because they learn that the power of music does not lie in its universal qualities but in its differences. Diversity brings power in nature, in culture, and in music (p. 144).

- When we sing together, our cooperation and interdependence become the perfect analogy for the interdependence and cooperation within nature. Children singing together are learning how to cooperate—literally how to live in harmony with one another (pp. 17–18).

There are many ways to bring music and singing into your classroom. Several Web sites are excellent sources of children's music, particularly the site of the Children's Music Network, which is committed to music that honors diversity, builds community, and helps give children positive messages about themselves, others, and the earth. Look at www.cmnonline.org particularly the songs under the section "Peace Resources." If you are not a singer, there are numerous CDs and DVDs of children's music you can use, and the Web is now an excellent source of music as well. All of the songs included here are linked from the Web site www.corwin.com/changetheworld. You can use the shared sites to learn the song yourself or, perhaps, to share it directly with your students (after you've seen it, of course).

"Love Grows One by One" (Johnson, 1981)

"Love Grows One by One" is one of my favorite songs to teach; the chorus to the song can be taught in sign language, and then the whole class can sing and sign along. The song talks about building community, one person at a time; growing; and expanding.

Rounds

Rounds (songs in which one group starts the song and another group or groups join in singing the same song only starting later) are a wonderful way to make a rich, exciting sound with minimal musical knowledge.

"Make New Friends" (Traditional Round)

This is a wonderful song about making new friends and keeping old ones as well. The teacher might want to discuss how we make and keep friends.

The three rounds listed below can be sung simultaneously (called partner songs). They sound wonderful together and provide a rich musical experience.

- "Frére Jacques" (Traditional French song)
- "Row, Row, Row Your Boat" (Traditional round)
- "Three Kind (Blind) Mice" (Traditional round, new words)

"Music Alone Shall Live" and "Let Us Sing Together" (traditional songs) are two more wonderful songs for teaching (and experiencing) community building.

CHILDREN'S LITERATURE

Why use books? Children's books provide many opportunities for encouraging the development of community. First, listening to a story together can build a shared experience within a group. It provides a common text to students who may have very disparate reading levels. Second, children's literature that deals directly with issues of friendship, inclusion, cooperation, and sharing can be used to model and teach appropriate skills in very accessible and nonthreatening ways. Class discussions about the book can help students generalize from the book to their experience or classroom: "How do you think Tom felt in the story when the other children told him he couldn't play?" "Has that ever happened to you?" "What was it that made Amos and Boris such good friends?" "What do you do to be a good friend to someone in our class?" Because most children enjoy story time and reading, and because many teachers already include a story or reading assignments in their daily activities, carefully selected children's books can become an important part of building the classroom community.

On the Town: A Community Adventure (Caseley, 2002)

Charlie's class is studying community. The teacher tells the class, "A community is a group of people who live or work in the same area or who have something in common with one another." Armed with their black notebooks, the children set out to explore their community and talk to people. Charlie interacts with the police officer; the barber; the garbage collector; and people at the bank, the fire station, and the pharmacy.

The neighborhood is diverse and could be a good way to begin discussing all the people who live in a community and are necessary to its smooth functioning. The book could also be used to talk about classroom communities and different roles and responsibilities. The teacher might lead students in a discussion of community rules: What do we have to agree on for our classroom to function smoothly?

There are many wonderful books about friendship, and this can be a valuable way to begin discussing how children interact in the classroom.

The Brand New Kid (Couric, 2000)

Katie Couric (2000) introduces this book by saying that "kindness can be taught, and perhaps we can all do a better job helping our children learn about tolerance and inclusion."

When second grade begins, there is a new boy named Lazlo S. Gasky. He is new to the school and the community. The children tease him, exclude him, and treat him very badly. "So these first weeks were lonely for this brand new kid. They made fun of him, all that he said and he did. So he kept his head bowed and stopped trying to please and simply prepared for the next taunt and tease."

But when Ellie sees Lazlo's mother who is crying and distraught about how her son isn't fitting in at school, she breaks the barrier and invites Lazlo to play. They have a good time together playing chess, and the next day, when the other kids continue to tease him, Ellie stands up to them and tells them they should get to know him.

This is an excellent book not only about friendship but also about being an ally when someone is being picked on (more on this in Chapters 5 and 8). Ellie breaks away from the crowd and initiates a friendship and connection with the new kid. When have you done that? What stands in the way of your doing that? How do our relationships in this class affect the overall?

Kindness Is Cooler, Mrs. Ruler (Cuyler, 2007)

When Mrs. Ruler sees some of her kindergarten students being unkind to one another, she keeps five of them in from recess and teaches them that "kinder is cooler" and challenges each of them to do five kind deeds for their families during the week, which they will report at show-and-tell.

The good deeds for family members grow to include good deeds in school—all of which are documented by hearts on the wall. Then they expand to include all of the children and acts of community kindness as well. Even David, a boy who has trouble getting started, gets into being kind and excels.

This book could easily be part of a class project, with acts of kindness written on individual hearts and used to decorate the classroom. This could also be used to report others positive acts in the community and the wider world.

Friends! (Scott, 2000)

This is a picture book for young children about making friends—the book shows kids playing together—skating, building with Legos, reading books, doing gymnastics. It asks questions: What new things have you learned from your friends? Are you friends with both boys and girls? (Boys bake cookies; children are of different races.) Have you ever included a new person in your group of friends? How would you feel if a friend told your secret? The book deals directly with issues of exclusion and cheating—friends asking you to do things you shouldn't (copy your paper). A note at the end of the book poses questions about exclusion and bullying in the context of friendship.

Not only could students read and discuss this book, but also they could add other questions and conduct their own surveys. With older students, the questions can be more sophisticated and student generated.

Amos and Boris (Steig, 2009)

Amos the mouse and Boris the whale are a devoted pair of friends. Not just despite their differences but because of them, they are able to help each other and find deep connection and friendship.

These books are wonderful ways to begin a discussion of friendship with students. What do friends do to help one another? What are some ways in which people who are quite different can interact and support one another? Teachers might want to engage students in creative writing or drawing about friends: make a picture of you and a friend doing something and tell us why you value that person. Write a story about a time when you were a good friend to someone and how you felt about it.

Two Good Friends (Delton, 1974)

This book is about Bear and Duck who are good friends, although they are very different. Duck is a meticulous housekeeper with a home that is always clean and neat, but he often has no food in the house. Bear, on the other hand, is an excellent cook but a terrible housekeeper, and his house is always dirty. After some initial difficulties in reconciling their differences, they reach a perfect solution: Duck cleans Bear's house for him, and Bear bakes delicious things for Duck to eat.

Teachers can use this book and others like it to begin a discussion of the tremendous variations in talents and skills of class members and the ways in which they can help and support one another. If Bill is wonderful at jump rope but has trouble remembering things (like his homework), perhaps he could give other students jump-rope lessons and someone else could remind him to take his books home every day after school.

LINKS TO THE CURRICULUM

In this era of high-stakes testing and ongoing assessment, it is important to see how every aspect of community building and social-justice teaching described in this book can be directly linked to national and state curriculum standards. Teachers need not sacrifice what they believe to be important content; rather, they can implement activities and curriculum in ways that can be directly linked to required standards. Or said another way, they can meet state and national standards by engaging in teaching and learning activities they find meaningful for students. It is possible to link all the activities, songs, children's literature, and goals in each chapter of this book to standards in the areas of language arts, social studies, and mathematics.

The standards of The National Council of Teachers of English (1998–2010) include the following:

1. Students read a wide range of print and nonprint texts to build an understanding of texts, of themselves, and of the cultures of the United States and the world; to acquire new information; to respond to the needs and demands of society and the workplace; and for personal fulfillment. Among these texts are fiction and nonfiction, classic and contemporary works.

2. Students read a wide range of literature from many periods in many genres to build an understanding of the many dimensions (e.g., philosophical, ethical, aesthetic) of human experience.

3. Students apply a wide range of strategies to comprehend, interpret, evaluate, and appreciate texts. They draw on their prior experience, their interactions with other readers and writers, their knowledge of word meaning and of other texts, their word identification strategies, and their understanding of textual features (e.g., sound-letter correspondence, sentence structure, context, graphics).

4. Students adjust their use of spoken, written, and visual language (e.g., conventions, style, vocabulary) to communicate effectively with a variety of audiences and for different purposes.

5. Students employ a wide range of strategies as they write and use different writing process elements appropriately to communicate with different audiences for a variety of purposes.

6. Students apply knowledge of language structure, language conventions (e.g., spelling and punctuation), media techniques, figurative language, and genre to create, critique, and discuss print and nonprint texts.

7. Students conduct research on issues and interests by generating ideas and questions, and by posing problems. They gather, evaluate, and synthesize data from a variety of sources (e.g., print and nonprint texts, artifacts, people) to communicate their discoveries in ways that suit their purpose and audience.

8. Students use a variety of technological and information resources (e.g., libraries, databases, computer networks, video) to gather and synthesize information and to create and communicate knowledge.

9. Students develop an understanding of and respect for diversity in language use, patterns, and dialects across cultures, ethnic groups, geographic regions, and social roles.

10. Students whose first language is not English make use of their first language to develop competence in the English language arts and to develop understanding of content across the curriculum.

11. Students participate as knowledgeable, reflective, creative, and critical members of a variety of literacy communities.

12. Students use spoken, written, and visual language to accomplish their own purposes (e.g., for learning, enjoyment, persuasion, and the exchange of information). (para. 8–19)

Each of these standards can be incorporated by having students read, write, and talk about the content in each chapter. For example, students can meet the standard of learning to write for different audiences (Standard 5) by writing letters to school officials, community members, and national leaders about issues of concern to them. Students can meet Standard 2 (about reading texts from different periods) to examine how a particular issue was addressed or described across time; how, for example, were children with disabilities included in texts or referred to in literature? Learning to respect diversity in language forms and patterns (Standard 9) can be addressed by reading children's books that are written in dialect, exploring how different people communicate and the power and beauty of different language forms.

One of the important goals of building an inclusive, cooperative classroom community is that students will learn the skills and attitudes that will help them strive for and build communities outside of schools. Learning to be a citizen in a democratic system requires learning to live in a community; taking responsibility for yourself as well as being responsible to others and learning to communicate, problem solve, and negotiate across differences and conflicts. The activities and curriculum in each chapter can be directly linked to the topics set forth by the National Council of Social Studies (n.d.). These include the following.

1. Culture

2. Time, Continuity, and Change

3. People, Places, and Environments

4. Individual Development and Identity

5. Individuals, Groups, and Institutions

6. Power, Authority, and Governance

7. Production, Distribution, and Consumption

8. Science, Technology, and Society

9. Global Connections

10. Civic Ideals and Practices

Each of these has learning standards directly related to the content of this book. For example, the goals in culture and cultural diversity are justified as follows:

> In a democratic and culturally diverse society, students need to comprehend multiple perspectives that emerge from within their own culture and from the vantage points of the diverse cultural groups within that society. These understandings allow them to make sense of the actions, ideas, and products of others as well as to relate to and interact with people within their diverse society and throughout the world. . . . The challenge of all people is, wherever and whenever possible, to consider the strengths and advantages that this diversity offers to the society in general, and to their own growth as a human being in particular. This consideration is especially important in societies that value human rights, the principles of democracy and equity, and the notion that individuals should act to promote the public good. (National Council of Social Studies, 2002, p. 19)

This rationale is then translated into learner objectives, such as the following:

- Have learners interpret patterns of behavior as reflecting values and attitudes that contribute to or pose obstacles to cross-cultural understanding

- Guide learners in constructing reasoned judgments about specific cultural responses to persistent human issues (p. 20)

And it becomes actualized through suggestions like the following:

Socially, the young learner can be actively and frequently interacting in appropriate ways with other students, some of whom are like the learner and some different. These interactions can be encouraged and monitored and can involve rather than avoid dialogues about the substance of one's own culture and perspectives and those of others. (p. 20)

Under the topic of individual development and identity, for example, the National Council of Social Studies (2002) teacher expectations include the following:

- Assist learners to describe how family, religion, gender, ethnicity, nationality, socioeconomic status, and other group and cultural influences contribute to the development of a sense of self
- Guide learners as they analyze the interactions among ethical, ethnic, national, and cultural factors in specific situations
- Help learners to analyze the role of perceptions, attitudes, values, and beliefs in the development of personal identity and their effect on human behavior
- Have learners compare and evaluate the impact of stereotyping, conformity, acts of altruism, discrimination, and other behaviors on individuals and groups (p. 24)

The guidelines describe possible activities as follows.

  o Teachers . . . can assist learners in examining how their thinking, feelings and actions are similar to and different from those of others and to consider what may have contributed to their own thoughts, feelings, and actions and to the thoughts, feelings, and actions of others.
  o Teachers of the middle grades can provide learners with opportunities to . . . examine behaviors associated with peer pressure, conformity, personal identity, self concept, deviance, stereotyping, altruism, social expectations, norms, and roles. They can assist learners to consider personality and individual differences and use sound concepts and principles to interpret and explain them as well as appreciate the commonalities and differences that exist among humans in different and the same cultures, age groups, and social contexts. (pp. 24–25)

Each of the classroom topics addressed in this book can be linked to historical and current initiatives and processes in the wider world. Helping students make these connections grounds their experience in a deeper context and allows them to see how their skills generalize outside the classroom.

It is important, for example, for students of all ages to realize that the goals of community building and the creation of safe, cohesive groups is one that transcends their experiences and time. Teachers can seek out examples of community building in the curriculum (Why were unions formed? What does the American Red Cross do? What role did churches have during the civil rights movement?) and relate these to current classroom priorities.

Students can study the ways in which there is strength in numbers, both through material examples and conceptual ones. A study of the earth, for example, could include a discussion of dam building; how do people work together when a flood is coming to make sure the river doesn't overflow its banks? Why are 500 sandbags more effective than one? Why are there certain ways of placing the sandbags that are more likely to form a cohesive barrier than a random placement of the bags? Teachers can seek out current event examples to make the connections between individual action and the strength of communities as well as incorporate discussions of community power, community unity, and general solidarity into social studies and mathematics teaching.

It is sometimes more difficult to see how standards in the area of mathematics can be related to issues of diversity and social justice, but the only real obstacle is lack of creativity or imagination. Mathematics educator Ellen Davidson developed a math unit on Martin Luther King, Jr. Day that was specifically designed to teach some of the skills that would be tested on the MCAS (Massachusetts's high-stakes test). Students were engaged in word problems that required working with fractions (the percentage of marchers in Washington, D.C., who were white/African American), dealing with large number sets (estimated crowd sizes), and problem solving around the number of reams of paper required to print flyers for the march. While they engaged in mathematics instruction, they were also talking and thinking about a historical event, a social movement, and a famous American.

3

Sharing Ourselves
With Others

It is Circle Time in Ms. Romero's first grade. All the children are seated on the floor in a circle discussing things they are excited or worried about. When it is Tyshena's turn to talk, she tells her classmates that she is scared because her father has just lost his job and her family might have to move out of town to live with her grandma. She is worried that she will lose her friends and have no one to play with. The other children listen sympathetically and discuss ways to stay connected with Tyshena if she has to move.

Clayton comes crashing into the room in the morning, shoving Denny and smacking Nicole. When one of his friends comes over to talk to him, Clayton tells him to go away. When the teacher inquires what's wrong, Clayton says, "Nothing. Leave me alone." Not until two weeks later does the teacher learn that Clayton's parents are getting divorced and that his life has been disrupted.

Roberto enters the room, his eyes shining and excited. When it is sharing time, he tells the class that he has just made his first communion. He explains the ritual to his classmates, shows a picture of all his relatives that came to town for the event, and describes the party that was held in his honor. He answers questions about the ceremony in his church as well as why this event is so important to him and his family.

Deborah is the only Jewish child in her class. Chanukah came "early" this year, and the teacher seems to have forgotten that Deborah is not caught up in the same Christmas excitement as most of the other children. When the teacher asks the children to write down what they've asked Santa to bring them for Christmas, Deborah makes something up. When the teacher has the children make ornaments to take home to hang on the tree, Deborah worries what her parents will say and what she should do with what she made. She never mentions that she doesn't celebrate Christmas or that two weeks ago her family had a wonderful Chanukah party with latkes, dreidels, and presents.

What is there about the classroom community that allows Tyshena and Roberto to share but somehow silences Clayton and Deborah? The key element is safety. Tyshena is able to talk about her worries and fears knowing that circle time creates a safe place for her and that her classmates will respond with support and encouragement. Roberto's teacher and class allow him to be comfortable sharing his ethnic and religious background, knowing that others are eager to learn about the ways in which he is unique. Neither Clayton nor Deborah is able to share what is going on for them. Clayton does not feel comfortable letting others in on his distress or seeking their support. Deborah does not feel safe sharing her religious practices with her class, and instead, she remains silent in the face of her teacher's insensitivity.

THE VISION

The vision of classrooms in which students can share themselves fully is a challenging one. The ideal is a place in which students feel comfortable showing themselves—and all their complexities—to the teacher and their classmates. If I am fully comfortable with people, then I can tell them or show them the following:

- Things I am good at—my strengths and talents
- Things I am not so good at—the areas in which I require help and support
- Things I am afraid of—my areas of concern or worry
- My goals for my future—what I hope to accomplish both today and in the future
- Things that make me happy—my passions and joys
- Things that make me unhappy—everything from pet peeves to deeper sources of sorrow

To do these things, I must be confident of how my sharing and openness will be received. I must be sure that I will face neither scorn nor blame nor humiliation for showing you the places where I am not strong, powerful, or brave. And I must be equally sure that my accomplishments and strengths will be celebrated by others, that it is safe to be proud of myself.

To build a classroom in which all children feel they belong, it is essential that every child have a voice. Many of the activities included in this chapter involve giving each student opportunities to talk and share with classmates. In the beginning, that sharing might best take place with a partner. Often talking to one person is less intimidating or threatening than addressing the whole group. As students gain confidence in themselves, then they can begin to share more and more of themselves with a broader audience through talking, writing, drawing, singing, and so on.

It is extremely important that students be given spaces and opportunities to share not only what is good and enjoyable in their lives but also what is painful and hard. We do not want to model the adage "If you don't have something good to say, then remain silent." Many children have difficult lives; racism, divorce, poverty, violence, and fear are part of their realities. Even children in more privileged environments often have concerns and worries—a parent with cancer; sexual abuse; a new, sick baby in the family; or the predicted downsizing of their parent's workplace. We want to create chances for students to share all aspects of themselves: the good, the laudable, the troublesome, and the confusing. Because community and cultural values and standards concerning what's appropriate to share are apt to vary considerably, it is important for teachers to be extremely sensitive in respecting children's differences. Students should always have the *right to pass* in sharing situations and to reveal only what they feel comfortable with.

What would a classroom be like in which students regularly shared their accomplishments and received affirmation from others? What would it take to create a space in which students could tell their classmates what was bothering them, confident that they would get support and help? What would stand in the way of this happening on a regular basis?

CHALLENGES TO THE VISION

Imagine a three-year-old who has just done a drawing and comes to show you, an adult, what she has done. With great delight, the child shows you the four kinds of flowers she drew, how she made the rings around the sun, and all the tiny little butterflies she drew. We would probably be thrilled that the child was that pleased with herself, would identify the child as having a good self-concept or self-image, and would be delighted that the child had chosen to share her accomplishment with us.

Now imagine a 38-year-old fellow teacher coming to you one day in the teachers' lounge. With great delight she announces, "You wouldn't believe what a great lesson I just taught. I had planned it so well and so carefully that every little detail was taken care of, and the kids loved it. I answered their questions so well and responded so thoughtfully to the issues they raised that the discussion was amazingly rich. I am just so happy with myself as a teacher—it was so great!"

What kind of a response would that teacher receive? Probably, her colleagues would label her a show off or a braggart and would describe her as full of herself, arrogant, snotty, or as thinking she's better than everyone else. It is unlikely that people would respond, "Oh, that's so great!" or "I'm so proud of you."

Why the difference? Why are we delighted with a three-year-old who is proud of herself but annoyed or repulsed by a 38-year-old who is proud of herself? What happened that makes it hard for us to show ourselves with complete confidence? What makes it difficult for us to support others who do?

One of the things that happened is that we were taught that there was a shortage of good things to go around. If you are doing well, I must, by implication, be doing badly. If your picture is terrific, mine must be awful. Therefore, if I have done something worthy of celebration or praise, you, by definition, must be not as good or worthy of congratulations. When teachers choose the best picture to hang on the wall, congratulate the child in the class with the highest grade, or focus attention on the child with the neatest writing, then other children may feel themselves slighted or diminished. What about the child whose writing, although far from neat, has improved greatly? What about the child whose painting is unusual or who took particular risks with the way she conceptualized the drawing? Why, in fact, should there be a best picture at all? Can we celebrate all children's accomplishments, neither minimizing their differences nor falsely elevating one child to the best?

It is difficult for people to share themselves fully (or at all) if they feel that their openness or revelation will be met with scorn or derision. If I admit to my classmates that I still sleep with a night-light or that I am completely baffled by time telling and they hoot, holler, or make fun of me, I am unlikely to share anything ever again. Or I may limit my sharing to trivial, safe topics. Or I may actually lie or cover up who I am so that no one ever really knows.

Safety cannot be mandated; it must be created. Students must have evidence that their sharing will be positively received. The same conditions for sharing are in place for the adults in the school environment. If a teacher shares that her husband has cancer and that she is very scared—and then finds that everyone avoids her in the lunchroom, she is unlikely to share again. In contrast, if the teachers in the school feel like a *community*, celebrating births and accomplishments and supporting people through sickness, death, and other difficulties, relationships among teachers are likely to be much closer.

Each of us is a complex individual. I am a woman, a Jew, a mother, a political activist, a teacher, a singer, and many other things as well. The reality is that I share each of those characteristics with many other people. My willingness to share those things about myself is tied in many ways to whether I feel that I am "the only one" and whether I will feel isolated, alone, stigmatized or "othered" by revealing things about myself. Some things about us are relatively easy to admit and share. Other characteristics or experiences are more difficult to share. The child whose parent is alcoholic may be very reluctant to share that information with classmates. First, he may be convinced that he is the only one and that admitting that will make him even more deviant looking in the classroom. Second, many of the things that children experience (abuse, poverty, divorce, and abandonment) make them feel that they are somehow at fault—that telling others that my mother lost her job will reflect badly on me. It is important to build opportunities for students to discover that they are not alone in their situation or experience and that there are others who will understand, be supportive, and reassure them that they are not to be blamed.

REFRAMING OUR WORK

Beginning With Ourselves

- When you were growing up, did you feel comfortable letting people get to know you?
- Now, as an adult, do you easily share who you are, things you love doing and what's hard for you?
- Do you ever worry that if people got to know *the real you*, they wouldn't like you? What do you do when you feel that way?
- Are there people around whom you feel like yourself, free to share openly and deeply? What are the conditions or situations that make that possible? What has happened for you to create that safety?
- What would it take for you to feel safer, more comfortable, and more accepted in a wider range of situations and circumstances?

Looking at Our Classrooms and Schools

- Do students willingly share their strengths and gifts?
- Do students volunteer information about themselves, their experiences, and their concerns?
- How do other students respond when people share? Are they supportive or scornful when large discrepancies of skill or talents are apparent?
- Do students know things about one another? Would they know who collects stamps and who has a dog? Are they aware of differences in religion, family background, and skills?
- Do students share what is hard for them? Do they tell people when they are struggling with the work or when they feel confused, hurt, or angry?
- What practices, procedures, structures, or events are in place that allow students to make themselves visible to others?
- Are there ways for students to signal to others (fellow students and adults) that they are in need of help or support? Do students avail themselves of these opportunities easily and frequently?

If teachers identify problems in any of the above areas, they can think about appropriate activities or discussion to address the concern, and they can raise these questions with the students themselves, perhaps at a classroom meeting: "I've been noticing that sometimes when people in our class share something about their families, some other children make faces or noises. I wonder what that's about and how it feels to you." "I'm wondering what hidden talents we have in our classroom that we still haven't uncovered—has anyone found a hidden treasure?"

What's the Big Picture?

- What are the ways in which the broader society keeps people from being able to show themselves fully?
- What would the world be like (and how might it be better) if all people were able to share, contribute and get to know one another easily?
- What kinds of personal, interpersonal, and other skills and experiences do students need to have to feel comfortable sharing their gifts, talents, and challenges with others?

HOW TO BEGIN

ACTIVITIES

News and Goods

Starting the day with individual student sharing can be an easy but important way to build classroom community. Teachers of almost any age (or subject) can begin class by having students say something that is "new" or "good" in their life that they are willing to share. All other students are expected to listen respectfully without comment. When this activity is first introduced, students often begin by sharing more trivial news, "I saw a good movie on TV last night," "I played basketball last night with my big brother," or "I got a new pair of running shoes yesterday." As community is built and students trust one another more, they often share about more meaningful parts of their life: "I just found out my aunt had her baby, and now, I have a new cousin," "I'm going to get to visit my Dad this weekend," or "I hit a home run in the game last night."

News and Goods should never be structured competitively (no prize for the best), and comparative statements ("Well compared to what Mike just said, this is no big deal!") should be gently discouraged. Help students understand that what is new or good for them is about them—not about someone else and that we can, as a class, celebrate and be glad for individuals and their success or pleasures as individuals.

When a student is having a particularly bad day (or week) and says, "Nothing good has happened," or "I have nothing positive to say," classmates can be encouraged to respond with sympathy and support: "We're glad you're here, Irene," or "I hope today is better, Darren." It is very important that students always have the option to pass and that this is emphasized consistently. Having the choice whether to share increases students' safety in the activity and will, hopefully, increase their long-term willingness to take risks with the group.

Two Truths and a Lie

Have every individual write down and then share three statements about themselves—two of which are true and one of which is a lie. Then, the rest of the class is asked to guess which statements are true and which one isn't. For example, I might say, "I'm a vegetarian, and I love to cook," "I can ride a unicycle," and "I learned to read Spanish before I could read English." After everyone who chooses to has made a guess: "I don't think you could ride a unicycle," or "Your background isn't Spanish, so why would you have learned to read it before English?" or "I'm pretty sure you are a vegetarian," I am asked to share the truth. I do ride the unicycle and have since I was 10 years old; I went to first grade in Spain and did learn to read in Spanish first (the truths), and I am a vegetarian, but I hate to cook (the lie).

The critical component of this activity is that it allows people to reveal things about themselves that they are willing to share, but they are not forced to reveal any particular item in any particular area. A student who is shy and not yet comfortable with the group can stick to more superficial facts (and lies) about himself: "I hate broccoli," "I was born in Ohio," and "I have two brothers and one sister." At a later point in community development, a student might risk sharing more personal information: "I want to be an artist when I grow up," "I'm adopted," or "I hate sports."

This activity allows students to share facts about themselves, revealing parts of their lives, interests, backgrounds, and concerns in a gamelike context. Because students themselves get to choose what they share, they are unlikely to be embarrassed or put on the spot. After each student's truths and lie are revealed, it is common for other students to say, "Me too," or "I didn't know that about you," opening the door to further conversations and connections. The activity also pushes participants to go beyond stereotypes and assumptions: The student who doesn't *look* like he studies karate may, in fact, be very skilled; the student who others see as shy or quiet may be the one who performs country-and-western music with her family on weekends. As new information is revealed, students can see beyond the surface to greater depth. (If teachers are uncomfortable about a positive usage of the word *lie* and worry that they might somehow be perceived as encouraging lying, this activity can be called "facts and fiction" or given another title.)

Little-Known Facts About Me

In this variation on the previous activity, each student is asked to write one (or two) pieces of information about themselves that they think that others in the group wouldn't know—"When I was two, I won a tap dancing contest," "I was born in Georgia," or "When I grow up, I want to have my own detective agency." All these bits of information are then put into a large box and shaken up. Students take turns drawing one slip at a time and reading it to the group. The group then has to guess who wrote the secret. As in Two Truths and a Lie, it is fun for students to find out new facts about their classmates and to find similarities and differences. Often when a slip is read, "I'd like to be a baseball player when I grow up," and the writer is identified, students find that they are not the only one for whom this fact is true.

Cultural Artifact Sharing

Children in the class can be encouraged to bring in something that represents them, their family, their religion, ethnicity, or some other aspect of their background. The children then share their object with the class and answer questions from classmates. Children have brought in pictures of their grandparents, a favorite family record or song, or a piece of clothing that has particular significance. Not only are children having an opportunity to show themselves but also they are teaching others about who they are as well. It is very important for teachers to model respectful listening and questioning, asking the Jewish child, for example, "Could you explain how you celebrate that holiday in your family?" rather than "How come your family doesn't celebrate Christmas?"

Collage of Me

All children can be given the opportunity to make a collage about themselves using old magazines, scissors, and glue. Ask them to cut out objects and phrases of pictures that represent them somehow and to make them into a collage. These are then shared with the class and hung on the wall. Many children who have difficulty talking about who they are can represent themselves graphically with more success, tapping into another kind of intelligence. I have found that grounding something on the page—a word or a picture—often increases the depth of sharing from which to speak. If some children are unable to cut or paste, they can work with a partner, preferably another student, perhaps pointing to images that seem appropriate to their collage. (This activity is a great introduction for a faculty workshop as well; teachers can make collages of their pathway to teaching and share these with colleagues.)

Lifelines

Each child is given a piece of paper and asked to draw a line—their lifeline. They are then asked to enter 6 to 10 points on the line that represent important events in their life that they are willing to share. They might include an early memory, a family vacation, the birth of a sibling, the time they fell off their bike and broke their leg, a move across country, the death of a grandparent or parent, the time they hit a home run, or when they made the team. There are no limits placed on what's important. That is the child's choice. Students then get together with another student and tell their life story. Extend this activity by then having the student who heard their classmate's life story introduce that student to the class: "This is Daquon. When he was four, he rode a horse for the first time, and he remembers that he was really scared. When he was six, his Mom got sick, and he lived with his grandma for a year in New Jersey. When he was eight, he became friends with Shay, and they're still best friends."

The activity provides opportunities for students to talk about themselves and to have others listen respectfully. Many students also enjoy the "famous person" status of having someone else talk about them the way people talk about celebrities or famous people. And because everyone's life is invariably different, there are no right answers or a right way to do the activity.

GAMES

It can be useful to find games that allow students to be in the lead, to take charge, or to be featured in some way.

Who Is It?

The teacher (or a student) describes a student, one detail at a time, and the other students guess who the mystery child is. Start out with general descriptions that fit many students and build suspense: "I'm thinking of someone who's wearing a T-shirt. And running shoes. And has curly hair. And glasses. And long pants." You may add useless clues, such as "This person has a nose," or "This person eats lunch every day," as a way to postpone the guessing and make clear how much we do have in common while we are each unique. When the person has been guessed successfully, the guesser (or another child who hasn't had a turn yet) can do the describing.

This can be a valuable activity for helping students to truly notice one another. By scanning classmates to determine who is being talked about, they may attend to details they had previously missed. The teacher can also introduce appropriate ways of talking about specific characteristics or differences through this activity: "This person communicates by using his hands," or "This person moved here from another country that's south of the United States but still part of North America."

Mirrors

Students are paired up and face each other. One student begins acting as the leader by making slow movements—the other person imitates those movements, moving in fluid form with the leader. After several minutes, the other person becomes the leader and the other the follower. This activity allows students the chance to be in charge and to have someone else pay close attention to what they are doing.

Elephant Toss (Weinstein & Goodman, 1980)

Students stand in a circle and one student begins by saying, "I'm throwing an elephant to Michelle." That student then pretends to throw an elephant (holding her hands out wide, supporting something heavy), and Michelle pretends to catch the elephant. Then Michelle says, "Now I'm throwing Jell-O to Fred." Both the thrower and the catcher have to make movements that would be appropriate to the object's size, weight, smell, feel, and so on.

Pass the Face (Sound, Movement) (Prutzman, Bodenhamer, & Stern, 1988)

Students sit in a circle. One student begins by making a funny face. The person to the left makes the same face as the first person and then makes his own funny face. The third person imitates the second person and then adds her own. Children, then, are making two faces—the one passed to them and their own. The game can also be played by passing sounds: clink; clink, harrumph; harrumph, snort or by passing gestures: wink; wink, handshake; handshake, pat; pat, tickle; and so on.

Group Introductions (Weinstein & Goodman, 1980)

This is a game of pure silliness. The group is told that the job of every single member of the group is to introduce every person in the room to every other person. This works best in a group that doesn't know one another well yet. Susan runs up to a boy and asks, "What's your name?" He says, "Eli." Susan grabs another person and asks, "What's your name?" The other person responds, "Becca." Susan then says, "Becca, this is Eli; Eli, this is Becca," and moves on. Because every person is making introductions or being introduced simultaneously, everyone always is busy and has a role. Although this game doesn't work well for learning names, it does create an atmosphere in which it is much easier to approach the person later and ask, "What is your name—I didn't really catch it before, but I know we were introduced!"

SONGS

"Here Is What I Can Do"

Children sit in a circle, and the leader starts by doing a motion for others to follow (clap hands, snap fingers, wiggle arms). The leader chants, "Here is what I can do. I can do it, so can you. Here is what I can do. Won't you do it with me, too?" Other ideas can come from the group. Each child can get a turn to lead the motions.

"Down by the Bay" (Traditional Song)

Students can be asked to write their own last lines, either individually, with partners, or in a small group, and then to share them when it is their turn. Students love the opportunity to be silly and make others laugh, and doing it within the context of the song may make that kind of "showing oneself" less intimidating. There are several great versions of this available on YouTube, including one done by the third graders at St. Patrick School in Decatur, Illinois.

"My Name's Sarah" (To the Tune of "Twinkle, Twinkle Little Star")

In this song, children have the opportunity to sing a verse about themselves and then get feedback from the group. This might sound like this:

> My name's Sarah, how about you? I like to swim, do you like that too?
>
> We are friends, and we have fun. We make room for everyone.
>
> My name's Sarah, how are you? I like to swim, do you like that too?

Ask students to nod or smile or raise their hand if they also like to do the activity that the child has identified. If a child is not able to sing or create his own verse, classmates or the teacher can make up the verse about the child, "This is Justin, how about you? He likes to watch cartoons, do you like that too?"

"Love Makes a Family" (Two of a Kind, 1996)

This wonderful song describes children who come from very different families. The song affirms that it is love that makes a family rather than any particular (or singular) configuration of family members. Use this song as part of a discussion of the many kinds of families represented in the classroom, and couple it with one of the books about families described below.

CHILDREN'S LITERATURE

One of our community goals is for students to feel comfortable expressing who they are, in all its fullness and complexity. It is important to teach students the differences between positive self-affirmations (what I like about myself, what I'm good at) and bragging talk that is designed to make others feel inferior or less than. It is important for teachers to create spaces (like News and Goods) for students to say things about their lives and their accomplishments without embarrassment or fear of humiliation and to learn how to talk about themselves in ways that are honest and true but not arrogant. The differences between "I had my swimming lesson yesterday and I'm really getting much better at the breathing part" and "I'm the only one in my class who can swim the length of the pool" are important for students to recognize and understand. Several books address issues of bragging and arrogance and can be useful in this discussion.

The children's books in this section fall into the following categories: (1) general books about differences, including different names, and (2) books about different kinds of families, including race, family composition, language.

Individual Differences and Gifts

It's Okay to Be Different *(Parr, 2001)*

This brightly illustrated book is designed for younger children but will likely be enjoyed by many older students as well. The book tells us that it's okay do the following:

Be missing a tooth (or two or three)

Need some help (a woman with a guide dog)

Have a different nose (an elephant)

Have wheels (a boy in wheelchair)

Be small, medium, large, or extra large

The book concludes, "It's okay to be different. You are special and important just because of being who you are". This book is very simple and completely accessible. The class could easily write and illustrate their own book (or take photographs) that reflects some of the diversities in their classroom (color, size, religion, skills, mobility, language, and so on).

Courage of the Blue Boy *(Neubecker, 2006)*

A blue boy lives in a blue land where everything is blue. "There must be more than blue," he sighs. He and his best friend Polly, a calf, set out to find other lands. They find places that are exclusively purple, orange, red, and pink but finally find a city that is all colors—except blue! Slowly, the blue boy finds a way to insert himself and his color into the landscape, making it (and himself) many colors.

Lead students in a discussion of this book as a metaphor.

- What is it like to live in a place of sameness?
- Why are some people more comfortable if everything (or everyone) is the same?
- What would you miss if there were so much sameness?
- What is it like to live somewhere where you don't see yourself represented at all? (Older students can explore issues of representation—Am I here? Do you see people with your skin color, type of family, appearance represented in books, in magazines, or on television?)
- What are the benefits of more heterogeneity and differences?

Jack's Talent *(Cocca-Leffler, 2007)*

On the first day of school, the teacher asks the students to share their special talents. The children share what they are good at: drawing, building sandcastles, catching insects, singing, and dog training. But Jack says that he isn't good at anything. But it turns out that Jack is very good at remembering the children's names and their special talents, and he is rewarded by being asked to pass out the name tags!

An excellent intro to children's individual gifts, this book could easily become a first day of school activity: Share your name, and draw a picture of what you're good at. These could make a great bulletin board or be compiled into a book. For those with access to computer technology, the children's photos or pictures and narratives could be made into a PowerPoint presentation.

Giraffes Can't Dance *(Andreae & Parker-Rees, 2001)*

Gerald the giraffe was not a good dancer, and every year, he dreaded the great jungle dance. All the other animals made fun of him and the way he danced.

But he persists, looking for the right music—when he exuberantly dances and amazes all the rest of the animals, he says, "We all can dance when we find music that we love."

I Like Me *(Carlson, 1988)*

This is the ultimate self-affirmation book. The main character, a pig, likes herself and likes everything she can do. "When I get up in the morning, I say, 'Hi, Good-looking.' I like my curly tail, my round tummy, and my tiny little feet. When I feel bad, I cheer myself up. When I fall down, I pick myself up. When I make mistakes, I try and try again."

This book could be a wonderful lead-in to a discussion about affirmations—saying nice things about yourself (and, hopefully, by extension, about others). The book also allows for a discussion of the importance of cheering yourself up and supporting yourself too. Teachers could follow this book with an activity in which students write self-affirmations that are placed on their desk—to look at when they need to be reminded that they are of value. This is an excellent activity for the teacher to model as well: "I am a good teacher, and I know how to be patient with my students," or "I try really hard to correct children's mistakes gently."

Rachel Parker, Kindergarten Show-Off *(Martin, 1992)*

Olivia is five years old and in kindergarten. She is very proud of the fact that she can read and write. When a new girl, Rachel, moves next door and can also read, trouble begins. Olivia is jealous of everything about Rachel—her puppet theater, her baby sister, and her grandfather who gives out candy. Olivia ends up calling Rachel a "show off" and they have a fight. But Olivia is lonesome without Rachel to play with. The next day in school, their teacher Mrs. Bee announces that both Olivia and Rachel will read to the class—together. After the girls struggle over the chair, they learn to support one another through tricky words and become friends again.

This is a great book on jealousy and different abilities. The book nicely promotes a discussion of pride versus arrogance and the importance of sharing the spotlight and the success. One need not be the only or the best to seek and attain recognition and respect; we are all deserving of respect and praise for our accomplishments, and we lose nothing by sharing that success with others.

We're All Special *(Maguire, 1995)*

This brightly illustrated picture book is all about diversity: "We come in many colors and shapes and sizes too. We all have different interests and different things we do" (Maguire, 1995). The book's examples cover a wide range of differences: different interests, skills, food preferences, sleeping preferences, and movement speeds and modalities.

This is an excellent book for having children self-identify their unique characteristics. This book could be read to students and followed by making a class book or collage.

The Storm *(Harshman, 1995)*

Jonathan, who has used a wheelchair since an accident, hates when he is singled out and treated differently. When the students talk about an upcoming storm, one of the students says, "It must be real scary for Jonathan!" (Harshman, 1995).

> This was what he hated. Just this. Being singled out. Different. And of all things, a storm. There were things he was scared of, but storms weren't one of them. He loved storms. He loved those evenings when he and Dad would watch a thunderstorm, and its spidering lightning, boom and lash the darkness into daylight. (Harshman, 1995)

When the storm becomes a tornado, Jonathan is brave and resourceful and rescues the horses in the barn. Although it is, in some ways, a hero narrative, it is also about him realizing that there is more to him and that others might see that also.

> He felt better than he had for a long time. He knew he had done a thing he could feel good about. He wouldn't care so much now when people looked at him. He knew they would. They would still see his "condition," but when they knew this story they might begin to see a lot more. They might just see him. Jonathan. (Harshman, 1995)

This is a powerful introduction to a discussion of multiple identities: none of us want to be seen in a one-dimensional way.

Discuss the following with students:

- When you see someone with a disability, what do you think? How do you know that your assumptions are correct? How could you find out? List all your identities and weaknesses too.
- What would it be like to be known and talked about only in terms of a disability or a problem? "Oh, that's the boy who can't read," or "That's the girl who's afraid of the dark."
- How can we get to know one another in all our complexities? What will it take? Time? Trust? Opportunities to work and play together? How can we make that happen?

One key way to honor students' names is through recognizing, learning to pronounce, and respecting their names. Several books can be very helpful in beginning this conversation and linking it to teasing, a common phenomenon in many classrooms. For the teasing to have a "hook," other students often center in on something that is different or noteworthy about the person they are teasing. Because teasing is never true, per se, but is an attempt to goad or irritate another person, teasing often centers on aspects of a person's appearance or life that could be treated with either relatively nonchalance, acknowledged supportively, or celebrated (Maria wears glasses, Lucille still sleeps with a night-light, Matthew's mom is in a substance rehabilitation program, or Jeremy has two moms). Children's books about teasing can be used to guide students into a discussion of the ways in which teasing hurts and the need to notice and support others in nonoppressive ways.

Chrysanthemum *(Henkes, 1991)*

Chrysanthemum (a mouse), from a loving and supportive family, starts school with great eagerness and enthusiasm but is quickly devastated by her classmates' teasing about her name. The classroom teacher reacts minimally: "Thank you for sharing, now put your head down" (Henkes, 1991), and this response does little to change the children's behavior. Although Chrysanthemum's parents try nobly to reassure her that she is wonderful and her name is perfect, the behavior of her classmates wears her down. When a new music teacher comes to the school, her proactive (yet gentle) response to the teasing brings an immediate change in the students' behavior.

Not only a wonderful book about teasing, name-calling, and respecting people's names, the book also provides two very different models of teacher behavior. It becomes clear that laissez-faire responses to teasing and exclusion are much less effective than taking a strong, but positive, stand by modeling and expecting children to be respectful and supportive of classmates.

A Perfect Name *(Costanza, 2002)*

Mama and Papa Potamus are having a hard time choosing the right name for their new baby. They explore many choices, including finding out what all the names mean! Finally, after much difficulty, they come up with the perfect name for the naming ceremony.

The book begins with a note to parents about the importance of names, and it encourages parents to help their children understand that each child is a gift. This is a perfect book for discussing children's names and talking about respect for people's names. The application activity could be a discussion of the following questions and answers: What is your name? Where did it come from? Why were you named this? What do you call yourself? Do you have nicknames? Do you like your name?

The Name Jar *(Choi, 2001)*

Unhei has just moved to the United States from Korea, and she is eager to make friends and fit in with the other students. But she is worried about her name and doesn't want to be teased or treated badly, so she tells the students she has no name and needs a new one. They volunteer many names for her that they put in a big jar for her to choose from. But after Unhei talks to the Korean grocer who recognizes that her Korean name means "grace" and an encounter with her classmate Joey, Unhei decides to keep her own name and introduces herself to the class with her name written in English and in Korean. Joey asks her to fill the jar with some Korean nicknames with good meanings so that the rest of the class can choose one as well.

This is a powerful book for talking about names, teasing, and the power of an ally. Little Joey turns out to be Unhei's friend and doesn't want her to have to change her name. This book could be used to explore children's names at length. In addition to the questions identified for the previous book, this book can easily begin a discussion of the oppression of immigrants to this country and the pressures they face to Americanize their names. Students could construct a wall chart of all the names contained in their extended families, including information about country of origin, name changing, and so on. For older students, a discussion of the immigrant experience at Ellis Island and the ways in which people's names were changed could deepen the understanding of the importance of respecting diversity in names.

Different Kinds of Families

There are many books on families and the different forms families take. These books can be very useful in helping students understand that differences in families can be shared openly and discussed in school. Books that specifically address some different kinds of families can be very useful in breaking through the isolation that tells students "I'm the only one in the world with a grandmother who doesn't speak English," or "No one else has a sister with cerebral palsy."

Celebrating Families *(Hausherr, 1997)*

This beautiful book of photos and text illustrates many kinds of families. There are children who move between two homes because their parents are divorced, multigenerational families, children living in a city housing project with their grandma, foster families, a mixed-race family with a mother who uses a wheelchair, a family with two mothers, a stepmother, a single mother, and a single dad. I particularly appreciated that some less common families are also shown, including families living in a homeless shelter, families living in a cohousing community, and a family in which the father is in prison.

The thoroughness and inclusiveness of this book should make most any child feel that their family is okay to share. The range of families pictured also provides opportunities to talk about some of the prejudices and stereotypes that others might have about different kind of families: "What do you think it would be like telling other kids that your father was in jail?" "I wonder what it's like for the little girl who is living in the shelter. What do you think happens when she goes to school?" "Can a family have people in it who have different skin colors? Let's look at all the colors of skin we have in our classroom."

Families Are Different *(Pellegrini, 1991)*

Nico and her sister are from Korea, and they are both adopted. Nico is troubled that she doesn't look like her mother and father. Then she looks around and sees that there are many kinds of families—some in which the kids look like their parents and don't, different configurations of families, and much more. (Note: There are no gay or lesbian families represented.) She feels better. Her mother explained that their family is held together with a special kind of glue, *love* as opposed to being related in other ways.

Although somewhat limited in the scope of families included, this book does provide the opportunity to talk about racial differences, skin color, and so on.

Who's in a Family? *(Skutch, 1995)*

In this picture book, many kinds of families are represented: single-parent families, children being raised by grandparents, children with gay and lesbian parents, and children of different races. Differences and connections are drawn with animal families as well: "In elephant families, the oldest female elephant is in full charge of a family consisting of only mothers, aunts, teenagers and babies. Male elephants live together in their own family." The book concludes, "Who's in a family? The people who love you the most."

The last page in the book offers, "Here's a place for you to draw a picture of your family." This provides a wonderful opportunity to develop an inclusive definition of family and to have students share their situations and connections.

Lucy's Family Tree *(Schreck, 2006)*

It is challenging for Lucy (who was adopted from Mexico) to deal with the teacher's family tree assignment. She feels too different from the other children and wants to be excused from the assignment. But her parents challenge her to find three families that are the same, and in her quest, she discovers the vast variety of families represented in her classroom. This book can be used to deepen the discussion of family diversity and to find ways to honor many kinds of families. The book also offers suggestions for parents and teachers about how to approach the family tree project more inclusively.

Shy Mama's Halloween *(Broyles, 2000)*

Anya, Dasha, Irina, and Dimitrii, new immigrants to the United States, anticipate their first Halloween with great excitement. But when their papa's illness keeps him from taking them trick-or-treating, they have a problem; their mama is terrified by many things in the new country, Halloween in particular. With great courage, Mama takes them out anyway and finds friendly people unperturbed by the children's accents or limited English. The family feels more welcomed and included after the evening's events.

The Tilbury House (the publishers of *Shy Mama's Halloween*) Web site (http://www.tilburyhouse .com/childrens/shy-mamas-halloween-teachers-take-note.htm) suggests the following excellent questions as discussion starters:

- Have you ever moved, or do you know someone who has? How do you think it feels to be in a new school—neighborhood—country?
- What would be some good experiences a person could have on his or first day at a new school? What would be some bad ones? How could you help someone new in your class feel more at home and welcome? How could you and your family welcome a new person or family into your neighborhood or building?
- Are there children at your school who originally came from other countries as immigrants? Look up where they came from on a world map or globe. Can you give these classmates a chance to tell you about the places where they came from? What do they miss about their old home? What do they like about their new home? Who or what helped them feel comfortable in their new home?
- How would you feel if someone made fun of the way you dressed, looked, or spoke? What could you do about it? What could you do to help if you heard someone making fun of another child?
- Mama was led out into the world by her children's desire to be part of Halloween. What have you discovered on your own that helped your parent(s) or a grown-up try something new?
- Do you think grown-ups feel frightened when they move or begin a new job? Interview a grown-up you know, and ask him or her to tell you about how it feels to face a change or new experience.

A Day With Dad *(Holmberg, 2008)*

A little boy is excited to spend the day with his father who lives in another town. They go to the movies, out to eat, to the library—and everywhere they go, Tim announces, "This is my Dad." At the end of the day, the father leaves on the train and Tim, although a bit sad, knows that one day soon the train will come back and he will spend another day with his dad.

The book doesn't say specifically that the parents are divorced or separated, but the boy's delight in spending time with his father is clear.

Milly, Molly and Different Dads *(Pittar, 2004)*

A little girl is upset that her father has left the family. The rest of the kids share all the different kinds of dads they have—two dads, adopted dad, dead dad, dad at home, dad with another family, dad in the army, deaf dad, dad in wheelchair, and so on, and everyone feels better.

Sam Is My Half Brother *(Boyd, 1990)*

Hessie is nervous when her father and his new wife Molly have a new baby, Sam. But she learns that having a half brother doesn't mean that she isn't loved fully and that she can love Sam fully as a little brother.

This book presents a broad concept of family and could be useful in discussing the range of kinds of families that might exist in the classroom.

Nana Upstairs and Nana Downstairs *(dePaola, 1973)*

A little boy is close to both his grandmother who lives downstairs and his great-grandmother who lives upstairs. He is very sad when Nana Upstairs dies. Although the older brother calls great-grandmother a witch, the little boy is very clear that she is not.

Diana, Maybe *(Dragonwagon, 1987)*

Rosie has never met her half sister Diana, who was born to her father and a previous wife. She knows that Diana is six-years older than she is and has brown hair. She fantasizes about what it would be like to have her as a sister—she would braid her hair and go shopping with her and support her when she's sad and be her ally. She hopes that Diana, somewhere, knows that Rosie is thinking about her. This book is a good combination of honoring different kinds of families and talking about the kinds of support people want from others.

An increasing number of excellent books deal directly and indirectly with families that have two mothers or two fathers. These can provide excellent starting places for conversations about family diversity in general and, when appropriate, explicit discussions about gay and lesbian parents and families.

And Tango Makes Three *(Parnell & Richardson, 2005)*

This true story tells the tale of two male chinstrap penguins, Roy and Silo, who live in the Central Park Zoo. Always the closest of friends and companions, Roy and Silo work together to hatch and raise a penguin chick when an extra egg is available because the parents can't successfully hatch two. The story makes it clear that there are many ways that families are created and that love is what holds them together.

King and King *(deHaan & Nijland, 2000)*

The queen decrees that it's time for the prince to marry, and princesses come from near and far to try to charm him. But in the end, it is another prince who catches his interest, and the book ends with a happy wedding for the two princes.

1, 2, 3: A Family Counting Book *(Combs, 2001b) and*
A, B, C: A Family Alphabet Book *(Combs, 2001a).*

These books are similar to other counting and alphabet books except that the families represented have same-sex parents. In the counting book, the Number 2 is illustrated by a house sign that reads "Welcome Home New Daddies!" and the Number 16 shows two women watching their children climb to the tops of 16 trees. In the alphabet book, *B* is for book: "Our moms read our favorite book to us at bedtime" (Combs, 2001a). *O* is for overalls: "I always wear my overalls when my dads take us to the playground." The whimsical illustrations are very matter-of-fact—these are children and families going to the zoo, playing in the snow, and going grocery shopping, but the families represented show two mothers or two fathers.

Issues of racial difference and skin color are introduced well in some children's book and can begin conversations about the many shades of skin that children have and that their skin doesn't necessarily match their parents. This can also be a relevant issue for discussions about adoption as well.

The Skin You Live In *(Tyler, 2005)*

This beautifully illustrated picture book shows children with many different skin colors (and families with assorted colors) playing, eating, and enjoying their variations:

> *Your coffee and cream skin, your warm cocoa dream skin . . . your chocolate chip, double dip sundae supreme skin!*

This book could be used to encourage children to really *look* deeply at their own and others skin and challenge the binary of black and white. Using multicultural crayons now available, they can make self-portraits that attempt to actually mirror their skin tones. Older students can be engaged in a discussion of racism and white privilege—what skin colors get represented positively in our culture—and the assumptions behind Band-Aids labeled "skin color" (*Whose* skin color?).

Two Mrs. Gibsons *(Igus, 1996)*

A little girl talks lovingly about the two Mrs. Gibsons in her life. One Mrs. Gibson was born in Tennessee, has skin the color of chocolate, sings all the time, and gives great big hugs. The other Mrs. Gibson was born in Japan, can write beautiful Japanese characters, and gives soft, gentle hugs. But what they both have in common is that they love her father and her; one is her grandmother and the other is her mother.

This beautiful interracial book is an excellent beginning to discussions about similarities and differences and the benefits of knowing (and loving and being loved by) all kinds of people.

Trevor's Story: Growing Up Biracial *(Kandel, 1997)*

In this photo essay, Trevor talks explicitly about what it's like growing up biracial. The book begins,

> Once in a while someone asks me, "What are you?" I usually answer, "Human." When one kid at school asked me, that's what I said. Then I asked him, "What are you? Alien?" I've always wondered, why do I have to be anything? We're all part of the human race. So far as I know, no one has proven that aliens exist. (Kandel, 1997)

Trevor Mark Sage-el is 10, and his mother is white, and his father is black. The book talks frankly about skin color, including the words *multiracial* and *interracial* (and that the word *mulattos* isn't used anymore). The book not only includes the difficult questions that other children ask Trevor but also shares about his challenges in math, the fact that he is on the wrestling team, and that his nickname is "Bean" because he is skinny.

Trevor's parents instruct him to walk away if someone picks on him because of the color of his skin and label those people as "not educated."

When he is asked to draw a self-portrait of himself at school, Trevor draws a yin-yang symbol, symbolizing both parts of him—he says it represents harmony of the universe.

The book talks directly about racism—how Trevor is treated differently when he is with his mom or his dad—how someone at the food court thought that his dad was trying to steal her purse or how the bank turned down their mortgage application when it was both parents applying and approved it when it was just the white mom. The boy's heritage includes his mother's family from Germany (and she has Jewish relatives too) and his history on his father's side of slavery. Stories are told about each of these— rich sources of narrative.

This is an excellent book for discussing skin color, name-calling, prejudice, and (for older children) Hitler, Nazi Germany, and the Holocaust (which are referenced here).

What Are You? Voices of Mixed-Race Young People *(Gaskins, 1999)*

This book for older students combines interviews, poems, and essays from 80 mixed-race young people. It begins with a powerful poem:

> *I'm mixed, but I'm not mixed up.*
>
> *I'm not about denying a part of me.*
>
> *I'm not about trying to pass.*
>
> *I'm no sellout, no traitor.*
>
> *No wanna-be, no mutt.*
>
> *I'm no tragedy and no exotic other . . .*
>
> *If anything, I'm just another hue of you.*
>
> —Sara B. Busdiecker (Gaskins, 1999)

The individual stories are powerful and provide multiple opportunities to talk about race, racism, prejudice, abuse, name-calling, and discrimination. Students could be encouraged to write their own narratives and to interview others.

I Hate English! *(Levin, 1995)*

Mei Mei is a recent immigrant to New York's Chinatown from Hong Kong. She is comfortable in Chinatown where everyone looks like those she knew in China and speaks Chinese. But school is a different story—everything happens in English, and Mei Mei is not happy about how English looks or sounds—so different from her native language. She refuses to speak English.

When she goes to the Chinatown learning center, Mei Mei refuses help in English, but she loves tutoring the little ones in arithmetic. When a new teacher comes to the center, she talks to Mei Mei in English, but Mei Mei continues to think in Chinese. Soon it becomes clear that some of her reluctance to learn and speak English is about her fear of losing her identity and her language. But the new teacher persists and shares much of her life with Mei Mei—in English—and eventually, Mei Mei wants to share her world as well, in the only language they have in common. The story ends as follows, "To this day, Mei Mei talks in Chinese and English whenever she wants" (Levin, 1995).

This could be a useful book for discussing what school is like for English language learners and ways that teachers and students can be responsive and supportive in the classroom.

Jin Woo *(Bunting, 2001)*

A little boy has mixed feelings about the arrival of his newly adopted brother from Korea. But through his parents thoughtful handling of the adoption, he learns that there is plenty of love to go around. The book contains some good information about the parents' attempt to preserve some of Jim Woo's culture. Parents write a letter to David (in the words of the baby):

> Dear David,
>
> It's going to be scary for me for a while. Everything will be so different. I'm glad I have you to help me. Mom and Dad told me how much they love you. And how much they will love me. They say they have so much love inside of them that what they give to me won't take any away from you. (Bunting, 2001)

Embarrassment can be a powerful impediment to keeping students from sharing fully who they and their families are. Several books deal with the ways in which children are embarrassed by their own challenges or differences and by their families' differences and stress the need for acceptance and understanding. Once children have identified the source of embarrassment, the teacher can lead a discussion about positive responses to differences and challenges and the need for people to show themselves fully.

Two Strikes Four Eyes *(Delaney, 1976)*

This book tells the story of Toby, a mouse who loves to play baseball but is afraid to wear the glasses he needs for fear of being teased. When he finally wears his glasses, he plays much better!

This book is a wonderful introduction to the importance of accepting our differences. What kind of atmosphere was necessary for Toby (acceptance, support) before he could be open about his differences? Because the children's teasing is painful for Toby, it also provides an opportunity to talk about how it feels to be teased and why such behavior should be avoided.

Apple Pie and Onions *(Caseley, 1987)*

Rebecca loves to visit Grandma and loves all the things from the old country that Grandma has. But when they go shopping and Grandma bursts into a loud conversation in Yiddish with an old friend, Rebecca is embarrassed and pretends she doesn't know her. Grandma tells Rebecca a story of being embarrassed when her father picked her up at school with a bag full of potatoes and onions. Then they have tea together and learn to love each other in spite of this.

This story provides another good opening for talking about embarrassment and differences and learning to be accepting of one another and of our families. Teachers might want to structure a conversation or a writing experience about the topic of embarrassment.

Daddy Has a Pair of Striped Shorts *(Otey, 1990)*

A little girl's father has a pair of striped shorts that he wears with his Hawaiian shirt and his smiley-face tie. She is very embarrassed by him. He is an outgoing guy who makes himself prominent at the PTO and with her friends. He is also a preacher. Finally, she realizes, "Funny, how people seem to like him no matter what he wears or how bright it is. And now that I've been thinking about it, so do I" (Otey, 1990).

This is a great book for a discussion about embarrassing parents. We are afraid that our parents are a reflection on us and that if people don't like our parents, they won't like us. The book provides a great jumping-off point for a discussion about diversity.

Jamaica and Brianna *(Havill, 1993)*

Jamaica has to wear her big brother Ossie's boots, and the other kids tease her. Then she gets new boots—cowboy boots—and her friend Brianna teases her about those too. It turns out that Brianna is not that happy with her hand-me-down pink boots either. The two girls finally talk, share what is going on, decide that they are both okay, and agree to play together in the snow in their boots.

This book provides an excellent introduction to why people tease and what's behind teasing. Because children often tease to cover up their discomfort, learning to ask, "What is this really about?" can be a useful lesson for students.

LINKS TO THE CURRICULUM

There are many ways to connect the importance of voice and safety to the curriculum. Teachers might want to explore the ways in which cultures and societies provide opportunities for people to share themselves: theater, music, and art are perfect examples. Teachers can help students understand the ways in which different groups have developed their own rituals of performance and sharing. Links can also be made to the many different gifts that people have when we are able to know them well. Obstacles to sharing ourselves can be explored at both institutional and interpersonal levels: What kinds of classroom rules and atmosphere do we need for students here to show themselves to us? What kinds of communities and societies do we need for people to feel safe to show themselves and their backgrounds? Links to the National Council of Social Studies standards in the areas of cultural diversity and individual identity can be easily made (http://www.socialstudies.org/standards).

Opportunities for students to show themselves can be built into all subject matters. Students can be asked to share their writing or their artwork with a partner or with a small group. During math class, the teacher can ask individual students to show how they figured out the problem. Role-plays and simulations, which can be a regular part of the social studies curriculum, can provide students with opportunities to be seen in a supportive environment.

4

Knowing
Others Well

> Shequanna, one of the students in Ms. Jefferson's first grade, is nonverbal. She communicates by pointing at objects on her communication board and is beginning to use a letter board and a computer to type words. The other students in Shequanna's first grade know from the sharing that has taken place that Shequanna is very interested in cats and kittens. Whenever they find a picture of one in their reading or come upon an advertisement for cat products in a magazine, they clip it out for her and bring it to her for her scrapbook.
>
> It is November, and a visitor comes to observe in Mr. Jackson's fourth grade. He inquires to one student about the project he sees three students working on in the corner. The student shrugs and responds, "I don't know their names, they're not in my reading group."

THE VISION

Although it is critical that students are aware of the ways in which they are unique and special, it is equally if not more important that they understand the many ways in which they are the same and the things that they have in common. Many years ago, I used to give workshops titled "Teaching Children About Differences and Disabilities" for teachers. We would look at children's books about disability, curriculum materials for teaching about differences, and activities for teaching children about individual differences. At the end of the workshop, a teacher approached me, and her comment radically changed how I approach my work with teachers. She said to me, "I teach students with learning disabilities. They are already painfully aware of all the ways they are different. What they have no idea about is the ways in which they are similar to other students." Perhaps in stressing individual differences so heavily we have failed to communicate to students all that they have in common.

The vision is of a classroom in which all children know one another well and connect freely and easily, a classroom in which it would be possible to assign any two students to work together and know that they have already been connected in many ways and have figured out how to have a relationship with one another. The vision is of children who reach out to one another with friendship and support, deeply aware of whom their class-mates are and what they need and want.

Our goals in this area are that children know that all human beings are *multidimensional* and that they are able to see many parts of other people, reaching beyond simplistic characterizations of others. Once students are aware of the multifaceted nature of human beings, we would hope that they would be able to *counter stereotypes* and crash through their prejudgments and assumptions about others. They would be able to say, "Mark dresses in overalls and work boots—and he's also a really good artist and a great baseball player," or "Eva doesn't talk with her mouth, but she types on a computer, and she's really smart." We would like to structure classrooms in which all students could *counter isolation* (their own and others), knowing that they are not the only one with a particular concern or challenge. And lastly, we would like to see classrooms in which all people find *places of deep connection and trust* with others, secure in their acceptance and their relationships.

Moving beyond the classroom, getting to know others well means broadening our friendships and connections, having our relationships reflect the diversity that surrounds us, and overcoming exclusionary or discriminatory practice or patterns. The goals of multicultural education in its broadest sense are going beyond *knowing* about differences to respecting and appreciating diversity and working together for social justice.

An inclusive, cooperative classroom in which children are working closely with one another (and across differences) can also, of course, lead to negative interpersonal interactions (including tattling, teasing, and bullying), which must be responded to firmly and with conviction.

Tattling

Many teachers report problems with tattling—a situation in which one child approaches a teacher to report on the misbehavior or transgression of another child. It is common, therefore, for teachers to make "no tattling" rules or to tell students that they will not respond to tattling at all. They often explain this further by saying that they don't want a student to tell them anything about another student and that students should pay attention to their behavior only. Although this may appear to make sense, the following story illustrates some of the complexities of the situation and the rule. A teacher was on the playground the first week of school and a child rushed up to her excitedly saying, "Teacher, teacher, Sasha . . ." and before the student could go on, the teacher responded, "I don't want to hear about Sasha! You take care of yourself." The student was insistent, "But teacher, Sasha . . ." and again, the teacher told the little girl to mind her own business and not to tattle. After several more attempts and the little girl's tears, it became clear what was happening; Sasha, a first grader, had climbed the monkey bars and was dangling by her knees and couldn't get down! The little girl was not tattling, but trying to secure help and support for Sasha!

This true story, about which the teacher felt terrible afterward, illuminates the real question: do we really want students to only be concerned with their own behavior, or are there times and situations in which it makes sense—and may be laudable—for one student to talk about or report on another student's situation or behavior? One teacher made the distinction clear by asking her students—when they were about to tell on another student—"Are you telling me this to get Damien *out* of trouble or *into* trouble?" Another teacher phrases it, "Is what you're about to tell me going to *help* Ella or *hurt* Ella?" The distinction can also be articulated as the difference between "tattling" and "reporting" (see Box 4.1).

In Kim Rombach's first-grade class, she has told the students that they can tell on someone "only if it will help that person." When her students explained this to me, they gave me examples of times when telling was helpful to the person ("Carolyn is stuck in the bathroom." "Greg has one of the very sharp knives.") and times when it wasn't ("Marquita took three cookies instead of two." "Donese is playing with her toys and not doing her math.").

In a caring, responsive classroom, the teacher would certainly want to know that Martha is crying in the bathroom because she's upset about her sick grandma or that Darnell is playing with the blade of the paper cutter. We don't really want to create classrooms in which students are concerned only about themselves; we want to develop empathy and mutual concern.

Teasing

Helping students discern the difference between teasing that is playful and affectionate and teasing that is mean-spirited and hurtful is essential. It is common for students (and adults) to say cruel things to one another and then defend themselves by saying, "I was only kidding!"

It is important for students to be able to do the following:

- Discriminate between kinds of teasing
- Learn how to respond when they are being teased
- Learn how to respond or support a classmate who is being teased

Some of the books described at the end of this chapter contain excellent starting points for discussions about teasing and its negative consequences.

The Bullying Prevention Handbook by John Hoover and Ronald Oliver (1996, p. 153) includes a page of "Teasing Do's and Don'ts," including the following:

Do

Tell others if teasing about a certain topic hurts your feelings.

Try to read others' body language to see if their feelings are hurt—even when they don't tell you.

Don't

Tease someone you don't know well.

Tease about a person's body.

Tease about a person's family members.

Tease about a topic when someone asked you not to.

My personal experience with teasing has been that teasing only feels okay when (1) my relationship with the person teasing is strong and positive (i.e., I know they like me) and (2) I am being teased about something that I know the teaser notices or values about me. Asking me, "So how many quilt stores did you find to go to in Australia?" acknowledges that the teaser knows that I am likely to seek fabric wherever I go, or asking me, "How many friends did you make in the airport on your trip?" is a way of recognizing that I am likely to talk to strangers and find connections wherever I go. Neither personal attribute is something I would deny or be troubled to have named. Teasing me about my weight, for example, or my religion, or something else about which I am sensitive would be a completely different experience. In the end, the person *being* teased gets to say whether the teasing is acceptable or welcomed.

A possible activity for students might be to ask them to respond to the following questions:

- Is there anyone in your life from whom teasing feels good or okay?
- Who are the people from whom teasing feels dangerous or painful?
- What's the difference?
- How do your answers to the first three questions inform your understanding of what kind of teasing is appropriate and when?

Bullying

Stan Davis, author of *Schools Where Everyone Belongs: Practical Strategies for Reducing Bullying* (2003), writes (in a foreword to the book *Just Kidding*, Ludwig, 2006) about the causes of teasing and what to tell young people who are being bullied, including the following:

- It's not the child's fault.
- There is a variety of things you can try, but you shouldn't assume that one particular thing will work.
- Bullying *does* hurt. It puts the lie to "sticks and stones may break my bones but words will never hurt me."
- You should ask for help from adults when you are bullied, and if you talk to an adult who does not help, keep telling adults until someone does help you.

The book also includes discussion questions, including some important ones such as the following (Ludwig, 2006):

- How can you tell if your friends like it when you tease them?
- How do you let your friends know when their teasing is hurtful?
- When do you think teasing is okay, and when is it not?

The book says,

For many families and friends, teasing and kidding around is a way of showing affection and creating a feeling of playful camaraderie with one another. Both the teaser and the person being teased can easily swap roles, there is no imbalance of power, and the basic dignity of everyone involved is maintained. Equally important, if the teaser sees that the person being teased is obviously upset or objects to the teasing, the harmless teaser stops immediately. (Ludwig, 2006)

CHALLENGES TO THE VISION

Deep connection, realizing our relationships with others, and reaching out to other human beings with joy and delight are all a part of our natural state. Think of a very young child who has not yet had negative experiences with other people—the toddler who goes up to all adults and says, "Hi"; the six-year-old who is eager to tell the people in the supermarket that he can read now; or the baby who catches adults' eyes and smiles, fully expecting that the smile will be returned. If this is how we begin our lives, what happens?

Many of the impediments to being closely connected to others come from personal, individual experiences. These impediments are similar to those that keep us from showing ourselves fully.

Isolation

If I am sure that I am the only person with a particular experience of fear or challenge, then it is difficult to reach out to others. I am sure that I am alone, that no one else will understand, and that it isn't safe to tell others who I really am.

Competition

If I think that I will be compared unfavorably to others, found wanting or unworthy, then I am also hesitant to reach for connection with others. Instead, I monitor my performance carefully and am reluctant to include others in my circle lest our relationship damage my own standing or status.

Shame

If I have somehow been made to feel that I am not a completely lovable and wonderful person, then it will be difficult for me to believe that others would like to know me and connect with me. If I have been made to feel ashamed about my appearance, my background, my family, my language, or my skills in any area, it will keep me from being eager to share those aspects of myself with others.

Some of the other barriers to connecting with others come from more structural or societal experiences we have been affected by.

Early Messages About Difference

Early on, most of us got subtle and sometimes not so subtle messages about people who were different from us. Perhaps we were told, "Don't stare at that man in a wheelchair, it isn't polite," or we were chastised for asking questions about differences in skin color or facial appearance. Perhaps the messages were more overt, and we were told, "We don't play with Mexican children—they're dirty," or "You can't trust Jews. They cheat." Or perhaps the messages we got were largely silence—no information about differences, no opportunities to ask questions and learn, and no encouragement to get connected with others. In many cases, however, we grew up ignorant about many differences, perhaps scared or embarrassed to find out, and perhaps overtly uncomfortable or reluctant to interact with people who had been categorized as different or "not like us." We failed to develop a language around issues of diversity: how to ask respectful questions, and how to listen well when we hear information that is different than what we previously thought or believed.

Think about the messages we have learned about same and different. Even a Sesame Street song says, "One of these things is not like the others / one of these things just doesn't belong" (Raposo, Stone, & Hart, 1969). It's good to be the same; it's bad to be different. It's safer to be the same; it's dangerous to stick out. To be different is not to belong.

Tracking/Segregation

Throughout our school careers, many of us were systematically separated from other students. Perhaps, in your school, all the students labeled "special education" were in separate classrooms in the basement with little opportunities to interact with other students. Or maybe your school had ability grouping so that there was a smart third grade, an average third grade, and a slow third grade. Or perhaps you grew up in classes with three reading groups, the Robins, the Cardinals, and the Vultures, well aware of which one was the high reading group and which was the low reading group. In any case, we were often kept from knowing the full range of students in our school, and we were given covert messages about how those students were different from us and the desirability of staying in our own group. This kind of labeling and segregation may have left us feeling cut off from many of the students in our school, connected, instead, to a much smaller subgroup of students. Whether we grew up thinking that most other kids were smarter than we were or more stupid than we were, or whether we learned that we weren't like the jocks or the brains or the popular kids, we often felt like we couldn't be friends or even peers with all other students. In Beverly Tatum's (1997) wonderful book *Why Do all the Black Kids Sit Together in the Cafeteria?*, she reflects on the ways in which high schools are very segregated by race. A high school teacher recently told me that in his science classes, students are actually segregated by *row*—each row having an individual label or characteristic, with little mixing or interaction.

But reassuringly, children are not born with prejudice; they do not come into the world believing that light skin is better than dark skin, that people who are large are self-indulgent and lazy, or that certain food preferences are disgusting and strange. Although even young babies notice difference, they do not instinctively attach positive or negative judgments to those differences. Think of the four-year-old who cheerfully (and loudly) announces in the supermarket upon seeing a bald man, "Mama, that man's head is so shiny!" The child is noticing a difference and has not yet been taught that in our culture being bald is not considered desirable and that it falls into the category of "differences we don't mention." What children *do learn* very early is that differences are something we don't talk about. We learn that silence in the face of difference is the desirable response.

All of these values are ones that we learned, through our families, the media, advertising, and personal experience. The good news, then, is that because these values are not inherent or inevitable, we can structure our classrooms so that they are not learned or, if necessary, so that they can be unlearned or replaced by different information.

REFRAMING OUR WORK

Beginning With Ourselves

- What early messages did you get about people who were different from you? What did parents, teachers, and other community leaders tell you about people of other races, religions, or neighborhoods? Were your questions about differences easily and comfortably addressed?

- Did you grow up knowing people who spoke different languages? Whose families were very different from yours? Who had physical, cognitive, or emotional challenges?
- In your life now, how diverse are your friends? Neighbors? Coworkers?
- Which of your identities (race, religion, class, gender, sexual orientation, language, and the like) have been sources of pride and positive experiences?
- Which of your identities have been sources of pain, prejudice, or ill treatment?
- What do you wish *others* knew about you that would make your life easier or more comfortable?
- Is there an area of difference (religion, ethnicity, sexual orientation, or the like) about which you know very little?
- What area of difference is challenging for you personally (i.e., makes you uncomfortable)?
- What plan could you make to address both your knowledge gaps and your comfort gaps regarding difference?
- If you were teased or bullied as a child (or as an adult), what response or intervention was made by the adults in your world?
- Were you ever taught explicitly what to do if you witnessed teasing, bullying, or exclusion?
- Now, as an adult, are there times when you witness teasing or bullying and are concerned or puzzled about what to do?

Looking at Our Classrooms and Schools

- How explicitly are issues of diversity addressed in the curriculum?
- How well do you know the other teachers and staff at your school?
- What efforts have been made to help school staff know one another?
- Do teachers have a safe space in which to discuss and address challenges that arise in the school relative to meeting students' individual needs and dealing with tensions between groups?
- How prevalent is bullying in your classroom? In your school? How sure are you about your answer to this question?
- Is there a schoolwide policy on bullying or harassment? Were students involved in designing it or in implementing it? How has the policy been shared with students and parents? How consistently is it enforced?
- Do students connect across differences? Girls with boys? Children of different ethnic and racial groups?
- Do children notice and attend to stereotypical statements about who can be friends with whom? (I.e., do they respond when someone says, "Boys can't play with girls," or "You wouldn't know anything about this game"?)
- Do students know things about one another? (I.e., "There was television show on last night about volcanoes, and I thought about Marcus's rock collection," or "I saw that there was a big problem on the West Bank, and that's where Rami's grandparents live.")
- Do students know how to ask *respectful* questions of one another, particularly about differences? ("Why do you eat that special cracker?" or "Can you explain why you and your sisters wear that special kind of hat on your head?")

If teachers are not satisfied with their observations in response to the previous questions, they can initiate specific lessons on making connections or asking respectful questions.

Teachers can also avail themselves of teachable moments to make connections: "How many of you saw the article in the paper this morning about Mexico? Remember when we talked about students in our school who have come here from Mexico?" or "Did anyone see the big menorah they've erected downtown? Remember when we talked about all the religions that are represented in our classroom?"

What's the Big Picture?

If our long-term vision is of a global community with citizens who are well informed about the vast range of human differences, then we must keep our eye on the big picture. We might want to ask the following questions:

- What hopes and visions do we have for how our children will understand and relate to diversity issues?
- How will our students' school experiences regarding diversity and inclusion prepare them to become citizens in a democratic, diverse community?
- What changes should we make in our classrooms, schools, and communities to provide all children with the rich experiences that will allow them to be both knowledgeable and comfortable with a wide range of people?

HOW TO BEGIN

ACTIVITIES

Many of the activities in Chapter 3, in which students were encouraged to show themselves fully, are closely related to these activities in which we hope that students will reach out to one another. As we show ourselves fully, we allow others to see us as well. And as we feel more comfortable and secure about who we are, we can reach out more easily to others. Many of these activities are also ideal for settings in which adults are also getting to know one another, including staff development workshops and faculty meetings.

No Name-Calling Week

Originally a project by the Gay, Lesbian, Straight Educators Network (www.glsen.org), this program has extended far beyond its original implementation. It is now an annual week of educational activities aimed at ending name-calling in schools. There are many resources available to start an important school dialogue about eliminating bullying in schools and larger communities. The program was inspired by a book, *The Misfits*, by James Howe (2006; described in Chapter 6) that tells the story of a group of friends trying to survive seventh grade in the face of ongoing teasing and harassment. The students create a new political party and run on a platform aimed at eliminating name-calling of all kinds. Although efforts at eliminating bullying should be ongoing and not limited to a week, the resources provided (see http://www.nonamecallingweek.org/cgi-bin/iowa/all/about/index.html) can be very helpful in beginning or deepening the effort.

Stand Up, Sit Down

The teacher calls out a category and asks all the students who belong to that category to stand up (if the class includes students with mobility difficulties, students might raise their hands instead or hold up a yes or a no card.) Then she calls the next category, and students in that category stand up, and students who are standing from the last category sit down if they no longer are members of the new category. It is possible to engage students in this activity at many different levels. A first-grade teacher began with simple categories:

- Stand up if you have an older brother.
- Stand up if you like ice cream.
- Stand up if you like kittens.
- Stand up if you have brown hair.
- Stand up if you like playing baseball.

As students sat and stood, they could see all the ways in which they were alike and different. Karen and Malik both stood for the older brother category, but Karen likes baseball and Malik doesn't. Then the teacher asked this:

- Stand up if you have feelings.

Everyone stood. They then embarked on a discussion about the fact that everyone in the class had feelings, and therefore, everyone in the class had feelings that could get hurt by teasing, isolation, or meanness. Later, she asked another question that brought all students to their feet and occasioned another rich discussion:

- Stand up if you want friends in this class.

For older students, the categories may be more revealing, and as trust grows in the classroom, students can be asked to call out the categories themselves; this can serve as a way of their finding out who in the class feels the same way about something, has had a similar experience, or has something in common with them. Possible categories might include the following.

- Stand up if you like hip-hop music.
- Stand up if you are worried about going to junior high next year.
- Stand up if you like skateboarding.
- Stand up if you are concerned about someone who is using drugs.
- Stand up if you want to learn how to play soccer.
- Stand up if you are scared to stay home alone.

This activity can allow students to feel less isolated and to find areas of commonality and connection (see Box 4.2 for an example). If students are permitted to generate the categories, teachers might also gain insight into some of the issues and concerns of their students, which could be addressed at some future point. Again, it is important to stress that students can choose to pass.

BOX 4.2

In Cathi Allen's third-grade class in Bountiful, Utah, building a sense of community takes a front seat beginning on Day 1. On the first day of school, she encourages students to share with one another—what they did during the summer, commonalities, differences in families, and the like. Cathi structures her class so that there are many kinds of sharing going on. Sometimes students share in partners; sometimes the whole class listens as one person shares. The dynamics of the sharing change with each new activity, as students are given a variety of opportunities to share with someone they haven't shared with before. The enthusiasm is contagious, and the beginnings of belonging are taking root as similarities and uniqueness are shared.

Chart of Commonalities

One teacher put up a giant bulletin board in her classroom with each student's name written both across the top and down the side, forming a huge grid. Throughout the year, the students' assignment was to find one thing they had in common with every other student in the room. In the spot in the grid where the student's names intersected (Leora and Leora), the student was asked to write one thing about themself that was unique. For some pairs of students, finding something in common was easy. For others, it was more difficult. The growth from the experience comes not from finding easy answers but from working with complexity and reaching beyond superficial solutions. The children's delight when they found the commonality was exciting for the whole class.

In inclusive, highly heterogeneous classrooms, the greatest leap is when children who thought they were completely different find something in common. If some children are nonverbal or have difficulty making themselves known, the teacher may need to assist with this aspect of the activity, encouraging students to see beyond the surface to know the real child beneath! One teacher reported how thrilled a third grader was when he found out that a child who had a string of disability labels liked the same TV show that he did. A bond was formed that led to future sharing and interaction.

What List Is This?

The teacher generates 8 to 10 categories and writes each one on a separate piece of paper: likes watching TV football, has an older sister, likes roller coasters, likes spinach, and so on. The lists are passed around (or students come up to where they are posted), and students sign any of the lists that apply to them. Then, when everyone has signed all the lists they belong to, the teacher reads the members of the list and the students must guess what the category is. In other words, the teacher reads, "Shon, Darren, Alanna, Sarah, Tashena, and Morgan," and the students guess whether that's the "likes broccoli" list or the "knows how to ice skate" list. See Box 4.3 for a variation.

The teacher must actively seek categories that will have multiple children assigned and that will span across a diversity of categories of interests, characteristics, and visible similarities and differences. None of the categories should be ones that are negative or stigmatizing (in other words, no list of "still wets the bed").

BOX 4.3

In Kim Rombach's first grade, they play the yes/no game. Kim puts a large "no" on one wall of the classroom and "yes" on the opposite wall. Then she calls out a question: "Do you like ice cream? Yes or no?" Students have to run to the wall of the room that has their answer. She includes questions about hobbies, food preferences, interests, and so on. She reports that one little boy inquired, "Can I stay in the middle if my answer is 'sometimes' or I'm not sure?" Once students are at the same side, they can discuss their answer—"What kind of ice cream do you like?"

Color Sharing

Students sit in a circle and are each given a scrap of paper of various colors (three to five different colors). The leader says, "We're going to go around the circle, and you're going to share something with us. What you share depends on what color of paper you have." Based on the age, experiences, and context of the group, the teacher might make the following categories:

- If you have a red paper, tell us your favorite food.
- If you have a yellow paper, tell us your favorite animal.
- If you have a blue paper, tell us your favorite TV program.
- If you have a green paper, tell us your favorite sport.

Older groups can be asked more complex questions, and groups that have developed more trust can be asked for more revealing answers as well: "If you have a blue paper, tell us your plans for this summer." "If you have a green paper, tell us what you would do if you won the lottery." "If you have a yellow paper, tell us what three wishes you would make if you found a magic bottle." This activity can also be done with M&M candies or other colored goodies if the teacher feels this is appropriate to the group and won't raise issues of allergies, sugar, or others. One creative teacher uses raisins, pretzels, and carrot sticks to generate the categories. After students have responded, they might want to switch papers with students and then answer another color's question.

Name Sharing

Students sit with a partner and are asked to share about their name. They might respond to any of the following questions:

- After whom were you named?
- Do you like your name? Why or why not?
- What's the ethnic or language background of your name?
- Do you know what your name means?
- Have you ever met anyone else with the same first name?
- What other names are in your family (sisters, brothers, other relatives)?

This is a wonderful opportunity for students to share aspects of their background, including parts of their ethnic, cultural, and linguistic heritage. The discussion often touches on historic events ("I was named after my father's friend who was killed in Vietnam"), family traditions ("I'm the fourth John Harrison Wilson in my family"), language differences ("My name is Roberto, not Robert—my family comes from Puerto Rico"), and cultural history ("My mother was a Bob Dylan fan, and that's why she named me Dylan."). Some excellent books about differences in names are shared in Chapter 3.

All My Labels

Students are asked to list all the labels that apply to them. A student might write boy, brother, Cub Scout, Methodist, football player, son, grandson, roller blader, and so on.

Another student might write African American, singer, babysitter, Baptist, and so on. Students are then asked to look at their list and identify the following:

- Which of these labels are ones that you chose (Cub Scout, singer)?
- Which of these are labels that describe an unchangeable characteristic (girl, African American, Italian)?
- Which of these labels have had positive connections or experiences associated with them?
- Which of these labels have had negative connections or experiences associated with them?
- Would you want to be defined by any one label? Why or why not?

This activity gives students the opportunity to talk about their multifaceted selves and to see that their classmates cannot be easily labeled or pigeonholed. For some categories, the label or identity has been both a source of pride and positive experiences and a source of isolation or oppression. The activity also provides a gentle introduction to thinking about the ways in which people are sometimes oppressed or discriminated against because of one characteristic or quality and to think about the importance of connecting across narrow borders or distinctions. When students really listen to one another and hear how exciting it is to be a salsa dancer, what it's like to be teased for being large, or how hard it's been to have moved every year since kindergarten, they often grow in compassion and understanding. It's common for them to say, "Jamal told me about his dad being in the army, and I never realized how hard that would be to have your father gone so much and be worried too."

GAMES

Make a Group (Weinstein & Goodman, 1980)

This activity should be done in a large space with plenty of room to move around. The leader calls out a category or a characteristic and tells people to move as quickly as possible into a group of three to four people who share that characteristic. For example, if the leader calls, "People who feel the same way about cats as you do," you might end up with many small groups of "love cats," several small groups of "hate cats" and several groups of "allergic to cats." If the category is "people who had the same thing for breakfast as you did," you might end up with many groups of "cereal," several of "eggs and toast," and several of "skipped breakfast." The key to this game is to call out the categories as quickly as possible so that people are always moving. If they haven't found a group the first round, they will find one the next.

The teacher should make sure to call out categories that will include all children. Children who don't have the mobility to form groups should be either helped to move into an appropriate group or can become the center of a group to which other people move.

Birthdays

Again, in a large space, the leader tells people to find all the people who were born in the same month as they were. After the 12 groups have assembled, each group is given five minutes to make a chant or a cheer for their group. After all groups have come up with something, the groups perform their cheers, starting in January and moving through the months. The groups are told to cheer after each presentation. You might end up with, "July, July, firecrackers, apple pie, that's no lie" or "In December it gets chilly—we play outside and we act silly."

Linking Up

One child begins this game by standing in the center and saying, "My name is Lanai, and I like to skate." Any other child who also likes to skate then goes and stands next to Lanai, linking arms with her, says, "Link! My name is Tashara, and I also like to skate. And I love pizza." Another child who loves pizza then jumps up and links arms with Tashara, saying, "Link! My name is Manju, and I love pizza, and I have three brothers." The group goal is to get the entire class linked up—if, at the end, there are several children and no obvious matches, the group has to figure out commonalities, even if that involves undoing the last several links and redoing them in a way that works. The last child in the link makes a statement that links him to the first child, thus, completing the circle and the game. Children who are unable to talk or share can be involved through an interpreter, by writing their like/love on a paper, or by having someone who knows them well talk on their behalf.

Snowballs

The teacher gives the students a piece of paper and asks them to write the following:

A favorite place—real or imaginary	Something you love to eat
A wish you have for the future	Something you like to do with your free time

After each student has completed this task (students can get assistance, dictate, or draw if this is more appropriate), the students are instructed to wad up their paper and turn it into a snowball. Students then have a snowball-throwing blizzard in which they toss the snowballs at classmates, retrieve them from the floor, and throw them again. After several minutes, the teacher yells, "Stop," and everyone must retrieve one snowball. Everyone must search for lost snowballs until they are all found, accounted for, and each child has one. Students are then instructed to move around the room until they find the person whose snowball they have. They can ask people, "Are burritos with cheese your favorite food?" or "Do you like collecting baseball cards?" After everyone has found the person he or she is looking for and has been found by someone, the students are instructed to form a circle (or it can end up being two or three circles) in which they place the person they found on their right (with the person who found them on their left). After the circles have been formed (which can take a while in and of itself because it constitutes a cooperative challenge), students are asked to introduce the person on their right and tell something they learned about them. If the teacher has concerns about the context of fighting even with paper snowballs, all the wadded-up paper can be placed in a basket and students can draw one from the basket and then look for the person.

Depending on the group, age, and context, many things can be in the corners of the paper. A teacher whose class had just finished reading *Charlotte's Web* asked students to write down: your favorite character, your favorite scene, what you thought about the ending, and another book that you love. Students interviewed one another about their answers and had a rich discussion about the book because of this activity. When a group has developed more trust, questions can be more detailed or intimate: Write down something about your family that makes you happy. Write something that you're good at that you don't always tell people. Write three concerns you have about our school, community, and country.

This activity can also be easily adapted to content matter in any subject area. Students studying electricity in science might be asked to write: an electric appliance you rely on daily, one concern you have about the energy crisis, three alternate energy sources you have learned about, and one unanswered question you still have about electricity. A unit on World War II could yield questions like: two reasons the war started, your opinion about the role of the United States in the war, one lesson you learned by studying about the war, and one thing you learned from your interviews with your grandparents and other elders.

SONGS

"Under One Sky" (Pelham, 1982)

Singer and diversity educator Sarah Pirtle (1994) uses this song to help students find commonalities. Pair students and ask them to find similarities. Encourage them to explore hobbies, food tastes, interests, families, favorite colors, and TV shows. Then, take the similarities students come up with and make them into a song. Sometimes, I group two sets of students (for a total of four) and have them write their own verse:

> Well, we're soccer fans
> We love pizza
> We have little sisters
> And we like to swim

It's also possible to write a class verse including everyone's similarities or to have small groups write their own verses in addition to a classwide verse. Often, verses will directly contradict each other—"we love pizza" and "we hate pizza" or "we have four brothers" and "we're only children." Not only is this fine, it actually is a wonderful way to make the differences in the class clear and noted. The return to the chorus, "We're all a family under one sky," emphasizes the commonalities that are overarching.

Note: When teaching this song in Australia, several teachers pointed out to me that the sky was, in fact, different! This led to a wonderful discussion of stars, constellations, the moon, the sun, and what we shared and what was different. Teachers can write verses about family configurations, languages spoken, countries of birth, religions, or any other area in which the class' diversity will be highlighted.

"Make Our Circle Grow" (Traditional Song, New Words)

Two students begin acting out this activity: They jump together holding hands for the first two lines ("make our friendships grow"). Then they shake their heads, nod their heads (up and down), and tap their toes. For the rest of the song, they link arms and turn each other around until the very last line when they each choose a new partner and continue the activity. After each round of the song, the people chose new partners until, soon, the entire group is involved. This activity is a wonderful way to demonstrate reaching out and unity. If the teacher has any concerns about a particular child being chosen last, it is possible to begin with that student or to begin the activity with multiple pairs of students so that the game snowballs more quickly.

"Sing About Us" (Pirtle, 1998)

This is a song in which students write the verse following the pattern: "My friends _____." Sarah Pirtle has students brainstorm by categories (e.g., "What foods do people in this class eat?") and then write verses such as, "My friends like to eat spaghetti, my friends like to eat burritos, my friends like fried tofu, too." A verse on students' family backgrounds might be, "My friends come from Puerto Rico, my friends are African American too, my friends have family in Italy . . ." Teachers might want to combine this song with an interviewing activity in which students talk to classmates to find out things about one another and then small groups or the whole class writes a verse.

"Walk a Mile" (Nigro, 1987)

This song expands on the idea that the only way to really know a person and what her life is like is to "walk a mile in her moccasins." The song encourages students to think about their classmates and see things from another perspective. This song could be coupled with a writing activity that involves taking another's perspective and writing from that person's point of view.

"I Think of a Dragon" (Schimmel & Fjell, n.d.)

This song is about seeking (and finding) courage when facing bullying or mistreatment. The child imagines that there is a dragon beside her, and that gives her the strength to act powerfully. A discussion could center on the following: (1) Times you have wished you had a dragon beside you. (2) Who or what is your personal dragon? (3) How could you be a dragon for someone else who needs support?

"When I'm Strong" (Two of a Kind, 2002)

This song talks about the kinds of strength and courage needed to stand up to peer pressure and bullying. Students could easily contribute their stories of times when they had to be strong. An extension activity could involve brainstorming different ways of resisting pressure to do things that are uncomfortable or wrong.

CHILDREN'S LITERATURE

The books annotated in this section fall into two categories. The first set of books are about people getting to know one another across differences, books in which characters reveal themselves and then become connected, sometimes in unlikely ways. The second set of books deals directly with issues of tattling, teasing, bullying, and the importance of learning to be an ally when students see a classmate being mistreated.

Getting Connected and Crossing Boundaries

Enemy Pie *(Munson, 2000)*

A young boy's perfect summer is ruined when Jeremy Ross moves in down the street, steals his best friend, and becomes his number one enemy. But the boy's father volunteers to bake an "Enemy Pie" that he guarantees will get rid of the enemy. The boy wonders what the pie will do to his enemy, but his dad won't explain. But the biggest challenge comes when his father explains that the one part of Enemy Pie that the boy must do is to spend a day with his enemy and be nice to him. Not surprisingly, after spending a day together jumping on the trampoline, playing basketball, throwing a boomerang, and playing in the tree house, the boys' friendship grows, and when the father invites Jeremy for supper and produces the Enemy Pie, the boy no longer wants his friend to be poisoned and steps in to save him.

This humorous story makes the point that getting to know someone may change your perceptions of them; the best way to get rid of an enemy is to make a friend. Possible follow-up questions might include the following:

- Have you ever initially disliked someone and then changed your mind after you got to know him?
- What actions can you take when your initial impression of someone is negative? What stereotypes do you tend to play out when you meet someone new? (Girls can't do sports, I can't be friends with someone who doesn't speak my language, it's no fun playing with someone younger, and so on.)

Wanted: Warm, Furry Friend *(Calmenson, 1990)*

When Ralph and Alice (rabbits) meet in the supermarket, they take an automatic dislike to each other. Meanwhile, Ralph answers a personal add and starts a wonderful correspondence with another rabbit. The two correspondents delight in their growing friendship. When they finally meet, Ralph discovers that he has been corresponding with Alice—and that there is more to her than meets the eye.

This is a wonderful book for talking about friendship, connecting, and finding things in common. It links nicely with some of the activities suggested in this chapter, particularly concerning getting past initial impressions and finding the commonalities among people. Teachers might want to extend this book by having students write personal ads and then have them develop pen-pal relationships with students in their class or another class.

Willy and Hugh *(Browne, 1991)*

Willy, a chimpanzee, was lonely. No one let him join in any games; all the gorillas tell him he is useless. When a big gorilla, Buster Nose appears and says, "I've been looking for you, little simp," Hugh stands up and says, "Can I be of any help?" Hugh and Willy go on to become good friends, and Willy thoughtfully and respectfully helps Hugh who it turns out is frightened by spiders.

Friendship and mutual support are the central themes of this story. Students could discuss ways in which they support one another and the need for friendship and solidarity. Hugh is able to protect Willy because of his size. Because Willy is not afraid of spiders, he is able to support Hugh. Both friends let themselves be supported in what's hard for them.

Stellaluna *(Cannon, 1993)*

Stellaluna, a little bat, is dropped by her mother when she is very tiny. She falls into a bird's nest and is raised by the mother bird. She tries to learn to be a good bird, hanging right side up and eating bugs. She is awkward at many of these things, but she learns. One day, she finds her real mother, who reintroduces her to the world of bats and to doing things the bat way. They think that what she does is weird—flying during the day, eating bugs, hanging right side up, and the other bird things. She says, "Mama bird told me I was wrong, wrong for a bird, but right for a bat." She goes back and reconnects with the birds, and teaches them to do it the bat way. They realize they have different strengths.

"How can we be so different and feel so much alike?" mused Flitter. "And how can we feel so different and be so much alike?" wondered Pip. "I think this is quite a mystery." Flap chirped. "I agree," said Stellaluna. "But we're friends and that's a fact."

This book is a perfect introduction to the idea that there are many different ways to do things. We can talk about learning to be bilingual or multilingual, knowing multiple ways to get things done. Although we can share those ways, there is probably one way that works best for each child. We can respect our differences, and those differences don't have to stand in the way of building friendships or connections.

Mrs. Katz and Tush *(Polacco, 1992)*

A warm friendship develops between Mrs. Katz, an elderly Jewish woman, and Larnel, a young African American boy who lives across the hallway. Larnel helps Mrs. Katz care for a little kitten, and together, they develop a close friendship. Mrs. Katz shares with Larnel the similarities in their cultures and experiences— they both escaped from slavery and have suffered exclusion and isolation throughout their lives. Their friendship culminates with Larnel's invitation to Mrs. Katz' Passover Seder.

This is a sweet book about friendship across differences of age, race, and religion. There are many good opportunities to talk about cultural issues (kashruth, holidays, mourner's kaddish, and so on) as well as the similarities between racism and anti-Semitism.

The Goat Lady *(Bregoli, 2004)*

Two children and their mother befriend an elderly woman who raises goats. The other neighbors are not kind about the Goat Lady's run-down house, but the children come to love the woman, Noelie, after witnessing how she cares for her goats. Noelie provides goat's milk for people in need and sends her extra goat kids to poor people in other countries through Heifer International.

This is not only a book about a friendship that transcends boundaries of age but also provides a wonderful opportunity to talk about community service and making a difference. This could easily inspire a discussion of service projects students might undertake.

The Mushroom Man *(Pochocki, 2006)*

This is a tender story about a man who works on a mushroom farm. He spends his days in the dark, and the children tease him and call him "The Mushroom Man." Eventually, the man, who is lonely, makes friends with a mole. This is another book about a unique friendship and provides another opportunity to discuss the importance of relationships.

Muskrat Will Be Swimming *(Savageau, 2006)*

The author of this book is of Abenaki and French Canadian heritage; it tells the story of a little girl, Jeannie, who, although she loves her home by the lake, is teased by schoolmates who call her a "Lake Rat." Her wise grandfather shares a traditional Seneca story that helps Jeannie value and appreciate her native identity and the roles played by animals in her world.

This beautifully illustrated book provides opportunities to both learn about and appreciate native culture and to discuss issues of teasing. Possible discussions might include the importance of sacred places in native culture and the role of animal stories to impart ancient wisdom.

Chester's Way *(Henkes, 1988)*

Chester is a mouse who has very particular ways of doing things: he always has the same thing for breakfast; he always double knots his shoes; he always cuts his sandwiches diagonally. He is best friends with Wilson, who does everything exactly the same way. They are two peas in a pod. Then a new girl, Lilly, moves in, and she does things differently. They reject her and won't play with her. In the end, she rescues them from some mean boys, and they decide to become friends. They teach one another all their things—she shows them how to cut their sandwiches with a cookie cutter instead of diagonally; they teach her how to do hand signals on her bicycle; she teaches them how to pop wheelies. Lily teaches Chester and Wilson how to talk backward. They teach her how to double knot her shoes.

This is a wonderful book about broadening the people we can be friends with and learn from. A natural extension would be for students to talk about what they can share with others.

Nutmeg and Barley: A Budding Friendship *(Bynum, 2006)*

Nutmeg, a chatty red squirrel, and Barley, a quiet gray mouse, are neighbors who appear to have nothing in common. Nutmeg repeatedly makes overtures of friendship to Barley, but Barley resists and remains alone most the time. But when Barley gets sick, Nutmeg goes to visit and mishears "would love some tea" as "should leave me be." After a while, though, Nutmeg returns, and finding Barley quite ill, Nutmeg gently and tenderly nurses him back to health with tea, extra blankets, and special books. Soon, the two animals realize that they do have something in common—a love for lively music to which they dance together.

This book is perfect for exploring commonalities and differences between people. It can also be used to discuss what happens when people miscommunicate and the importance of persisting in finding common ground. This can be particularly important in classrooms that have students who speak different languages or who communicate in ways other than vocal speech (sign language, communication devices, and the like).

The following activities could be undertaken:

- Match students by passing out stickers (two of each kind) or some other small objects and have them find their partner.
- Have the partners find two things they have in common and two things that are different.
- Have partners share with the group what they found out about one another.

Given the possibilities of miscommunication that can easily occur when people speak different languages or come from different cultures, engage students in a discussion of the following:

- A time they were misunderstood and what that felt like
- A time they misunderstood someone else and what happened

This could also be another great time to talk about cultural differences—the different meanings that people attach to words, gestures, and expressions:

- One person's friendly closeness is read as too close and intrusive by another
- One person's friendly questions are interpreted as prying by another.

Have students generate strategies for improving their communication skills with people whose method or style of communication might be different, whether because of ability/disability, language, culture, or other characteristics: (1) How can you make sure that you are understanding someone well? (2) What can you do if you think you have misunderstood someone or she misunderstood you?

Owen and Mzee: The Story of a Remarkable Friendship *(Hatkoff, Hatkoff, & Kahumbu, 2006)* and Owen and Mzee: Language of Friendship *(Hatkoff, Hatkoff, & Kahumbu, 2007)*

Owen (a baby hippopotamus) and Mzee (a tortoise) formed a special bond after the tsunami in the Indian Ocean orphaned Owen. Mzee initially resisted Owen's overtures at friendship, but eventually, they bonded, and Mzee began to act in the role of an adoptive parent, teaching Owen what to eat and where to sleep. Within a year, the two had become inseparable, eating, sleeping, swimming, and playing together. Scientists have been astonished both by their close bond and by the ways in which they have developed a special vocal communication system.

These books, illustrated by photographs, are perfect for exploring the ways in which people (or animals) who are very different can come into one another's lives and form deep and meaningful relationships.

Ask students the following questions:

- Are you friends with anyone who is very different from you in some way (age, race, appearance, religion, background)?
- What would it be like to have your friendship limited to people who others think are just like you? What would be lost? Explore stereotypes like "boys can't be friends with girls" or "Arabs and Jews can't be friends."

Have students explore and write about friendships that cross traditional boundaries and what each person gains from the relationship.

Horace and Morris but Mostly Dolores *(Howe, 1999)*

Horace, Morris, and Dolores are the best of friends. They have many adventures together and can't imagine ever not being friends. But one day Horace and Morris join the Mega-Mice (no girls allowed), and Dolores joins the Cheese Puffs (no boys allowed). They are not really happy about it, but they feel somehow compelled to segregate by gender. One day, though, Dolores decides that the all girls group is boring and, gathering a confederate, Chloris, approaches the Mega-Mice and ask who wants to go exploring. Horace, Morris, and Boris join them, and the five of them build a clubhouse of their own that is called "The Frisky Whisker Club: Everyone Allowed."

This is a wonderful book for exploring issues of exclusion and segregation. Students could have a rich discussion of why Horace and Morris decided that they could only be with other boys and then Dolores only with girls. What are the pressures they experience to choose friendships and activities based on rigid conceptions of gender and gender-appropriate activities? What happens to children who cross the line: the boy who wants to dance or the girl who wants to play football?

Slightly older students can engage in an activity in which they explore sex-role stereotypes in children's books and in advertisements. Who plays with what toy? What kinds of activities do girls engage in? Boys? What are the negative results of this kind of rigid enforcement?

Several books about food provide wonderful opportunities to talk about what we have in common—needing food, liking to eat, eating with family—and the ways in which what and how we eat may be different. Although we do not want to reduce multicultural education to food, this can be a wonderful place to begin a discussion of similarities and differences.

Everybody Cooks Rice *(Dooley, 1991)*

A little girl goes out looking for her brother Anthony to bring him home for dinner. She goes to the homes of all her neighbors—from Barbados, Vietnam, China, and India. In every house, they are cooking rice in some form, and Carrie learns something about each family and their history. The book includes recipes for rice from each country.

Bread, Bread, Bread *(Morris, 1989)*

This is a photo book of all the places that people eat bread and all the different kinds of bread people eat—flat breads, round breads, bread with holes, and so on. A glossary at the back tells something about the country where that kind of bread is eaten.

A logical activity would be to prepare a class meal of different kinds of rice and various kinds of breads. If possible, parents could assist with this or students could follow recipes from home or from books. The meal could be connected to a social studies activity (mapping the location of various countries from which they bread comes) and with math activities associated with measurement (cooking, doubling and tripling recipes, estimating serving sizes, and so on). For older students, a discussion of world hunger, the uneven distribution of food in the world, world food banks, and the politics of hunger could be initiated. Working in a soup kitchen or collecting food for a food cupboard might also be possible (see Chapter 8).

Tattling

Don't Squeal Unless It's a Big Deal: A Tale of Tattletales *(Ransom, 2005)*

The story, which is excellent for exploring this topic, begins, "There were nineteen students in Mrs. McNeal's class. And nineteen tattletales." When the kids come to her to tattle (actually they are pigs!), she tries different things. She reminds them about class rules about borrowing things only after you've asked; she encourages them to tell their classmates what they want and how they feel. It gets a little tricky when one pig tells the teacher that "Frankie called Sookie a fat sow." While the teacher says it's good that the piglet remembers the class rule about not calling each other names, she says, "Also, we don't try to fix problems that don't belong to us." She says,

> I know you're trying to help, but if Frankie and Sookie have a problem, it's their job to fix it. If they can't, it's my job as the teacher to help them. Your job, Mrs. McNeal added, is to take care of you. That's the most important job you can have!

Finally, when it all erupts, the teacher makes a new rule: don't squeal unless it's a big deal. This is her attempt to do a bit of tattling triage—She tells them they *can* squeal "when someone is hurt or in danger, or when a person is hurting you, or hurting a pet, or hurting something that doesn't belong to them or that belongs to all of us."

At the end of the book, the teacher slips and falls. The piglets recognize that it's an emergency, and they call the nurse and get another teacher—proof that they can tell the difference between annoying tattling and an emergency that requires outside help.

This excellent book contains a section on the differences between tattling and telling.

Two other books discuss the issue of tattling.

Armadillo Tattletale *(Ketteman, 2000)*

Armadillo, who is blessed with long ears that hear everything, loves to eavesdrop on other animals and tell tales about what he heard. But Armadillo's long ears also make it difficult for him to move, and he is slow. The other animals, who dislike him for telling tales, beat him to the watering hole every day and force Armadillo to scrounge for water to drink. But time after time, Armadillo overhears conversations not intended for his ears and reports them to the animals, creating lots of anger and confusion. When alligator gets angry about the tale bearing, he nibbles on Armadillo's ears until they are small—they hear fine, but they don't hear everything.

Although the story is somewhat problematic—the solution to the problem is a bit violent—the story certainly could be used to discuss the dangers and damage that comes from repeating things that are said by others. Students could share a time that someone said something about them that hurts their feelings or a time they repeated something someone else had said and later wished they hadn't. It would also be wonderful to couple this discussion about ways we could pass on positive comments and compliments— the ways in which it is great to repeat things other people have said!

Tattlin' Madeline *(Cummings, 1991)*

This book, with an African American protagonist, describes some of the consequences and again discusses the difference between tattling and reporting and the importance of reporting when someone or something is being hurt or going to be hurt.

An excellent activity for these books would be to make a list of things someone might tell about and have students decide whether they represent tattling or reporting. With young children, this could be done with response cards (hold up the *T* card for tattling and the *R* card for reporting) while older students could work in small cooperative groups to sort the statements into two piles.

Words Are Not for Hurting *(Verdick, 2004)*

Although intended for very young children, this book raises issues of how words can be used to help or to hurt. A section in the book for teachers includes activities about communication (including body language), learning to express feelings, tone of voice, and apologizing. Of particular interest is the section "Words that Hurt," which includes ways of initiating a discussion of sticking up for yourself and others who are being teased.

Just Kidding *(Ludwig, 2006)*

A young boy, DJ, is bullied at school by other boys who call him names and make fun of him. His father talks to him about some possible ways to respond to the taunts (with some support from his older brother), and they also talk to the teacher about what's going on. DJ is reluctant to be a tattletale but the teacher reassures him that "tattling is when you're trying to get someone in trouble. Reporting is when you're trying to help someone in trouble. In this case, DJ, you're reporting because you're in trouble and you need help."

The Sissy Duckling *(Fierstein, 2002)*

Elmer is a different kind of duck. He loves building things, painting pictures, helping around the house, and decorating cookies. He is not like the other boy ducks, and although his father tries to get him interested in sports, he isn't interested, and the other ducks call him a sissy. His mother explains to him, "Sissy is a cruel way of saying that you don't do things the way others think you should." Elmer continues to be tormented at school and rejected by his father as well, and finally, he decides to run away from home. But when his whole family migrates, his father is shot by a hunter, and Elmer rescues him and nurses him back to health in a little cave he has found to live in. When the rest of the family returns, Elmer is a hero, and his father is his defender and champion. Elmer concludes by saying, "I want to make one thing perfectly clear: I am the same duck I have always been. I have not changed. I am a BIG SISSY and PROUD of it!" But the father says, "You haven't changed, but maybe I have."

Although the taunt of sissy is highly problematic, this is a tease heard in schools and could begin an important discussion of name-calling and differences. Although not explicitly about issues of sexual orientation, the way in which Elmer is presented may engender a discussion of gender expression and the ways boys who do not fit the cultural stereotypes of masculinity are often excluded and oppressed. The ending of the book, however, does raise an important point, which is that Elmer doesn't get "cured" or "transformed" but rather that his qualities and skills come to be seen in a new light.

Bullying

There have been many books about bullying published in the last 10 years, and this reflects both the magnitude of the problem and the increasing recognition of the importance of attending to the social emotional climate of the school to make schools safe learning environments for all students.

As it is impossible to review or name all of the books available about bullying, the following questions may be useful in evaluating books to determine if they are consistent with your and/or the school's values and policies. Consider the following.

1. Does the book in any way blame the target for the bullying behavior? Avoid books that imply that it is the victim's fault that he is bullied. Although children's behavior may be annoying or problematic, there is never any justification for bullying. Do not fall into the trap of "if only Jed didn't X, then other kids wouldn't pick on him."

2. Does the targeted student have any allies? Do any other students witness, care, or involve themselves in figuring out a solution or offering support? Does the book open a discussion or provide models of what one might do when witnessing the bullying of others?

3. What language and words are used as part of the bullying? If negative terms or words are used in the book, do you *have* and will you *take* sufficient time to debrief the book so that there will be no doubt that this language is unacceptable? In other words, you don't want to use a book that will be a model for new name-calling possibilities.

4. Is the solution provided by the book realistic or feasible? Will students see the outcome as possible or desirable? Books in which a bigger bully, for example, comes to the rescue of a child being targeted or something terrible happens to the bully are neither realistic nor helpful in modeling kind, collaborative problem solving and loving support.

5. Are adults in the book seen as involved, caring, and alert to how students are treated? Is reporting bullying behavior modeled as an acceptable and desirable strategy? Avoid books in which students are shown as or feel abandoned by the adults in their vicinity.

6. Last, will the students relate or connect to the characters in the book, particularly in terms of the characters' age, race, school context, or language?

The following books are some that I feel may be useful in working on bullying issues with students.

For Younger Students

Nobody Knew What to Do: A Story About Bullying *(McCain, 2001)*

A young boy is upset when he sees kids in his class picking on Ray, a classmate. He reports that the teachers don't notice. He says, "Ray was trying hard to be brave. I hoped he could keep going until he fit in." But the bullies escalate their violence, and the boy recognizes that the bullies' behavior is designed to intimidate the other children: "They used words and fists to make us all so afraid, that nobody, not one of us, would ever say, 'This is NOT okay.'" Finally, the boy knows he must do something and he goes to tell the teacher. The teacher affirms that he did the right thing. When Ray returns to school after staying home, the boy acts firmly.

> When Ray came back, he looked nervous and afraid. So I said, "Play with us at recess." And he did. You know what? When the kids who bullied came around . . . so did my teacher. So did my principal. And she called the parents of everyone who had been mean to Ray. Nobody bullied that day.

We won't let it happen. Together we know what to do and say to make sure bullying is NEVER okay. We work together to make it end.

A discussion at the end of the book gives suggestions on bully prevention including "While 'tattling' just spreads stories that don't help, telling lets adults know what happened in a bullying situation and enables them to address the problem." Children sometimes have trouble understanding this distinction, so they need reminders that it is always okay to talk to parents, teachers, and other familiar grown-ups.

Louder, Lili (Choldenko, 2007)

Lili is a very quiet girl—she is barely heard when she speaks, and she is way too shy to assert herself. A bossy girl, Cassidy Clummer, becomes her partner but continues to take advantage of her—taking her lunch, making her do the disagreeable parts of projects, and so on. Her only real friend is the Lois the guinea pig. But one day, when Cassidy threatens to seriously abuse Lois, Lili finally finds her voice and yells, "Stop it!" really loud. Everyone is astounded, including Lili, and it becomes clear that she will learn to stand up for herself and others from now on.

- Use this book to explore quiet/loud children.
- Talk about the ways Lili is abused and taken advantage of by others.
- Ask students, "Has that ever happened to you?" What finally made you find your voice? What would be so bad that you would finally say something? Are there tipping points for speaking up?
- Talk about the role of allies when someone is quiet or can't speak. There is a poster that says, "Not being able to talk doesn't mean you have nothing to say."

The Bully Blockers Club (Bateman, 2004)

Using animal characters, this book tells the story of Lotty, who begins the school year with great excitement only to be bullied repeatedly by Grant Grizzly. Various family members suggest strategies, some of which Lotty tries; while she rejects her brother's suggestion of a karate chop, she does try ignoring the behavior, being nice to Grant, and telling the teacher. But when Lotty realizes that most of the bullying takes place when the teacher isn't there, she has the brilliant idea to enlist her peers in a Bully Blockers' Club; the club members keep an eye out for one another and reach out to anyone who is lonely or threatened.

The book includes a section for teachers that discusses the importance of awareness of the bullying issue. The strong focus on building allies and looking out for one's classmates makes this a very useful conversation starter with students.

My Secret Bully (Ludwig, 2005)

Monica's bullying by her "friend" Kate is hard to detect; most of Kate's bullying is done very secretively and even when Monica asks her about it, Kate is evasive. When Kate's bullying expands to include enlisting other students to exclude Monica, Monica finally confides in her mother. Her mother listens to her very well, doesn't minimize her problems, and shares stories of her childhood. She practices speaking powerfully with her mother, and the next day she confronts her bully confidently and effectively. The happy ending does not include reconciliation or friendship with Kate, but Monica learns to take care of herself and be assertive about her right to proper treatment.

The book's exploration of *emotional bullying*, which includes rumors, intimidation, humiliation, exclusion, and the silent treatment, will be particularly useful for exploring girl bullying in the classroom.

Two other books by the same author, *Just Kidding* (Ludwig, 2006) and *Trouble Talk* (Ludwig, 2008), are also excellent for exploring rumors, bullying, and cruelty.

For Older Students

What Do You Know About Bullying? *(Sanders & Myers, 1996)*

This book is one in a series of "What Do You Know About" books, and this one addresses the following questions:

- What is bullying?
- Why do people become bullies?

Bullies like to be powerful. Sometimes they may be jealous of others and use bullying as a way of getting at them. Bullies will pick on anyone if they think they can get away with it. They will look for situations that allow them to do this.

- Standing up to bullies?
- What will happen if I tell?
- How do schools deal with bullying?
- Why do some people get picked on more than others?
- Racist bullying: Bullies will often pick on people simply because they are different in some way. It may be the kinds of clothes they wear, the food they eat, or the neighborhood they come from.
- What can I do?

The book combines photos, cartoons, and simple text and offers many opportunities for discussion.

Jake Drake, Bully Buster *(Clements, 2001)*

This book tells the story of fourth-grader Jake who is bullied by Link. Jake's attempts to deal with the bullying are not successful, but when the two boys are made partners in a social studies project, Jake sees a different side of Link, and they are able to form a (limited) relationship. The book explores the real person underneath the bully, and although it does not have a clear solution, it certainly makes it clear that bullies are complex.

Diary of a Wimpy Kid *(Kinney, 2007)*

This novel in cartoons (and the subsequent books in the series) tells the story of Greg, a young boy who enters middle school, encountering many students who are bigger, taller, and meaner. As Greg navigates challenges with bullies and other difficult situations, he provides a unique (and also typical) reaction to the challenges of middle school. Students will have lots to talk about and discuss after reading this engaging, easily accessible story.

Amelia's Bully Survival Guide *(M. Moss, 1998)*

This creative book looks like a graphic novel, a student's journal, and a scrapbook, and tells the story of Amelia's attempts to deal with the class bully. Written with great humor and insight into the real lives of students in school, this book will spark lively conversation among readers in the upper elementary grades.

Bullies Are a Pain in the Brain *(Romain, 1997)*

This book of jokes and cartoons uses a humorous approach to address how students can respond when confronted by bullies in their schools and neighborhoods. It contains important truths about bullies including that they love power and control, that they are sore losers, and that ignoring them won't make them go away.

Stick Up for Yourself! Every Kid's Guide to Personal Power and
Positive Self-Esteem *(Kaufman, Raphael, & Espeland, 1999)*

This self-help book for upper-elementary students contains sections on "How to Get and Use Personal Power" and "How to Build Positive Self-Esteem," and it is full of quizzes, tips, and anecdotes about dealing with bullies, using positive self-talk, and talking about feelings. Although this book is primarily didactic, it could provide an excellent starting point for discussing these issues with upper-elementary students.

Stand Up for Your Friends: Dealing With Bullies,
Bossiness, and Finding a Better Way *(Criswell, 2009)*

This book is targeted primarily at girls, although the information is useful for all. The book includes a helpful discussion of what to do in the face of inappropriate, mean behavior.

Goodbye Bully Machine *(Fox & Beane, 2009)*

This brightly colored, collaged book address what bullying is, why people bully, and how to stop the "Bully Machine." The book is immediately engaging and contains an excellent section on moving from bystander to ally.

Cootie Shots *(Bowles & Rosenthal, 2001)*

This collection of short stories, poems, plays, and songs for upper-elementary and middle school students raises issues of teasing, bullying, and exclusion in engaging and interactive ways. Students could create a performance piece for themselves and to share with students in other classes.

LINKS TO THE CURRICULUM

This topic has direct links to all aspects of the curriculum: How do we find out about other people? Through reading, writing, talking, and interacting, how can we learn more about the people in our classroom? In our community? In our city? In the world? When we notice that we have an initial negative reaction to another person or another group, how can we find out more about that person or that group? How is the process of getting to know others connected to forming relationships and working together?

For language arts study, students might learn interview skills and seek to find out about others in their communities. Young children might interview one another, and then move on to interviewing students in other classes or at different grade levels. Older students could use interviewing as a way of getting to know people outside the school. They might start with interviewing parents or grandparents and then go on to interview other elders in the community and other people who work or reside in their neighborhoods and town. Getting to know people beyond superficialities and first impressions can be an important lesson for students (and everyone).

With older students, I have often initiated what I call *mini-investigations*. Students are asked to talk to three to five people (who must be diverse) about a specific topic and then to record what they heard and report it in class, either verbally or graphically. Sample mini-investigations might include the following:

- Talk to three people who are more than 50 years old, and ask them what they studied in school that has been important to them as adults and what they wish they had learned.

- Talk to three people who are from religions different from yours, and ask them what it has been like to grow up as a Lutheran, Jew, Christian Scientist, or whatever religion.
- Talk to three people, one in their teens, one in their 20s, and one in their 30s, and ask them what kinds of chores they had to do as children.

Mini-investigations can also be linked to specific subject matter but can again emphasize getting beyond superficiality:

- *Science:* Talk to three people of different ages, and ask them what electric devices or appliances they use in a day. Ask them if their use of electricity has changed in the last 10 years.
- *Math:* Talk to three people who do different jobs, and ask them what kinds of math they use in their work. Ask them when and where they learned the math they use.
- *Social studies:* Talk to three people whose parents were not born in the United States, and ask them to tell you what they learned from their parents. Ask, in particular, about family customs, language, experiences as immigrants, and the like.

5

Places Where
We All Belong

Marta, a third grader, is excited about the upcoming puppet show her class is doing. Some children have written the script, others have painted the scenery, a few children will work the puppets, and others will make programs and sell tickets. Marta, who uses a wheelchair and a computerized touch talker, is the play's narrator. When it is her turn to talk, Marta activates the touch talker and the next piece of the story plays.

Antoine, a kindergartner, is already a fluent reader. He is very proud of his skills and especially loves books about animals. After the third week of school, he asks his mother for warmer school clothes. She inquires further and finds out that the teacher sends him into the hallway by himself during reading time because he can already read and the kindergarten reading lessons focus on sound and letter recognition.

Noah, a fourth grader, loves studying insects and reading books about classifying insects. Because he wears glasses, is quiet, and prefers reading to sports, several of the other boys in the class have teased him, calling him "sissy" and "faggot." They shove him out of the "boys' line" and tell him he doesn't belong with them.

In Mr. Watkin's class, Valentine's Day is celebrated as a day of friendship. Because last year there was fierce competition about who got the most valentines and many hurt feelings, Mr. Watkins now has another system. Each student cluster (four to five students who sit together) is assigned to plan a surprise treat for another cluster, and they are required to use resources available in the room or with no cost.

THE VISION

Students differ in many ways. Regardless of what it says on the door—third grade or kindergarten—the reality is that all classrooms are actually heterogeneous. In your class, you may have students who live in different family situations, some living with two parents, some with one parent, some with grandparents, and some in foster care or shelters. Children may have two mothers, two fathers, many siblings, stepbrothers and sisters, or no siblings at all.

Your class may contain children from different racial or ethnic groups, children of different religions, and children of different socioeconomic levels. You may have students with different dietary requirements, children who speak different languages, and children whose parents are struggling with drug or alcohol abuse.

Without a doubt, your students differ in appearance, size, interests, skills, abilities, and challenges. Your classroom may have students who are athletic and coordinated and students who are not, students who read easily and those who struggle, and students who make friends quickly and those who wrestle with forming relationships.

Although all classrooms are really heterogeneous already, many schools are moving toward even more purposive heterogeneity, attempting to limit the negative effects of tracking and recognizing the value of teaching children to interact comfortably with a wide range of people. This philosophy, sometimes referred to as *full inclusion,* represents a commitment to creating schools and classrooms in which all children, regardless of individual educational needs or disabilities, are educated together (Sapon-Shevin, 2007).

What makes a classroom inclusive? Many people use the word *inclusive* to refer to the ways in which special education services are provided. From that perspective, an *inclusive classroom* can be described as one in which all children, regardless of performance level, are educated with their chronological peers in a typical classroom. That is, children are educated in third grade even though they do not read at the third-grade level and individualized or specialized services that may be required are provided in the context of the general education classroom.

But inclusion can be defined much more broadly so that it refers to welcoming all students, acknowledging the many differences students bring to the classroom (not just characteristics labeled as disabilities), and accommodating all those differences in a shared community. Addressing student differences related to race, class, gender, ethnicity, language, family background, and religion are all part of creating an inclusive classroom. A broader definition of inclusion refers to a classroom in which all children are part of a shared community and the following characteristics are present:

- Open discussion of the ways in which people are different and the kinds of support and help they need and want
- A commitment to meeting children's individual needs in a context of shared community and connection
- Explicit attention to the ways in which students' differences can become the basis for discrimination and oppression and to teaching students to be allies to one another

The goal of having an inclusive classroom is *not* to homogenize those differences, pretending that they aren't there or don't have impact on students or their lives. The goal is to acknowledge those differences and create a classroom community that works with those differences (and sometimes around those differences) so that every student can feel a sense of connection and belonging. By setting inclusion as a goal for all our classrooms, we can acknowledge the heterogeneity we already have (and receive support and help for responding to challenges), and we can set a vision of full membership and participation in the forefront of our thinking and planning. Rather than conducting business as usual and then needing to retrofit or revise our curriculum and our teaching when we recognize students' differences, we can plan for and with those differences from the beginning.

A mother approached the human relations coordinator of a large urban school district and said, "I'm so proud of my son. He's been in kindergarten for four weeks now, and he hasn't noticed that his teacher is black." The human relations coordinator was taken aback. She asked, "Is he visually impaired?"

Of course, the kindergartner had noticed his teacher's dark skin. What the mother probably meant was that his observation hadn't interfered with his ability to connect and respond to his teacher. But noticing itself is fine.

The goal mustn't be not noticing. The goal should be to notice, understand, respond, and connect. Sometimes, in an effort to act casual or accepting, we pretend not to have noticed differences among ourselves. But we can make a distinction between noting that Nicole's hair is bright red and making fun of Nicole for being a "carrot top." There is a difference between noting that Nancy's shoes are shaped differently to accommodate her feet and looking away quickly in embarrassment when she mentions buying new shoes. Telling someone that you don't notice how they are different is not a compliment if it means that you are failing to see all aspects of who that person is. We have moved far beyond the oft-stated goal of "colorblindness" because it is neither possible nor desirable (not to mention that the word *blindness* is problematic).

In inclusive classrooms, differences are acknowledged and accommodated, and teachers both talk honesty and openly about differences and still retain a strong sense of community. Previous chapters have discussed classrooms in which students are comfortable showing themselves fully and knowing others well. These two conditions are essential to creating classrooms that feel inclusive to students, where they know that their individual needs will be met without exclusion from the community, shame, or humiliation.

Consider the following two possibilities for Marsha, who has diabetes: In Classroom A, the teacher makes special arrangements to buy some sugar-free cookies for the class party and quietly dispenses those to Marsha so that other students won't know.

In Classroom B, all the students know that Marsha has diabetes, and they understand why and when she takes insulin. When they are discussing the class party, the students themselves volunteer, "Let's make sure we get snacks that everyone can eat," and they list Marsha's needs, as well as those of Sarah, who is a vegetarian; Robin, who is allergic to wheat; and Amman, who doesn't eat pork or pork products such as lard.

The goal is not to hide Marsha's unique needs but to think about Marsha as both an individual and as a member of a cohesive, classroom community.

Similarly, think of how teachers respond to children noticing differences in academic requirements for different children. In one classroom, children who ask, "How come Matthew gets to do his math on the computer?" or "Why does Sharissa only have five spelling words?" are told to mind their own business. In an inclusive classroom in which the teacher has helped students to know one another well, other students *know* that Matthew works on the computer because his processing difficulties make that strategy much more successful for him than pen and paper. Sometimes they partner with him and work on the computer together. They also know that people learn spelling in many different ways and that five spelling words for Sharissa is just the right level of challenge. And because students' spelling words are drawn from their personal writing and not from a standardized list, it makes sense to them that different people have different lists.

One sometimes hears it said that the *successful* inclusive classroom is one in which "you can't tell the kids with disabilities apart from the regular kids." Although the underlying sense of equity and fair treatment reflected in that goal is admirable, the goal itself is often unattainable and probably undesirable as well. Some of the children included in typical classrooms have differences that are quite noticeable, and no amount of community building or successful accommodation will mask their unique characteristics. Setting a goal of "invisibility" for children with disabilities doesn't help us think well about how children's differences are responded to or how they are incorporated into the daily life and activities of a classroom. Encouraging Rowena to hide her hearing aids behind her hair so that no one knows will not help other students learn how to best communicate with a classmate with a hearing loss, and it communicates to Rowena that wearing hearing aids is somehow bad or shameful. The goal of inclusive classroom is that all students feel that they belong and are able to contribute to the class.

The same must be said for the accommodations required to meet the needs of a wide range of students. Setting a goal that "no one will notice" that Quentin does his math differently or that Rahima uses a different form of communication implies embarrassment or shame related to accommodations and modifications. The goal, instead, should be easy acceptance and understanding of students' differences (by the teacher and other students) so that modifications and adaptations occur in an overall framework of community and honest communication. Attempts to make sneaky modifications communicates a lack of understanding of the nature and importance of diversity in classrooms. Although we certainly want adaptations and modifications to be implemented in thoughtful and respectful ways, they need not be kept a secret and can become part of the daily discourse of the classroom.

Making inclusion work also means attending to the beliefs and experiences of parents, whose own school history may not have included extensive relationships with students they perceived as different. When it came time for Stacy, a typically developing child, to go to school, her parents wrestled with not only whether Stacy should be in an inclusive classroom but also whether she should go full-time to the gifted program that the district offered (see Box 5.1).

BOX 5.1

My husband and I weren't sure that we wanted her to go full time [to the gifted program], and we did a lot of talking to the teachers, the principal, and other parents, and we eventually decided that we didn't want her to participate because we didn't want her in an isolated classroom away from her friends where she would feel different from everybody else. So my husband and I decided not to send Stacy to a gifted program, but to keep her in a regular second-grade class. And guess who her seat partner was? It was Madison! We were blown away because here was this kid of ours that we decided not to send to a gifted program, but her seat partner couldn't read or write. So we decided to get with the program and figure out what all this [inclusion] was about. (Staub, 1998, p. 21)

Later that year, after Stacy and Madison, a child with Down syndrome, had become good friends, Stacy's mother reflected,

For Stacy, it was a turning point. I mean I don't know if a seven-year-old can have a turning point in their life, but I think it was for her. Their friendship was a connection immediately and wasn't something that we could explain to Stacy. We couldn't explain to Stacy about Madison, but she found out for herself. In spite of us, the kids wanted this relationship to happen and it did. (Staub, 1998, pp. 21–22)

Parents, like students, can learn through inclusion that children are children and that individual accommodations need not be overwhelming or frightening. For Stacy's mother, as for Stacy, learning to be comfortable with differences was a growing process (see Box 5.2).

BOX 5.2

About six months into their second-grade year together, Stacy must have asked a dozen times if Madison could come over and play. I had so many excuses why Madison couldn't come over—dance practice, piano lessons, Madison lives too far away, etc., etc. Finally, after Stacy's persistence, I asked Madison's mother. I was quite embarrassed, but I just blurted out, "You know, Stacy really wants Madison to come over and play, but what does she eat? What do I do if she chokes? What if she wants to go home? Does she know how to use the toilet? Will she be okay being away from home?" You know, our generation is just so ignorant about these things. I was terrified the first time Madison came over to play. Well it took all of about 10 minutes to put my worries to rest. Madison was really just another kid. Nothing secret, nothing surprising. (Staub, 1998, p. 165)

And Madison's mother shares what it means to her having Stacy and her mother in their lives: "For the first time in Madison's life, a parent who does not have a child with disabilities was interested in my daughter and how she could make Madison feel like a welcome guest in her home." (Staub, 1998, p. 180)

A wonderful new film, *Including Samuel* (Habib & Desgres, 2009) tells the story of the Habib family's commitment to include nine-year-old Samuel in all facets of school and community. As one sees Samuel in school and playing on a T-ball team in the community, it becomes clear how important inclusion is for *all* of us; learning to be comfortable with differences and being able to have relationships with a wide range of people enhance all our lives. It is not a favor we do for those who are different but a gift we give ourselves, the gift of understanding and compassion. This is what building community is all about.

Creating an inclusive classroom means attending to many aspects of the classroom: what is taught and to whom, how the room is arranged, how students are grouped, what kinds of teaching strategies are used, and how assessment is done. Why is it that in the same school, one teacher seems to do well with a very diverse group of students—the one who just moved to the United States from Vietnam, the painfully shy little girl emerging from an abusive family, and the child with cerebral palsy—at the same time that a teacher down the hall struggles whenever he has children who are even slightly different or performing below grade level? What is there about that first teacher's classroom that makes inclusion so much easier?

I sometimes hear teachers and administrators say,

"If we include a student like Daniel, we'll have to modify the curriculum."

"If we include students like Tara, we'll have to change our teaching methods—lecture just doesn't work for those kids."

"If we want to include a student like Noelle, we'll really have to deal with a lot of social issues—the kids in my class can be so cruel." (Sapon-Shevin, 1996a)

All of the statements are true! Attempting to integrate students with significant educational and behavioral challenges or other characteristics that could lead to rejection and exclusion shows us what kinds of changes are needed in our schools. When we see how certain children struggle in our system, it points out to us all the ways in which our schools and classrooms are unimaginative, underresourced, unresponsive, and simply inadequate. I use the metaphor of a disclosing tablet, the little red tablet that students are asked to chew after they've learned to brush their teeth. When chewed, it reveals all the places that haven't been adequately brushed—the areas that need attention. Similarly, inclusion of all kinds of diversity is the disclosing tablet of our schools—it helps us see the places where our programs, our curriculum, and our classroom environments aren't working for all children. And the kinds of changes we make for Daniel, Tara, and Natasha are almost always changes that benefit many other children as well. Thinking about our curriculum, our pedagogy, and our social climate in terms of inclusion can help us meet the needs of *all* children better.

CHALLENGES TO THE VISION

There are many challenges to implementing inclusion. Long-held notions of how people learn, how teachers can best teach, and how differences should be responded to can keep us from reinventing schools as cooperative, inclusive communities. Many of the existing structures of school (gifted programs, special education, remedial education services) also make inclusive classrooms difficult to operationalize. This next section details myths about inclusion, grouping, and teaching that can get in our way as we move to creating more diversity-friendly classrooms.

Myths About Ability Grouping

There is such a thing as ability.

Many educational systems are based on a notion of fixed ability levels that define the best a student can do. When we talk about children "not working up to their ability" or sometimes, ironically, "overachieving" (doing better than we predicted they would), we are evoking an image of fixed immutable potential. This belief system leads to classes for the "gifted" and for the "handicapped" where we adjust our curricula and expectations accordingly.

In actuality, all people vary along a wide number of dimensions, and ability is not a particularly useful construct. How well any child does is a function of many factors, including the nature of the curriculum, the child's self-concept, and the flexibility and support of those who surround the child. In other words, if conditions were right, we could all do better. Hunt (1961) notes,

> It is highly unlikely that any society has developed a system of child rearing and education that maximizes the potential of the individuals which compose it. Probably no individual has ever lived whose full potential for happy intellectual interest and growth has been achieved. (p. 346)

We are, then, *a world of underachievers*, and it makes sense for teachers to find ways to help all children achieve more and to create classrooms that nurture and support diversity (Sapon-Shevin, 1994a).

Students learn better in homogeneous groups.

Some teachers believe that by narrowing the range of abilities in the classroom, children will learn better because tasks will be more appropriate. In her famous book

Tracking Inequality, Oakes (1985) showed that despite the fact that many teachers grouped students by ability, overwhelming research results suggested that homogeneous grouping did not consistently help anyone learn more or better (Massachusetts Advocacy Center, 1990). Now, more than 20 years later, Oakes has reviewed the research on tracking and the "tracking wars" and has found that although many believe that tracking has been eliminated, the deep structure of tracking still remains powerful. Organizing children into high-, average-, and low-ability groupings continues to *create* differences in what children learn by exposing them to different kinds of materials and vastly different expectations. Although some children in high-ability groups may benefit academically from such arrangements, those who lose the most are those placed in average- and low-ability groups. Such grouping practices tend to compound racial, ethnic, and economic differences in schools, as poor children and children of color are least likely to be served in enriched, gifted, or high-ability tracks and are more likely to end up special education and low-ability groups. Oakes (2005) says, "Through tracking, schools continue to replicate existing inequality along lines of race and social class and contribute to the intergenerational transmission of social and economic inequality" (p. xi).

Ability grouping also takes a serious toll on children's self-concepts and their opportunities to form meaningful relationships across groups. Children in the lower groups or in special education classrooms are often painfully aware of the limited expectations adults have for them and are often subjected to teasing, ridicule, and humiliation by their classmates. Similarly, children who are in the top groups or removed to gifted classes are often labeled as "brains" or "nerds" and are sometimes equally excluded or isolated. Grouping children according to some putative ability level creates artificial distance among them as well as amplifying and solidifying whatever differences actually exist.

Teaching is easier in homogeneous groups.

Most of us were educated in highly tracked schools and classrooms and have gone on to organize our instruction that way. Having three reading groups or grouping by ability for math may seem natural and familiar, but it has been increasingly challenged through the development of multilevel, multimodality instructional models, the use of cooperative learning, and the increasing recognition of the many intelligences students bring to their learning. Although organizing instruction in heterogeneous groups definitely involves a different kind of planning and preparation, many teachers report increased enthusiasm in their students, greater learning, and deeper involvement when curricula and instruction are organized around diverse learners working together (Sapon-Shevin, 2007).

Myths About Inclusion

Inclusion means dumping all students back into the regular classroom.

Unfortunately, in some schools, children previously educated in special education settings have been summarily returned to general education classrooms with little or no teacher preparation or support. This is not inclusion but is, in fact, "dumping," and it should be resisted. Inclusion requires ongoing preparation and support for teachers and the reorganization of support services for both students and teachers so that resources are available in the regular education classroom.

*It takes a special person to work with special
children, those with disabilities, and the gifted.*

Idealizing the special education teacher or the teacher of the gifted as someone with unique personality characteristics and a set of instructional tricks foreign to general education teachers has served to deskill general education teachers, removing the motivation and necessity of developing a wider repertoire of skills. Increasingly, the research shows that all children need "good teaching" and that the characteristics of that teaching (learner centered, responsive, and engaging) cut across all categories of students.

*Inclusion is beyond the reach of the already
overburdened general education teacher.*

There is no question that many general education teachers are overburdened and undersupported. Adding student with disabilities or other special needs without committing the necessary resources and support is unethical as well as ineffective. We must make huge improvements in the kinds and quality of support we provide to teachers, particularly planning and collaboration time with other teachers, modified curriculum and resources, administrative support, and ongoing emotional support.

*The curriculum of the general education
classroom will be watered down and distorted.*

There is fear that inclusion will force teachers to "dumb down" the curriculum, thus limiting the options for typical students and especially for gifted and talented students. The reality is that curriculum in inclusive classrooms must be structured as multilevel, participatory, and flexible (see Chapter 7). We must abandon the assumption that all children in the same grade will be working at the same level, completing the same project in the same way, and being evaluated according to the same criteria. We need new models of instruction and assessment. We must find ways to respond to the requirements and constraints of high-stakes testing programs and standardized curricula in the framework of inclusivity and diversity, seeing student differences as occasions for creativity and flexibility not exclusion.

*Inclusion is a favor we're doing for children with
disabilities at the expense of other children's education.*

There is currently no evidence that the education of other students suffers in any way from the inclusion process. The film *Educating Peter* details the classroom experience of Peter, a boy with Down syndrome during his third-grade year. Al Shanker (1994), former president of the American Federation of Teachers, raised the following question:

> I wonder whether the youngsters in that class had spent a whole year in adjusting to how to live with Peter and whether they did any reading, whether they did any writing, whether they did any mathematics, whether they did any history, whether they did any geography.
>
> And it seems to me that it's a terrible shame that we don't ask that question. Is the only function of the schools to get kids to learn to live with each other? Would we be satisfied if that's what we did and if the youngsters came out not knowing any of the things they're supposed to learn academically?

Will any of them, disabled or non-disabled, be able to function as adults? (p. 1)

Martha Stallings (1993, 1994), Peter's third-grade teacher, reports that the students in her class all had a wonderful year; learned their math, history, and geography; did a great deal of writing and reading; and learned to be decent human beings as well as learned to understand and support a classmate with major behavioral and learning challenges. That seems like an incredibly successful year to me.

Will any of them be able to function as adults? Yes, they will function as adults who, in addition to knowing long division and the states and their capitals, know how to actively support a classmate who is struggling and know not to jump to early conclusions about whether someone can be a friend and a classmate.

Myths About Teaching About Differences

If we don't mention differences, students won't notice them.

Ask any teacher whether the students know which child comes from a poor family, which child is overweight, and which child reads really hard books. Children are extremely aware of their classmates and their differences. Not noticing differences simply tells students that differences are things we shouldn't talk about with the teacher or in class; such discussions become the focus of playground whispering and bathroom secrets.

Mentioning differences calls negative attention to them and makes things worse.

We probably all have a memory of a teacher who attempted to address children's social interactions and made things worse: "Now I don't like the way you're treating Sasha. I want you all to be nice to her," or some other well-meaning but ineffective and embarrassing attempt to address friendship and exclusion issues. But there are effective ways to deal with students' social interactions and their differences, ways that are respectful and sensitive and that allow students to develop repertoires of perspective taking and problem solving.

People are naturally more comfortable with people who are just like them.

Since most of us grow up in a highly segregated society in which differences in race, religion, social class, and ability are rarely addressed, it is not surprising that we gravitate to others who look like us. But this is neither inevitable nor desirable. Thoughtful teachers can implement strategies designed to help students learn to be comfortable interacting with and socializing with others they perceive as different—girls and boys, students labeled as able-bodied and those with disabilities, children of different racial or ethnic groups, and the like. But before they can do this, teachers must see the value and importance of this intermingling and connection and not accept as inevitable the ways in which children often separate themselves. Many teachers still refer to their class as "boys and girls" although they would never consider saying, "blacks and whites," or "Christians and Jews." Our framing of difference—what we think matters—will be clearly communicated to our students.

Children are cruel and cannot accept differences.

We have all seen (and experienced) horrible examples of teasing and cruelty between children. But many of us have also seen the opposite—a child gently supporting the head of a classmate with cerebral palsy, a junior-high girl stepping in to defend her overweight friend who is being harassed, and children figuring out ways to include their classmates in projects and field trips. Children learn their responses to differences from the adults with whom they interact—parents and teachers—and it is clear that they model their behavior closely on the behavior of those adults. Children can be systematically taught and supported in learning repertoires of kindness, support, and caring in classrooms that value those behaviors.

REFRAMING OUR WORK

Beginning With Ourselves

We all received messages—some overt and others more covert—about other people in our lives. We learned to distinguish *us* from *them*, often with damaging or at least distancing consequences. As we look at this area of our work, we can begin by asking ourselves the following questions, comparing our responses, and thinking about how our experiences have shaped our thinking. We can also identify gaps in our knowledge base and formulate individual and collective ways to address these limitations in our experience and understanding.

- What early messages did you get about who you were relative to other people (smarter, less athletic, nicer, and the like)?
- What messages did you get about how you should relate to people who were different than you were?
- What were your early experiences with being excluded? Can you recall specific times or places during which you were excluded? How did you feel?
- What were your early experiences of excluding someone else? Can you recall specific times or places during which you excluded others? How did you feel then? How do you feel now about what you did or didn't do?
- Did your parents, teachers, or other elders talk to you specifically about how you should relate to others not in your group or not like you in some way?
- When you were in school, were you grouped according to ability or skill level? What was that experience like for you? What connections or relationships did you have with people who were in different groups?
- Was there a special education room in your school? What do you remember learning or knowing about that room and the students who were taught there? Was there a gifted program? What was your understanding of who was in that group and why?
- When you were a student, if a child in your class was experiencing difficulties of some kind, did the teachers talk to you about this or include you in problem solving?

Looking at Our Classrooms and Schools

Answer these questions about your school or teaching situation and then compare notes with others in the same setting. After discussing what you said, think about what changes you could make in your school to make it more inclusive.

- Does the school have a mission statement that refers explicitly to issues of diversity and inclusiveness?
- Are all school facilities physically accessible to all students?
- Are classrooms identified in ways that are nonstigmatizing and avoid labeling particular groups of students?
- Are students tracked or grouped according to ability for instruction?
- How much contact do students in one program or group have with other students the same age? Different ages?
- Do all children participate in schoolwide functions such as assemblies, field days, school trips, and award ceremonies?
- Have faculty and staff received professional development related to diversity issues, including racism, sexism, homophobia, and ableism?
- Does the curriculum explicitly address issues of diversity with students at all grade levels?
- Would all students feel represented and acknowledged by the school decorations and displays?
- Are school activities organized so that they take into account students' differences in financial resources? Religions? Family backgrounds? Language skills? Physical and cognitive abilities?
- Do all students have access to extracurricular activities including sports, music, drama, and art programs?
- Do students interact with a wide range of other students?
- Do students have repertoires for including all classmates in academic and play activities, including those with challenging behaviors and diverse learning abilities?
- Do students know about one another's uniquenesses and call attention to these in positive and thoughtful ways?
- Do students engage in inclusive thinking: "How will we get Catherine's wheelchair on the bus to go on the field trip?" "What can we have as refreshments for the class party that everyone can have?" "How can we figure out roles in the puppet show so that everyone who wants a part has one?"
- Do students actively take on an advocacy role when confronted by examples of exclusion in their lives?

As a group, identify questions in the previous list to which you had a negative answer or, perhaps, didn't know the answer. Individuals or partners might want to investigate the previous questions and report back to the group with their findings. Asking different questions may increase awareness: The daddy–daughter dance is now identified as problematic for some students, or perhaps the placement of segregated special education classrooms concentrated on one corridor becomes a more obvious symbol of lack of inclusiveness.

What's the Big Picture?

After looking at our individual experiences and the school, we can ask bigger questions about how the goals of an inclusive classroom connect to other issues.

- What experiences could we provide to students that would help them both know about one another and feel a sense of connectedness and mutual responsibility?
- How do the lessons our children learn about inclusion in schools help them understand and be proactive in addressing global issues of exclusion and segregation?

HOW TO BEGIN

ACTIVITIES

Many of the typical structures of the classroom can be changed to support more inclusive behavior in students. Although no single change will make a highly segregated classroom inclusive or turn children who feud into children who love one another, each element of the classroom can make a difference in community building and inclusion (Sapon-Shevin, 1996c).

Mix It Up at Lunch

In this project of the Southern Poverty Law Center (n.d.), once a year, students sit with people at lunch that they don't usually interact with. In 2007, an estimated four million students in 10,000 schools participated in this program. The Web site (http://www.mixitup.org) provides resources for structuring this program in your school. The belief is that one way to reduce prejudice among youth and improve intergroup relations is by organizing specific opportunities that enable students to cross typical boundaries of cliques, race, class, religion, and ability. By participating in a recognized, school-structured activity, the challenges of crossing these boundaries are minimized, and support is provided for the richness of the connection.

Seating Possibilities

Many teachers allow students to choose their seats, often resulting in patterns of segregation (boys on one side, girls on the other; blacks and whites on opposite sides; and all the special education students at the same table). Although student choice and autonomy are important, teachers can also be more proactive in arranging seating. To begin with, rather than organizing chairs or desks into rows, student desks can be pushed together to form clusters of four or five. These natural communities can be used to promote sharing and interaction. Each group can choose a group name, emblem, or cheer, and these can be displayed above their desks.

Students can be assigned to these clusters in many ways that promote inclusion and interaction. Some teachers make very intentional decisions about whom to seat together, attempting to place students together who represent a range of characteristics and who might support one another. Steve is very shy and tends to keep to himself. Rolando is more outgoing and seems to be able to draw others into activities. Claryce likes some of the same sports as Mark, and Riana is a peacemaker, skilled at resolving conflicts. Thinking about students according to a range of characteristics usually makes more sense than a rote assignment of one high reader, two middle-level readers, and one slow reader, which is how some teachers attempt heterogeneity. Students can be grouped heterogeneously in terms of skill levels, interests, social skills, racial and ethnic backgrounds, gender, and personalities.

It is generally considered desirable for groups to stay together for at least a six- to eight-week period so that students can really get to know and understand their seatmates. Switching students too often can interfere with that bonding and learning process. If students in a group are having difficulty getting along—"Clark always takes over"; "Carla just sits there"; "Tori thinks her ideas are the only good ones"— the teacher must actively intervene to teach social skills and to help groups learn to work together.

Some teachers alternate six- to eight-week periods of teacher choice with equal periods of student choice for seating, thus allowing students to sit with a wide range of classmates.

Groups can also be formed more randomly, by drawing names out of a hat or by placing names on tongue depressors and drawing these from a can. Teachers can also use color-coded cards (all the people with red dots on their cards will sit together), stickers, or little animal erasers to form groups. Because these random methods can result in some unfortunate seating arrangements, many teachers prefer that seating clusters be done in a more thoughtful way (see Box 5.3), although they may group students more randomly at other times during the day (see Box 5.4).

BOX 5.3

When fourth-grade teacher Debbie Quick wants to change her home groups, she asks students to complete a *confidential* form (and she teaches them what confidential means—you don't tell anyone what you wrote). She asks them to list two students they would like to sit with, two students they don't know very well, and one student that they think would be a problem for them to be placed with. She reports that this survey gives her important information about how students in her class are interacting and seeing one another, and she makes her seating clusters based on this information. Interestingly, she reports that very few students name a student as someone they can't sit with.

BOX 5.4

Jo Marie Vespi, a fourth-grade teacher, talks explicitly to her students about why she groups them the way she does. She tells them that as a classroom community, she wants them to learn to work with lots of people and to get past any initial stereotypes or prejudices they might have. She talks about not groaning when new groups are called, and if such behavior occurs ("I don't want to sit with George"), she immediately responds to it, reiterating her belief in kindness and inclusion.

Kindergarten teacher Anne Dobbelaere helps students connect with a wide range of other students by determining where students sit in the morning "hug ring." The children have cards with their names on them, and by placing these cards on the circle in very thoughtful ways, Anne can help students sit next to one another who can support one another or who need to know one another better. At snack time, she places their personal napkin rings at certain places at the table to make purposive seating combinations at that time also.

Classroom Jobs

It is typical in many classrooms for jobs to be designated—line leader, lunch count, cleanup, office messenger, and so on. By thinking carefully about the nature of those jobs and how they are assigned, teachers can use classroom jobs to build community and connection.

To begin with, every student in the classroom should have a job, and having a job should be part of being a classroom member, not an opportunity that has to be earned. If only students who have finished their work or received high grades are allowed to have classroom jobs, then certain children will probably never get to do a job, feel useful or valued, or be seen as valued by classmates. Careful job assignment can allow students to develop the skills and attitudes of being a full member of the classroom that may actually help them to complete academics and other assignments better.

In many classrooms, jobs are assigned to individuals—Shoshana is the line leader, Imani collects lunch money, Frederick takes care of the rabbit, and so on. But jobs can be assigned to pairs or even to groups of students. When two children are assigned as office messengers, the time they spend going to the office together can be important connecting time. In inclusive classrooms, there are also likely to be individuals who could not manage a particular task by themselves but could easily do so with a partner. If Rolando, for example, is prone to wandering and might not make it to the office, by being paired with Liliana, they can both walk to the office together, and he can have that experience at the same time that he and Liliana are getting to know each other better. If teachers assign pairs of students to jobs, it is generally best to assign pairs to all jobs, thus avoiding pairing as a stigma, done only for children with special needs or other challenges.

Jobs can also be assigned to groups of students, particularly if students are seated in home groups or clusters. The Leapfrogs might be in charge of cleanup for the room while the Rainbows are in charge of materials distribution or pet care. By assigning tasks to groups of students, children can learn to work together in their small group to accomplish a task important to the whole class.

The teacher should set up a system for deciding how often tasks get shifted and how they are chosen. Some teachers simply rotate through their class roster in order; others pull sticks or name cards. Some teachers assure students that every person in the class will eventually get to have every job—and then make that happen. Routines in which the previous jobholder gets to pick the next jobholder are best avoided because they often lead to hurt feelings, accusations of favoritism, and a sense of exclusion.

The teacher can decide the classroom jobs, or the students can develop them themselves. Thinking about what kinds of things have to happen in a classroom to be an inclusive community can help students (and teachers) to think of jobs that aren't traditionally designated. Some classrooms, for examples, have "greeters," who talk to any visitors, show them around the room, and answer questions. Having a job like this demonstrates the importance of students' voices in the classroom and gives them opportunities to interact with a wider range of adults. Other classrooms have a Missing Persons Committee that makes notes of absences, gets copies of papers or handouts for those who aren't there, and organizes get-well cards if those are called for (see Box 5.5 for a variation). This kind of job acknowledges that everyone is important to the community and that people who are absent are missed and valued!

BOX 5.5

In Mary Schlitz' fourth-grade class, each student has a peer buddy who is charged with supporting them and helping ease back into the classroom after an absence. If one child is out at speech and returns in the middle of a reading lesson, the peer buddy already has her reading book out on the desk, opened to the right page. If a student who is absent misses a paper that is handed out, the peer buddy takes a copy and puts it in the student's folder to be retrieved on his return.

Classroom Rules

Almost all classrooms have rules. In some classrooms, the teacher makes and posts the rules before the year begins; sometimes classroom rules are posted but rarely noticed and never referred to. In other classrooms, however, students are actively involved in making the rules, and the rules are actually used to guide behavior and establish class norms.

Teachers can begin the school year by asking students what classroom rules they think they need to function well as a community. The teacher can help guide the students toward positive phrasings of the rule, if that seems appropriate ("What should people in our class do?") rather than soliciting a long list of negatives: Don't take other people's things, don't hit, don't yell, and the like.

The teacher can also help students look for ways to generalize rules so that there aren't 45 rules in the class (see Box 5.6).

Outside a first-grade classroom at H. W. Smith Elementary School, there are only two classroom rules posted: (1) We don't hurt people's insides. (2) We don't hurt people's outsides. These rules allow the teachers and students to have powerful discussions about the many ways in which people can get hurt, not just by hitting, kicking, and scratching, but also by teasing, name-calling, and exclusion.

Teachers should be respectful of students' need to make specific rules that reflect problems and challenges that they perceive in their own situations. In one fourth-grade classroom, for example, the students generated elaborate rules about "cutting" in line (when cuts were allowed, how many, in what kinds of lines, and so on); although these rules seemed complicated and overly complex, the students I spoke with understood them perfectly and followed them conscientiously.

Here are some questions to ask yourself (and students) as you make rules for the classroom:

- Who made these rules? Whose voice is represented?
- Do the rules tell students what to *do*, or simply what *not* to do?
- Do the rules hold students to high expectations for how they will interact and treat one another?
- Are the rules explicit enough or well enough understood that everyone agrees what constitutes rule following or rule breaking?
- Are there few enough rules so that they can be remembered and internalized or so many that they are overwhelming?
- What will the classroom look and feel like if these rules are followed rigorously?
- Is the teacher's behavior included in the rules? Does the teacher also have to "use kind language" or "respect children's property"?

Rules can also address more sophisticated concepts related to exclusion and friendship. Vivian Paley's (1992) book *You Can't Say You Can't Play* describes her experiences talking to students about having such a rule in their classrooms. Paley, a kindergarten teacher, was concerned about patterns of exclusion she observed in her classroom—"You can't be in our group," "We don't want you to play in the block area with us," "You're not my best friend anymore," and the like. She came up with a possible solution—the rule "You can't say you can't play," and she approached her kindergartners with two questions: (1) Is it fair? (2) Would it work? The book details her conversations with her kindergarten students as well as her experiences talking to all the other students in her school, one grade at a time, about the rule and its utility and meaning. See Box 5.7 for the story of one teacher team that used this book in practice.

Four teachers at Ed Smith Elementary School in Syracuse, New York, embarked on a project using the book, *You Can't Say You Can't Play* (Paley, 1992). The teachers, all of whom have inclusive classrooms that include children with significant disabilities as well as a wide range of other student differences, read the book together, discussed it, and then implemented the rule in their classrooms. Anne Dobbelaere, the kindergarten teacher, reported that the children accepted the

(Continued)

(Continued)

rule easily, and incorporated it into their problem solving. When two children were playing a game and a third approached, the students decided they would play in teams. When the fifth child approached the game, they made him the coach. Anne introduced the rule using role-plays with her teaching assistant. They presented a scenario of exclusion from their classroom and asked students to brainstorm, "What could we do instead?" She reports that the students quickly grasped the language and the meaning of the rule and would point to where the rule was written on the wall when any child attempted to exclude another.

In Mary Mastin's first-grade classroom, implementing the "you can't say you can't play" rule meant removing the limits from the learning centers. Mary realized that putting up a sign that said only four children could be in the block corner or only six in the reading center was de facto exclusion. She and the children brainstormed what they would do if many children wanted to use the same center at the same time. After a brief chaotic period during which 12 children tried to be in the science corner together, the students figured out ways to share materials and activities. Mary reports, "The focus now is on *how* to include other students, rather than on *whether* to include them. Students report that they play with 'more different kids' now that they don't have to 'save places.'"

In Kathy Goodman's second-grade classroom, she introduced the rule following a *teachable moment* of exclusion in her class. Kathy's classroom is already called "The Helping Hands Classroom," and this rule felt like a natural extension of that idea to her. In addition to implementing the rule, Kathy has modified many of the activities in her room so that all children *can* be included. For example, students were reluctant to include a child with a physical disability in their bingo games because his uncontrollable movements often knocked the markers off the pages. Instead, Kathy got bingo markers (the kind that stamp) for all the students, thereby including this student more easily and making the game fun for everyone.

The fourth graders in Cathleen Corrigan's class were more reluctant about adopting the rule. They highly valued their autonomy, and while they agreed the rule was "fair," they weren't sure it would work. A turning point occurred on the playground when a fourth grader from another classroom (who didn't have the rule) told one of Cathleen's students he couldn't play. When Cathleen's students responded, "You can't say you can't play," the student insisted that this rule didn't apply to him. Cathleen's students returned after recess and passionately discussed the importance of the rule for them and the necessity of spreading the rule beyond their classroom.

The four teachers report that the rule was by no means a cure-all for exclusion, but it did provide the basis for discussion and was useful as an organizing value in classroom problem solving. Although the rule was certainly helpful in setting a tone of inclusion for all students, they observed that students still need to be taught specific repertoires of asking to play ("Can I be in this game?") and asking others to join in play ("Do you want to play with us? Do you want to be one of the wild dinosaurs?").

(For a full description of this study, see Sapon-Shevin, Dobbelaere, Corrigan, Goodman, & Mastin, 1998.)

Cathi Allen reports that in her third-grade, class meetings become an important part of the inclusion process and develop into a powerful force for the students to take action on issues close to them. She explains, "The first time a student comes in with the familiar recess complaint, 'So-and-so said I couldn't play,' recess becomes the focus of the community discussion. I usually start by directly stating the issue, having a student state the issue, or maybe begin the discussion with a work of literature relating to the issue." It then becomes a "suggestion or sharing" circle with each person sharing a suggestion with regard to the issue or sharing a similar experience. I become a silent part of the circle. The students know I want them to share freely and to generate solutions, not my solutions. My role is that of recorder and facilitator only. Generally, after discussion, they will take the ideas back either to their group for reflections or as self-reflection, with any decision to be made the next day after they've given the suggestions some thought. This was how the birth of the "you can say, you can play" idea came about. The students took the ideas and feelings shared and decided as a whole class that they wanted to adopt the rule. Interestingly, as they began to see the power in adopting the rule as a class, they start looking toward bringing the rule to the whole school. When the discussion turned toward whether the rule should be imposed schoolwide because it was important for everyone to feel included, they became adamant about giving the student body a choice, just as they were given a choice. Their comments were insightful: "When we get to choose, we want to do it more," and "It's part of us! Everyone should be given the choice.'"

GAMES

Inclusive games are those in which everyone participates, no one is "it" or left out, and everyone is needed to make the game work.

Sticky Popcorn

The students all begin huddled on the floor, pretending to be kernels of unpopped corn. The leader then "turns the heat up" on the floor and the kernels start popping. As it gets hotter and hotter, they pop bigger and higher (jumping up and down). Then the leader can "pour hot caramel" on the group, trying to turn them into a giant popcorn ball. As they hop and jump and touch one another, they stick until they are all stuck together in one giant, jumpy popcorn ball.

Students love this game, and it is very inclusive. Students in a wheelchair, for example, can still be jiggled and then included in the popcorn ball. Nonverbal students are at no disadvantage either nor are non-English-speaking students. The popcorn ball image of unity is powerful—we can stick together in this class, no matter how different we are.

Riddle Matches (Cooperative Memory Game)

Students are each given a large card (8½″ × 11″). Half the cards have riddles on them; the other half have the answers to the riddles. Students are instructed to mill about the room until they find their match. The partners then link arms and form a giant circle of riddles. When all the partners have been matched, the class can hear *dramatic readings* of the riddles and their solutions.

Careful attention should be given to the riddles chosen. Choosing humor that isn't sexist, racist, or offensive provides a wonderful model for students that *having fun* and *making fun of* are totally different activities. To find appropriate riddles, check children's joke books:

What did the ocean say when the plane flew over it? Nothing, it just waved.

Why were the little strawberries upset? Because their mother and father were in a jam.

Why is the letter "A" like a flower? A bee ("B") comes after it.

How did the ghost get into the room? With a skeleton key.

This game is both cooperative and inclusive; everyone's card is needed for the game to be complete and the riddles to be heard.

To build unity for a large class, or to support individuals for whom this task might be too challenging, each child can have a partner (i.e., two children sharing a card and looking for their match). Nonreaders can participate in this activity if someone reads them their card and/or tells them what match they are looking for. Helping students is called "cheating" or an unfair advantage in a competitive activity, but in a cooperative activity, many methods of achieving success are acceptable and appropriate. You might want to tell a student, "Your match is wearing blue pants and a red shirt," or "Your match has the word "pig" on their card." Students often help one another during this game, "I think I saw your match over there," and even students who simply stand there immobile will have people coming over to read their card and see if they match. This game can also be played as a Cooperative Concentration Game. All students stand in a circle with their cards held up to their chest (the writing not showing). The group goal is to make all the matches as quickly as possible. A student begins by calling on another student to reveal her card and read it (or the whole group reads it aloud). For example, Riana calls on Justine, and the class reads, "Broom service." Then, Riana calls on another students in the circle, Alfie, who reveals his card that reads, "What did the polluted water say to the filter?" As a group, students decide whether this is a match or not (It isn't!). The turn then goes to the person next to Riana who calls on two people, again trying to make a match. The chooser can call on himself second if the first person he calls on turns out to match his card. The rule is that students can get help from the person on either side of them when it is their turn to choose, so the decision is really made by a collective of three. When a match is made, students cheer, and the match is put in the center on the floor. Students who no longer have cards are still active as guessers, helpers, and choosers.

This game (and the matching game) is infinitely adaptable. Virtually any content at any level of difficulty can be used. Young students might match a picture of a dog with an identical picture of that dog. They might then progress to matching a picture of a dog with the word "dog" or a picture of a Dalmatian with a picture of a golden retriever (recognizing that these are both kinds of dogs).

A brief list of possible topics and levels of challenge includes the following:

- *Math:* numerals and a number of objects, an equation and the solution, a geometric shape and its name, a story problem and the answer, a story problem and the kind of operation you would need to solve it, a drawing of a clock and the time it represents, a kind of measure (quart, gallon) and a liquid measured that way, or a fraction and its equivalent decimal.
- *Language arts:* synonyms or antonyms, rhyming words, storybook characters and what happened to them, books and authors, words and definitions, sentences and the kind of punctuation they require, or descriptions of characters and the name of the character.
- *Social studies:* places and events that happened there, cultural artifacts and their significance, conflicts and precipitating factors, Indigenous people and their contributions, or individual rights from the Bill of Rights and an example of its protection or violation.
- *Science:* land formations and their names, chemical formulas and substances, pictures of machines and names (lever, incline), geographical terms and their definitions, foods and their nutrients, or animals and their kingdoms.

The possibilities are endless, both in content and level of complexity. Students can move beyond simple matching (states and their capitals) to more complex matches that require real discussion and debate "Immigrant groups that have faced major discrimination in our country" with the names of different ethnic groups, for example.

SONGS

Simply by talking about *full inclusion singing*—we need and welcome every voice—singing can be a wonderfully inclusive activity. Rather than focusing only on those children with particularly strong or melodious voices, teachers can actively work to teach all children to sing and to recognize the ways in which group singing in harmony provides a powerful metaphor for cooperation and diversity.

"The More We Get Together" (Traditional)

Children can repeat the song several times, inserting other words (play, work, laugh, sing, and help) in place of *get*. Students can also substitute words for *happier* in the first and fourth lines: *stronger smarter, better, safer,* or *powerful*. The songbook *Children's Songs for a Friendly Planet* (Weiss, Prutzman, & Silber, 1986) suggests using the song to help students learn one another's names. Beginning at Line 3, they can go around the room and sing, "There's Deeana, and Zila, there's Tracy and Tomaso, and Christina and Kasheef," using all the names in the class and then singing the last line.

"We Won't Leave Anyone Out" (Pirtle, 1998)

This is a wonderful song for talking (and singing) about issues of inclusion and exclusion. Sarah Pirtle (1998, pp. 132–135) suggests that students can make up motions to go with the "click, clack, zoon" section, perhaps by working with partners. The teacher might want to precede the song with a discussion of the ways and places in which students are left out. The group could then brainstorm ways to address each of these situations and propose solutions.

"Oh, Give Me a School" (To the Tune of "Home on the Range," Sapon-Shevin & Shevin, n.d.)

Oh, give me a class, where each student can pass, and we all help each other to learn.

We work and we play, and we stay friends all day, 'cause we know that we'll all have a turn.

Chorus:

Home, this feels like home.

It's a vision of what school can be.

People caring and fair,

Always willing to share,

And we're starting right here, you and me.

Oh, give me a school where to share is the rule, and no teacher must feel all alone.

Where seldom is heard a comparative word, and where your success adds to my own.

Oh, give me the earth, where each person has worth, and where all of us know we belong.

We can work as a team, but it starts with a dream, and that why we are singing this song.

Last Chorus:

Home, this feels like how.

It's a vision of what life can be

People caring and fair,

Always willing to share,

And we're starting right here, you and me.

This song can be a class or schoolwide anthem (some schools have performed it at their concerts). It might be part of a discussion of all the ways in which a school can be made to be more like a loving, supportive home (bearing in mind that some students do not have homes like this).

"Inclusion Round" (To the Tune of "Oh, How Lovely is the Evening," Sapon-Shevin & Shevin, n.d.)

> *Oh, how lovely is the feeling (is the feeling)*
>
> *When inclusion bells are peeling (bells are pealing)*
>
> *Welcome Home (repeated three times)*

First, the song is taught and practiced as a three-part round. Then people get in three concentric circles and hold hands. For the first line of the song, people move to their right; for the second line of the song, people move to their left, and for the third line, people raise and lower their joined hands so it looks like they are ringing bells. Then the dance is done as a round. The inner circle begins by singing the first line (moving to the right); then the middle circle begins the first line (again, moving to the right), and finally, the outer circle begins. Everyone sings the song through three full times. After each group has sung the song three times, they repeat, "Welcome home, welcome home, welcome home," until all three groups are singing together. The effect of the dance round is very beautiful as students make harmony in song by singing the round and make visual harmonies as they walk past one another during the dance.

"Inclusion Hokey-Pokey"

This new version asks students to name the things that they would like to "put in" their classrooms and the things they would like to "take out."

> *We put kindness in; we take teasing out.*
>
> *We put kindness in, and we shake it all about.*
>
> *We do the hokey-pokey, and we turn ourselves around.*
>
> *That's how we change our class.*

After introducing one or two examples, have students come up with their own, for example hugging/hitting, compliments/put-downs, inclusion/exclusion, nice words/mean words. The song can promote an excellent discussion of ways to change the class to make it more inclusive and a kinder place. (With thanks to Verne McArthur).

CHILDREN'S LITERATURE

There are many children's books that deal with issues of diversity and individual differences. Some of these books are specifically about disability issues; others address other kinds of differences, and some are more general or deal directly with issues of inclusion/exclusion.

Books Addressing Inclusion/Exclusion Issues

Wilson Sat Alone *(Hess, 1994)*

Wilson is always alone. When the children in Wilson's class push their desks into groups, Wilson sits alone. He eat alone, plays alone, walks alone, and reads alone. When a new girl comes to school, she sits alone, eats alone, and plays alone but only for one day. Then she joins the other students and becomes part of the group. One day she approaches Wilson and tries to bring him into the group. The other children tell her that she shouldn't do that because "he likes to be alone." But this turns out, of course, not to be quite true, and she is successful at bringing him into the group.

The girl, Sara, is basically an inclusion facilitator! She brings Wilson into the group.

Activities

- Generate strategies for how to get someone to join a group who has excluded himself.
- Talk about all the reasons someone might be excluded or feel excluded in the classroom.
- Discuss the differences between being alone and being lonely—between aloneness that is genuinely self-chosen and aloneness that is about exclusion, not feeling welcome, and the like.
- Talk about how kids get a reputation—that kid is mean, likes to be alone, hates us, isn't smart, and so on. Ask students about a time they felt they had gotten a reputation that wasn't true or helpful or felt good. Talk about how you can change your reputation and/or challenge the reputations that others have also.

Our Friendship Rules *(Moss & Tardif, 2007)*

Alexandra and Jenny have been best friends for a very long time. But a new girl at school, Rolinda Sparks, draws Alexandra's attention, and she betrays Jenny by telling her most important secret. Alexandra is distressed by the pain she has caused and works to find a way to regain her relationship with Jenny. Together Alexandra and Jenny create their friendship rules—which, incidentally, allow them to welcome Rolinda to play with them as well.

An important book about friendship, forgiveness, and negotiating the tricky terrain of inclusive and exclusive relationships, this book is sure to provoke important discussions. A Web site at (http://www.tilburyhouse.com) has activities and games for using this book in the classroom.

Jamaica Tag-Along *(Havill, 1989)*

Jamaica, an African American girl, wants to go play ball with her big brother Ossie and his friend Buzz. Ossie tells her no, to find her own friends, and she's too little to play. Rejected, she goes to build a sandcastle and tells a little boy who asks to help that he is too small. Then she realizes that she has done the same thing as her brother and lets the little boy help. After a while, Ossie comes over and asks to help too. Jamaica says, "Yes."

This book provides another entry point into a discussion of issues of exclusion, rejection, and the ways in which we pass on the hurts that have happened to us. An excellent book to accompany the implementation of the "you can't say you can't play" rule discussed earlier, this book can help students to move beyond immediate patterns of exclusion.

Two excellent books address children who want to do things that others don't see as typical or appropriate; these books can be used to challenge stereotypes and introduce the concept of prejudice.

Oliver Button Is a Sissy *(dePaola, 1980)*

Oliver Button doesn't like to do the things other boys do. Instead, he likes to read, draw, jump rope, play with paper dolls, dress up in costumes, and dance. His father tells him he is a sissy. The other boys don't want him on their team. Then his mother enrolls him in a dance class. The boys continue to tease him, especially the older boys. The girls defend him, and the boys tease about that: "Gotta have help from girls." Then, Oliver enrolls in a talent show. Although he doesn't win, he does well. When he gets back to school the next day, the other students have erased the wall where they'd written "Oliver Button is a Sissy" and replaced it with "Oliver Button is a Star."

This book could provide a wonderful discussion starter for talking about what happens to people who go against the grain. Why do other people feel challenged or uncomfortable with people who don't fit stereotypical ideas about behavior or interests? What kinds of support did Oliver need? Has there ever been a time when you've wanted to do something different? Did you get support? What support would you have liked? A discussion of gender roles and rigidity can also be helpful here.

Amazing Grace *(Hoffman, 1991)*

Grace loves stories, and she loves acting them out. When her class decides to put on *Peter Pan*, Grace knows who she wants to be. "When she raised her hand, Raj said, 'You can't be Peter—that's a boy's name.' But Grace left her hand up. 'You can't be Peter Pan,' whispered Natalie. 'He isn't black.' But Grace kept her hand up." Grace's grandmother takes her to the ballet to see an old friend dance. Their friend Rosalie, who is black and from Trinidad, dances in the ballet of *Romeo and Juliet*. More confident about her desire to play Peter Pan, Grace does a wonderful job at the audition and is cast for the part!

Both a book about others' limited expectations and prejudgments and about prejudice and stereotyping, this book is a useful beginning to discussions about exclusion and possibility.

Come Sit by Me *(Merrifield, 1990)*

Nicholas, a young boy at the day-care center, has AIDS, and some of the children won't play with him. Karen's (another child) mother gives her accurate information, and there is a parent meeting so those children can warmly welcome Nicholas. The book includes a description of AIDS and pictures of ways you can't get it—hugging, sharing toys, mosquito bites, and so on.

By addressing one of the reasons a child might be excluded from school or play situations, the book and subsequent discussion could be powerful tools in the fight against prejudice toward people with AIDS. Lessons about health and disease can be learned as well as those about compassion, understanding, and the need for accurate information.

The Big Orange Splot *(Pinkwater, 1977)*

Mr. Plumbean lived on a street where all the houses were the same. The people on the street like it that way. "This is a neat street," they would say. But when a passing seagull drops a can of bright orange paint on his roof and leaves a big splot, rather than painting over it, Mr. Plumbean decides to paint his house to reflect his dreams. By the time he has finished, his house has stripes and pictures of elephants and lions and a clock tower on the roof. The other people on his street are not happy, and one by one, they come to him to try to persuade him to repaint his house so that the street can be neat again. But instead, after they sit under his palm trees with him sipping lemonade and talking about their dreams, they go back and redesign their houses to look like their dreams. By the end of the story, the street is very diverse: a house that looks like a ship, one like a castle, and another like a hot air balloon. Whenever strangers came to the street after that and said, "This is not a neat street," Mr. Plumbeam and his neighbors would reply, "Our street is us and we are it. Our street is where we like to be, and it looks like all our dreams."

This is a beautiful book for talking about the dangers of conformity and the beauty of diversity. The way in which Mr. Plumbean disarms his critics—by talking to them gently about who he is and why he does what he does provides a powerful model of dealing with conflict and diversity. Students could easily generate role-plays about conflicts that arise from differences (people who look different, dress different, have different ways of talking or behaving) and the ways these could be discussed and resolved nonviolently. A natural follow-up activity would be for each student to design the house of their dreams and to create a wall or bulletin board that reflects all the students.

Old Henry *(Blos, 1987)*

When Old Henry moves into a dilapidated old house, the neighbors wait anxiously for him to clean it up and restore the property. But he doesn't. They offer their help, and he rejects it. Finally, disgusted, he moves out. They miss him.

His house looks so empty, so dark in the night.

And having him gone doesn't make us more right.

That Henry.

Maybe some other time, we'd get along

not thinking that somebody has to be wrong.

And we don't have to make such a terrible fuss

because everyone isn't exactly like us.

Henry misses them too, and he writes to the mayor, asking if he mended the gate and shoveled the snow would they not scold his birds and could he let the grass grow?

A wonderful companion piece to the *Big Orange Splot* (Pinkwater, 1977), this book is all about accommodation and different people learning to get along. This book could also be part of a discussion about making peace with those who aren't just like you and the huge diversity of people who can live together successfully with respect and tolerance.

Books With Characters With Disabilities

Thirty years ago, when the preliminary moves were being made to include children with disabilities in more typical classrooms and schools, many books were written specifically about children with disabilities. Although some of these books are excellent, the rapid shifts in understanding about disability and changing social policies make some of these older books inaccurate and not consistent with the move toward inclusive schooling. Although we should celebrate the growing numbers of books published in this area, not every book will do! Two phenomena can be noted in general:

1. Because the problems of avoiding stereotypes and difficulties of writing fictional books that present whole characters rather than unidimensional views of disability, many of the books that meet the strictest criteria for accuracy and breadth are *nonfiction* books.

2. It is easier to write accurately and positively about physical disabilities than it is about cognitive, emotional, and/or behavioral differences. But because there are many more students with these invisible disabilities, accurate portrayal and information is even more critical. My previous research in this area (Sapon-Shevin, 1982a, 1982b) as well as an excellent recent article by Chloe Myers and Hank Bersani Jr. (2008/2009) can help us raise questions and guidelines for selecting appropriate books, including the following.

   • *Visibility:* Are people with differences and disabilities represented at all in books and other media? Countering the invisibility of people with disabilities is the first imperative.

   • Does the book promote ableism (defined by Hehir, 2002, as prejudice by able-bodied and able-minded people—that distorts perceptions of people with disabilities and helps maintain biases and myths about disabilities) by ignoring people with disabilities? Always ask, "Who isn't here or who is missing from this book or illustration?" It can be as simple as noting that in an illustration of a class none of the children wear glasses. Help students to notice issues of representation and marginalization in everything they see and hear.

   • *Accuracy:* Even in books for younger children that must use nontechnical, simplified language, we must ask whether the information on the causes, treatment, and prognosis for the disability discussed represent current professional thinking. A person can be born with Down syndrome, for example, but a child cannot be born "retarded" because this refers to issues of future growth and development. A close examination of copyright dates is helpful, but do not assume that more recent books are automatically more accurate or appropriate. There are some excellent older books (sadly now out of print) and also new books that have stigmatizing and inaccurate language.

- *Appeal:* No matter how accurate a book is, if it is not readable or appealing, it will not be useful. Some books about disabilities are overly wordy or contain too much text. It is important that the text and illustrations are appropriate to the intended audience.
- *Breadth:* Does the book show the child with a disability as a real person, a full participant in a family and a community, or is the book limited to details about the disability itself? People with disabilities have hobbies, interests, families, food preferences, and individual personalities just like everyone else; they should be presented and represented as full people not simply a label.
- *Language:* Issues of language are critical. An avoidance of labels, jargon, and epithets will lead to the reader's increased ability to see beyond the disability. In *Hey, Dummy* (Platt, 1977), for example, the words "dummy," "retarded," "brain damaged," and "moron" are used interchangeably and indiscriminately. Some of the descriptors of people with disabilities that were once considered acceptable have been rejected and replaced as a function of increasing sensitivity to the problems of labeling. The terms "crippled," "wheelchair bound," and "handicapped" have been replaced by more descriptive terms. It is considered more respectful to use "people first" language—putting the person before the disability. Michael is child who has a visual impairment (rather than Michael is blind); Cara uses a wheelchair; David has Asperger's syndrome (rather than "David suffers from autism.").
- *Role:* Why is the person with a disability in the story, and what role do they play? Some stories in which a character with a disability emerges as a superhero are problematic. It can raise the bar so that it's only okay to have a disability if you save the day. People with disabilities should be presented with the full range of attributes and skills—some exceptional and some quite ordinary. It is also problematic if the person with a disability is in the story to be rescued or saved by another person, thus reifying images of helplessness or victimhood. Think about what message readers (both those who are temporarily able bodied and those with disabilities) will take away from this book? Will they feel empowered and hopeful or diminished and humiliated?
- *Authorship:* Who wrote this book, and what are his qualifications? Many books in this category are written by parents and siblings of children with disabilities, and although this can add authenticity, there is also the risk that individual stories are presented as universal or typical. First-person accounts, although more limited, can be powerful stories to share.

Excellent books that present accurate, positive images of people with disabilities have been written and more continue to be written as community integration and sensitivity increase. Myers and Bersani urge us to use and create teachable moments about issues of disability, asking, for example, "What if the prince stayed blind? Could he still marry Rapunzel?" or "Did you know that President Roosevelt had a disability that was not mentioned in the book?"

Picture Books and Books for Younger Readers

We'll Paint the Octopus Red *(Stuve-Bodeen, 1998)*
and its sequel The Best Worst Brother *(Stuve-Bodeen, 2005)*

In the first book, a six-year-old discusses what it will be like to have a new brother or sister and has many expectations about what she will do with the baby. When the baby is born with Down syndrome, the little girl tries hard to understand what that will mean for their relationship and the possible things they will do.

The little girl says, "Isaac won't be able to play kickball with me." My dad said that Isaac might not walk as soon as other kids, but he could probably learn to kick the ball when he's older.

He won't be able to ride in the back of the mini-van and eat fruit snacks and stick out his tongue at cars. My dad smiled and said that he figured Isaac would be very good at both things. (Stuve-Bodeen, 1998)

As she explores each of her expectations, her father reassures her that all of those things were possible for her new brother.

The book ends with some questions and answers about Down syndrome. This is a very positive, upbeat book—good for exploring what it means and doesn't mean to have a disability.

The sequel continues telling the story of the relationship between Isaac, who is now three, and his older sister, Emma, who is sometimes frustrated by his slow language and motor development. Isaac's family attempts to teach him sign language, but he doesn't seem to make much progress. By the end of the book, Isaac has learned, and Emma also grows in her understanding of his disability and his successes. The sequel is not as positive but might still initiate good conversations.

Moses Goes to a Concert *(Millman, 2002)*

A young boy who is deaf goes to a concert with his deaf classmates and explores music. The children hold balloons on their laps to feel the vibrations. The book has standard text and includes inset photos of the story in sign language. It turns out the percussionist who is performing is also deaf. The book includes the sign language alphabet. Although Moses attends a segregated school (which we know from another book, *Moses Goes to School*), this book could be helpful in exploring deafness, sign language, and inclusion.

Mama Zooms *(Cowen-Fletcher, 1996)*

This book tells the story of a little boy's relationship with his mother, who zooms him everywhere in her wheelchair. The interactions between mother and child are sweet and typical—she just happens to do her mothering from a wheelchair.

Dad, Jackie and Me *(Uhlberg, 2010)*

This story, based on Uhlberg's experiences growing up as a hearing child of deaf parents, is about a young Dodger fan (a recent Chinese immigrant) who is excited about the addition of Jackie Robinson to his team's lineup. The narrator's father (who is deaf) is also a fan and sees parallels between his struggles as an outsider and those of Robinson. As the father and son attend games, their relationship grows, and the son overcomes some of his embarrassment about his father's awkward cheering. The book provides a wonderful opportunity to talk about different kinds of prejudice and the ways in which exclusion has been both painful and damaging to the fabric of our society.

Books for Older Readers

Joey Pizga Swallowed the Key *(Gantos, 1998)*

This book paints a sympathetic portrait of the life of a boy with attention deficit disorder (ADD) whose life is out of control. When his erratic behavior becomes dangerous, he finally receives the help and support he needs and is eventually able to rejoin his class. Written in the voice of the student himself, this book could be used to discuss some of the invisible disabilities that make life challenging for students and to initiate conversation about how to support someone whose behavior is unpredictable and puzzling.

The Giver *(Lowry, 2002)* and Gathering Blue *(Lowry, 2006)*

These two novels, both set in the future, raise powerful questions about what it means to be normal, the consequences of repressive societies, and the power of a young person with a vision to transform culture. *The Giver* tells the story of young Jonas who was born into a "perfect" world in which perfectly matched couples have exactly two offspring and the community elders control all major decisions. But Jonas painfully discovers that the elderly who are "released" and babies who are not developing on schedule are all being killed. When he is appointed to the position of "Receiver of Memory," he finds himself able to expose the hypocrisy of the society and to escape from it.

Gathering Blue is the story of another future society in which young Kira, newly orphaned and described as "lame since birth," discovers the secrets of the society in which she lives and is able to act powerfully to form alliances and transform her world. Both books can be used to discuss students' conceptions of perfection and how they feel an ideal society would deal with those who are seen as different.

Rules *(Lord, 2008)*

Catherine is embarrassed by the behavior of her younger brother David, who has autism. To help him negotiate life, she makes up rules for him to follow. As her life grows to include friendship with a boy, Jason, who uses a book of pictures to communicate, her understanding and acceptance of difference grows as well. This book is an excellent discussion starter about issues of difference and acceptance and could be the centerpiece of excellent conversations with upper-elementary students.

Freak the Mighty *(Philbrick, 2001)*

This book tells the story of a friendship between Maxwell Kane, a large eighth grader who describes himself as a "butthead goon," and Kevin, a small boy with a birth defect that requires him to use braces and crutches. By combining their gifts (size and imagination) and their bodies (Freak rides on Max's shoulders), the two boys become an invincible duo. Although parts of the story are somewhat maudlin (Kevin dies at the end), the embedded lessons will provoke good discussions about disability, friendship, and mutual support.

The Misfits *(Howe, 2003)*

This story is about the relationship between a group of students who are all outsiders in their seventh grade and have been taunted and subjected to name-calling. When the four of them decide to run against their more popular peers in the upcoming student council election, one of the members, Bobby Goodspeed, who is called "Lardo" and "Fluff," talks from his heart about the devastating effects of nicknames and taunts, and teachers and students finally listen.

This is a powerful book about stereotyping and the horrible effects of degrading labels. Sure to initiate a powerful and emotional discussion about bullying and exclusion, the book is both real and hopeful.

Reaching for Sun *(Zimmer, 2007)*

Told in the voice of a seventh grader with cerebral palsy, the story revolves around Josie's growing friendship with Jordan, a boy who shares her love of nature. Although it is Josie who has the label "disability," Jordan has his own challenges, allowing for a discussion of the ways in which many young people struggle with a multitude of challenges. Written in poetic verse, the book explores issues of disability, isolation, friendship, and the power of collaboration.

LINKS TO THE CURRICULUM

There are many ways to link issues of inclusion and exclusion to the curriculum. As evidenced by the previous list of children's books, there are many literary examples of people who have been excluded for a variety of reasons: color, gender, ethnicity, size, political beliefs, and so on. Such works of literature can be studied with reference to issues of exclusion and related to classroom practices and patterns.

Social studies curricula typically include many historical examples of exclusion (see Chapter 7). By studying the exclusion of people of color from baseball (the story of Jackie Robinson), the exclusion of woman from participation in voting, and the exclusion of Jews from certain colleges and universities, parallels can be drawn to inclusion and exclusion practices in the classroom.

Students can be encouraged to examine all aspects of their school day for evidence of inclusion and exclusion and to explore with the teacher and with one another alternative solutions and possibilities. Examples of exclusion can provide immediate examples of situations requiring problem solving and advocacy (see Chapter 8). Seventh-grade students at Roxborough Junior High School in Cleveland Heights, Ohio, were asked to complete an accessibility checklist for their school. They discovered that the elevator only went up (and not down), thus making it impossible for students with disabilities to take classes above the first floor. They wrote letters to the principal and to the school board detailing what they found, why it mattered, and what should be done about it. They were also given the task of going through a typical day and noting whether all their activities would be accessible to a person using a wheelchair. They made systematic lists of which movie theaters, restaurants, and stores were accessible, and they wrote letters to those that were found to be inaccessible. Rather than implementing the standard curriculum of letter writing by having students write pretend letters to nonexistent businesses, students were learning advocacy skills about their power to change things which are inequitable or unjust.

6

Setting Goals and Giving and Getting Support

Cameron is struggling with his math. As he tries to do the problems at his desk, he becomes more and more frustrated. Finally, he throws up his hands and announces loudly, "I just don't get it!" Two students come over to see if they can help explain the problem to him.

The students in Mr. Maguire's third grade become aware of the fact that Theresa is afraid of the dark and sleeps with a night-light. They find every opportunity they can to tease her about this: "Fraidy baby, scaredy cat" is a common refrain when she walks by. Last week, when she was in the bathroom, two kids waited until she was sitting on the toilet and then turned the bathroom lights out.

Everyone in Miss Scalone's room is aware that Mark has lots of trouble controlling his temper. When they see that he is about to "lose it" during a game or activity, one of his classmates encourages him, "Calm down, Mark. This happens to lots of kids when they're losing, but it's going to be okay. We'll help you figure it out." Another classmate puts his arm around Mark's shoulders and gently leads him away from the person he was about to hit.

THE VISION

The vision statement for this aspect of classroom community centers on two areas: (1) goal setting and (2) giving and getting help.

All people have goals—things they are working on, hoping to learn or improve, or mileposts they would like to reach. In a broad sense, curriculum guidelines are a kind of goal, but hardly personalized ones. Some children have individual goals drawn for them as part of the individualized educational program (IEP) process of the special education system.

I recently visited a third-grade classroom that included a girl, Casey, who had some significant learning and behavioral challenges. I was surprised to notice, posted on the chalkboard, a large piece of paper listing Casey's goals: Casey will learn to recognize

117

colors and shapes. Casey will count to 10 independently and count objects 1 through 10. Casey will initiate social interactions with other students, and so on. Posting these goals was probably intended to serve several functions: (1) remind Casey's teachers what goals she was working on and prompt them to include those goals in day-to-day activities, (2) remind Casey of her goals throughout the day, (3) provide a reminder to other adult staff of Casey's goals, and (4) encourage Casey's classmates to understand what she was working on so they could encourage her to work on those goals. Although there was nothing wrong with the goals set for Casey or with the idea of garnering support for her, posting them publicly in the room seemed problematic: What messages were communicated to children, adults, and Casey herself by the public posting of her goals? What would Casey's parents think if they saw her goals posted on the wall like that? Was such a posting even legal, or did it violate the right to privacy component of the special education process? And perhaps most significant, *why was Casey the only student in the class with explicit goals?*

Certainly, we want students to understand their goals and those of other students. We definitely also want their support and help in meeting goals. But shouldn't that be happening for *all* students, not just the student with a special education label? How could we take the best of this example (the sharing; the openness; and the implicit structuring of help, support, and encouragement) and make goal setting more normalized and standard?

One teacher I have worked with has all students generate a goal for the week, which they place on a 3 × 5 card taped to their desk. These goals might include academics (get working on my social studies report or master the new computer program), study or learning skills (remember to take my homework books home each night or spend silent reading time actually reading), and social goals (find someone to play with at recess and stay out of fights or stay calm when I don't understand my math). Because the goals are self-generated, students were afforded an opportunity to think well about themselves as learners and people. And because everyone had a goal, goal setting was not something reserved for people in trouble or at risk. Because students choose which goal they want to work on and post, they are free to pick something they feel comfortable sharing and can also engage their classmates in an open discussion of what kind of help would be appreciated—"Ask me if I have my books when it's time to go home," "Come over and check in with me if you see me getting frustrated during math," or "Offer to work on the computer with me." It can also be extremely positive to have teachers set goals for themselves also. This establishes teachers as growing, learning members of the classroom community and ones who also needs help and support!

All people need help. None of us is really independent, although the myth of "making it alone" keeps many people from asking for and getting the help they need and deserve. A positive vision around help involves the following assumptions:

- All people need and deserve help—even people who are considered intelligent, competent, and mature.
- People should be allowed to specify the kinds of help they need and want and when they want it.
- Both giving and getting help are positive and can help bring people closer together.
- There should be no stigma or shame associated with needing other people's help, support, encouragement, or appreciation.
- All people need to develop (and be taught) repertoires of asking for help appropriately, accepting help graciously, rejecting offers of help kindly, and offering help respectfully.

A mistaken belief that independence is the goal (or even that independence is possible!) sometimes keeps us from embracing all the opportunities classroom communities present to foster interdependence and peer support. And our cultural lenses about the values of independence and separateness often keep us from seeing other possibilities.

Many years ago, an American visitor to a Chinese preschool observed that the smocks the children wore buttoned *up the back.* The American visitor said, "But with smocks like that, they can't learn to dress independently." "Precisely," replied the Chinese teacher, "This way they learn to help one another." The same observer noticed that small groups of three to four children were sitting on the floor pushing a toy car back and forth among themselves. Concerned about the apparent scarcity of play materials, the American approached the Chinese teacher and offered kindly, "I can see that you don't have enough cars for all the children. When I get back to the United States, I could see about collecting some toys to send you." The Chinese teacher took the American visitor to the classroom supply cabinet, opened the door, and revealed an entire shelf of toy cars and trucks. She explained patiently, "We give them materials to share so that they will learn to work together."

Our notions of scarcity and abundance can interfere with thinking about the ways in which children and adults can relate to one another if they accept their interdependence as a given. If we really believe that it is *best* when children have their own package of crayons, then we might not think creatively about ways for children to share crayons and the skills they will gain by negotiating and problem solving around "scarce" resources, such as, "May I please use the blue crayon when you're done?" "How about if I color the grass and the trees green and you use your red crayon to do the roof and the flowers?" When we truly value interdependence and working together, then we can look for multiple opportunities to foster such interactions.

Structuring interdependence also allows different kinds of interpersonal feelings and responses more likely. In my classroom, for example, when a child cut her finger, I always asked another child to provide "medical attention." The ritual of helping the child wash her finger, applying antiseptic, and putting on a Band-Aid provided multiple opportunities for tenderness and concern on the part of the caregiver and appreciation and acknowledgment on the part of the one receiving the care. (Although current concerns about infectious diseases may make teachers more cautious about which parts of the tending students can do, other students can always offer verbal support and consolation.)

A visitor to the Regio Emilio Preschools in Italy noticed that when it was time for outdoor recess, the children in the class approached the teacher with their coats, and the teacher helped each student put on the coat. The American observer saw this as an unnecessary lack of independence and a burden on teacher time and offered to show the teacher the independent way children can learn to put on their coats by laying them on the floor, standing behind them, inserting their arms, and flipping them over their head. "Thank you for the idea," said the Italian teacher. And taking the visitor's coat from her, she helped her put her arms in the sleeves. "If the children dressed themselves," she explained, "I wouldn't get to do this to each one before they went outside," drew the coat around the visitor, and kissed her warmly on the cheek.

A Vietnamese story describes the difference between heaven and hell as this: in hell, all the people have arms that do not bend at the elbow. They sit in front of steaming bowls of soup, but because they cannot bend their elbows, they cannot feed themselves and whimper plaintively from hunger. In heaven, on the other hand, the people's elbows still do not bend, but there they have learned to feed one another.

CHALLENGES TO THE VISION

Establishing new norms related to goal setting involves actively resisting some cultural preconceptions and assumptions about the ways in which human beings can and should interact.

Barriers to Shared Goal Setting

As children, other people mostly set the goals for us. Our parents told us to clean our rooms; our teachers told us to study, and church or synagogue leaders may have set other tasks in front of us. For this reason, many people react to the idea of goal setting with skepticism and hesitation; they don't like the idea that someone else will be telling them what to do.

But goal setting can be an empowering act as well, one in which we get to think well about ourselves, our hopes, and our desires. We can take the time and be provided the structure to think about what we really want to accomplish for ourselves.

Goal setting tends to be a private act, as well, and many people are hesitant to share their goals with other people for several reasons: (1) They don't want other people's advice or intrusion on what they perceive as personal. (2) They don't want reproach or humiliation if they perceive that they are failing at their goals. (3) They become competitive or embarrassed about the nature or caliber of their goal ("I'm only trying to learn to print—Nancy is already on cursive," or "I'm trying to run a 10-minute mile, but even if I do, I'll still be one of the slowest students in the class.").

In a supportive learning community, however, goal setting can be a positive act. Goals can be set by students themselves or by students working with other students or with teachers. Goals can also be shared and students taught specific repertoires for supporting and helping classmates' to reach their goals and to celebrate successes and respectfully honor challenges.

Barriers to Getting and Giving Help

The barriers to developing classrooms in which help is freely asked for, offered, given, and accepted or rejected are tremendous, and many of them precede children's entry in schools. Some of the cultural norms of competition already discussed as barriers to showing ourselves fully and knowing others well apply here as well. If being of value is closely linked to "being the best" or the "fastest," then helping is clearly dysfunctional. If I stop my work long enough to help you, then you might win instead of me. I can hardly afford to take time from what I'm doing to help you. Furthermore, if I help you, you might do better than I do and make me a loser. In a competitive system, it is really to my advantage to have others do badly—so why would I help them?

Asking for help is no easier. If one's sense of self-esteem and worth hinges on a notion of competence—individual competence—then by asking for help, I am making public that I am weak, limited, or needy in some way. Why would I want others to know this about me if it will lead to scorn, teasing, or mockery? Better, then, to struggle along by myself, give up, or somehow cover my challenges or weaknesses and hope that others won't notice.

These issues apply as much to teachers as to students. An accomplished inclusion teacher recently confided to me that when she went to her school's inclusion support meeting and announced that she was struggling with a particular child, another teacher said derisively, "Oh, and we thought you were the expert!" That comment radically decreased the first teacher's safety in sharing her problems and needs. And who lost by that interchange? Everyone. The child who may now never get the help he needs, the teacher who will likely not share her concerns in the future, and other teachers who observing what happened to this teacher will also hesitate to share their struggles.

REFRAMING OUR WORK

Beginning With Ourselves

- What are some things you need help with to make your life go well?
- How easy is it for you to ask for help when you need it?
- How do you feel when others ask you for help?
- What are some ways that people have offered you help that have made you feel either grateful or humiliated?
- What is your personal history with goal setting? Do you make goals? Do you share them with others?
- What are some ways that people have supported you in reaching your goals? What has that taught you about support?

Looking at Our Classrooms and Schools

- Do students set realistic and reasonable goals for themselves?
- Do students think critically about what goals would make sense for them?
- Do students recognize that different people in the class will (and should) have different goals?
- Are students able to articulate their goals clearly?
- Are students able to explain other students' goals clearly?
- Are students supportive of one another's goals? Do they offer concrete and responsive help to their classmates?
- Do students freely ask for help when they are struggling?
- Do students ask for help appropriately rather than whining or complaining?
- Are students alert to others who require assistance?
- Do students offer assistance respectfully to classmates?
- Do students accept help from others graciously?
- Do student reject unwanted offers of help politely?
- Do student have well-developed repertoires for providing support and assistance to classmates who are quite different from themselves (i.e., those with physical and educational challenges, those who speak another language, and the like)?
- Are teachers and other staff members encouraged to set individual and collective goals for themselves?
- Do the teachers and administrators in your school easily support one another?
- What happens when a teacher or other school staff member is in need of help or support?
- What channels or procedures are in place in the school to provide nonstigmatizing help and support to those who need it?

What's the Big Picture?

- What is your vision of what the world would look like if people freely offered and asked for help to others?

- What does support look like at a local level? A national level? A global level?
- What messages do you want future citizens to get about how they can support one another?

HOW TO BEGIN

ACTIVITIES

Peer Listening

Peer Listening is a way for two people to structure a block of time so that each gets a turn to talk and each to listen. This process can work with students of any age or with adults. There are three general guidelines:

1. Time is divided evenly. The listening period can be anything from 2 to 10 minutes, with smaller intervals generally being easier for beginners. It is useful to use a timer so that the time is spent equally. If the teacher merely tells students to take turns, it is inevitable that the "high talker" will use more time and never get to experience being a listener as well as denying the "low talker" their chance to share.

2. The role of the listener is to listen. Good eye contact, nodding, smiling, and asking for clarification are permissible, but the listener is not to give advice or to interrupt the talker to tell a story. Neither is the listener to evaluate or judge what the talker is saying.

3. Whatever is said during the peer listening activity is confidential and doesn't leave that space. Younger children may need extensive examples of what confidentiality means, but they can be helped to understand that "you don't tell anyone else what Marsha just told you."

Some teachers use peer listening to start the morning every day so that each student's voice is heard in the classroom (see Box 6.1). For some students, the opportunity to tell someone what is happening is invaluable in helping them to put issues aside to enter the learning environment able to learn. Teachers may occasionally assign topics for listening partners to talk about, particularly if an incident or situation has arisen in the classroom that evokes strong feelings. For example, when a fight broke out on the playground one day at recess and the students returned to the classroom angry, upset, and confused, the teacher asked them to each take three minutes with their listening partner. After partners had each spoken, the teacher led the whole class in a discussion of the issue.

BOX 6.1

A third-grade teacher from Texas who teaches in a community overwhelmed by violence, abuse, and drugs formed his class into what he called "friendship groups." The groups met each morning for 10 minutes. The ostensible reason for the meeting was to go over the homework from the night before and to give students a chance to unwind and talk. The teacher reported that, over time, his class changed from one in which there were high levels of interpersonal violence to one in which students grew to support and care about one another. Sometimes after sharing in small groups, students would share with him information they thought would be helpful. When other teachers challenged the teacher's use of time for this activity and asked what subject matter he listed it as part of, the teacher replied, "Health—mental health." He maintained that it was time very well spent.

Helping

We need to establish classroom norms and practices that are based on the assumption that all people need help, that giving and getting help are good things, and that helping others creates a win–win solution bringing people closer together. For children, we constantly need to reiterate that there is no such thing as true independence—all people function in community and are interconnected. Because not everyone is good at the same things (as discussed in the previous chapters), then it makes sense for people to help one another in respectful ways. Recent economic challenges have sparked a huge resurgence in the concept of bartering: I will do something for you, and you will do something for me. In the same way that adults now trade snow shoveling for investment advice or catering for childcare, children can begin to see how they can be of service to others and avail themselves of others' skills and expertise.

Classrooms that include students with visible disabilities and challenges can provide positive models of helping that apply to all children. It is obvious to students that Clarence, who is in a wheelchair, needs some help getting places and manipulating objects. As they problem solve with Clarence about what kinds of help he would like, how he would like that help offered, and what kind of interpersonal behavior will feel most respectful, students can answer these same questions for themselves: "When I don't understand a word, don't just fill in the paper for me—help me to figure it out myself," or "Don't tell me I'm doing it wrong when I tie my shoes the way I do—I know it's not like you do, but it's my way, and it works fine, even though it may take me a while."

Rather than thinking or talking about the class as "we're all the same except for Clarence who needs help," we can *normalize* helping by explaining and demonstrating that all people need help, although it may be help of different kinds: Clarence may need help getting materials, Kinesha may need help staying on task, Morgan may need help finding people to play with on the playground, and Justine may need help with her math. One teacher shared with me that she routinely asks for help from the classroom aide and from the students to model both appropriate help-seeking behavior and that the teachers are allowed to have help without losing respect. The intended message, "Well, the teachers are smart and grown up, and they're allowed to say they don't know and need help, so it must be okay for me too."

Teachers will need to think carefully about which tasks genuinely require students to do things by themselves and which tasks can or should be done with help or support. When I was teaching third grade, I observed that two of my students, Mickey and Paul, always did their math together. One day I wandered over and asked them why they always worked together. Mickey explained, "Well, Paul understands the math, but he has really messy handwriting. I don't understand the math, but I write really neat. So he figures out the problem, and I make two clean copies."

This conversation really made me pause—I had very mixed feelings. On the one hand, there was a problem because I wasn't sure that Mickey would learn math that way. On the other hand, these two boys had figured out exactly the way the world should work—we develop relationships and communication skills so that we can help one another accomplish our goals through our individual gifts and talents. It is not always clear when help is appropriate and when it is keeping a child from learning or growing himself, and there are no pat answers here. Rather, we must continuously ask ourselves what it is we are really trying to teach; how we can best establish those skills; and then, perhaps as a separate question, when will skills be needed and will they have to be performed relatively independently? We shouldn't, however, confuse skill acquisition with skill display; even if students will eventually have to complete a task independently, they may still learn that behavior best by working with others. In other words, learning to make change by working with a partner makes a lot of sense even though when you are standing in line at the checkout counter, you have to be able to look at what the cashier has given you and tell independently (relatively quickly) whether the change is right.

There are clearly tasks or jobs that most people do perform by themselves most of the time—filling out a job application, paying for purchases, and the like. But students can learn to do these with lots of help and support. And there are some people who will always require different kinds of help and support to perform specific tasks (to say nothing of everyone who ages and needs help), and it makes sense to help students become thoughtful about how to ask, offer, accept, and reject help appropriately.

All people need to develop four repertoires related to help and support:

1. Asking for help appropriately: "Could you please help me with this?" or "I'd appreciate it if you would catch me at the bottom of the slide," as opposed to "Can't you see I need help, for goodness' sake!" or "Help me, stupid."

2. Offering help respectfully: "Would you like a hand with that?" or "Would it help if I read each problem aloud for you?" not "Let me do that for you—you're obviously too short/clumsy/stupid to do it yourself," or, without asking, simply doing something for a person who was actually eager and prepared to do it herself.

3. Accepting help graciously: "Thanks for noticing I needed help with that," or "Yes, it would be great if you'd put your finger on that part while I'm trying to glue the other section," rather than "Well, it's about time you noticed I was struggling!" or "No, I want to do all the work myself!"

4. Rejecting help kindly: "No thanks, I have my own way I'm trying to do this," or "Thanks for asking, but I'd rather do it myself," as opposed to "Leave me alone, I don't need your help!" or "What do you think I am, stupid or something?"

Teachers can systematically teach and structure each of these repertoires in several ways.

Classroom Yellow Pages

Children can generate their own yellow pages with listings of the things they can teach or share. Under "jump roping," for example, Beth's name might be listed as an indication that she is willing to teach/show people how to jump rope. Dominic's name might be listed under "rockets" or "stamp collecting." Sophie's under "origami" or "memory tricks." The teacher's task is to help students generate what they are good at so they can make entries. This is a particularly important activity when there are students who feel (or who may be perceived) as incompetent or not good at anything! Classmates can help generate students' strengths for the yellow pages, which can be very affirming to the student who is feeling less than or unvalued.

Classroom Classifieds: Help Wanted and Help Offered

Students can write their own classified advertisements for skills, interests, and needs. For help offered, you might get something like these:

> Want to learn origami? My family and I do this all the time, and I can show you how to fold swans, frogs, and bears. After you've learned the basics, I can teach you more complicated animals and even some with moving parts. See Mai Li.

> Do you have trouble bringing home the right book and assignments? I can help you get organized. I have a system for recording homework and assignments, and I'll share it with you. See Carlos to set up an appointment.

Want to make inexpensive presents for your friends and family? Interested in learning to make friendship bracelets? I can teach you how. I know four different styles and can use thick or thin threads. It's easy, and I can teach you in one lesson. See Jamalla.

Help-wanted ads might look like these:

I want to learn how to play soccer. I see other kids playing, but I don't even know the basics. I need a patient, calm teacher who will help me get started. Must have soccer experience and be willing to work with a real beginner. See Gladys if you can help.

Do you like to play pretend games? I do. I am looking for other people who want to meet at recess and invent fantasy kingdoms and act out roles. I have some ideas but want to meet other people who have ideas too. See Nicodemeus if you are interested.

Do you have little brothers and sisters who are always getting into your stuff? I do, and it's getting me very upset. Does anyone have suggestions about how to share a room without getting into fights all the time? Please see Peter if you have ideas.

This activity works well for teachers too—who also deserve help and support and to share their skills and gifts with others proudly. Think about your teachers' lounge. Is this where people sit and complain about children and their families, or is it a place for giving and getting support and sharing accomplishments and successes? One school posted a help wanted/help offered board in the teachers' lounge, and the teachers wrote ads like this:

Help! I'm drowning in paperwork. I can never seem to keep track of forms to fill out and reports to file. They all get heaped up on my desk and sometimes lost! Does anyone have a system he or she can share before I drown in paper? See Gretchen Wilson in Room 2.

Always wanted to do puppetry with your students but didn't know where to start? I have many ideas for making inexpensive, easy puppets and having students write their own puppet plays. I can help you figure out how to do puppet plays on any subject matter with all age groups. See Dan Najinksy in Room 12 if you are interested in joining the world of puppetry.

I need ideas for reading and writing activities for students who are ELL. I am having trouble adapting materials for two students from Vietnam whose English is very limited. Do you have materials or ideas? I'd really appreciate any help I can get with this. See Karen Boyd in Room 246.

Want to get parents more involved in the classroom? I've come up with some ways to get those hard-to-reach parents into my classroom. I've been especially successful with parents with limited reading and writing skills and those for whom school wasn't successful. I have strategies for transportation, communication, and activities. See Elena Sanchez in Room 43.

Note to teachers: The same principles of safety and trust apply for teachers. To ask for help or support, teachers must be confident that their acknowledgment of need will be treated with respect rather than scorn ("Boy—I can't believe that Mrs. G. is asking for help—after all the years she's been here, you'd think she'd know how to handle that kind of a situation"). And for teachers to claim and celebrate what they know and are willing to share, they must also be confident that their sharing will be met with appreciation and support rather than jealousy or hostility ("Who does he think he is, saying that he's the IEP expert in the school now," or "Sure, if I only taught 15 students, I'd be able to put on lots of plays too!").

CYCLES OF SUPPORT

It is possible to think of support in terms of a cycle, depending on when it occurs with relation to a specific task or occasion.

BEFORE → DURING → AFTER

Teachers can conduct specific lessons with students on three categories of support:

1. Encouragement

2. Help

3. Appreciation

What is encouragement? What does encouragement look like or feel like to you? How do you want other people to encourage you? A sample lesson on this topic might look like this:

1. The teacher introduces the word *encouragement* and asks students what it means. The teacher and/or students complete a word web on the board or on paper.

2. The teacher asks students to think about a time that someone encouraged them and to share their story with a partner (self-chosen or assigned, making sure that everyone is partnered).

3. The teacher elicits stories of encouragement from the whole group, asking students to share either what they told their partner or what their partner told them.

4. The teacher leads a discussion of what kinds of encouragement people like, what they don't like, and how each of these sounds (specific words or phrases) or looks (gestures, physical contact, or the like).

5. The poster on ways to encourage is posted in the classroom and referred to by the teacher consistently. Students are also encouraged to add to the chart or to share at class meeting about specific ways that people encouraged them.

This same lesson can be conducted using the other two words, *help* and *appreciation*, with the same sharing and development of guidelines or charts. During the discussion of help, it is important for students to articulate the differences between help with respect and help without respect, or ways people sometimes help them that don't feel helpful (for example, doing something for someone can sometimes be helpful and appropriate and can sometimes feel dismissive and punitive).

The discussion of appreciations can be used to elaborate kinds of appreciation that feel good as opposed to those that often contain an element of put-down ("You catch pretty well for a girl," or "Boy, I never thought you could do that—I'm so surprised"). At the end of a workshop I led once, a woman in the group commented, "I saw you before, and you've gotten a lot better." Although perhaps she meant well, it somehow didn't feel like a real appreciation.

APPRECIATIONS (SEE BOX 6.2)

Teachers can develop various appreciation rituals with students. These might include the following.

'Round the Circle

Have students sit in a circle and say one thing they like or appreciate about the person to the left (or right).

Drawing Names

Have students write their names on slips of paper. Each student draws a name and says something he or she values or appreciates about that person.

Flood of Appreciations

This activity is particularly wonderful for someone having a hard day, the "kid of the week," and the like. One child sits in the center of the circle, and people from the circle say nice things about him.

Book of Appreciations

Each child (either one a week, or all at the same time) makes a little book for himself or herself or has one made by the teacher. Classmates write positive notes, comments, or appreciations in the book. For young children, the teacher can have them dictate using a standard format: "What I like about Latisha is . . ."

Appreciation Box

The students create and decorate a box into which spontaneous appreciations can be dropped throughout the day or week. The teacher might pull some out some to read at a class meeting, or a "letter carrier" could deliver them to their intended recipients. The teacher might want to develop a system to ensure that all students receive appreciations at some point.

BOX 6.2

Third-grade teacher Cathi Allen says, "We work on developing real appreciations—ones with heart. We celebrate those types of appreciations. Last year, I had a student who was really struggling socially—she was an in-charge type of person. How exciting it was when she was the first to genuinely go deep and share, 'Thanks, Sandy, for listening when I was sharing my story. I could tell you were interested by the questions you asked, and it made me feel important.'"

Proud Board

Rather than posting only the top papers or the perfect spelling or math scores, the teacher can create a *proud board*. Students can be asked (daily or weekly) to post something on the board they are proud of and to explain to the rest of the class why they are proud: "I'm putting up this story because I've never written anything like this before, and I was pretty nervous, but I like the way it came out." "I put up my spelling paper because it's a lot better than I did last week, and I really studied this time." "I put up my math homework, 'cause even though it's not all right, it's the first time I ever did it without getting upset." Students can learn to value and appreciate accomplishments and improvements rather than seeing that only perfection or being the best as worthy of recognition.

Goal Setting

Setting goals with students can take many forms. Goals can be short term (finish my math today), long term (make more friends in class), or situation specific (respond calmly the next time Craig tries to pick a fight with me).

As described earlier, teachers can help students set daily/weekly/monthly goals for themselves. These goals can be private, semiprivate, or public. A private goal is one that only the student knows. The teacher may encourage students to write their goals in their journal and then to check in with themselves about whether they are reaching those goals and, if not, what kind of support or help they would like. Semiprivate goals are ones that are shared with one other person (or perhaps several). The teacher might sit down with students individually, for example, and help them generate a goal. Or two students (or a home group) might become privy to another student's goal. Public goals can be posted either on the corner of the student's desk or on a wall chart.

Teachers need to make thoughtful and specific rules about how students are to respond to one another's goals. For example, students might be coached to ask another student, "How are you doing with your goal of studying spelling every night?" or "Are your ideas for finding people to sit with at lunch working?" The teacher can also model this same kind of respectful questioning, following it either by congratulations or with an offer to problem solve or support the student who is not being successful.

COLLABORATIVE PROBLEM SOLVING

Collaborative Problem Solving (CPS) is a process developed by Salisbury, Evans, and Palombaro (1997) in which children and adults work together to resolve conflicts and problems. Salisbury and colleagues say that through CPS people "develop concern for others; accept differences as well as similarities; learn how to work with others to resolve problems; are empowered to create change; and find ways to meaningfully include everyone in activities." The process has five steps:

1. Identify the issue: An issue arises whenever there is a discrepancy between what is happening and what we would like to happen. To identify the issue, state the desired outcomes. For example, the

class has a commitment to having all students involved, and during an activity, one student is sitting with nothing to do.

2. Generate all possible solutions: Brainstorm potential solutions to the issue. Discuss all solutions with no value judgment at this time as to whether the solutions are viable. The intent is simply to identify any possible alternative to what is currently happening.

3. Screen solutions for feasibility: There are two main components to this step.

   a. Once all the solutions have been proposed, review each recommendation in light of the following criteria:

      i. Does the solution match the value base of the group? For example, does the solution demonstrate concern for others, foster inclusion, and/or respect differences?

      ii. Is the solution feasible? Can the individual or group implement the solution? Are all the materials available? Can it be accomplished in the setting where the problem arises? Is there enough time to do it?

   b. Predict the possible outcomes/success of the solution. This allows the participants to identify the potential benefits or detriments of the proposed solutions and assists in deciding which one to implement.

4. Choose a solution: Reach consensus on which solution to implement. By having all stakeholders involved in the process of identifying potential solutions and agreeing on which one to use, we increase the likelihood that participants will support and be committed to the solution the group has identified.

5. Evaluate the solution: Participants need to evaluate whether the proposed solution had its intended effect. In other words, was the issue successfully resolved, did the child or adult get what they needed, or are there remaining concerns? How do members of the group feel the process went? In light of what the group has learned from this experience, is further action necessary?

An example of the CPS is shared in Box 6.3.

BOX 6.3   SCENARIO

1. Identify the Issue

   Third graders are getting ready to begin a unit of study on the rainforest. Because part of their studies will focus on the destruction of the rainforest, their teachers have decided to set the lesson by "time traveling" to the rainforest of the past as well as the future. In preparation for time traveling, students have been asked to make a large clock face that they will wear around their neck. Students in one class are busy working on their clocks in small groups at their tables. Stacy, a student in this class, is sitting in her wheelchair working with an aide, Mrs. Jones, on visually responding to materials presented by reaching out her arms and trying to grasp them. Megan, another third grader, is watching Mrs. Jones and Stacy as she waits for a brightly colored marker Mrs. Jones is using.

   "Mrs. Jones, isn't Stacy going to time travel with us?" asks Megan.

   "Sure she is," says Mrs. Jones. "Why?"

   (Continued)

(Continued)

"Well, aren't you going to have her make her clock then?" asks Megan. "I mean she's got to have a clock to time travel."

"I know. We have to make one, you're right. But I'm not sure what to do."

"I'll help her do it. I'm done with mine," says Calvin who is sitting next to Stacy.

"Well, maybe you could all help," says Mrs. Jones. "I want to make the clock something meaningful for Stacy. You all are going to be learning about the rainforest and time travel. I want Stacy to learn something too. How do we make the clock so that Stacy can learn something from it, too?"

2. Generate All Possible Solutions

"Why don't we make the clock and then someone can explain to Stacy what it's for?" suggests Jared. "You know, like write on it that it's for time traveling."

"No, that's no good, Jarred," says Sean.

"Any idea is good," Mrs. Jones tells the group. "We won't know which one will work until we try it. Let's just try to think of a bunch of different ideas and then decide which one we should try."

"Hey, how about you make the clock on that bright fluorescent paper Stacy likes to look at? Then you know she'll really pay attention to it! We could get her to watch it and follow it with her eyes. Then she'd be doing something we work on with her. I mean she'd be learning something."

"No, I know," said Megan. "What if we put bright colors and things she could feel on her clock? Like we could get her to look at it and then reach for it and feel the stuff on it."

3. Screen for Feasibility

Mrs. Jones thanks them for all the ideas and asks them which one they think they could use. After some discussion, they rule out making the clock from the fluorescent paper because they only have one sheet of it.

They also talk about whether they should just write on the clock what it is for and have someone read it to Stacy. They agree that then she's not doing anything but sitting and listening, and they don't like that idea.

The students begin hunting to see if there is anything in the room that is brightly colored that Stacy could feel. They take some cotton balls, yarn, and felt out of their art supply box. They also find some corrugated cardboard that someone suggests they could color.

4. Choose a Solution to Implement

"Well, what did you decide?" Mrs. Jones asks.

"We're going to have her make her clock with this stuff," they say as they point to the assortment of materials on the table.

"Yeah while we're making it with her, we can see which one she likes to feel best and then we can put a lot of that one on it," says Calvin. "Then we know she'll want to reach for it."

"We're going to let her choose what color she wants to color the cardboard too, so it's the one she likes best."

The students at the table work to make Stacy's clock once they have finished their own. When it is finished, it has numbers on it like all the others but some of the numbers are made of pieces or cardboard or yarn. The back of clock is covered in bright red felt.

When the class time travels the next day, Megan uses Stacy's clock with her, having her reach out for the numbers to set her clock to the time the teachers have asked for.

5. Evaluate the Solution

When the class exits the time travel machine, Mrs. Jones asks Megan and Calvin how it went. They talk about the fun they had, and Calvin adds, "You should have seen Stacy. She really liked her clock. She was looking at it and talking and everything."

"She loves that felt on the back, Mrs. Jones. She would really watch it when I moved the clock away from her," said Megan.

"Well, I'm glad it worked so well. It was a great idea, guys. Thanks for helping me."

Although this scenario deals with problem solving around curricular inclusion, the same strategy can be used for problem solving other issues in the classroom, including conflicts, social exclusion, management concerns, and so on.

Peer Tutoring and Partner Learning

Peer teaching/learning can be established in a single classroom, across classrooms, or within an entire unit or school. Peer teaching generally refers to any approach in which one child instructs or teaches material to another child; the terms can include both cross-age and same-age tutoring or support. Peer teaching can also be understood as a form of *peer collaboration* in that students are working together toward a shared goal.

The benefits of peer tutoring programs have been well documented. Benefits to the tutors include increased academic understanding, improved social interaction skills, positive self-esteem, and teaching experience (perhaps we are nurturing future teachers!). Tutees typically show improved academic skills and benefit from developing a close relationship with another student, often one from a different grade level or age. The peer experience can also help students learn how to understand another person's perspective, key to the development of empathy. See Box 6.4 for examples.

BOX 6.4

In Winooski, Vermont, a formalized peer training and supervision program involved more than 80% of the student body as tutors and tutees in 18 of 21 classrooms. One fourth-grade teacher established a peer tutoring system in her class that involved all of the students as tutors and tutees. Then, a first-grade teacher linked up with the fourth-grade teacher, with the fourth graders providing math review for the first graders for 30 minutes every other Friday. Each tutor worked with three or four first graders, allowing all students in the class to receive tutorial instruction. Supervisory responsibility was shifted from a support person to the first-grade teacher, and eventually, to the fourth graders themselves, who became responsible for creating their own instructional materials.

At the end of the school year, a number of the fourth-grade tutors approached their newly assigned fifth-grade teachers, requesting permission to continue their tutoring roles.

It is important to note that the tutors were not all high-achieving students but included many students with special needs of their own that teachers believed were helped through the tutoring experience (including high-achieving students who needed a creative problem-solving experience;

(Continued)

(Continued)

students themselves requiring special education services; and students identified as withdrawn, shy, or having low self-esteem). A sixth grader in one Vermont middle school served as a cross-age tutor for the last 45 minutes of the school day. His tutoring was made contingent on displaying appropriate classroom behavior as specified in his behavior contract. Although his teachers still described him as presenting "intensely challenging" behaviors, the second-grade teacher described him as a model of appropriate behavior and a valuable instructional asset. The sixth grader chose to miss his class party to attend the second-grade class party where he presented individual presents to each student in the class and a large stuffed teddy bear to the teacher (Villa & Thousand, 1986).

■ ■ ■ ■

In an urban school in Rochester, New York, each sixth grader was partnered with a first grader for math instruction. The sixth graders met with their math buddy once a week and were required to write lesson plans and lesson evaluations for each session. The first graders thrived on the attention and their math learning increased dramatically. The sixth-grade teacher reported that even the students who weren't very skilled at math studied and prepared hard to be competent teachers to their first-grade friends. One sixth grader was overheard saying, "I've got to make sure I understand this so I can teach it to Matthew." Other benefits included serious changes in the overall school atmosphere. Gone were the chants of "first-grade baby" in the hall; the older students looked out for their little friends and seemed to adopt a protective attitude toward the younger students. One sixth grader said to another, "Don't mess with Dwayne—he's my friend." The first graders were especially thrilled to know big kids in the school, and the satisfaction on their faces was clear when they would spot one of the older children in the hall and wave, "Hi, Mitch!"

■ ■ ■ ■

Mary Schlitz, a fifth-grade teacher, and Lori Keevil, a first-grade teacher, have combined their classes for curriculum study and projects. The teachers worked together to develop a multilevel curriculum that met the educational needs of both group of students. For one unit, the fifth graders developed learning centers on the five senses for the first graders. The older students took the younger ones through the centers. The fifth graders had to learn how to teach; their teacher explained to them about time on task, word attack, praising, wait time, and redirecting. She said to them, "Here's how I teach you—now, you get to do these things with little kids." The teaching has not been all one-way; for a unit on fossils, the first graders showed the fifth graders how sand was made (part of their curriculum study) while the fifth graders built models to demonstrate volcanoes in the ocean. For another unit, the fifth graders made games that used the younger students' sight-word vocabularies; the older students learned how to write direction paragraphs on how to play the game. They designed and built the games themselves, tried them out with the first graders, and then evaluated them and made changes based on what they observed. The year culminated with a party celebrating the cross-age friendships. The teachers made T-shirts with each of the peer partner's pictures on them so that Jamal and Nicole both had identical shirts with both their pictures.

The teachers report that the teasing between the groups has stopped completely and that the students now seek one another out in the neighborhood as well. Mary says, "They used to be scared of the bigger kids—now they're their friends."

Peer Advocacy

Students can learn to act as advocates for their peers in both planning for instruction and resolving conflicts. When children with special educational needs have been successfully included in a classroom, their peers can often function as valuable resources to future teachers and students about what works and what doesn't (see Box 6.5).

BOX 6.5

When Bob, a student with multiple disabilities, moved to a public school from a segregated residential facility, the student body of the small junior high school met with school staff in small groups to plan Bob's transition. "The students' participation in the planning helped develop a genuine sense of ownership and responsibility for Bob's success among his future classmates. The advice they gave faculty members greatly facilitated his immediate acceptance, and suggestions ranged from providing an augmentative communication device that they thought would help Bob communication to what kind of notebook, backpack, and musical tapes he should have to fit in." When, after two years, Bob's family moved to a neighboring community, his classmates offered to talk with teachers and students in the new community to help him adjust and be accepted. They did this by talking to Bob's new peers (Villa & Thousand, 1986).

MAPs (Pearpoint, Forest, & O'Brien, 1996)

A MAP (Making Action Plans) is a collaborative planning process for people that brings together the key players in a child's life. This includes the student, the student's family and teachers, and significant people in that student's life, including peers. MAPs have been used extensively for students who are transitioning into general education classrooms, for students experiencing academic and social difficulties or isolation, and for children who are interested (or whose parents are interested) in having multiple perspectives for planning and shared responsibility for implementation.

The first part of the MAPs process consists of four steps:

1. What is a MAP? The facilitator guides the participants in thinking about what a map is, eliciting that a map helps you to know where to go and what to do.

2. What is the story? The facilitator asks participants to share what they know about the student so far—what has his or her life been like? What pieces of information are important to be shared?

3. What is the dream? This is the most significant portion of the MAPs process. The facilitator aims to create an atmosphere in which the family, student, and friends can share what their hopes, dreams, and wants for the student really are. One parent, for example said, "My dream is that my child be happy, be included in school, walk or ride to school with his sister, be invited to birthday parties, have a hamburger with a friend, and have the phone ring just for him."

4. What is the nightmare? This segment of the process is difficult because it asks participants to lay out their worst-case scenario. Parents often share that their worst fear is that their child will end up alone, isolated, and without friends. Articulating the nightmare can both help avoid it and help participants identify shared goals and a common humanity, recognizing that belonging and friendship (and probably not fractions or American history) are critical to this child's success.

The second portion of the MAPs process is action oriented, and it includes the following questions:

5. Who is this student? All participants are asked to share what they know about the student, and all voices are recorded. Labels that are not really descriptive (such as cognitively delayed or speech impaired) are replaced by more descriptive language that is more likely to lead to connection and effective programming: "He loves animals," "He's very active," "She likes snacks," "She loves rock music," and the like.

6. What are the student's strengths and unique gifts? Again, multiple perspectives are solicited and noted.

7. What does the student like to do? What is she good at? What are her needs? As in Question 5, the attempt is to solicit concrete ideas and suggestions: he needs a friend, she's good at listening to others, he needs someone to play ball with him, and she needs support for going to school events.

8. The plan of action. This is the planning portion of the MAPs session. What specific plans will be made for this child, and who will be available and willing to provide support?

It is important to note that a MAP is not a substitute for a formal IEP meeting, but it involves a wider range of people, including the nonprofessionals who may actually know the student better (and from a wider variety of contexts and perspectives). By including other students in the MAPs process, all students can see their roles in the inclusion process.

Note: While MAPs have typically been organized for students with special needs, they have also been done for any student facing behavioral and/or social challenges in the classroom or school. Done with a respectful tone, such a process can help students realize the critical roles they plan in one another's lives and can enlist their caring and support in a more formalized, personalized way.

Circles of Support

Any member of the classroom community, including the teacher, may call for *a circle of support*. The students are gathered in a circle and the initiating person says, "I'd like to call a support circle for myself around . . ." and then shares their concern or problem. Students might ask support around a particular situation (How can I learn to deal with my mom's remarriage and getting three new brothers?), an ongoing situation (I'd like to learn some sports so I have something to do at recess and after school), or a specific problem (I'd like some help in learning to keep my temper when I'm angry). Students in the support circle are encouraged to ask questions to (1) clarify the problem or situation, (2) ascertain what kind of help the person thinks he needs, and (3) determine what role the support circle can play in the solution. The person calling the circle is in charge of deciding what solutions or ideas seem appropriate, desirable, or feasible. Because the student is at the center of the process, the process should be conducted so that having multiple people problem solving feels like a show of support rather than being "ganged up on" by other students. By enlisting other students' problem-solving help and support, blaming and recriminations are minimized, and the focus is on change and help.

It is extremely important to note that structures and procedures for generating help or support for individual students should be normalized; that is, it should be available to all students and should not depend on students' failure or crisis to be initiated. In addition, it is critical to build reciprocal relationships and support systems, avoiding the situation where there are some students who are always the helpers and some always the helpees. Teachers and students must create an atmosphere in which all students give as well as receive support. Van der Klift and Kunc (1994) emphasize that one-sided relationships should be avoided and that helping someone does not necessarily promote friendship:

There is nothing wrong with help; friends often help each other. However, it is essential to acknowledge that help is not and can never be the basis of friendship. We must be careful not to overemphasize the helper-helpee aspect of a relationship. . . . Unless help is reciprocal, the inherent inequity between helper and helpee will contaminate the authenticity of a relationship. (p. 393)

Yoga and Meditation for Kids

There has been increasing recognition that establishing a peaceful atmosphere for students is a critical step in helping them solve their problems, support others, and be peaceful with themselves. A method called YogaKids is growing quickly in the United States. The promotional materials describe the program as follows.

> YogaKids is a unique approach to integrative learning using yoga as a pathway. Reading, storytelling, music, creative arts and earthcare blend seamlessly with yoga movement to educate the "whole" child. The YogaKids curriculum provides children with an exciting new way to explore and appreciate their academic and creative potential. (YogaBeez, 2007, para. 1)

Educator Linda Lantieri has created techniques to help student increase self-esteem, improve concentration and awareness, and enhance their empathy and communication skills. She does this through exercises that teach children to quiet their minds, calm their bodies, and manage their emotions better. In her book (Lantieri & Goleman, 2008) that comes with a CD for teacher and student use, she shares meditations, activities, and rituals that are geared toward students from five through adulthood. These activities are not instead of the curriculum; they are useful for helping students be able to profit from instruction and learn life skills that will help them interact with others and be peaceful in their bodies. See Box 6.6 for another example.

BOX 6.6

At Seymour Elementary School, seventeen children are sitting in a circle on little (half-size) yoga mats with their eyes closed. Their teacher, Midge Regier, sounds a chime, and when the sound stops, they open their eyes.

They take five breaths together. While holding out their hands with fingers splayed, they "blow out" their fingers, one at a time. "Why are we doing this?" asks their teacher. "To calm ourselves," they reply. Then they take quick bunny breaths, for energy; grab the sunshine with their hands; and pull it in.

In chorus, they recite their yoga pledge, each line accompanied by a different yoga pose; their pledge includes naming all the ways yoga makes them feel—energized and powerful, balanced and centered, strong and flexible, calm and focused, peaceful and loving, and all connected. They end by pointing to one another: "Your heart and my heart are one. Namaste."

Today's lesson is about birds and perseverance. The children squat on their mats, pretending they are birds, and then they are the eggs. They come out of their shells, stretching, wet, and tired. They cheep. Midge walks around and feeds them worms as they fly across the room to different mats. Then they are eagles, diving down to eat a chipmunk; then they are flamingos on one foot; then storks, with one leg raised, as they balance on the other.

The children freeze and flow, dancing on their mats to music and then freezing in various yoga positions that the teacher calls out—down dog, eagle, flamingo, stork, cat, cow, bear, tree, and butterfly. They are moving through their curriculum with their bodies.

They hear a story and act out the different animals. Finally, after about half an hour, it is time for calming down, for meditation. The children lie on their backs, breathing quietly. Midge walks around and places a Beanie Baby on each child's stomach, so that the animal moves up and down as the child breathes. The room is quiet, and the little bodies are still. The focus is on breathing.

Cultivating Emotional Intelligence

Positive Noticing

Tattling is a frequent issue in elementary classrooms. As discussed in Chapter 5, students often seem to take particular delight in noticing one another's transgressions and reporting these to the teacher. Teachers are often confused about how to respond to such interactions, especially when there are times when they do want to know what they are told and times when the tattling is clearly inappropriate and destructive of relationships.

It helps to begin by thinking about why students tattle. There are several possible reasons: (1) They are perceptive and attentive observers of one another's behaviors. (2) They seek and enjoy the adult attention they receive for tattling. (3) They are seeking, somehow, to connect with the child whose behavior they have observed. All of these impulses are fine, although when they are actualized as tattling or tale bearing, they become problematic. The goal, therefore, is to channel these instincts into appropriate, socially acceptable activities.

Good Deed Tree

A tree (or other structure) can be erected in the classroom, either freestanding or on a bulletin board. Students are told that when they see someone in their classroom doing something good or helpful (or some other defining category of behavior) they are to write down what they saw and attach it to the tree with a clothespin. At the end of the week (or the end of each day), the teacher reads the deeds on the tree.

This activity provides an opportunity for two children (or more) to be recognized. When the teacher reads, "At lunch, Hannah shared her sandwich with Nicole after Nicole's sandwich fell on the floor," the teacher can appreciate both Hannah for her kindness and can recognize the person who noticed Hannah's kindness for his alertness and observation. (To avoid turning this activity into one in which children are seeking an external reward by being nice, it is important to treat the process as providing multiple teachable moments, helping students to develop an understanding and appreciation of what it means to be kind, thus setting the stage for the internalization of these behaviors.)

Frog in the Box

The class can adopt a small stuffed animal as a recognition tool (a beanbag-size animal is perfect). The rule is that when you see someone doing something nice, you put a little note on the frog and put it in that student's cubby or on her desk. When the animal appears in your cubby or desk, you have 24 hours to notice someone else doing something nice and pass it along. Students sometimes like doing this activity secretly (from inside one desk to another) so that there is an element of mystery attached to it. The activity encourages students to be on the lookout for one another's good deeds rather than attending largely or exclusively to what others have done wrong. (Again, teachers might want to implement a rule to make sure that the frog gets around to everyone rather than be exchanged between a small group of students).

Secret Friend

Many classrooms have a secret Santa program during the Christmas holidays in which each child picks another child's name and does nice things for them for a period, prior to a special day when identities are revealed. But there is no reason that such an activity—of thinking well about another student—shouldn't happen throughout the year, in a more secular way. Students can either pick another child's name, or if students are organized in home groups or base groups, each group can pick another group to plan surprises and nice things for. These surprises should be without cost—they might draw pictures for group members, write them nice notes, and the like.

BOX 6.7

In Melissa McElroy-Elve's preschool classroom at Jowonio school, there is a special *hug spot* designated on the rug. Any child who wants to give or get a hug can go there! What a wonderful way to have your needs met! (Perhaps we need a hug spot in the teachers' lounge as well.)

BOX 6.8

At Latchmere Primary School in London, there is a special area of the playground where children who are looking for someone to play with can go. It provides a clear place where those who have not yet found someone or something to engage with can find the other "unattached" children to play with.

GAMES

Frozen Bean Bag (Harrison, 1976)

Players places a beanbag (or a rolled up sock or a paper plate) on their head. Music is played (preferably lively music that makes you want to dance!), and players move to the music. If anyone's beanbag falls off his head, he is frozen and must remain frozen until another player notices the situation, comes over, and without losing her beanbag retrieves the fallen one and replaces it on the frozen person's head. If, however, in rescuing the frozen person, the rescuer loses her beanbag, then she is also frozen until another person appears to rescue them both.

The object of the game is to keep all players actively engaged in the activity. All players are charged with noticing people who are in trouble and needing help and rescuing them so they can return to play. Unlike so many games in which eliminating other players is the goal, the goal here is to keep everyone included and involved. This game can be played by a very heterogeneous group of players, including people of all sizes, ages, and levels of mobility. I have played this game with a group of over 100, ranging from 2-year-olds to 80-year-olds. The nice aspect of this game is that it demonstrates that everyone is able to be helpful and supportive, and it disrupts typical hierarchies of classrooms in which some people are always the helpers and others are always the helpees. In addition, younger children can, in this activity, help older children or adults, which is also noticeably different from how things usually are.

Knots (Harrison, 1976)

Players stand in a circle of six to eight people, and everyone closes eyes (optional) and moves together, each child taking a different child's hand in each of his or her hands. When each child has two hands, they all open their eyes and try to untangle themselves without dropping hands. The group must work together to get out of the knots. Students must help one another by actively problem solving, "If Wei lowers his right arm, then Peter can step over it," and by moving together cooperatively.

Students typically end up either in one large circle or two circles, either separate ones or interlocked. It is best to start this game with a small number of players so those students can experience success before tackling bigger and harder knots. An easy way to teach this activity is to begin by having all players hold hands in the circle and then, still holding hands, to knot themselves up by ducking under and over arms and hands. Such knots are easier to undo, and players know that they were a circle before and so can easily revisualize and reform the circle they had. After students are more experienced with this activity, the number of players can be increased, although groups of more than 10 tend to become unmanageable.

Hot and Cold

This classic game can be used to help students develop helpful repertoires. One child (or several) leaves the room and the other class members hide something or chose some object in the room. When the student returns, the rest of the class guides that student to the hidden object by telling them "hot" (you're close) or "cold" (you're not close). More sophisticated versions can include a range of clues like hotter, colder, completely frigid, boiling, and so on. Teachers in the older grades might want to have students give clues in terms of directions (Go north, south, southwest, and so on). This is a win–win game, in which good directions lead to a successful find, and students must work together to give accurate cues. This game can also be played by having children clap (loud for near and soft for far) or hum (louder and softer).

This game develops skills of following directions and providing accurate feedback. Unlike many activities that involve an "it" player, in this game, all of the individuals are engaged in a facilitative activity, trying to help the it or its find the hidden object. That is, they are all working directly for the other student's success. This is a wonderful game for demonstrating cooperation: the success of the individual and the success of the group are not only compatible but one is also the function of the other.

Obstacle Courses

A small group of students creates an obstacle course for their classmates. They might, for example, design a course that goes around a wastebasket, under a pole, over a stack of books, through a narrow space created by a desk and the wall, and between two coat racks. Each student who has built the course then takes a turn acting as a guide to a classmate who is blindfolded, giving them *clear* directions to allow them to complete the course. This involves lots of practice giving directions: What does "go left" mean? When you take two steps forward, how big of a step do you mean? "How high do I have to lift my leg when you say, 'step over the object'?" The course should be designed so that no one could actually get hurt (i.e., walking into a wastebasket is unlikely to cause injuries), and the responsibility and seriousness of being someone else's guide should be stressed. Debriefing the activity can include giving feedback to the guides about the quality and accuracy of their directions and also a discussion of what it felt like to trust another person to give you directions and what it means to be responsible for someone else.

Standing Ovation (Weinstein & Goodman, 1980)

This is as much a class rule as a game. The originators of the game suggest teaching the game as follows.

> Let's make an agreement . . . At any time during the remainder of this (class, activity, play period), anybody can get to their feet and say, "I want a standing ovation!" and no matter what we're doing, we'll stop and give it to him or her. There's only one rule about that: you can't be real wimpy about it. If you're going to ask for one, then take it like you deserve it—jump on a chair . . . or get two people to hoist you up on their shoulders, and hold your hands over your head in a gesture of victory—go for it in a big way. (Weinstein & Goodman, 1980, p. 52)

Although teachers might want to limit the periods where this rule applies, the idea that any student who is feeling depressed or, conversely, like they have something they really want to celebrate can initiate that support for himself is exciting! Teachers can also modify this activity with students and suggest other ways in which students can ask for appreciations or support: "I need some people to tell me what they appreciate about me," or "I need a hug" (a good time to reinforce appropriate touching and boundaries).

SONGS

"Here's a Hand" (Pirtle, 1984)

This song is best sung in a circle with students actually encouraged to feel the support in their classmates' hands. It is a good song for a well-established classroom community where holding hands will be acceptable to students. The song might follow a discussion of the ways in which people support one another. It reminds us that no one has to be perfect to have support and help from others.

"Kindness Is Everywhere" (Donkin, 2007)

This song talks about all the ways that children can show kindness to one another. The song provides a wonderful way to brainstorm ways that we could be kind, helpful, and supportive to one another.

CHILDREN'S LITERATURE

There are many wonderful books that model ways in which people in trouble ask for and receive support. Two of the important themes that emerge in these books, each of which could be a focused lesson, include the following:

1. Even people who are very different can support and help one another.

2. Help and support often come from unexpected sources.

3. Asking for the help directly can be an important strategy for getting the support we need and deserve.

Helping Others

Do Unto Otters: A Book About Manners *(Keller, 2007)*

This cleverly illustrated book describes basic manners based on the premise that one should "do unto otters, as you would have otters do unto you." This book is an excellent introduction to some of the nice ways we can talk to and treat one another.

Ordinary Mary's Extraordinary Day *(Pearson, 2002)*

Little Mary may be ordinary, but when she does a good deed, the recipient does something nice for five other people who then do nice things for others—the numbers are exponential, and by the end, one good deed has turned into thousands. The recipients and givers of the kindness include the old and the young, storeowners and the homeless, a boy using a wheelchair, strangers, and family members.

This would be a wonderful book for talking about kindness and helping others. It could be used to start a kindness chain in the classroom. One student could initiate it, and then the rest of the class could document how it grew. Also this book is helpful for discussing what constitutes a good deed, help, and the like, including discussions of respect, dignity, and mutuality.

Give a Goat *(Schrock, 2008)*

This true story extends the idea of helping to the broader concept of philanthropy. The book tells the story of a class of children going through all the steps necessary to give a goat to a family in need living thousands of miles away. Discussion could include the importance of doing good deeds at the national and international levels, the importance of preserving people's dignity when engaging in charity-related behavior, and the significance of understanding other people or cultures before attempting to be helpful. The adage "give a man a fish and he eats for a day; teach a man to fish and he eats for a lifetime" could be a good starting point for this discussion.

Keep Your Ear on the Ball *(Petrillo, 2009)*

This book describes how Davey's classmates learn to provide help to him in ways that respect his abilities and his desire for independence. They creatively brainstorm how to include Davey, who is blind, in a kickball game when that becomes challenging. The book provides wonderful opportunities to talk not only about students with visual impairments but also, more significant, about the importance of providing help in ways that are respectful and actually helpful. Possible discussion questions might include are (1) anyone ever tried to help you in a way that you didn't appreciate? (2) How can you communicate to others what kind of help you actually want or will accept?

Mean Soup *(Everett, 1995)*

Horace has had a really terrible day at school—forgetting an answer, getting stepped on, and so on. By the time he gets home, he is really mad and feeling mean. When his mother sees his terrible mood, she suggesting that they make soup. He doesn't like this idea, but they do it. Together, they scream into the pot, they stick out their tongues at the pot, they bang on the pot with a spoon, and eventually he feels better. His mother says it's called mean soup, and together, they stir away a bad day.

Discussions of this book could center on how you can cheer up yourself or someone else when they are upset.

Possible Activities

- Have students share a time they have been upset.
- Have students discuss what makes them feel better when they are upset or disturbed.
- Have students talk about a time when someone else has helped them feel better.
- Make an illustrated book, a chart, a digital storybook, a readers' theater, or in some other way compile the ways of feeling better students generate.
- Refer back to this when a child is upset. Encourage people to appreciate others for helping them feel better as well as talking about ways to ask for what you need when you are upset: "I am really feeling sad, and I just need someone to sit with me for a while." "Someone just said something mean to me, and I would like someone to tell me what they like about me."

Alexander and the Terrible, Horrible, No Good, Very Bad Day *(Viorst, 2009)*

Everything goes wrong for Alexander—he gets gum in his hair, trips on his skateboard, and drops his sweater in the sink—and that's all before he goes to school. When things go from bad to worse, he is discouraged and sad. He eventually gets reassurance from his mother, who assures him that some days are "just like that." This book would be excellent to discuss bad days and what we can do for our classmates when we see that they are having one. Students could even deliver *happy grams* or smiley faces to students who they perceive as in need of cheering up. This can be explicitly contrasted with making fun of people whose days (or lives) are going badly!

Bravery Soup *(Cocca-Leffler, 2002)*

Carlin is afraid of everything and goes to see Big Bear, the bravest animal in the land, for advice. Big Bear tells him that he must take a perilous journey and bring back the secret ingredient for Big Bear's bravery soup. Carlin sets off with lots of things to support him (armor, a basket of food, and a raft) but soon finds that these things actually slow him down. When he enters the cave to find the box, he finds a monster there who is more afraid of him than the other way around. He brings the box back for the soup and finds out it is empty. He asks if his journey was for nothing. Big Bear tells him, "Your journey was not for nothing. You faced the forest and you faced your fear. It is not what is inside the BOX that makes bravery. It is what is inside of YOU!" And then Big Bear tells him that bravery soup is only served to the brave!

Discussion

- What are you afraid of?
- What would you have to do to get over your fear?
- What help or support would you need?
- Students can each create a personal quest—something that they want to do to face their fears. For one student this might mean going to the library alone, for another, it is approaching a friend and asking them to play, for another it is telling someone about something that is bothering them. They can each generate a plan and a support plan as well.
- Then set up a day to celebrate Bravery Day—and make soup!

Sink or Swim *(Coulman, 2003)*

Ralph the cow is trying to learn how to swim, and it's very hard for him. The things that seem to work for the duck family don't work for him, and he keeps trying different things to be successful. When the log doesn't work and the lily pad is too small, he ends up getting a surfboard, and he is able to find his own unique way to get around the pond.

This is a wonderful book to talk about differences in skills and abilities—and the usefulness of adaptations and modifications. This could easily transition into a discussion of adaptive devices to help people do things. Where there's a will there's a way. There are many ways to make this happen!

Crazy Hair Day *(Saltzberg, 2003)*

Stanley Birdbaum is excited because it's crazy hair day at school, and he has great plans. His mother works on his hair for a long time, styling it with elastic bands, gel, and two cans of Halloween hair spray. He can't wait to get to school to show off his fancy hairdo. But when he gets to school, he is devastated. It turns out that today is school picture day, and Crazy Hair Day is *next* week! He is mortified and hides in the bathroom after everyone laughs at him, including his best friend Larry Finchfeather. Mr. Winger, the teacher, sends Larry to the bathroom, instructing him to be a "peacemaker instead of a troublemaker" and persuade Stanley to come back to class. After a long time and lots of anguish on Stanley's part, he returns to class only to find out that the *whole* class has made crazy hats and hairdos for themselves—wastebaskets, books, newspaper, and the globe! It is a day none of them will forget.

This is a wonderful book to talk about solidarity and support. Through their behavior, Stanley's classmates turn his huge embarrassment and shame into an experience in community and support. Discussions could include ways in which people can support one another, including stories of people who have shaved their heads in solidarity with students who are losing their hair because of chemotherapy. A possible link could include the song "Manuel Garcia" (David Roth, 1993) that tells the story of a man whose friends all shave their heads to welcome him home from the hospital after he loses his hair because of his cancer treatment.

There's a Big, Beautiful World Out There! *(Carlson, 2004)*

The book begins, "There's a lot to be scared of, that's for sure!" and then details all the things children might be afraid of, including mean-looking dogs, thunderstorms, roller coasters, and scary stories in the news. The list of things to be scared of includes "people who look different from you." The author says, "All this scary stuff can make you want to hide under your covers and never come out." But all this is countered with all the things you might miss by hiding under your covers: the rainbow after the storm, the fun of the roller coaster, and all the new friends you'll never meet. The book concludes, "There's a lot to be scared of, but there's even more to look forward to . . . So throw off those covers!"

This book was written on September 12, 2001—(the day after the destruction of the World Trade Centers in New York City in a terrorist attack). The book provides a good chance to talk about fear, where it comes from, and how it can be debilitating. This book could also be used to talk about the fear and anger after September 11th and how that got applied to people who look different!

Jenny Is Scared! When Sad Things Happen in the World *(Schuman, 2003)*

Jenny and her brother Sam are frightened by events in the world (not named), and their parents help them to talk about their fears and how to feel better. The book discusses various ways that the children behave because they are afraid (getting mad, not being able to do homework or concentrate, not wanting to hear more or talk about it) and some of the ways that they can feel better, including going back to regular routines of chores, school, soccer, baths, and the like. The mother in the book says, "It might help, too, if we send some loving thoughts to other people, because some other people are not very happy." This book was also written after the events of September. 11, 2001, and contains a detailed note to parents by Ann Rasmussen, talking about how children react to disturbing events and how parents can help. Most of the suggestions for parents are equally valid for teachers, including the following:

- Be honest.
- Listen openly and respectfully.
- Find out what they know.
- Use simple words.

A Rainbow of Friends *(Hallinan, 2006)*

This book is about all kinds (and colors) of children being friends. The book is illustrated by cartoons and written in verse, and although the text is brief, parts of it are very powerful relative to issues of support:

> *A rainbow of friends*
> *is a chance for us all*
> *to help one another*
> *when we stumble or fall*
> *our goals can be reached*
> *with the greatest success*
> *by trusting that others*
> *are doing their best*

This poem could easily be posted on the board and followed by a discussion of all the ways we can help one another, making sure that all students recognize their dual roles as people who need help and people who can provide help.

You Hold Me and I'll Hold You *(Carson, 1992)*

A phone call comes telling a little girl's father that his aunt has died. Together, they travel to Tennessee for the funeral. The little girl feels sad—like she did when her mother moved away—and wonders what the funeral will be like. She has already buried a hamster and was the preacher. The funeral is hard, and people start to cry. She wants to cry too, which she finally does when her father takes her on his lap. The father says, "You hold me and I'll hold you." It was good to be held, and it was good to be holding too.

"You hold me and I'll hold you. It's what I'm going to say if I ever have to preach at another funeral. It made me feel better."

Another wonderful book about giving and getting support; the father is both the comforter and a person in need of comfort. The positive role of physical support and touch are well demonstrated. Teachers could enlist students in a discussion: "When you're upset or hurt, what are some things that make you feel better? Hugging? Back rubs? A hand to hold?"

Making the Team *(Carlson, 1985)*

Louanna wants to try out for cheerleading, and Arnie wants to be on the football team. They help each other practice, but Louanna is better at football, and Arnie is better at cheerleading. At the tryouts, they both try out unsuccessfully for what they want, but then get a chance to do the opposite: Luanne on the football team and Arnie a cheerleader.

This book provides not only a wonderful example of students helping and supporting one another; it also challenges sex-role stereotyping and rigid sex roles. How can we help people to do what they want to do and what they want to learn, regardless of traditional notions of who should learn or do what. Carter should feel comfortable asking a girl to teach him to play jacks without being teased or called a "faggot." Kari should be allowed to play football with the other students, even if they are predominantly boys playing.

Regina's Big Mistake *(M. Moss, 1995)*

Mrs. Li, who is Asian, gives everyone in the class a sheet or paper and tells them to draw a jungle or a rainforest. Regina, an African American student, is immobilized by fear of making a mistake. Other children are not helpful; they tease her and accuse her of copying. Finally, she overcomes her fear and starts to draw, and it keeps coming and coming. It turns out well, and she even turns another mistake (a funny-shaped sun) into a moon, thus drawing the rainforest at night. Everyone else likes her painting, and Mrs. Li hangs it (and all the others) on the wall.

This is an excellent jumping off place for a discussion of mistakes, being afraid of making them, the kind of support we want when we're scared, and the like. Although Regina's classmates are mostly negative about her struggles, this could initiate a good discussion on the kinds of support people want/need when they're having trouble.

The Cow That Went OINK *(Most, 2003)*

All the other barnyard animals laugh at the cow that goes "oink." One day the cow meets a pig that goes "moo." They teach each other their sound, and at the end, they are the only animals that can make two sounds, and they have "the last laugh."

The strengths of this book are the conception of *bilingual education* and the ways in which the animals teach each other. A bit troubling is the way that the animals keep laughing at the two nonstandard animals, and the concept of having the last laugh seems somewhat ungenerous. Perhaps this could be used as part of discussion of teasing and support and the ways in which mockery and derision damage community.

Now One Foot, Now the Other *(dePaola, 2006)*

Bobby loves his grandfather Bob. When Bobby was little, Bob taught him how to walk. When Bob suffers a stroke, Bobby is frightened and confused by the changes in his grandfather, who can no longer walk or talk. With Bobby's help, Bob relearns walking and talking.

This is a wonderful introduction to how scary differences can be responded to with love and compassion. The importance of support and help and the reciprocal nature of helping are clear.

It is also important to point out to children that although adults are often the ones assisting or teaching children, the reverse can happen as well.

Ira Sleeps Over *(Waber, 2000)*

Ira is very excited about the planned sleepover at his friend Charlie's house. They make elaborate plans for games and activities. But Ira struggles with whether to take his teddy bear that he always sleeps with. His parents reassure him that it would be okay, but his sister teases him. Ira leaves the bear at home, but while he is at Charlie's and they are telling ghost stories, they both get scared and Charlie pulls out his teddy bear. So Ira runs home to get his bear, now confident that he won't be teased.

This is a wonderful book about how common it is for people to want and crave support and acceptance of those needs. The book also takes a powerful stance against sexism, showing young boys supporting one another and still needing support themselves.

Mirette on the High Wire *(McCully, 1992)*

The famous Bellini, the high-wire walker, who once crossed over Niagara Falls on the high wire, has lost his nerve. While staying at a small pension in France, he befriends Mirette, who begs him to teach her to walk the high wire. When she finds out that he has stopped performing because he is afraid, she encourages him to "make it [the fear] leave." When he does arrange a performance, he freezes on the wire, and Mirette walks from the other end to encourage him. Together, they perform for the crowd.

This is a sweet book about support and mutual help. It becomes clear that fear must be overcome in a community and not in isolation. Mirette models cutting through Bellini's fear and isolation to help him. Support can come from unlikely people in unusual ways.

LINKS TO THE CURRICULUM

Part of the vision statement for this chapter was that students would recognize that all people have goals. Students can link this to the curriculum by setting goals for themselves in each subject matter: "By the end of October, I want to have learned how to multiply two-digit numbers, written at least two poems, found out why the local lake is so polluted and if anyone is doing anything about it, and read at least three books by authors who were born outside the United States." Students might want to try setting a goal specifically around helping—"I want to see if I can help four different people this year."

Examining the role of goal setting throughout history can also make links to the curriculum. What goals have others set for themselves that have changed the course of history, through invention, civil rights struggles, creative endeavors, and the like? Students might want to engage in creative writing or play writing on the question, What if a specific goal had not been met—how would things be different now? What if Jonas Salk had not succeeded in developing a polio vaccine? What if the Panama Canal had not been built? What if Rosa Parks had not initiated the Montgomery Bus Boycott?

The theme of helping is also well represented in the curriculum. History is full of examples of people helping one another; people have worked together in hundreds of ways to fight for justice, to support one another during periods of crisis or hardship, and to provide moral, physical, and financial help during periods of need.

When the Red River of the North overflowed its banks, virtually destroying the town of Grand Forks, North Dakota, thousands of people worked together sandbagging and attempting to reinforce the dikes. When this was unsuccessful, they worked together to clean up after the flood. Although the mayor's initial goal was to prevent the flood, when this became clearly impossible, the community set a new goal: no one will die. They were able to meet that goal by working together. One resident told me, "Although what happened to our community was terrible, I wouldn't want to live anywhere else. Now, I know that I live somewhere where people really care about one another and help each other. No matter what happens, I know I can count on my neighbors."

Teachers can encourage students to make connections to both current and historical events in which people have helped one another. You might want to create a bulletin board called "People Who Have Helped" and have students draw, write, or otherwise identify people to go on the list from their reading, the curriculum, the media, and so on.

Many of the activities in this chapter can easily be linked to writing, reading, and other language arts activities. Teachers might want to create a class book on helping with students making entries whenever they see a good example of helping. Students often enjoy writing their own Dear Abby columns, in which one student writes in about his problem and other students offer solutions. Help columns can be initiated on many topics: health and beauty, sports, friendships, and so on.

Within every subject matter, teachers can actively ask students to (1) help teach the material, (2) help others who are experiencing difficulty, and (3) discuss strategies that have helped them master the material. Students might want to develop role-plays or skits showing good helping and poor or ineffective helping, offering these to the class for comment or critique.

7

Working Together to Learn

Four students are gathered at a table in their classroom. They have been charged with identifying and classifying the animals on the large paper in front of them; they are discussing whether the animals are mammals, reptiles, amphibians, or marsupials. Their task is to color each type of animal family with a different colored crayon: mammals blue, reptiles green, and so on. As a group, they must agree on the name and category for each animal and share the limited crayons to complete the chart. As they work together, they practice asking one another for feedback: "Tony, do you think this is supposed to be a koala bear? Are they mammals?" "Are the reptiles supposed to be yellow?"

Julia is sitting at her desk trying to figure out how to color in the map the teacher has given her. Although the teacher gave instructions, Julia didn't really follow them; and now, she is confused. She leans over to the student sitting to her left to ask her about how to do the task. The other student puts her hands over her map to cover it up and announces loudly, "Teacher, Julia's cheating—she's copying from my paper."

Mr. Killington announces that there will be a reading contest in his sixth-grade classroom. The student who reads the most books by the end of the three-week period will get a prize. He is surprised when he sees, at the end of a week, that half the class hasn't read anything, that several of his top readers are quickly consuming preschool books, and that students are snappy and testy with one another when they are asked to stop their work to answer a question from a classmate.

The whole class is discussing how they want to organize the end-of-the-year class picnic. First, they list all the tasks that need to be done, and then they discuss how they should assign tasks to individuals and groups. They agree that everyone should get to do at least one task they like and that they should also have each person do one thing they don't usually do, with a partner supporting them. They keep in mind that Carson, who uses a wheelchair, can do many things even though he needs help with fine-motor activities. They agree that Carson will print the invitations on his computer using his head switch to program the device. They decide to encourage Marcie to help do the decorations even though Jennifer and Albert are best known in the class for their artistic skills. They end their meeting by each appreciating someone in the class who has helped them.

THE VISION

Essentially, teaching can be organized in three ways: *individually* (the focus is on what each individual child needs to learn), *cooperatively* (the focus is on teaching children to work together toward achieving shared goals), and *competitively* (the focus is on having students work against one another to see who accomplishes the most or the best work). Creating a cooperative, inclusive classroom involves carefully structuring how instruction takes place. In classrooms that value diversity and seek to develop a climate of mutual support and caring, two of the three instructional designs are a good fit—individualized and cooperative learning. Having students compete with one another is not consistent with a vision of inclusion and respect for diversity. Regardless of how instruction is organized, it must take place in an atmosphere that honors and recognizes differences and values how people treat one another.

This chapter contains strategies for *differentiating* instruction within instruction that is structured more individually and within more formally organized models that use *cooperative learning*.

A differentiated classroom is one in which teachers support the learning of individuals in diverse classrooms by providing curriculum, instruction, and assessment that is carefully tailored to individual students' learning needs. Each student is viewed as having both strengths and challenges, and the aim is to provide appropriate but also challenging teaching in a context of community. Oyler (2001) refers to the organization of teaching so that every child is productively engaged as *accessible* instruction. The teacher may vary the goals she sets for individual students, the materials used to meet those objectives, and how students demonstrate their mastery of the lesson.

Tomlinson (2003) describes differentiation as follows:

> A fuller definition of differentiated instruction is that a teacher proactively plans varied approaches to what students need to learn, how they will learn it, and/or how they can express what they have learned in order to increase the likelihood that each student will learn as much as he or she can as efficiently as possible. (p. 151)

A classroom can be described as cooperative when all members are actively engaged in their own learning and in supporting the work of their classmates. Sometimes goals are individual, and sometimes students work together to achieve mutual goals. These goals can include academic learning, social problem solving, and conflict resolution. The poster "none of us is as smart as all of us" embodies the essence of the cooperative classroom. The language and principles of cooperation—working together—shared goals—mutual support—problem solving—infuse every activity of the classroom. For teachers to work well with heterogeneous groups of students, an atmosphere of cooperation is essential; competition and competitive structures make diverse classrooms even more challenging.

I choose to use the term *inclusive teaching* to include all the ways that teachers organize grouping, instruction, curriculum, and assessment so that all students are (1) flexibly grouped, (2) actively engaged, (3) appropriately instructed, and (4) authentically assessed. Rather than viewing inclusive teaching as an activity that is done on Wednesdays from 10 to 11 or as a specific teaching strategy for teaching math or social studies, inclusive teaching can be conceptualized broadly to include everything that happens in the classroom. It is about what is on the walls, how tasks are assigned, how goals are set, how praise is delivered, and how students line up for lunch. It represents a set of decisions about both process and content and includes careful thinking about the daily activities of classroom life as well as broader, conceptual frames.

Instead of assuming that all students will be engaged in identical learning experiences for the same unit and evaluated according to the same criteria, the curriculum can be conceptualized as broad and inclusive. If the class is doing a unit on space, for example, the teacher can organize space activities and projects on many different levels. Children who have exceptional reading and research skills might be asked to write a report on the origins of the galaxy. Other children might be asked to draw and label the major planets in the solar system. A child with limited language skills might be required to be able to point to pictures of the sun, the moon, and the Earth in different arrangements. Every student would share their completed projects with the whole group so that everyone benefits from the diversity of activities.

Teachers need continually to challenge the traditional curriculum and ask themselves: What does each child need to know? What aspects of this unit can be modified or adapted? Can students participate in the same activity with different levels of evaluation and involvement, or does an alternate, related activity need to be provided?

Many teachers have also found that broadening their teaching approaches and encouraging flexibility and adaptations have been beneficial to a far larger group of students than they first predicted.

A teacher assigned one student each day to take a set of notes for the class (a carbon copy of personal notes) to meet the needs of a deaf student who could not take notes. The teacher later found that these notes were also helpful to students with learning problems who could not both listen and take notes, students whose handwriting left them with very inadequate notes, and students who were absent and needed to catch up. Another teacher, on the advice of the learning disabilities teacher, began writing key words on the board and teaching them before beginning a new lesson. She found that all students benefited from this preteaching motivation and organization. Another teacher, in helping one student get himself organized by teaching him to use an assignment notebook and to check with peers for assignments, found that many students in her class could benefit from a similar system to keep themselves on task and on track. Such classroom modifications and adaptations benefit children's learning and demonstrate that all students are valued. We do not abandon people who are having difficulties.

Rather than limiting the school play or the science fair only to high-achieving students, teachers have found ways to transform exciting activities so that they include everyone. Modeling after Judy Chicago's Dinner Plate project that involved creating place settings for famous women, a third-grade teacher created a similar project for all the students in her inclusive classroom. Each student chose a famous woman and made a placemat that represented that woman, found out information about her, and represented that woman on an evening when parents and other invited guests walked around and engaged with the famous women. This way of organizing instruction made the project— and the learning—accessible to children who represented a huge range of reading, writing, and speaking abilities.

The aspects of classroom life illustrated in Box 7.1 need to be considered as part of creating a cooperative, inclusive classroom that meets the needs of many students (Sapon-Shevin, 1990).

> **BOX 7.1 BROADENING THE CURRICULUM**
>
> Mr. Lorenzo has set up a classroom store. All children work in the store completing various tasks, including bookkeeping, inventory, sales, promotion, and the like. Tasks are assigned to children based on their particular individual educational needs and skills: Carlos is in charge of advertising, using his considerable artistic skills; La Tasha is learning to make change; and Jason is working on the social skills involved in meeting and greeting customers. Mr. Lorenzo allows children to work in their area of strength while also challenging them to participate in activities on their learning edge.

We need to rethink what constitutes the curriculum, broadening and diversifying our notions of appropriate learning. We will need to move away from lockstep, skill-driven deficit models of reading and language, for example, and toward approaches that allow students to engage in reading and writing tasks at different skill levels. For example, a dinosaur reading unit might include books and print materials about animals at many levels, as well as CD-ROMs and Internet exploration. Literacy, broadly defined, allows us to recognize that a child learning to point to and recognize different dinosaurs is meeting a valid educational objective, as is a child working to put together a three-piece dinosaur puzzle and then sharing it with the class.

When students are all asked to do the same task in the same way, many are unsuccessful. But providing 30 different learning activities to 30 individual students to complete in isolation feels overwhelming to teachers, leaving them exhausted, frustrated, and convinced that the only solution is to remove or lessen the diversity. Developing curriculum that is more participatory, interactive, hands-on, and designed around multiple intelligences and modalities is conducive to both differentiated, cooperative learning approaches and the inclusion of children working at many levels.

What Are We Really Teaching?

Although virtually any content can be taught differentially or cooperatively, the real question is, do we want to teach just *any* content, or do we want to teach students lessons of value, including the values of cooperation, differentiation, and inclusion? Simply because a lesson is implemented differentially or cooperatively does not assure its worth. What a waste of children's cooperative learning time for them to spend group time completing the same mindless, rote-memorization-oriented worksheets or dittos they used to do individually. Rather, why not use cooperative learning to teach meaningful academic content and to teach *about* cooperation and differentiation. Students can explore the things that divide us, the ways that we are kept from seeing one another as full human beings, including racism, sexism, and discrimination based on age or physical condition. Cooperative learning can be used to learn about the many ways in which people, throughout the course of history, have worked *together* to resolve problems, create magnificent art and music, and negotiate a whole series of tasks and challenges (Sapon-Shevin & Schniedewind, 1989/1990, 1990, 1993). The lessons of differentiation can also be made explicit, engaging students in discussions of how and when we allocate tasks to different individuals, the difference between equality (everyone does the same thing or gets the same thing) and equity (everyone does or receives the instruction, materials, support, or structure that they need). We can talk explicitly about what's fair, what input students should have into their own learning, and what kinds of support feel helpful. We can openly acknowledge differences in students' levels and skills rather than hiding them or homogenizing them under an umbrella of sameness.

For example, we can use the jigsaw method (when students learn different portions of material that they then teach to classmates) to study *not* generic famous people but to focus on people who have cooperated with others to make positive contributions or to build a better world. We can go beyond lists of famous men to think about which famous people are typically taught and why, and we can extend our study to include people of color and women who are often excluded from our learning. We can make inclusive teaching, cooperative learning, and the content compatible and complementary.

Looking at the Whole Classroom

At a cooperative learning workshop, a teacher confessed to me that she had found herself yelling at a group of students, "Stop helping one another; we're not doing cooperative learning now!" She reflected, with honest embarrassment, that there was no reason her students shouldn't help one another most, if not all, of the time. It makes sense to look at all aspects of the classroom environment and ask, "Is this practice or this activity consistent with a vision of cooperation and inclusion?" Consider spelling bees in which most children are eliminated, posting only the best work on the board, star charts that provide graphic representations of people's progress on a specific task, and choosing the "row of the week" for an award—coupling these with "doing cooperative learning" may lead to confusion for both students and teachers; what *are* the values in this classroom, and how do they interrelate?

In one fifth-grade classroom I visited, the teacher informed me that his class "did cooperative learning." The students were seated in groups of six, and they worked together on shared projects. At the end of every assignment, he gave points to the group that had done the best. The group could also get demerit points for rule infractions or bad behavior, and students were permitted to tell on other groups so that they lost points. A student's accusation that "Matthew didn't push his chair in when he went to lunch!" was followed by the teacher giving demerit points to Matthew's whole group. At the end of the week, candy was awarded to the group with the most points and the fewest demerits. Predictably, there was little classroomwide cooperation or goodwill; students were in constant competition across groups, and there were multiple recriminations in groups: "If you had shut up when the teacher came in, we wouldn't have lost two points!"

Teachers need to be encouraged to look at all aspects of their classrooms rather than just to implement a cooperative learning program or system in their classrooms. Looking at the whole picture will help teachers make all classroom activities and procedures consistent with the values of help, cooperation, and high achievement for all (Sapon-Shevin & Schniedewind, 1993).

Inclusive teaching is a principle and a vision not only for students but also for teachers and support staff as well. Creating inclusive classrooms asks teachers who have worked in isolation to learn to work together. Territorial barriers and roadblocks presented by different preparation and areas of expertise must be overcome for teachers to work together successfully. Just as cooperative classrooms model the belief that "none of us is as smart as all of us," teacher collaboration is based on the principle that teachers working together cooperatively are better prepared to handle the challenges of inclusion and diversity than any one teacher (no matter how skilled) working in isolation (see Box 7.2). Teacher collaboration and teaming require changes in how teachers are prepared and in how schools are staffed and supported.

BOX 7.2 CHANGING TEACHER ROLES

Mr. Chang, the speech therapist, used to work with other students by removing them from the regular classroom for individual therapy three times a week. Now, he works in the regular classroom, meeting students' needs on a "welcomed-in" rather than a "pull-out" basis, collaborating with not only the regular classroom teacher but also involving other students in his teaching and therapy activities.

Inclusive schools are organized so that teachers are no longer identified as "special" or "regular," each serving discrete groups of students. For example, two former regular class teachers and one former special education teacher might become the fifth-grade *team*, serving 60 students, some of whom require special educational services. The teachers do not wear labels saying whether they are special or regular, and neither do the students!

When teachers plan cooperative lessons for their students and collaborate to provide educational services, they must learn to cooperate with one another, learning some of the same social skills required in children's cooperative groups: listening, giving constructive feedback, sharing what they know, negotiating and compromising, and respecting one another's expertise and experience. It is difficult to teach students to cooperate if their teachers are unable to do so or do not model collaboration with other adults. A climate of collaborative respect and cooperation must infuse the school as a whole. Inclusive classrooms are like blended families in that they bring together adults and children who have previously been separated. Individual histories and ways of doing things must be merged or negotiated, and trust must be established.

I believe that most teachers are truly interested and capable of reflecting about their classroom practices and the consistency between their long-range goals and their teaching methods. Teachers need opportunities to think together, to problem solve, and then to consider their teaching practice: How successful was my lesson at getting students to learn? To work together? What messages about diversity or collaboration did my students learn from this activity? What else can I do to make my classroom fully cooperative? See Box 7.3 for one example.

BOX 7.3

In Melissa McElroy-Elve's preschool classroom, she and her coteachers look for every opportunity to promote positive social interaction and interdependence. For one activity, they divided the children into pairs. One child in each pair got yellow playdough, the other red. Together they made orange, and each got to bring some home. One day they played a game where two children wore one *big* shirt together. They each had to use one hand to take a ball and put it in a wastebasket together! Partner songs and activities are common and children who must leave the classroom to do some kind of physical therapy get to bring a friend with them to the therapy room.

Inclusive teaching in diverse, heterogeneous classrooms will result in more student-student interaction and, therefore, possibly more student conflicts. This illuminates the necessity of teaching students conflict-resolution skills. Good classroom communities are *not* those in which there are no conflicts. Conflicts are inevitable when people work, learn, and live in close proximity to one another. Rather, good classroom communities are those in which children have been given opportunities and repertoires for resolving conflicts productively and peacefully.

Inclusive teaching can help us to rethink much of what goes on in the classroom. How might we need to rethink how we label and separate students identified as "learning disabled" or "gifted"? How can grading and evaluation be done so that all learners have accurate feedback about their progress but are not alienated from or compared to peers in hurtful, damaging ways? What is the relationship between cooperation and diversity? What are the implications of having an inclusive classroom on the ways in which students learn to work together?

Teacher Lauri Pepe Bousquet (personal communication, 1996) offers the following summary of the ways in which competition has shaped our past and cooperation might shape our future.

Area	Ghost of Classrooms Past	Specter of Classrooms Past	Spirit of Classrooms Future
Athletics	Boys compete; girls cheer	Girls and boys compete; girls cheer	All play cooperative sports and games
Discipline	Dunce cap; sent to principal	Checkmarks on the board	Community membership
Diversity/ population	Segregation	Integration	Cross-racial/ethnic friendships
Grouping	Long term	Pull-out gifted and special education programs; some heterogeneous groups	Full inclusion; heterogeneous grouping is standard
Motivation	Fear	Extrinsic rewards; stickers	Intrinsically motivating curriculum
Evaluation	Grading on a curve; norm-referenced tests; class rank	Norm-referenced tests; criterion-referenced tests	Self, peer, and teacher performance assessments
Beliefs about intelligence	IQ is fixed	IQ is not fixed	Multiple intelligences honored
Reward structures	Competitive	Individual	Cooperative
Values stressed	Obedience	Responsibility for self	Responsibility for self and community
Celebration of excellence	Best student	Contests; spelling bees; science fairs; Olympiads	Exhibitions; everyone wins
Curriculum values	Competition explicitly taught	Competition implicitly taught	Cooperation taught explicitly and implicitly
Curriculum on diversity	Biased; exclusive	Somewhat inclusive	actively antibias
Curriculum integration	Fragmented	Some integration	Fully integrated and relevant
Teacher cooperation	Isolation	Teams	Variety of peer support methods

Having a Big Vision

Let's think about inclusive teaching as more than a teaching strategy and dream big. How can we examine and reinvent schools as moral communities, communities in which children and adults learn how to value, respond to, and take responsibility for other people, even those they perceive as different from themselves? How can we use the principles of cooperation, shared vision, and mutual support to help think about building a socially just and equitable world? Asking whether inclusive, cooperative schools are possible is the wrong question. The more compelling question is, "What gets in our way of making such schools a reality?"

CHALLENGES TO THE VISION

Most of us were raised in competitive environments, and even if our families didn't force us to compete at home ("Let's see which of you can get into your pajamas first"), by the time we finished school, we had many experiences with competition. From these experiences, we learned certain things, and it is difficult, as adults, to step back and look critically at the messages we received (Kohn, 1986).

Myths the Competitive System Taught Us to Believe

What myths were we taught, and how did they keep us from connecting well with others and feeling good about ourselves?

There's not enough to go around.

In the game of Musical Chairs, discussed previously, we are confronted with a situation of scarcity—eight people and only seven chairs. And we are told that people must have their own individual chair to win. Although the scarcity is completely artificial—the teacher is the one who has organized the environment so there isn't enough to go around—we rarely question this starting assumption. Instead, we struggle to get a chair and eliminate the competition.

Schools set up other totally false conditions of scarcity, telling us that there isn't enough success/praise/achievement to go around. The teacher posts only the best spelling paper on the wall, the child who is fastest at running the mile gets the prize, and praise goes to the person who did the best.

Out of this scarcity model, we receive the messages that only some of us are smart, only some are capable, and only some are good. When I interviewed teachers in a public school about the gifted program in their school, one told me, "They don't ask if they'll get to go. By this age, they already know who's smart and who's not!" What a horrible indictment of our school system that many children have already been convinced at an early age that they are not as smart or valued as some of their classmates.

Additionally, because success is defined using a scarcity model, we get the message that if we're not the best at something, we might as well not try. How else do we explain the fact that in kindergarten *all* of the children love art, but by sixth grade most students say, "I'm not a good artist," and they avoid opportunities to engage in creative endeavors. If only the best counts and I'm not the best, then why bother?

In truth, there is no reason, other than our traditional ways of thinking about schools, that we cannot create classroom learning environments in which everyone is successful, everyone receives praise, and everyone is valued. Since all students are individuals with individual strengths, challenges, and goals, then why is success determined comparatively? Why can't we be thrilled that Carlos has learned to do double-digit subtraction without referring to the fact that Teesha reached that goal three weeks ago? And what about inclusive classrooms in which students' goals are so diverse that there are huge discrepancies not only in when goals are achieved but what the goals are. How can we celebrate that Dylan was finally able to lift his arm high enough to turn on the switch of his tape player if we compare his achievements to students who run, write, throw, and move their arms with ease?

We don't need to compare students all the time. We don't have to have an honor roll that is only for the top 10% of students. We don't have to organize gifted programs that are available to only 3% of the population. We don't have to teach physical education in ways that eliminate large numbers of students from active play and convince them that they are losers who shouldn't even bother learning to use their bodies. We can organize our classrooms and our schools so that all students succeed.

Other people stand in the way of our success.

If activities or learning are organized competitively, then other people *are* actually in our way: "If you hadn't been such a good reader, I would have won the prize." "If only you hadn't been so good at math, I would have gotten a better grade." Is it any wonder that under such a system we learn to look at others suspiciously, constantly sizing them up: "Is this going to be a person who does better than I do and, therefore, keeps me from being successful?" This atmosphere, of constant suspicion and ranking, is certainly not a wonderful way to build a sense of trust and connectedness!

In a competitive situation, it is important to find out our opponents weaknesses and vulnerabilities so we can use them against them; I discover you are weak on your left side so that's where I attack; I find out you are terrified of public speaking, so I assign you that task to humiliate you. In such a situation, we are unlikely to show people where we are weak or vulnerable lest that be used against us.

In a cooperative structure, other people are not in our way. Other people are the ones who help us be successful. Others support us in achieving our goals, celebrating our successes, and being sympathetic and supportive when we struggle. In a cooperative situation, if I tell you I am weak on my left side, you'll support me there. If I tell you I am frightened by certain activities, you will seek ways to support me. In cooperative, supportive environments, people are far more likely to show us who they really are and find ways to connect with us.

The system is fair; you get what you deserve and deserve what you get.

Think back to the children playing Musical Chairs. Not only does the structure teach them to push, shove, and exclude, but it also convinces them that you get what you deserve. Rather than realizing that the game was rigged—that there was no way that everyone could be successful—we internalize messages about our worth: "Of course I didn't win; I'm just not good enough/not smart enough/not strong enough." A competitive situation not only creates few winners and mostly losers, but also it teaches children (and adults) to doubt their value. For many children, no matter how hard they try or how well they do, they will never be the winner. People who say, "You can't win them all," are usually people who win at least *some* of the time. Children who win rarely or not at all are not likely to perceive themselves as valuable human beings or competent learners.

It's not safe to get too close or connected with other people.

If everyone around me is a potential obstacle to my success, then it doesn't make sense to get too close to other people. And if everyone around me is evaluating *me* all the time, trying to decide if I am a potential threat to their status or success, then it will also be difficult to connect and form warm relationships and friendships. When there is only room for one singer or one athlete or one smart person in a group, then people spend a lot of time jockeying for position, constantly evaluating and reevaluating their standing or status: "I wonder whether that new boy who just came to our class will be a better reader than me—I've always been the best reader in here." "I wonder if the girl who moved into my neighborhood will be a better athlete than I am—then other people won't want me on their team the way they always have before."

Competition also keeps us from connecting with a wide range of people who have different skills and abilities than we do. I believe that people who are better at something than I am won't want me around—I'd just drag them down. And if I help someone who is not as good at something as I am, then that person might get better, thus displacing me or using up my time that I could be using to get ahead. It's not surprising that in competitive reading contests, for example, students hesitate to help other students find good books, read difficult words, or understand what they're reading. Time spent on others will simply take away from my personal success.

In a cooperative environment, people can comfortably interact with people who are at very different skill levels. I sing in the Syracuse Community Choir. It is an inclusive choir; anyone may join, there are no auditions, and all people support one another. When I sang in more competitive groups, I noticed that if I didn't understand a part of the music or was struggling, I either kept quiet or made a discrete note to myself to practice the part that was troubling me when I got home, all the while trying to make sure that no one else knew that I didn't really understand it. In our cooperative choir, I am a section leader. My job is to help everyone be successful. If I notice that someone is struggling with a particular section, I will offer to sit next to her and help her stay on pitch. If I myself am uncertain about a part, I easily turn to others (even though I am the leader) and ask them to sing in my ear. In this cooperative, inclusive choir, we realize that all of us will sound better if we help one another. The goal is beautiful music and friendship, not a competitive hierarchy of best singers and worst singers locked in competitive struggle.

Cooperation counts less than individual achievement.

We have already discussed the belief that doing things by ourselves somehow *counts* more than doing things with other people. In higher education, where publications are important for promotion, coauthored articles count *less* than singly authored articles, even though most people would acknowledge that writing with someone—combining ideas and writing styles—is both more difficult and likely to result in a better publication.

This belief—that alone is better—filters down to elementary schools as well. I was distressed to see a commercially produced teacher stamp that says, "Done with help." I couldn't understand what meaning that was possibly intended to convey—don't get too excited parents; your child didn't do this by himself or herself! My vision is of a time when we would respond to boasts that "I did it myself" with the response that "Doing it by yourself is great sometimes. But there are also lots of things that you can only accomplish if you do them with other people."

Part of the "alone is better" message is that asking for help is a sign of weakness. This leaves people who realize that they need help or support in a very difficult situation; if asking for help is invalidating and doing things with support is devalued, what are you supposed to do when you don't understand something? The alternatives aren't great—muddle through, fake it, or somehow avoid the task all together. These are hardly conducive to creating a learning environment in which all children are safe, nurtured, surrounded by support, and take on greater and greater learning challenges.

Competition is motivating.

One of the major arguments made in favor of the necessity of competition is that it is motivating and that, without competition, people would simply not try or would settle into complacency and laziness. This is not only a pessimistic view of people, but it isn't even accurate. Human beings, by nature, strive for growth and competence. Observe the three-year-olds in a well-resourced preschool. They eagerly paint, look at books in the book corner, ride the vehicles, engage in singing and movement activities, and set the table for snack time. No one has to promise them rewards or prizes (or threaten them) to get them to actively engage in their learning. What is true is that we often resort to competition and external motivators because what we are asking people to do has no inherent value to them or makes no sense to them. Alfie Kohn (1993), in his book *Punished by Rewards: The Problems of Gold Stars, A's and Other Bribes,* puts to rest many of the myths that surround the use of competition as motivation. Kohn argues not only that rewards and punishments have undesirable side effects but also that they don't work to establish long-term, intrinsically motivated, self-initiating learners and workers. Skeptics may want to read his book for many examples of the ways in which extrinsic rewards have backfired over time.

In most classrooms, competition doesn't really motivate. Imagine this scenario: the teacher announces that there will be a prize for the best math paper. Of 30 students, 20 immediately take themselves out of the running, knowing that they aren't strong enough in math to win the prize. Perhaps several of the top math students are in fact motivated—but they are motivated to win rather than to learn. Sometimes this leads to very undesirable behaviors: cheating, sabotage, and outright hostility to the perceived opponents.

Johnson and Johnson's (1989) research on competition demonstrated that three conditions must be met for competition to actually be motivating to learners:

1. Participants must perceive that they have an equal chance of winning.

2. Competitors must be able to closely monitor one another's performances.

3. The outcome of the competition must be relatively unimportant to all of the participants.

If we think about these conditions and the typical school competition that is structured, we can see how infrequently competition is likely to be motivating to students. When the teacher announces a writing, reading, or art contest, how many children actually see themselves as having a chance of winning? In an inclusive classroom in which the range of differences is very wide, the likelihood of each child being an equal contender is further diminished. And competitions in which students do individual work and are then comparatively evaluated certainly don't meet the criteria of opportunities to know how others are doing. Most important, even though the rewards offered by the teacher—stickers, candy, food—may seem small, they may loom large for the students, particularly those students who have limited home or family resources. All that really fits the criteria is the low-key footrace between two children who challenge, "Race you to the corner," and then they both try hard and remain friends regardless of the outcome. In other words, competition isn't usually motivating to most students, and even when it is, it brings with it high costs in personal interactions and feelings of unity and connections.

It's not fair to set different goals for different students.

Competitive schooling also instills the idea that *fairness* means the *same*—that students should be asked to learn the same material, in the same way, and be assessed identically. If success is limited, then any accommodations are considered unacceptable because they increase a particular student's chances of success. Of course, equal treatment is patently unfair given students' individual differences, but it is a hard notion to dislodge. This myth keeps us from setting individual goals for students and for valuing their different accomplishments. When we move to more cooperative models, then it is possible to see that each student's contribution is laudable and that the sum of all students' accomplishments is greater than the combined total.

Competition helps prepare students for the real world.

It is not unusual to hear people argue that the real world is competitive and that is only fair or appropriate that we teach children to be ready for that world by exposing them to large doses of competition. But this assumption can be challenged in many ways.

First, many aspects of the real world are extremely cooperative. Every time four cars approach a four-way stop, they must cooperate or have an accident. Many of the major scientific discoveries of the last century reflect the work of many people collaborating, problem solving, and combining research results and ideas. Even many of the major corporations are now realizing that the skills of cooperation are critical to success, and they are training their employees in teamwork and collaborative decision making.

In addition to the aspects of the world that are already cooperative, many huge problems cry out for cooperation and collaboration. Finding a cure for cancer or AIDS, working with other nations to address environmental pollution and to protect the environment, and figuring out ways of allocating scarce resources so that everyone has enough food—these are all problems that will only be resolved by people, organizations, and nations working together. During the horrible ice storms in the Northeast, hundreds of thousands of people lost their electrical power and, thus, their heat. Six families in Montreal shared one generator—each family used the generator to warm their house to 65 degrees and then passed it along to the next house. Rather than one family hoarding the precious generator, they figured out a system that sustained six families through the crisis. Who thought of this solution? The world our students will live in will be a world they create. They are not passive recipients of the world as it is; the beliefs they bring—about other people, about working together, and about the value of cooperation—will create the world as they know it. And the skills of cooperation—listening, problem solving, and conflict resolution—will be required for them to create safe and just communities and societies.

Barriers to Conflict Resolution

In addition to the barriers to implementing a more cooperative model, there are additional barriers to devoting time to teaching the conflict-resolution skills students will need in cooperative, inclusive classrooms. One of the most powerful barriers to developing conflict-resolution skills and using them is the idea that "nice people don't have conflicts." Many of the early messages we received in our families were about the importance of avoiding conflicts: "If you two can't get along, I'm sending you both to your rooms." "Children should be seen and not heard." "I'll give you something to cry about." "If you just ignore him, he'll stop doing it." Is it any wonder that many of us are conflict avoidant—willing to do almost anything to avoid getting into an argument or a fight, even if it means abandoning our hopes, goals, or plans and stewing quietly?

If we act, instead, from the premise that conflict is inevitable; that conflicts can be resolved in ways that do not leave one person humiliated, hurt, or devalued; and that people can learn and grown from their conflicts, then it makes sense to teach students repertoires of conflict resolution.

Another barrier to teachers' spending time on conflict-resolution skill teaching and practice is the notion that this is a waste of time and not as important as the "real" academic subjects that must be covered. One often hears teachers lament, "I just don't have time to respond to every little altercation, or my whole day would be taken up with conflict resolution." This perception is very accurate and points to the importance of teaching students to resolve their own conflicts as often as possible so that the teacher does not remain the only mediator or negotiator of conflicts.

In the game of Musical Chairs, students are taught that in a situation of scarcity—not enough chairs for every person—the only possible solution is to push and shove, excluding some people, and leave them without chairs. But imagine the game of Cooperative Musical Chairs (described earlier) in which eight children must figure out how to get everyone seated. The higher-level thinking skills of that activity far surpass the skills involved in kicking someone off a chair. Now imagine that these same children, who have experienced Cooperative Musical Chairs, board a bus and see that there are more people than there are seats. One solution, clearly, would be to push and shove to secure a seat, not worrying about the people left standing. But there are many other solutions as well: People could share seats; they could talk to one another and see if there are any particular needs that could be taken into account ("I'm not feeling well; I need to sit down"); they could agree to each sit/stand for half the trip, or they could creatively come up with other solutions ("I'll stand if you can hold my backpack"). One person per seat seems simple, but it is *not* the only solution and, arguably, not the best. The experiences we provide students with today—of shared problem solving, mutual support, and caring—will create the citizens of tomorrow. We must ask ourselves, "What would a cooperative, inclusive classroom look like? What would a cooperative, inclusive community look like? And what would a cooperative, inclusive world look like?" The answers to these questions can guide us in our decision making today.

REFRAMING OUR WORK

Beginning With Ourselves

- Were your school experiences primarily individualistic, competitive, or cooperative?
- How did you feel about classmates who did better than you did at academic and other tasks?

- How did you feel about classmates who didn't do as well as you did at various tasks?
- Were you encouraged to help others who were struggling in school?
- Did other classmates help you when you were experiencing difficulty?
- What are the things you do in your adult life that involve cooperating, collaborating, or working with others?
- What skills do you have as an adult that you think contribute to your working well with others?
- What early messages did you get about resolving conflicts in your life?
- Did the adults in your life help you resolve conflicts that arose for you?

Looking at Our Classrooms and Schools

- Do students use the language of cooperation ("I'll help you," "Let's do it together," "Come work with us," or "I think there's room for both of us here")?
- Do students conceptualize tasks as cooperative, looking for others to work with ("Who wants to help me?" "Mario and I did this together"), or as competitive ("Only I can do it"; "I'm doing it best"), or individualistic ("I can do this myself")?
- Do students constantly compare their work to others ("My picture is better; yours is dumb"), or are they able to support the efforts of their classmates ("You draw really well")?
- Do students display the skills necessary for working in cooperative groups: listening, problem solving, taking turns, encouraging others, asking for clarification, and disagreeing nicely?
- Do students turn to one another as sources of help when they have academic or personal problems?
- Do students consistently empower other students and give them opportunities to do things rather than insisting that the best person do something all the time ("Lianna hasn't had a chance yet—let's see if she wants to do it")?
- Do students have repertoires of cooperative games that they know how to play and will initiate with others?
- Are students critical and thoughtful about community and world events that are structured or conceptualized competitively, pointing out that there might be alternative, more cooperative ways to accomplish the same goal?
- Do students have repertoires for resolving conflicts collaboratively?
- Do teachers establish shared goals for themselves, perhaps across grade levels or with particular cohorts of children?
- Are teachers encouraged to cooperate and collaborate, or are they set up to compete with one another through competitive merit pay or other reward systems?
- What support is there in the school climate for collaboration and cooperation?
- How are conflicts between teachers, staff, administrators, and parents resolved in the school environment?

What's the Big Picture?

- How will the attitudes and skills that students learn about collaboration and conflict resolution help them to view their adult challenges differently?
- What are some global problems that could best be resolved through cooperation and collaboration?

HOW TO BEGIN

Looking at Everything We Do in the Classroom

Implementing cooperative learning, creating spaces that invite children to work together collaboratively, giving children the language of cooperation, and teaching children *why* they are being asked to cooperate are all important components of creating a cooperative, inclusive classroom.

If desks are in rows and children are told not to talk to one another, it is not surprising that the class doesn't *feel* cooperative. If behavior management programs are organized that pit student against student, resulting in a few winners and the rest losers, it isn't unusual to find students who are resentful of one another's successes. We need to ask ourselves, about every classroom decision, "Will this activity/rule/process bring children closer together, or will it isolate and separate them?"

A teacher approached me after a workshop I had given on cooperative classrooms. In this class, we discussed how to make all aspects of classroom life cooperative—from class jobs to wall decorations to music to art. She said that she had been to cooperative learning training before and thought that just following the nine-step model she had been given was all there was to it. Now she said, "I can see that it's about *everything* I do, not just what I do when I'm *calling* it cooperative learning."

Many of the ideas in previous chapters apply here: class jobs can be given to pairs or groups, seats can be arranged so that students have easy access to one another for help and support, and students can be taught to peer tutor and do peer listening. All of these help create a cooperative rather than a competitive atmosphere.

Teachers can look at everything that goes on in their classrooms, reshaping what they say and do and how and what they teach students about being cooperative and understanding the meaning of cooperation in their lives. The more aspects of the curriculum, pedagogy, and classroom practices that are cooperative, the more likely teachers are to be successful giving students consistent messages and creating cooperative communities (Sapon-Shevin, 1990).

Making a classroom cooperative has two main components: (1) eliminating all the vestiges of competition generally associated with teaching, curriculum, and classroom practices and (2) implementing cooperative structures in each of these areas. The following are some examples of the dos and don'ts:

Don't put up star charts that show which students are doing the best. *Don't* read student scores aloud, return papers in order of score, or write classroom averages on the blackboard.

Do put up a "Proud Board" (described in Chapter 6), or keep students' achievement progress privately. *Do* think about what messages students, parents, and other visitors get from looking around your room. *Do* the "visitor test": what would an outsider see and know about your beliefs and values from looking around your room? If a visitor coming to the class could look at the board, the walls, or the seating arrangement and know who is doing well and who isn't, the classroom bears rethinking.

Don't encourage students to compete with one another by saying, "Let's see which row can get their desks clean first," or "I wonder who will be able to answer the most math questions in two minutes." *Don't* use competitive language about individual students, groups, or classes ("You're the best fourth grade in the school." "You read better than any sixth grader I've ever taught"). *Don't* use individual people as examples ("I hope everyone noticed what a nice job Sarita did on her project," or "Tino is the only student in here who knows how to act like a first grader").

Do appreciate people for their individual gifts or group accomplishments ("I am so proud of the way this class is working together to design the world map for the playground." "Leslie—I love how you read with so much expression and feeling in your voice"). *Do* encourage students to work together and define tasks as group goals: "Let's see if we can get all the desks cleared in less than two minutes, and then we'll have time for a game," or "What are all the things we need to do together to get ready for the field trip?" *Do* encourage students to see one another as sources of information, instruction, and support. Put students' desks in groups and make a rule: anyone in the group who has a problem must consult with the group before coming to the teacher for help.

Don't organize competitive games in the classroom (spelling bees, around the world flash-card competitions, and the like).

Do teach students to play cooperative games, and stock your classroom library with student-made or commercially available cooperative games.

Don't accept without question the competitive aspects of the outside world or bring them into your classroom (beauty pageants, color wars, schoolwide contests).

Do encourage students to think about alternative ways of viewing the world, conflicts, and collaboration (a school mural instead of a coloring contest, a poetry day instead of a poetry competition). *Do* structure many class projects: plays, murals, group projects, field trips, or group singing.

Don't accept competition in your life as a teacher just because it's always been done that way (competitive merit raises, teacher of the year).

Do continue thinking about what a more cooperative world might look like, including for you as a teacher. Think about ways to make your life as a teacher more cooperative and supportive.

Differentiated Instruction/Multilevel Teaching

Differentiated instruction refers to a way of organizing teaching so that the content, activities, and products are developed so that they can respond to varying learner needs. All students are engaged in challenging work, but there is more flexibility in how specific tasks are accomplished. Students might, for example, work at learning centers; each learning center focusing on a specific skill or task. Or students and teachers might develop individual contracts with students that make specific what each child needs to do to meet the academic goals set for that individual.

Teachers using differentiated instruction often use flexible grouping, including learning in pairs, triads, or quads; in student-selected groups; in teacher-selected groups; in random groups; and as a whole class. Rather than having students permanently pigeonholed into a particular learning group (often a group organized to be homogeneous around a particular skill or lack thereof), flexible grouping means organizing instruction so that students move through a variety of different groups every day. Sarah and Tanner might both be in a very short-term group working on the use of apostrophes, part of different cooperative learning groups that are working on a volcano project, paired with different students as reading buddies during quiet reading, and involved as peer tutors with younger children during part of math time.

One of the leading proponents of differentiated instruction, Carol Tomlinson (2003) remarks that it is our similarities that make us human; it is our differences that make us individuals. This philosophical value becomes manifest when students work is all valued but differs in how it is tailored to individual students' needs, strengths, and abilities. In this context, success is viewed as individual growth, not as a competitive comparison between individuals.

Instruction can be differentiated in many ways, and many of these are structural. That is, it makes sense to design the curriculum and teaching strategies by thinking about *all the* students in the class from the very beginning rather than designing lessons or projects and *then* thinking about the students for whom it won't work and trying change things.

Universal Design

As an architectural construct, universal design refers to creating structures that are accessible to all—a ramp with railings, for example, works for those who can walk, those who use wheelchairs, those pushing strollers, and those who need extra time or support. And a ramp can be beautiful. It doesn't have to be a signifier that something is wrong or that some people are different (i.e., regular people enter here, and those with disabilities use this entrance). The ramp can be the way that *everyone* enters the building.

In instruction, universal design means that the curriculum and teaching can be broadly designed so that all students can access it and be a part of it. The principle of universal design can be contrasted with the idea of retrofitting the curriculum after the fact. Rather than designing the lesson and then saying, "Uh-oh, this isn't going to work for Holly because she can't read or for Wei because he doesn't speak much English—what shall we do for them instead?", we design the lesson *from the beginning* so that a wide range of learners can access it. For example, instead of assigning each student to write a five-page report on 1 of the 50 states and then realizing that this assignment doesn't work for (at least) several students in the class, we can design the United States project as one in which each student will be learning something about one of the states and representing that work to the rest of the class. Although this might include a report, it could also include posters, videos, songs, cartoons, dioramas, travel brochures, and on and on. And the materials that students access to learn can also vary widely and include print materials, audio books, interactive software, personal interviews, and more.

Using the principles of universal design communicates that all students belong in the classroom and that the curriculum is designed for all of them. By providing broad, diverse options from the beginning, as part of the original design, teachers are much less apt to be surprised or distressed by the variation in their classrooms.

How Can We Differentiate?

Teachers can differentiate in many ways, including (1) the content or curriculum students are asked to learn, (2) the learning activities or strategies that students use to learn, (3) the materials students use to learn, and (4) the product or evidence that students show to allow the teacher to assess their learning.

Differentiating Content/Curriculum

Modifying the curriculum goals for individual students involves clear assessment of their current level of skill or performance. Once that has been established, teachers can figure out the next logical objective for that student. Carmen's learning objective is to learn the difference between floating and sinking; Nora is working on more advanced principles of flotation, and Aileen is learning to design flotation experiments and test hypotheses. Differentiating the curriculum is useful in helping students of all ability levels engage in meaningful learning tasks (generally around a shared theme) at their own levels. It is crucial, however, to make sure that we are differentiating for individual students based on high expectations and a commitment to inclusion rather than tracking students (i.e., "We will all study the Civil War, and Marco will color in the corner").

Differentiating Strategies/Activities

Students will meet their objectives by engaging in different learning tasks. Some of these tasks might occur individually, and some might be differentiated in a shared activity. In a science unit on floatation and water pressure, for example, Carmen's objective is to sort objects into categories of "those that float" and "those that sink," and she has a bucket of water, a set of objects, and a chart for recording her findings. Nora is designing a boat that will float using Styrofoam, wood, and glue and writing the directions clearly enough for others to follow. Aileen is creating a prediction chart about floating and sinking that her classmates will use for the experiments she is designing with a variety of objects.

Differentiating Learning Materials

In a unit on the Holocaust, for example, the materials the students are using to access information may vary widely. There are children's books written about the topic that range from those appropriate at the very early grades to those accessible only to very advanced readers. Rather than having all the students in the class read the same book (some of them unable to read it at all and some of them bored by it), the teacher could provide a range of books. Since not all students will access print, the available materials will include films, music, artwork, and audio archives. The richness and diversity of the resources will ensure that students' learning will be appropriate for them and will *also* enrich the whole class's understanding.

Differentiating Products

Just as students are using different materials and working on different projects at different levels, they will show their learning in different ways. Daniel produces a readers' theater he has written of voices from the Holocaust. Ju Hyun creates a visual display of images of the Holocaust and accompanies each with an audio narration that viewers access by pushing a switch. Sasha creates a poster showing the similarities and differences between the Holocaust and the genocides in Rawanda and Darfur. Jafeth demonstrates his learning by finding computer images to accompany his new vocabulary words of *discrimination, allies,* and *community.* All of these products are shared with the whole class, allowing the teachers and the other students to learn more as well as providing an assessment of individual student learning.

All of the forms of differentiation explained previously can be incorporated into different inclusive teaching structures.

Learning Centers

Differentiation can occur at learning centers by having students go to different learning centers (i.e., Marco goes to Centers 1, 3, and 5; Lianna goes to 1 and 2; and Shay goes to 3, 4, and 5). The tasks at the learning centers can differ in levels of complexity or how the activity is completed. Or there can be differentiation within a learning center (i.e., the alphabetizing center can have plastic letters that need to be put in alphabetic order, word cards that need to be sequenced, and a dictionary activity that involves finding words and noting what page they are located on). Specific students could be asked to complete different tasks at the learning center. Although all would be working on alphabetizing, there would be differences between how hard the alphabetizing was and whether it also involved reading, writing, or manipulating objects.

Teachers and other adults can each staff a learning center, or an adult can help an individual child move through learning centers or complete tasks. Students can also move through learning centers with a peer buddy or support.

Project-Based Learning

When learning is structured around projects, it becomes much easier to create activities that are appealing and appropriate to each student. When a fifth-grade classroom, for example, decided to create a carnival for the younger grades, the students were involved in reading about the history of carnivals, designing the booths (measuring, building, and advanced math), creating advertising posters, printing tickets, making refreshments, and staffing the booths. Students engaged in a variety of reading, writing, and math activities as well as thinking carefully about the students who would come to the carnival and how they could make sure that the activities were appropriate to them. It was not hard for the teacher to assign students tasks that were appropriate to their learning strengths and challenges. A student who struggles with social interactions was encouraged (and succeeded) at being the ticket seller, and a student with advanced math skills designed the Skee-Ball booth so that the angle of the ramp was just right. Other students worked on writing skills by writing invitations to the other classes and drafting the instructions for the setup and takedown for each booth.

Individual Learning Contracts

Rather than expecting all students to accomplish the same thing, teachers can write individual learning agendas or contracts with students. Some teachers provide a wide menu or options for a curriculum area and allow the student to choose three, four, or five things they will do. Or the teacher might say, "I get to choose two things on the list for you, and you can choose three for yourself." Some of the items on the learning contract can be done in collaboration with others. Learning contracts can also be designed so that everyone in the class is doing three of the same objectives, and the other objectives are individualized.

For example, for the unit on community helpers, a first grader's contract might specify that the student do the following:

- Draw a picture of three different community helpers
- Talk to an adult who is a community helper and report at circle time what he or she learned
- Design a skit with a friend that shows a community helper doing his or her job

A fifth grader's learning contract on South Africa might include labeling a map of South Africa with the key cities, reading a book about apartheid and writing a reaction to it, listening to the South African national anthem and explaining why it is written in three languages, and watching a video about Nelson Mandela and sharing what she learned through a speech to the class. Other classmates might have objectives that included learning some words in Zulu and making a word chart, interviewing parents and elders about their understanding of apartheid, or making food from South Africa to share with the class.

Curriculum Boxes

Teachers at a school in Oshkosh, Wisconsin, who were trying to meet the needs of a wide range of learners (including those labeled as gifted) designed the box project. Each teacher took one of the curriculum content areas and assembled a box of materials on the topic. The Underground Railroad box, for example, contained books (at various levels) about the topic, music from the era, several quilt design books and projects that focused on the use of quilts during the period, several plays about the role of Harriet Tubman, timelines, costumes from the time, slave narratives, and children's books about the topic. When the teachers taught that content, they simply opened the box and had an amazingly differentiated set of possibilities for students. Rather than having students (and teachers) view modifications and adaptations as something that they make only for students with special needs, the box contained materials for everyone, and the vast range of ways of engaging with the material provided depth rather than stigma for those who were doing something different from the rest of the class. One teacher said, "I found myself asking, 'Why would I want 25 copies of the same textbook when I could use those funds to buy a wide variety of materials?'"

Because each teacher only had to design (and fill) one box—and these boxes were then shared—the design of curriculum was shared and the individual burden decreased. It was also possible for students to access the same curriculum multiple times without the sense that they were repeating something because the range of activities was large. After any teacher used the box, the class generally added to the contents—puzzles they had designed, a readers' theater they'd written, a video they had found, and so on. So the boxes grew and grew!

Teaching the Big Idea and Essential Questions

Rather than setting narrow objectives (students will be able to plot Columbus's journey on a map, or students will be able to explain Clara Barton's contribution to American history), it is possible to think about teaching *big ideas*. For example, a big idea might be that individual people can make a difference even when the odds are against them.

Within that big idea, students can engage with materials and activities at a variety of levels. Students might read biographies of various people who have made a difference, they might interview community leaders who are trying to improve the city, and they might write about ways in which they would like to be remembered 30 years hence.

As Kluth (2005) explains,

> the openness of the questions stimulates thought, permits and encourages inventive thinking, encourages different responses from different students, and allows for the pursuit of authentic learning and investigation. Further, students with a wide range of needs can answer "big questions"; some learners will provide answers that are more concrete while others will be able to answer in ways that are more complex and abstract. (para. 9)

Wiggins and McTighe (2005), writing about essential questions ask, "How can we avoid the twin sins of activity-based and coverage-based design" (p. 105)?

For the essential question, for example, "What is a true friend?" students might access a variety of print, audio, and visual resources to answer that question as well as talking to others (young people, elders, and so on).

The science question, "What does it mean to say our air or water is clean?" could lead to explorations involving physical phenomenon, reading about pollution, visiting a water treatment plant, studying water pollution across different residential neighborhoods, and so on.

Using Multiple Intelligences

The theory of multiple intelligences was developed by Howard Gardner of Harvard University in 1983. Gardner (1999) argued that the traditional notion of intelligence—as one clear continuum that could be measured by standardized IQ tests—was too narrow. He suggested, instead, that there are eight different intelligences that could be used to describe the many and divergent ways in which children and adults interact with the world and display their gifts. These have been identified as (1) linguistic intelligence (word smart), (2) logical-mathematical intelligence (number/reasoning smart), (3) spatial intelligence (picture smart), (4) bodily-kinesthetic intelligence (body smart), (5) musical intelligence (music smart), (6) interpersonal intelligence (people smart), (7) intrapersonal intelligence (self-smart), and (8) naturalistic intelligence (nature smart). Other educators have since added spiritual intelligence to this list (see www.howardgardner.com).

Multiple intelligence is not a strategy of teaching but rather a way of thinking about the many ways that intelligence can be fostered and displayed. Schools typically privilege those students who display exceptional linguistic and logical/mathematical intelligence and, therefore, don't fully recognize children who display other forms of intelligence. Embracing the idea of multiple intelligences means valuing the many kinds of smart that occur in a classroom and finding ways for students to master and display these gifts.

Thomas Armstrong (1994) has been one of the major translators of the theory of multiple intelligences into educational practices that can be used to reach and teach a wide variety of learners. Armstrong believes that schools (and education) would be radically transformed if teachers were trained to present their lessons in a wide variety of ways, particularly ways that actively tap into the multiple intelligences (www.thomasarmstrong.com).

A study of the civil rights movement, for example, might include studying the songs of the time and possibly writing a song, developing role-playing activities about key moments in the desegregation struggle, or constructing a timeline of events that link the civil rights movement with the women's movement. Students might draw a cartoon strip that tells the story of a particular event in the movement, interview elders in the community about their memories and perceptions of the 1960s, or develop a contemporary ad campaign that addresses continuing issues of racism and discrimination.

The good news about conceptualizing curriculum and teaching this way is that all students can be actively engaged in meaningful learning—in ways that all contribute to the overall learning of the class. Segregation into ability groups becomes unnecessary, and oftentimes, expectations of whom can benefit from which project of kind of instruction are challenged. It turns out, for example, that the child with a cognitive disability is great at participating in role-plays that reinforce his knowledge of the content being studied. Or perhaps, a struggling reader discovers that reading from a script—as part of a cast of readers—greatly enhances her understanding of what she is reading and what it means to coordinate her reading contributions with others—understanding that reading has communicative function.

Virtually any content can be analyzed and taught through a wide variety of intelligences, but this does not mean that individual students should be limited to learning or demonstrating their achievement in only one area. We must be careful, in other words, to avoid de facto tracking and segregation through a new theory! If Marcus is always asked to draw what he has learned, he may never develop his writing skills. If Carmelita always writes songs, she may not learn to draw or to express herself with other kinds of writing.

IMPLEMENTING INCLUSIVE COOPERATIVE LEARNING

Cooperative learning does not mean putting students in small groups and telling them to cooperate. Unless students have been systematically *taught* how to work together, simply demanding their cooperation is likely to be a formula for chaos and disaster. Rather, cooperative learning means creating *heterogeneous groups* (as small as two people) who work toward a *shared goal* that is structured so that there is *task interdependence* (we need one another to succeed) and *individual accountability* (everyone has to learn something) and for which the teacher has provided and later processed the necessary *social skills teaching*.

Characteristics of Cooperative, Inclusive Instruction

For cooperative learning strategies to be truly inclusive, we must look carefully at each of the previous components and design them so that they really can include *all* learners.

Heterogeneous Groups

Cooperative learning activities are typically done in heterogeneous groups, that is, groups that are mixed. Why should groups be heterogeneous? What about the logic of grouping students who are the same for easier teaching? First, heterogeneous grouping allows students to learn from and teach one another. Less-advanced students can benefit from the more advanced skills of other group members, and in a well-designed cooperative learning activity, high-level performing students are not simply reduced to tutors who are slowed down by other students but can actively engage in higher-level cognitive skills that *may* include supporting or teaching other students. Second, heterogeneous grouping avoids the stigma of being in the slow group or the arrogance of being in the high group. Most important, the world is heterogeneous. Students must learn to work with others who they (or society) perceive as different. I do not know of any communities that have a "gifted" video store or a "learning disabled" grocery store. In the real world, we work, play, worship, and interact with a wide range of people who may share certain characteristics with us and differ on others. Learning how to interact successfully with people who talk, move, look, or learn differently than we do is crucial to students' success in negotiating a diverse world with ease and comfort.

Although some teachers tend to limit this to mixing students according to a clearly specified skill level (one high reader, two medium readers, and one low reader), there are many ways to think about heterogeneity. Groups might be mixed by race, by ethnicity, by reading levels, social skills levels, learning styles, and so on. Teachers can make thoughtful choices for cooperative learning activities, and the student groups the teacher forms for project may not necessarily be the same groups students are with at their desks.

In inclusive classrooms, it can make sense to build a group *around* a particular student. I can think well about Shakeera, who has cognitive delays and expressive language difficulties; who would make sense as a group member or partner with Shakeera? Then I can think of a third person who will mesh with those two. It is important to remember that *heterogeneous is not the same as random.* Random grouping is rarely the most useful for successful cooperative learning. It might be my goal that, at the end of the year, my students have developed so many collaborative skills, such deep knowledge and appreciation of their classmates' differences, and such a commitment to cooperation and inclusion that I could place any four students together and have them function well as a group. This is rarely where one begins in September.

It makes sense to think about students along many different continua, rather than only one (intelligence or reading level). So although I might be one of the stronger music people in a group, doing music, I would not be one of the most proficient in a group engaged in an activity involving spatial design. I can teach others in my group about reading, but I would need to learn from others about art or mechanical repair. Thus, activities should be designed to take advantage of many different kinds of skills and abilities so that the same students are not necessarily always the most skilled or proficient. Shaking things up like this rattles students' ideas about who is smart and who is valuable, disrupting the sense that there is only one continuum or smartness in the classroom.

In my ideal classroom, an outside visitor who asked, "Who is the smartest kid in here?" would be met by a blank stare and the question, "Smart at what? We all have different gifts." If students do respond to the question with, "Laverne is the smartest, and Phillip is the dumbest," this is an indication that the tasks students are asked to perform may be limited to a narrow range of types of intelligence or skill. Teachers should not attempt to hide that students are different or bring different contributions to projects and activities, but there is a difference between acknowledging, "I think Taylor will be a good person here to help your group think of ways to draw this," and "Let's see, I need two people who are good at math—how about Lindsay and Tequa."

Shared Goal

Having a shared goal means that all of us are working together to accomplish something. It's not me against you or us against them (or even our cooperative group against your cooperative group).

Most of us have had experiences in life that are cooperative. When two people are canoeing and they approach a rock, the shared goal is to get the canoe around the rock without hitting it. The whole canoe—not just *my* half of the canoe! Both paddlers must work together to maneuver the canoe around the rock. Singing in a chorus, being in a play, or marching in a band—these are all examples of cooperative activities. It isn't considered a successful orchestral performance if the clarinet player boasts, "I finished four measures before everyone else!" The idea behind being part of an ensemble is that we watch one another, modify our behavior to mesh well with others, and are working for a shared outcome that will make us all pleased.

Whether the shared goal is cleaning out the flooded basement in time to save important books and letters, organizing a political campaign to get a candidate elected, or working as a team to support a critically ill friend, the goal for all participants is the same: a dry basement, an elected official, and a well-supported friend. If everyone in the group will be happy/pleased/satisfied/proud if the task is accomplished, then it is likely to be a shared goal.

Task Interdependence

Task interdependence means that every member of the group (which could be as small as two) is needed for the task to be accomplished. It might mean that each person's voice is needed, each person's body, each person's information, or each person's particular gift—but the task should be chosen, constructed, or defined so that one person could not do it alone with the same results. Teachers who ask four students to complete the same worksheet, when the worksheet is one that any particular student could actually fill out by herself, should not be surprised when students have trouble working together.

In thinking about diversity, it is important to remember that although each person's contribution is necessary for the group's success, each person in the group doesn't have to do the same task. Think of four people gathered around a table trying to complete a 500-piece jigsaw puzzle. The shared goals are clear: complete the puzzle and have a good time. But the tasks that people take for themselves can be quite different: some people are good at edges and create the border; then there are the "color experts" who can scan the entire table of pieces and find, if requested, "a little piece that's mostly purple with red in one corner." Other people are good at spatial relations—the person who can offer, "I think if you turned that whole section around, it actually belongs up here next to the sky section." And there are also the encouragers and supporters, who come by with pats on the back, encouragement, admiration, and cold drinks. A good way to know if an activity is cooperative is to listen to what people say when someone accomplishes a portion of the task: If they say, "Wow, that's great," or "Thanks, that helped," then it is clear that individual contributions are being made toward what is perceived as a group goal.

In an inclusive classroom, students can be engaged in cooperative activities in which different students do different portions of the task.

Individual Accountability

In the cooperative task, it is important that each person's contribution is important to the group's success. And each person must be accountable or responsible for his contribution. Just as all members in the group are not necessarily performing identical parts of the task, accountability will vary with each person. Take the example of five children sitting around a table working on a map of North Dakota. As a group, the children are labeling cities and rivers in the state, identifying the Canadian border and adjacent states

(Montana, South Dakota, and Minnesota), and discussing the Native American residents of the state and the places that have Lakota names. As a group, the students work together to construct a visual representation of the number of students in the class who have been outside the state and where they went, including location and type of transportation. Three of the children are responsible, at the end of the activity, for being able to take a blank map and fill in the names of the four major cities (Grand Forks, Fargo, Minot, and Bismarck) and all the adjoining states. Benji, who has learning challenges, is asked to paste the city and state names (which are printed on sticky paper) on a blank map using the already completed map as a guide. Allison, whose academic skills are very advanced, completes some of the standard parts of the task, and she is asked to explain the differences between domestic and international borders and the differences a traveler would experience traveling from North Dakota to Canada as opposed to North Dakota to Minnesota (passport, customs, and different currency). She constructs a chart that all the children can use that explains these differences.

Each student, in other words, is responsible for having learned something, but not every student is expected to have learned the *same* thing. Accountability through portfolio (students demonstrating what they learned relative to some previously established learning goals) would provide the kind of personalized accountability described.

Collaborative Skills

I often talk to teachers who say, "I tried cooperative learning, and it didn't work. The kids just couldn't get along; they had fights, and one or more of the children ended up doing all the work." Invariably, when I ask about the ways in which they structured that cooperative learning experience, prominently absent is any social skills teaching before the lesson or processing of social skills after the lesson.

You can't just put kids in cooperative learning groups and instruct them (or yell at them) to cooperate. If the behaviors necessary for cooperative learning (listening, encouraging, problem solving, and negotiating) are not in students' repertoires, then simply telling them to cooperate will not be successful. The good news is that the social skills necessary for successful cooperative learning are all teachable—we need not simply lament those children who don't display them, saying, "If only their parents had taught them to . . . , then I could just teach math/social studies/science." Children come to us the way they do, with a wide variation in their academic and their social skills, and teaching social skills is a critical (perhaps *the* crucial) component of cooperative learning.

Unfortunately, many teachers do not do any explicit teaching of social skills (Sapon-Shevin, 1986). There are a number of reasons for this.

- They don't know how. Although most teachers took courses in math methods or teaching reading, very few of us had formal preparation in teaching friendship skills or how to help children learn to appreciate one another. This gap in our educations sometimes makes it difficult for us to know *how* to teach children the social skills they need

- Some teachers think that teaching social skills just isn't (or shouldn't be) part of their job. Although it would be wonderful if all our students appeared with wonderful social skills, eager and ready to work together to learn, confident in their conflict-resolution skills, and cheerfully encouraging of one another (and us!), it just isn't so. Think about the adults you know. How many of them have social skills that are lacking? If many of the adults we know don't know how to share the work, encourage others, or resolve conflicts, why should we expect young people to know how to do these things instinctively?

- We believe that teaching people how to say nice things to one another somehow trivializes the experience or makes it insincere. When I first began teaching, I remember seeing a list of 100 ways to praise children. The chart contained simply a list of expressions: "Way to go, you're awesome," "I'm so proud of you," and the like. My first reaction was, "That's pathetic. If teachers need a list of nice things to say, they shouldn't be teaching." But, I have really changed my mind on this. If saying nice things to other people doesn't come easily and naturally, it makes perfect sense to prime the pump and to provide reminders and structures to help us be kind, supportive, or gentle. When one of my daughters was a young adolescent, I placed a note on my dresser reminding me not to criticize her (something that was easy for me to do) because it helped to make the behavior of appreciating her more likely. When children are first learning the skills of appreciation, for example, they may start out sounding superficial or contrived, "I like your sweater," but through experience, affirmation of themselves as learners, and multiple opportunities to see their classmates' strengths and the results of appreciation, they will progress to deeper, more sincere statements of affirmation, "I really appreciate how you made a joke when we were all getting frustrated."

- Some teachers believe social skills teaching is just a waste of time and that there are so many curricular demands that they can't afford the time to teach children how to listen, ask questions, or say nice things to their classmates. Although the time and teaching pressures on teachers are overwhelming and very real, many teachers have come to realize that time spent teaching social skills is time well spent, resulting in tremendous payoffs (and time saving) for other parts of their instructional day.

Even if cooperative learning is well structured and students work beautifully together, they still need time and practice in processing that interaction as a way of naming it, honoring it, and internalizing what they learned. The kind of analysis necessary to say, "The reason our group worked well today—better than yesterday—is that we really listened to one another a lot better, and we made sure everyone got a turn," or "I think that we spent so much time arguing about the first part of the assignment that we ran out of time to do the rest. Next time, I think we should let the leader read the assignment aloud and explain it before we get into an argument," is critical to students' ability to take what they have learned and apply it in other situations. See Box 7.4 for an example.

BOX 7.4

In Cathi Allen's third grade, the students use the agreements from the TRIBES program (Gibbs, 2001): attentive listening, mutual respect, appreciations/no put-downs, and right to pass. She explains, each of these agreements then becomes a *collaborative* focus, first individually for several days and then as part of the daily routine. As each activity is introduced, an agreement is used as a collaborative focus, often with the students deciding which is most appropriate for the given activity. They may select attentive listening as the focus and will actually define what it will look like, sound like, and feel like during the activity. They will most likely point out that teammates will be leaning in close together, looking at one another, and not talking when it is another member's turn. So important to facilitating this process of working together and helping one another is the reflection they do as a team when they finish the activity. You can hear them commenting, "We did a great job really getting close so we could hear and understand one another. We even had our seats off our seats so we could get close."

Including All Students in Cooperative Learning

The first step to including all students in cooperative learning activities involves conceptualizing the curriculum broadly. I once testified in a due-process hearing for a young man with Down syndrome. Sean was in the sixth grade, and although he had been in regular classes up to this point, the sixth-grade teachers now wanted him removed to a more segregated setting in a neighboring community. Although Sean could speak, read, and write, his skills weren't at grade level, and the teachers were unable and unwilling to figure out how to accommodate his learning needs in the classroom. When I inquired whether they had tried doing any cooperative learning, one teacher replied, "Oh, we do cooperative learning all the time, but he can't do the tasks in the group." Although I do not doubt that this teacher had made a sincere effort to include Sean within the group, clearly, the conceptualization of cooperative learning was still one in which each member of the group had to do essentially the same task, a task that was beyond Sean.

Students with learning and behavioral challenges may need particular kinds of modification or supports to be successful in cooperative learning activities (Sapon-Shevin, Ayres, & Duncan, 1994).

Physical assistance: It may be necessary to think about how a child will physically interact with her environment and other students (see Box 7.5). Will the child need a walker to move? Does the student need someone sitting next to her to sit on the floor and participate in an activity? Is a special kind of chair or standing device needed to be able to access materials?

BOX 7.5

Carrie, a student with cerebral palsy, has difficulty walking. One of her individualized education program (IEP) objectives has to do with increasing her mobility skills. You assign Carrie and another student, Grace, the role of materials gatherers, and Grace supports Carrie as they move around the room, collecting materials and delivering them to the other groups.

Equipment of adaptive devices: Some children will require different kinds of input or output devices to participate in an activity. While other children are writing, a child might use a computer, a touch talker, or a tape recorder to add his input (see Box 7.6). A child might need a talking calculator or a brailler to contribute to the group.

BOX 7.6

Mitchell, a boy who uses a computer talker, is part of a cooperative learning group that is generating ideas for the school fundraisers. He makes his contributions by typing on his computer, and another student shares what he has written with the group.

Emotional support or encouragement: Although all students require ongoing support and encouragement to participate, some children may require special thinking about the kinds and amount of support needed to keep them participating successfully (see Box 7.7). Partner buddies can be used to provide support as can careful thinking about grouping and tasks.

BOX 7.7

Karen is a student who has a lot of difficulty staying on task and often gets upset if she doesn't understand what's being asked of her. As part of your cooperative learning activity, you teach students how to encourage one another and make sure that all students receive positive feedback from one another.

A change in the rules: When students are engaged in *competitive* activities, a change in the rules is called cheating. Cries of "Why did you let Marnie use the calculator if I had to figure it out in my head" are common when students perceive that others will be unfairly advantaged by changes in the rules of participation. But in cooperative activities, when the success of the group depends on the success of each individual, then students are generally eager for all of their group members to be successful and changing the rules constitutes helpful, thoughtful modification and not cheating (see Box 7.8).

BOX 7.8

The class is playing a cooperative matching game, milling around the room trying to find the person whose card matches theirs (the cards have rhyming words on them). Most of the students are readers, and the activity, for them, involves recognizing rhyming words and word families. For Gretchen, who doesn't speak or read yet, the activity is structured so that she is told who her partner will be, and her task is to move around the room trying to find someone who fits the description she's been given: "Look for someone with blue pants and red sneakers and a green and white striped shirt."

Making thoughtful choices about grouping: Bearing in mind the previously mentioned notion that heterogeneous doesn't mean random, it is perfectly reasonable for teachers to think carefully about which students they will place together as learning partners or cooperative group members (see Box 7.9).

BOX 7.9

When you are thinking about putting together your cooperative learning groups, you carefully consider who to place with Miguel. He is new to the school, speaks little English, and is very shy. You decide to place him with Carly, who is warm and outgoing, and with Boris, who came to your class from the Soviet Union earlier in the year and has become skilled at navigating a new language and a new community.

Thinking well about challenging behaviors: Knowing one's students well often makes it possible to predict what kinds of difficulties students will encounter during specific tasks. I know, for example, that Clavon has trouble sitting still for long periods and that I must design learning activities and roles for him that involve movement and activity. I know that Vito does best when he has a partner (but not two!) and that the partner should be someone who also has a strong personality. Rather than designing an activity and then worrying about discipline or management strategies, preplanning can often avoid problems before they begin (see Box 7.10).

BOX 7.10

Before you plan your cooperative learning lesson (which is a science experiment), you think about Darren and the fact that if he doesn't have something to hold, he often fiddles and rips up paper. Before the lesson begins, you teach Darren to use the stopwatch, and you give him the role of time-keeper in his group. This keeps him very busy, gives him some authority, and occupies his hands by giving him something to hold at all times.

Assigning roles that promote active participation: Because not all students in the cooperative group have to do the same tasks or do them in the same way, it is possible to think about how to mesh the group's goal (broadly conceptualized) with any particular learner's needs and skills. It doesn't make sense that any particular group member is expected to be an observer or a bystander to the group's activity; every student must be actively engaged throughout the task (see Box 7.11).

BOX 7.11

Your cooperative learning math group is doing complex three-step story problems. One of the group members is Marissa, whose math goals include reading and writing numerals 1 through 10. She is given the task of recorder for the group. She must write the answer on the answer sheets as it is dictated by her group members. She is also asked to read the answer back to them to check for accuracy.

Talking about inclusion and cooperation to children: Although many teachers embrace a vision of cooperative, inclusive classrooms, they often don't articulate that vision to their students. Sometimes cooperative learning is perceived by students as "something our teacher makes us do" rather than as part of a framework that is discussed and revisited on a regular basis by the teacher (see Box 7.12).

BOX 7.12

In Kathy Goodman's second grade, the children explained to me, "We're the Happy Hands Classroom. That means we help one another." When I asked them what a teacher should do about a class where the children are mean to one another and don't get along, one child advised, "She should give those kids cooperative activities to do so they'll have to work together and that way they'll get to like one another." Clearly, this teacher had done a great job of explaining why she does what she does and enlisting children's active support and participation in the process.

There are many excellent books on cooperative learning, including several that address cooperative learning with diverse learners (see Thousand, Villa, & Nevin, 1994). The modifications and adaptations discussed previously can be used as part of most cooperative learning models. In addition to specific models of cooperation, teaching children to work together and support one another can be a central organizing value throughout all aspects of the school day. As the previous six chapters have described, models of support and caring should not be limited to specific periods of cooperative learning.

Many of the music activities already shared have involved students in working together to write songs, singing together, and making harmonies through rounds. All of these can be viewed as *cooperative music*. Teachers can also focus on *cooperative art* by initiating projects in which students actively work together to complete a common project (see Box 7.13). Groups can be as small as partners or as large as the entire class; the focus, rather than on individual achievement, can be on making something together. In a classroom I visited recently, the students had made an underwater scene on the bulletin board, each child contributed something that could be found under the water. The range of contributions included scuba divers, underwater plants, fish, buried treasure, and so on. Students had worked together to create an aesthetically pleasing display that incorporated all students' work. Many of the dramatic activities already described (role-plays, skits, and the like) can also be understood as cooperative by encouraging students to work explicitly on the social skills needed to make things go well.

BOX 7.13

At Narrangansett School in Gorham, Maine, Diane Knott teaches a first-, second-, and third-grade multiage program that includes children with multiple handicaps. The district uses exhibitions as part of their assessment system. Students prepare a personalized demonstration of their learning in a common theme. One year, the theme was "community connections," and student's individual projects ranged from calligraphy to pizza making to building nesting sites for loons. After each child's demonstration, there are questions and answers from the observers. Because the assessment is personalized and authentic, each child's contributions and learning can be honored with dignity and respect.

Conflict Resolution

Thinking about conflict resolution issues in your classroom should also not be considered something separate or apart from the day-to-day classroom environment, structures, and rules. Helping students know one another well, creating structures of cooperation and mutual support, and organizing instruction so that students work together and value one another's' differences—these are all part of setting the groundwork for productive conflict resolution.

The Children's Creative Response to Conflict Program (Prutzman, Burger, Bodenhamer & Stern, 1988) offers the following concepts as undergirding what they do:

1. Conflict exists. Conflict is a part of our everyday lives. Even though we learn skills to deal with conflict, it will continue to exist.

2. We can grow through conflict. When we learn and practice the skills of communication and conflict resolution, we learn to deal with conflict creatively.

3. There isn't necessarily one right answer to a problem. We are trying to teach about the complexity of conflict and to encourage children to learn how to solve their problems. We encourage people to explore various solutions and to decide on the solution that is best for them.

4. We all can learn the skills to solve our problems. By learning communication skills and creative conflict-resolution skills, we can become better and better at solving problems.

5. There are many alternatives. Through practice, we can learn the skill of generating many creative alternative solutions that usually do not occur to us.

6. Feelings are important. Sometimes we cannot even begin to get at the reason(s) for a conflict until we deal with the underlying feelings.

7. How we define a problem relates to how we will solve that problem. The more specifically we define a problem, the more specific the solution will be.

8. With practice, we can become better and better at resolving conflict. We are not born problem solvers. We can learn these skills and grow in our use of them.

9. Sometimes, we can all win. We can create win–win solutions when we use our conflict-resolution skills.

There are many excellent resources for teaching students specific conflict-resolution skills, including *The Friendly Classroom for a Small Planet* (Prutzman et al., 1988), *Creative Conflict Resolution* (Kreidler, 1984), and *Linking Up!* (Pirtle, 1998). It is important to remember that most of the components of good problem solving (listening, respect, turn-taking, and collaborative decision making) are the same skills that have been highlighted throughout the book. Using these same skills for a conflict is but one more application of the principles of community building and inclusion (see Boxes 7.14 and 7.15).

BOX 7.14

In Kim Rombach's first-grade classroom, there are two "talking chairs" at the front of the room. Students who are having a conflict can ask the teacher if they can go to the chairs, sit down, and talk about their problem. Several first graders explained to me how the chairs work. One boy said, "Sometimes it takes us a long time, but we try to be friends again."

Outside Kim's room is a bulletin board that the students created (activity taken from Kreidler, 1984). The bulletin board is titled "Say Something That Is Respectful to Someone," and there are two columns: "Words We Might Say Before We Think" and "Words We Would Say When We Think First." Cooperative groups of students brainstormed different ways to say things. For "You're not being fair," they have substituted, "Can you please be fair?" For "I don't want your help," they've written, "I don't need your help, but thank you."

(Continued)

(Continued)

At the Jowonio School, when two children have gotten into a conflict, they are asked to hold Heart-to-Heart Hannah, a large doll with a heart on her dress (and there is also a heart-to-heart box). They are asked to respond to the following questions:

1. What are you feeling?

2. Who are you feeling it about?

3. What happened?

4. What do you wish happened?

5. Can you think of something that you like about the other person? (optional question)

Although this strategy doesn't give the students a solution, it provides them with an opportunity to air the problem and explain their feelings. They feel that they have had their say and been heard, important prerequisites to problem solving. (Go to the website http://www.corwin.com/changetheworld to hear Robin Smith's song "Heart to Heart" based on this activity [used with permission].)

BOX 7.15

A fourth grader who was being trained as a conflict mediator on the playground was explaining to his family and an invited guest over dinner about what had happened at recess that day. He described how two children had entered into an angry dispute about a ball—who had it first, who it belonged to, and who could and couldn't play. The guest asked, "So who won?" The young boy responded quickly, "I don't think you understand. We were looking for a win-win solution!"

✖ ✖ ✖ ✖

At the Muscota School in New York City, older students from P. S. 218 (a service learning academy) come down on a regular basis to teach mediation skills younger students. First, they reviewed what they had done last time (observations skills, listening skills, and learning to ask more open-ended questions), and then they brainstormed some places and situations in which problems had come up. Then they reviewed their three-step model for what you do when you see a problem.

Tell them your name, and find out their names (introduction and setting the tone). "Hi, my name is Kasheef. I'm a problem solver. I'm here to help figure out what happened."

Find out what happened (the what happened step). Listen to both sides, ask open-ended questions about what happened, and then paraphrase. Tell it in different language.

Find a solution. How can we stop the fighting, even if you don't agree? What are we going to do right now?

Students then broke up into groups of four (two of the older students and two Muscota students) and developed role-plays in which two children fought and two mediated.

Community developer Bill Eyman started a group called the Playfair Squad in Wilbur, Rhode Island. A wide range of students learned to resolve conflict on the playground and in the lunchroom, two places where the loose structure often led to problems. When asked what they do, the students explained, "We got trained. We are the pioneers. Everyone can play fair. We start games. We're not the police. If someone wants to play, we brainstorm it, like 'How can we change the game so that Bill can play?'" Now, the kids from Playfair are training students at another school how to develop a Playfair squad. They explained, "Some kids are bullies, but it's hard to be a bully on the playground with Playfair because you stick up for everyone."

The following section contains games, songs, and children's literature that can all be used to help students develop the principles and skills of conflict resolution.

GAMES

Cooperative games can be used to show students that having fun doesn't mean excluding people and working against one another. The games selected for inclusion here focus on four specific behaviors, which can be identified as teaching objectives for social interaction:

- Including children who have been left out, opening one's games or activities to others, and finding a part for another child to play
- Sharing and taking turns
- Touching other children gently, helping other children who have fallen down or who are experiencing difficulty
- Talking nicely to classmates, calling classmates only by names they like, and noticing and commenting on classmates' strengths rather than weaknesses

Each game is described by how it is played, the social behaviors structured by the game, and how the game can be modified or adapted.

Recreational Games

Cooperative games can be used to teach social skills, to model appropriate social interactions, and to provide the opportunity for teachers to discuss issues of cooperation and competition. One teacher, for example, played competitive Musical Chairs with her class and then followed it by Cooperative Musical Chairs. She led students in a discussion of how each game felt and how people treated one another during the two situations. She used this experience as an introduction to the concept of cooperation and the ways in which mutual goals are the occasion for different social interaction patterns than are mutually exclusive goals. Even without discussing the games, however, playing cooperative games can provide students with positive social interactions that may transfer to other times during the day and other settings.

Hug Tag

One or more children are called "huggits" and are given a red flag (or a sock or something visible to hold). They try to give their flag to another player (who becomes the new huggit). Other players are "safe" only when they are in a hug group of two or three (hugging one another). The teacher calls switch, and each group must disband and then regroup while the huggits try to give away their flag by tagging someone with it. After people have played for a brief period, the rules can be switched so that each hug group stays together only as long as all the members can hum on one breath. When anyone in the group runs out of breath (which will happen faster and faster as people get out of breath from running around), the group must disband.

This wonderful inclusive, cooperative game can be played by people of all ages, sizes, and speeds. Children in wheelchairs can easily be included (pushed by another student). Because no child is likely to be left being the huggit all the time, the "it" role is not a stigmatized one but an active one. All players are involved at all times. The message is "We stay safe by being closely connected to others!"

Cooperative Musical Chairs and Musical Laps

Both of these (described in Chapter 2) are excellent examples of games in which children must work cooperatively to achieve a shared goal. Either of these games can be used to begin a discussion of the meaning and value of cooperation.

Tug-of-Peace (Learned From Bill Brown)

All the participants group themselves around a rope that has been tied in a knot to form a circle. Players squat down around the rope, holding onto the rope with both hands. At the count of three, all players lean back, and using the energy of the group, stand up. When everyone has stood up (and cheered), players can, at the count of three again, carefully lean back and return to a squat.

This game is a wonderful contrast to a tug-of-war in which players are pitting their strength against one another in an attempt to humiliate and beat the other group by dragging them through the mud. In the Tug-of-Peace, it is clear that together we accomplished something that we couldn't do alone. The counterbalance support players provide to one another is a graphic representation of mutual support and cooperation.

Hula-Hoop Circle

Players hold hands in a small group and attempt to pass a hoop (placed over their joined hands) around the circle without letting go. Players must figure out how to coordinate their movements (lifting and lowering their hands and their bodies) to pass the hoop around. After players are successful with one hoop, two or more hoops can be added to the circle with the same goal—keeping all the hoops moving around the circle.

This game is an excellent model of the communication skills needed in cooperation. Both parties—the one passing the hoop and the one receiving it—must work together to achieve the goal. Players of different heights need to figure out how to pass each hoop differently (i.e., a short person passing to a taller player must do things differently than a tall person passing to a shorter player).

Instructional Games

In addition to games that are for fun, teachers can structure instructional games to be cooperative as well. The following games present a basic format, and each is adaptable for students of different ages and with different subject matter. Each game annotation includes a description of the materials needed, how the game is played, what cooperative behaviors and what cognitive skills are structured by the game, and how the game can be modified with regard to skill and/or subject matter.

Cooperative Stories

Students sit in a circle and one player starts a story. Each player adds a little piece to the story, moving around the circle. Depending on the age of the students, the game can be played so that each player adds a single word (the most challenging), a sentence, or several paragraphs. Players must listen carefully to one another so that the sentence makes sense.

After students are familiar with the basic format, teachers can identify the subject or topic for the story. For example, as a review of a book the class has just read, players could take turns telling the story of the book. One child might begin, "There were three brothers, and they lived on a farm in the South." The next student adds, "One day, their grandfather told them a secret about the past." Players take turns adding information until the story has been told. Topics or subjects for the story can also be assigned where there isn't a particular right answer or correct sequence. For example, "Let's make up a story about a conflict that could occur in a classroom, what happened and how it was resolved," or "Let's tell a story about how the future might be if there are no cars or electricity allowed anymore."

A modification of this game is called Because (Arnold, 1972) in which the first player describes an event, the second player must give a reason for the occurrence of that event, and the third player must give a probable effect of that event, such as, "The toast burned." "Because the toaster was too hot." "So everyone had charcoal for breakfast."

These two games can be used in many different content areas. Students who are nonverbal can contribute by signing (if there is an interpreter), by using a touch talker, or by having the previous person stop when there is a clear place for the story to continue (i.e., "And suddenly, the ghost appeared and said, 'I want something to eat. I want . . .'" and turns to the child to supply the food, through sign or gesture). Or a child with limited verbal skills could be given the role of deciding a crucial plot turn: "Marcus, when the giant saw the three dragons, did he run away or try to make friends with them?"

Cooperative Shapes, Numbers, or Letters (Orlick, 1978)

Groups of children are asked to use their bodies to form various shapes (circle, square, letters, or numbers). The students can be placed in groups of three, for example, and told that everyone's body must be in the shape for it to count. Thus, students have to work together to include people in the activity.

Cooperative String (Cornelia "Sam" Arhelger)

In this version, groups of five are given a piece of string or yarn that has been joined in a circle. They are told to make shapes or to represent various words or feelings without talking. These might include, for example, square (and five people have to agree, without speaking, how to make four sides!), circle, octagon, triangle, and so on. Feeling words can then be use. "Show me angry, excited, scared, boring, jealous, eager," and the like. More abstract words can also be used: *peace, conflict, harmony, rhythm, sharing,* and the like. For each word, students must work together, without talking, to figure out what they are doing. Usually, one or more people will take the lead, but all players must follow or agree so that one consistent shape or idea is represented.

Nonverbal Birthday Lineup (Harrison, 1976)

In this activity, the leader gives only the following instructions: "Without talking, line yourselves up according to the month and day you were born. The idea is to have one line starting with January and ending with December with everyone in the right order." The participants must figure out a way to communicate without words so that they know where to begin and end the line and where everyone fits.

This activity really stresses nonverbal communication, including others, and gentle touching. It is always fascinating to see groups working on this activity. Players often hold up fingers for months and days; some have stamped their feet different numbers of times, acted out their months, and so on. I generally urge the group to do an internal, nonverbal check on themselves before the oral countdown at the end. This often results in much heated gesturing and repositioning. Sometimes one or more leaders emerge who attempt to get the group in the right order. This is sometimes the occasion for silent negotiating and compromise, as there can only be one beginning to the line and one end.

Other Lineups

It is possible to have students line themselves up for many other things. Each student might be given a card with a word on it, for example, and the group asked to put themselves in alphabetic order. This can be made easy with words like *apple, dog,* and *frog* or more difficult with words like *adventurous, adventitious,* and *admonishment.* Students might each be given an event from a story and asked to line themselves up in chronological order, occasioning discussions like, "Did Margarite see the vision before or after she met the old woman on the road?" Events from history can also be used, particularly as a review of a previous lesson or as a way of discussing a current-event situation: "Did the peace talks begin before or after this battle? At what point did the leaders agree to this resolution?" Other ideas for asking students to line up include the following:

- *Language arts:* Students are given cards with scrambled sentences and asked to line up to make a coherent sentence.
- *Geography:* Students are given cards with places on them, and they line up by distance from the school (can be local places like the video store or the drugstore or more distant places, such as neighboring cities or countries).
- *Science:* Students are given cards with names or pictures of animals and asked to line up in size; students are given geologic events and asked to line up by how long ago each happened.
- *History:* Students line up according to events in history and the order in which they happened; students are asked to order the steps in passing a bill through Congress or holding an election.
- *Math:* Students have cards with numbers on them and line up from smallest to largest (easy: 1, 3, 5; hard: 0.345, 0.347, 0.349). Students line up using mixed cards of fractions and decimals: ½, .37, 3/8, and 0.45.

Caution: Although there are many ways, times, and topics for doing lineups, care should be taken to avoid lineups that can stigmatize students or make them uncomfortable. For example, asking students to line up by height or weight can be embarrassing for many students. Asking students to line up according to personal information that may be a product of family income or status can also be a problem, for example, "Line up by the number of 'rooms in your house,' or 'Barbies you own,' or 'other countries you have visited.'" Ask yourself before any particular lineup activity whether the results of the lineup will somehow mirror some oppression or unfairness (size, income, family background, or the like).

What Am I?

Prepare cards or sticky labels with the names of famous people, parts of the body, different animals, famous events in history, and so on printed on them to attach to people's backs.

Pin one card on each player's back. Participants circulate asking only yes-no questions of others, trying to guess what/who is on their back. Participants can ask only one question of a person before going on to another player. When players know who they are, they continue to circulate, answering questions for other players.

Students must know how to phrase questions that can be answered by yes or no and that yield productive information. Students must talk to and interact with a broad range of people because of the one-question-per-person rule. There is likely to be laughter and amusement as people ask and answer questions and general congratulations when players figure out who/what they are. Students who experience difficulty asking questions can be identified to the group so that other players can rally around them. Although it is not considered standard to give players the answers, it is okay for players to help others know in which areas to ask questions (i.e., "Why don't you ask me if you're a male?" "Why don't you ask if you fought on the sides of the allies?"). Students who experience difficulty answering someone's questions can be encouraged to consult with another player ("Bill just asked me if the person on his back has ever held public office, has he?" "Is what's on Diana's back a mammal?") or to check with the teacher or another reference. The emphasis is consistently on pooling information and cooperating to find out the answer.

Depending on the age and level of the pupils, the hidden cards could have names or people in the news ("Am I a man or a woman?" "Am I in politics?"), kinds of fruit ("Am I red?" "Am I a citrus fruit?"), parts of the body ("Am I part of the circulatory system?" "Do people have two of me?"), holidays ("Am I a national holiday?" "Are there parades on my day?"), or any set of items that belong to a general category. This game can be played with all ages, even with preschoolers or nonreaders, using pictures of the object to be guessed rather than the word(s).

Sequence Games

Prepare a set of cards on which a story or sequence has been written so that each card provides the clue for what follows it. For example, one card says, "When someone jumps, you say, 'boo.'" The next card says, "When someone says, 'boo,' you faint." And the next card might say, "When someone faints, you say, 'Quick, get some water.'" The cues can be words, actions, gestures, or anything else that would be visible or audible to other players. One card must indicate who stars, for example, "You go first by _____" or something like, "When everyone is quiet, you say, _____."

Have people sit in a circle, in chairs or on the floor. Shuffle the cards and distribute them to the players. Every player should have at least one card, although it is all right for players to have more than one (or cards can be assigned to carefully chosen pairs). The player whose card signals the beginning does whatever is on her card. Other players watch, follow the sequence, and do what is on their cards until all the cards have been used and the sequence is completed. Students must attend closely to the words and/or movements of their classmates. They must coordinate their part of the sequence with that of other players. Like a play, the sequence will probably not work smoothly the first time. Students generally want to repeat the sequence over and over after redistributing the cards until the sequence flows smoothly and quickly.

This game is infinitely variable according to the age, level, and reading skills of the students. More advanced students often enjoy writing their own sequence games for other class members (see Box 7.16).

BOX 7.16

A group of fifth graders in Kalamazoo, Michigan, wrote two sequence games for their classmates. They had been studying Inuit culture and wrote a sequence game that included all the content of their unit: "When someone tells their dog to 'mush,' you pretend to be preparing seal skin," and the like. They had also been studying metamorphic, igneous, and sedimentary rocks, and they wrote a sequence game including that content: "When someone shouts, 'The volcano is erupting!' you yell, 'Here comes the molten lava, get out of the way!'"

Nonreaders can be included in various ways. The entire sequence game can be done with pictures: The top picture (the clue) is someone combing his hair, which is the clue for the person to perform the bottom picture (brushing her teeth), and so on, with students cueing one another through the picture clues and actions. Cards can also have jokes on them: each card has the punch line of the previous joke and the introduction to the next joke. Players have to figure out which punch line goes to which joke. Cards can also have pieces of a story or a rhyme that ends on one card and is continued on the next: "If you lived in Holland, then you would be Dutch; a rabbit is an animal that lives in a _____." The next card says, "Hutch. If you lived I Finland, then you'd be a Finn, a word that means the opposite of 'out' is _____." Students with disabilities can be included by giving them cards that they can perform either by themselves or with a partner. For example, in working with a group of nontalking students who used communication devices of various kinds, I programmed Rachel's touch talker so that when she got the clue, she pushed a button and her machine spoke, "Ten, nine, eight, seven, six," down to one. Another student was paired with a typical student, and when their moment came, they both hopped around the circle like bunnies, with one student supporting the other physically. Teachers can be thoughtful in both designing and writing sequence games and in how parts are assigned. If each card goes to partners, one of the partners can cue or assist the other partner with their action or sentence.

Cooperative Equations or Word Sentences

Prepare a set of cards with different words on them. These might be separated by parts of speech (i.e., nouns on red cards, adjectives on green cards, pronouns on yellow cards) or, for cooperative equations, a set of cards with different numerals and numerical symbols or operations on them. Again, these might be color coded.

There are various possibilities for play. The cards can either be dealt so that each player (four to six players works best) has cards of one kind (i.e., Billy has all the verbs, Allison all the adjectives, and so on).

Players can either take turns or cooperate to make the longest possible sentence (or equation); the funniest sentence; or a sentence in which there is at least one, two, or three of each part of speech. After a sentence has been written, all the players read it, or after an equation has been made, all players work together to solve it. Rules can be varied according to the teacher's objectives for the game: "Make as many equations as you can that equal 10"; "See how many verbs you can use in one sentence"; "See if it's possible to write a question without using who, what, why, when, or where."

The cognitive skills involved in writing, reading, and/or solving sentences are self-explanatory and can be modified according to the level of the players. The cooperation involved in deciding what to write, what should go where, who can add something, and the like are the most important cooperative behaviors likely to be observed. Teachers can add rules designed to encourage greater degrees of cooperation. For example, to get credit, each sentence must include at least one of each person's cards (thus ensuring that everyone is included and no one takes over) or that every member of the group must be able to read the sentence to the teacher to get credit (taking advantage of peer teaching and support). Teachers will also want to experiment with determining what constitutes the optimum number of players in a group to ensure cooperation.

This game can be thoughtfully modified to include students working at very different levels. One child, for example, might be given only the few joining words she can read (*and, but, or*) and the group be required to include at least one of those words in each sentence. Or one child could be given final punctuation marks and be told by a peer what mark to add: "Cherie—we need a period here."

Cooperative $20,000 Pyramid

In advance, prepare six large cards, each with a category written on them (one category per card). For example, holidays, tools, citrus fruits, presidents who were assassinated, things found in a bathroom, or items on a job application.

This cooperative game is a take off of the popular television game show. The object of the game is for one group of players to devise clues that they will give to other players in an attempt to get them to say the name of the category. The clues are members of the category. One group of players takes the large cards (or simply a list of the categories) and sits down together. As a group, they generate clues that they think will get the other players to say the name of the category. For example, for the category citrus fruits, they might come up with clues such as lemons, limes, grapefruit, and the like. For the category tools, they might list hammer, screwdriver, saw, pliers, and wrench. A group member records the clues for the group. After the group has come up with what they hope will be enough clues for each category, a number of players who were not part of this group are selected to receive clues. They sit facing the class on chairs. The clue givers hold up the large card with the category for the rest of the class (but not the clue receivers) to see, and they begin reading off their clues for the first category. Any member of the clue-receivers who thinks he or she knows the category immediately consults with the group. When they agree, they guess. If they are right, they go on to the next category. If they are wrong, they continue getting additional clues.

The skills involved in generating a list of members of the set without giving additional clues can be challenging. Many teachers have reported that although young students know about Christmas, Halloween, and other major holidays, they do not know the generic term *holiday*. The clue givers must also think carefully about clues that might be misleading and in what order clues should be given. For example, for the category "things found in the bathroom," the clues *sink, toilet, a bathtub,* and *soap* might work in that order. If, however, the clues given were *soap, toothpaste, deodorant,* and *hairspray* (all of which are found in the bathroom), the clue receivers might very logically incorrectly guess the category to be "drugstore items" or "things you use on your body." The group of clue-givers must work cooperatively to generate a good list. Any single contribution must be considered and considerable discussion is likely to take place: "Is a nectarine a citrus fruit?" "Was Robert Kennedy an assassinated president?" Although members of the group may contribute unequally to the total list of clues, single contributions count, and thus, a child who thinks of only one clue, but a good one, will be appreciated in the group.

The level of difficulty of the categories will alter the game substantially. Very young players might have categories like fruit or animals while more advanced players might have categories like words with silent letters, items on a French menu, or what Joan of Arc might have said. Categories can be designed for any subject: in math, prime numbers; in history, famous labor struggles; in literature, female Shakespearean characters; in geography, land formations formed by erosion.

The rules of the game can be modified to change the level of difficulty. As a challenge, a time limit can be set (let's see if all the categories can be guessed in X number of minutes) or by giving only five or fewer clues for any one category. Students can attempt to set cooperative records for the fewest number of clues required or the shortest amount of time needed. The exciting thing about this game is the way that it epitomizes cooperation. If the clues are good, the guessers are successful, thus, everyone wins!

SONGS

Singing together is inherently a cooperative activity. Many of the songs in this book involve students writing verses together, making rounds together, and, in general, creating a joyful sound together that can't be made by one person alone.

Three songs by Sarah Pirtle specifically address issues of conflict and conflict resolution. For the first song, have students stand facing a partner.

"Let's Get Together" (Pirtle, 1998)

Educator Sarah Pirtle suggests that students work in small groups of four to eight. Younger students might need to work in a large group. Students are asked to find ways to connect with other people with their hands and bodies so that no one is left out. She stresses that not everyone has to do the same thing, but all must be involved. Students are told there are only two rules: (1) keep it friendly and (2) keep it fair! Students engage in extensive problem solving to figure out new and creative ways to link up with one another.

"Two in the Fight" and "There is Always Something You Can Do" (Pirtle, 1998)

These songs can both be used to discuss alternatives to violence in resolving conflicts.

"Heart to Heart" (Smith, n.d.)

This song was inspired by teacher Carolyn Messina-Yauchzy's creative method of conflict resolution using a heart-to-heart box with young children. (For more on this strategy, see the earlier section, Conflict

Resolution, page 176). Teachers can use this song to help students remember the model and to reinforce creative problem solving instead of fighting as a solution to conflict.

"I've Got Peace in My Fingers" (Salidor, 2005)

This simple song talks about all the ways that we can connect with one another peacefully and gently.

"Circle the Earth (With Peace)" (Hammil, 1994)

This song talks about the ability to make peace throughout the world and includes the word for peace in much different language. This is a great song for talking about what each person can do to live more peacefully.

"When I Feel Mad" (Lockhart, 2002) and "When I Get Mad" (Greenberg, Vaughan, & Connier, 2004)

These two songs both talk about what it feels like to be angry and what the alternatives are to responding violently or aggressively. Discussion could center on students' experiences trying to de-escalate conflicts and specific strategies they have found that are successful for them, including breathing, walking away, and the like.

"Pitfalls" (Heitler-Klevans & Heitler-Klevans, 2009)

This song describes the things that get in the way of peaceful conflict resolution. There are many examples of ways to step back into the "circle of peace" rather than engaging in blame and recrimination.

"Most Valuable Player" (O'Leary, 1981)

This song talks about the ways in which being a good sport is what makes someone a valuable player, rather than her skills on the playing field. An excellent song for discussing what it means to be a team player and the challenges that competitive games create for relationships and fair play (pair with the book *It's Just a Game* [Farrell, 1999] in the next section).

CHILDREN'S LITERATURE

There are many wonderful children's books that model various aspects of cooperation.

- People working together can do something difficult that they couldn't do alone.
- Different people, working in close cooperation, can each do different things to help the whole group succeed.
- We can learn to cooperate and work together, even with people we don't initially like or who we see as very different from ourselves.
- Even young students can make a difference when they are working together with others.

It's Just a Game *(Farrell, 1999)*

A soccer team is having lots of fun before the game, singing, practicing, and enjoying their new uniforms. But once the game begins, the coaches are yelling at the students and some of the parents are being critical as well. The children are the ones to remind them:

"It's just a game! It's just a game!

We're only kids. We're not the pros.

We joined the team to learn and play and have some fun.

We'll try our best to win, but if we don't, there is no shame.

Please remember this:

We're only kids. It's just a game."

This book can provide a wonderful discussion about competition:

- What is the difference between competition that is fun for all and competitions that make people feel bad about who they are and how they perform?
- Has there ever been a time when you've tried really hard and been criticized for losing?
- What can the kids themselves do when they see a situation turning competitive in a way that isn't fun anymore?

Teachers can play some of the cooperative games in this chapter and also look for others. It might be particularly interesting for students to contrast cooperative versions of games they have always played competitively, such as baseball or volleyball.

Playing War *(Beckwith, 2005)*

A little boy, Luke and his friends are playing at "war" using sticks for guns and pinecones for bombs and grenades. But Sameer, a child new to the neighborhood, tells them that he has recently come from a country where there is a real war, and the children begin to examine their game. This book provides an excellent opportunity to talk with children about the ways in which their violent games are related to violence in the wider world and the consequences of real war. Opportunities to discuss the experiences of refugees and immigrants are also presented by the book; how do we welcome people to our community and what values do we want to convey by our actions?

The Peace Book *(Parr, 2009)*

This simple picture book about what it means to live in peace and make peace will inspire discussions about the ways in which we make peace locally (in our classrooms and schools) and more globally (in the world).

We Can Work It Out: Conflict Resolution for Children *(Polland, 2000)*

This is a book of photos for young children. Each set of two pages has a key word: *compliments, arguments, kindness, lying,* or *excluding,* and it asks two or three key questions, like the ones listed here.

- *Excluding:* If someone invited your friends to a party and they didn't invite you, how would you feel? Would you want to get even and leave that person out of something special?
- *Selfishness:* What do you do when someone grabs one of your favorite things? If you could have one thing that belongs to a friend, what would you pick? How do you think your friend would feel if you just took it?
- *Acceptance:* Is it okay to feel jealous sometimes? How can you make yourself feel better when you feel left out?
- *Teasing:* Why do some people like to hurt other people's feelings? What is the meanest thing anyone ever said to you? Is it hard or easy to forget those words? What is the meanest thing you've ever said to someone?

Having students respond to these questions and discuss them represents an exceptional curriculum.

Peace Jam: A Billion Simple Acts of Peace *(Suvanjieff & Engle, 2008)*

This inspirational book describes the work of Peace Jam, an international organization that pairs youth with Nobel Laureates in peace, including The Dalai Lama, Archbishop Desmond Tutu, and Rigoberta Menchú Tum. Peace Jam programs include those for children from ages 5 through 19, and all include education, inspiration, and action components in which children are actively involved in projects related to ending racism and hate, halting the spread of global disease, rights for women and children, controlling the proliferation of weapons, and breaking the cycle of violence. The book is accompanied by an inspirational DVD with examples of the students' projects. This project can enable students to see the relationship between their inter-personal behavior and bigger world issues as well as to understand that they can make a difference!

The Blue Ribbon Day *(Couric, 2004)*

Two best friends try out for the soccer team, but only one girl makes it. The other girl is crushingly dis-appointed, but her mother assures her that she will find something else to do that she's good at, another place to shine. In fact, she develops a science fair project that wins a blue ribbon and is proud of herself and able to celebrate her soccer-playing friend's achievements.

Follow-up for this book could include discussions of multiple intelligences and the ways in which people have unique gifts. Students could generate a chart that says, "What I'm good at" and "What I'm trying to get better at," or even "Not my best thing!" Developing realistic assessments of our skills is crit-ical, as well as a sense of humor about the places we struggle!

Friends *(Heine, 1997)*

Charlie Rooster, Johnny Mouse, and fat Percy the pig are good friends. "Good friends always stick together." That's what the friends said. They play hide-and-seek; they find an old boat and play pirate and other similar things. They cooperate in all these activities: they ride a bicycle with one animal on each pedal and one steering. The animals cooperate to sail a boat and to go cherry picking, each standing on another's shoulders. But when the friends try to spend the night together, negotiating sleeping in a pigsty or on a perch, they find that even good friends sometimes have to part.

This is a wonderful book about friendship, support, and fairness. The three animals work together to accomplish things, drawing on the strengths of each member. But they also realize that they are different, that fairness doesn't mean sameness, and that they must accommodate to one another's differences as well.

This book could provide a wonderful starting point for a discussion of both friendship and cooperation: "What are some of the ways you and your friends work together?" "Do you always do things the same way?" "What are some examples of times when you did different things to help one another succeed?" This book could be used for constructing a similarities and differences chart: How are the animals alike, and how are they different. It could also provide an opportunity to discuss problem solving; students or the teacher could generate scenarios or situations that require problem solving and negotiation, and let students work in groups to figure them out and then present them (either through role-play or drawings) to the whole class.

Big Al *(Clements, 1997)*

Big Al is a big scary fish, and all the other fish are scared of him. He tries various solutions to make himself more acceptable to others—wrapping himself in seaweed and hiding himself in the mud. But it doesn't work. Then one day, the little fish are caught in a net, and big Al rescues them by biting through the net. They appreciate him, and then he is caught in the net. But the fishermen take one look at him and let him go. And then he has lots of friends.

This is a nice book about the acceptance of differences. Beyond that, it is a book about how people we don't know or who look different or scary can still be our friends and allies. The relationship between people who are different and fear is an important one to make; when we actually get to know people, we are generally less frightened by them.

Many wonderful books about conflict resolution include the following themes:

- Problems can be resolved without fighting.
- Most problems, even complicated ones, have very elegant solutions if we can put our heads together to think.

- When people try to resolve conflicts through violent confrontation, the results are often painful and always unsatisfactory.
- People often have very different perspectives on a situation; through listening and negotiation, they can work things through.

Barb Streibel (1977) reviewed children's books in an effort to see how these books handled the resolution of conflict and to explore the potential of using children's books to teach alternatives to fighting. She describes goals and guidelines for analyzing and evaluating children's books on problem solving and conflict resolution. The goal of peace education is teaching children methods of creative problem solving. The following questions were used to facilitate evaluation of the books in this category:

- Who, if anyone, accepts responsibility for finding a solution to the problem/conflict?
- How are fears of rejection/failure or needs to save face resolved?
- Is the problem solved? How do you know it is solved? What are the implied standards for a successful solution?
- Is the solution realistic? (Could the same behaviors in real life lead to similar resolutions?)
- Is the solution a direct consequence of someone's actions, or does it occur by chance or by magic? Does the story imply that actions have consequences or that things happen regardless of any plan or problem-solving approach?
- What is the role of adults in the story? What does this teach about children's abilities to solve problems; what does it teach about adult problem solving? Are children encouraged to depend on adults or authority figures for solutions to conflicts?
- Are there patterns along age, sex, ethnic lines in passivity activity, leadership, decision making, or power in dealing with conflict?
- What is the role of aggression or violence (either physical or verbal)?
- What is the role of cooperation or competition?
- Is any decision-making *process* shown? Does this process include exploring alternatives, or is only one solution presented? Are consequences of actions visualized before the solution is enacted? Are any standards presented for evaluating the best alternative?
- Are everyone's needs taken into account in the solution? (Streibel, 1977, pp. 2–3)

This set of challenges can help us think well about all books with conflicts and the lessons they are teaching our students. The following books offer some positive examples; even if they are not perfect, they can be used as teaching tools by thoughtful teachers.

The Butter Battle Book *(Seuss, 1984)*

There is a wall between the Yooks and the Zooks because they are at war. Zooks eat their bread with the butter side down, Yooks with the butter side up. The battle escalates; they make more and more weapons; and at the end, they each hold the ultimate weapon of destruction and stand poised ready to totally destroy each other.

The book ends with ambiguity but makes a wonderful statement about the dangers of escalation and how each side gets angrier and angrier and the situation worse and worse. It is a wonderful tie-in to social studies themes: What does it take to stop the escalation of war? What is the role of weapons in fighting? What are the risks involved in fighting? In stopping the fighting?

Tusk, Tusk *(McKee, 2001)*

A powerful metaphor about war and peace. All the black elephants and white elephants try to kill one another—and they succeed when all are dead. Only the peace-loving black and white elephants survive, and they create gray elephants—what we have now. This book could be linked to a discussion about war, killing, peace, prejudice, and racial violence and hatred.

The True Story of the 3 Little Pigs (Scieszka, 1996)

This retelling of the three little pigs by A. Wolf describes what really happened. It seems the wolf had a cold and sneezed, and the houses just happened to fall down, and the pigs died so he had to eat them for supper. The wolf explains that he is much maligned and people made up the whole story about huffing and puffing and so on.

This is a great book for talking about both sides of the story. Although, when children are upset, they are certain that their perception is "the truth," there is always more to the story than we think, and different people have different perspectives. Teachers could conduct a wonderful unit using the original story of the Three Little Pigs, this book, and the Spanish version, which tells yet another story. This book could also be coupled well with the next book.

The Three Little Wolves and the Big Bad Pig (Trivizas, 2004)

In this wonderful reversal of the traditional story, the big bad pig is after the three little wolves and destroys all three of their houses. After he had blown up the third house (made of stone and concrete), the wolves decide to build a house of flowers. When the pig goes to blow it down, he breathes in the sweet scent and becomes a good pig! The wolves invite him in; they become friends and decide to live together.

This story could be used in several ways. First, it provides a wonderful example of different perspectives and could be used to initiate role-plays and discussions about conflicts that arise when people see the same situation differently. The sequence of the story, in which stronger and stronger houses are no match for the pig, but he is finally transformed by flowers and kindness, could be a wonderful place from which to launch a discussion of de-escalation and the ways in which unexpected kindness to our enemies might be the most disarming strategy of all.

Wolf's Chicken Stew (Kasza, 1996)

A very hungry wolf with a craving for chicken stew decides to fatten his prey by leaving wonderful food (pancakes, doughnuts, and cake) on the chicken's doorstep. But when he finally appears at the chicken's house to eat her, she opens the door and exclaims, "Children, children! Look, the pancakes and the doughnuts and that scrumptious cake—they weren't from Santa Claus! All those presents were from Uncle Wolf!" The baby chicks jump all over him and give him a hundred kisses, grateful for the goodies he has brought them. Unable, then, to follow his original plan, he stays for supper and plans to make the little chicks cookies for the next day.

The surprise ending of this story is about expectations and possibilities. Enemies, once humanized, can never truly be enemies again. Teachers might want to lead students in a discussion about the ways in which not knowing a person or a group can make them appear scary and the ways in which close connection and relationship can alter that perception.

Sam Johnson and the Blue Ribbon Quilt (Campbell Ernst, 1992)

Sam, a farmer, discovers he likes to sew and wants to join his wife's quilting club. They reject him, and he rebels and decides to start his own Rosedale Men's Quilting Club. The two clubs end up competing with each other in the quilt contest. But on the way to the contest, both quilts blow into the mud and get mucky. The only solution is for the men and the women to combine parts of both quilts and complete one beautiful quilt together. They do, and they win the contest.

This is a book with many uses. Issues of sexism and gender exclusion are the most obvious themes: Why can't boys quilt? Why can't girls play football or build rockets? The larger lesson, about cooperation and collaboration, is graphically illustrated by the final, combination quilt and could lead to a rich discussion of teamwork, diversity, and redefining success as working with others toward a shared goal.

Pinky and Rex *(Howe, 1998)*

Pinky and Rex are the best of friends. Pinky collects pink things, and Rex collects stuffed animals. They each have big collections. They go to the museum with Pinky's dad and his sister Amanda. A conflict develops at the museum gift shop when they all want to buy the same stuffed animal. The finally reach a solution by combining their money and agree to shared custody—one on Monday, Wednesday, and Friday the other Tuesday, Thursday, and Saturday, and Amanda on Sunday (she put in 50 cents).

This is another great example of problem solving, compromise, and fairness. The math component of buying shares and partial ownership could easily lend itself to a broader discussion of different economic principles such as rental versus ownership, landlords, and so on. It is also nice to see boys caring about stuffed animals and hugging and kissing them, thus, challenging some stereotypical notions of boy behavior.

LINKS TO THE CURRICULUM

We can think about cooperation not just as something we *use* to teach but something that we teach *about* as well. Nancy Schniedewind and Ellen Davidson (1987) in their powerful collection of teaching activities *Cooperative Learning, Cooperative Lives* share a variety of cooperative teaching strategies and link these directly to the content of cooperation as well.

They suggest having students create learning materials for one another in all subject areas. In math, for example, groups of students might make word-problem books for another group to solve. Students can be encouraged to write world problems that have cooperation as a theme. In spelling, students can take turns creating fill-in-the-blank sentences (which are antiracist and antisexist), which use the spelling words to be learned. In science, students in heterogeneous groups might make ecology booklets. The booklets might contain ideas for encouraging people to recycle, how to dispose of trash, and so on. Regardless of the content, Schniedewind and Davidson (1987) suggest that the following questions could guide students in a discussion of the process:

- In what ways was making up sentences and problems with a group easy? Difficult? Satisfying? Frustrating?
- How was it different to make up examples where people were cooperating? How, if at all, did you have to change your thinking?
- How did it help to have a group making up the examples rather than doing it yourself?
- Were there are anyways that the group made it harder? If so, what could you do about that the next time? (p. 115)

Teachers can think creatively about the examples and problems they give students to solve and ways to introduce concepts of cooperation, inclusion, and antibias teaching into all aspects of the curriculum. Schniedewind and Davidson (1987), for example, have students do the following family math problems:

- Your mother has been complaining that she has to do all the cooking. She has a full-time job and is tired when she gets home. She doesn't think it's fair. So you all decide that each family member will cook dinner one night a week. That works out well because you live with your grandfather, both your parents, and your three siblings. You have a wonderful eggplant recipe from camp. The problem is it serves 42 people! You realize that's too much. You decide to make one-sixth of the recipe. Here's the original. Rewrite this recipe so it makes the correct amount for your family.

- Your family is hosting a block party for a new family in the neighborhood. They are the first Hispanic family to move there, and they've received a few rude phone calls. You hope that gathering friendly neighbors will help them feel at home in the neighborhood. You decide to arrange flowers. You make three arrangements that each have four daffodils and twice as many tulips. You make two arrangements with seven lilies in each. You make four arrangements that each have four jonquils and eight daisies. How many flowers do you need? (pp. 222–223).

Although the math may be standard, the context and the story of the problems provide additional opportunities to talk about issues of racism, sexism, and working together.

Cooperative Learning, Cooperative Lives (Schniedewind & Davidson, 1987) also includes more elaborate curriculum projects that revolve around the theme of cooperation throughout history. Students might study the Underground Railroad (see Chapter 8) as an example of people working together to bring people to freedom. Or students might study about how boycotts are used to present strong messages that a company's product or practices are not acceptable. During the boycott of the Nestle Company for their practices in improperly selling infant formula in Third World countries, children at one school talked directly about the issues involved and how their cooperation (eating other chocolate, writing to the company) could be powerful in making a difference.

8

Speaking Truth and Acting Powerfully

Two days before their big field trip, the students in an inclusive fourth-grade classroom in New York City found out that no accommodations had been made to provide transportation for Tina, who uses a wheelchair, and that she had been told to simply stay home that day. The students insisted that either the field trip be canceled or that alternative transportation arrangements be made. "Tina's in our class," they said, "and it's a class field trip."

When Wilson Elementary School holds its annual book fair, children from each classroom go down to the cafeteria to buy new books. There is often teasing, "I got more books than anybody!" and whispered comments about kids who can't afford any books at all. One child comments defensively, "It's not my fault if I have more money."

Two second graders walk by the desk of a Jewish classmate and draw swastikas on her paper. When the Jewish girl tells the teacher, the teacher yells at the boys to stop. The boys become more covert in their teasing and assaults.

When students in a third-grade classroom realized how badly some of the children from single-parent families felt about the daddy-and-daughter dinner dance at the school, they insisted that the practice be changed. The event was modified so that girls could come with any adult who was important to them in their lives, thus enabling a far broader group of students to attend.

THE VISION

We have already talked extensively about the importance of classroom communities in which children feel safe, nurtured, and respected. The goal of creating classrooms in which children are comfortable with who they are, able to connect well with others, and work to support and help one another is important in and of itself. But the goal of forming close communities goes beyond the community itself. It is in communities that people form relationships and begin to understand some of the ways they are connected to other people. In communities, people learn to draw on the strength of others and to offer their support. Being in one community can also helps us to think about other communities of which we are a part. As I begin to know and care about the people in my classroom community, I can appreciate that there are other communities in which people care about one another, and I can see that I am part of not just my classroom community but also a neighborhood, a city or town, a country, and the world. I can also realize that I can be a part of many communities simultaneously and can make contributions to many different groups. Understanding the nature of community and having a positive experience with other people in a nurturing, safe space can help students set high standards for themselves and for the world. One child commented, "I want my whole life to feel like what it feels like at camp—everyone is nice to one another, and people say appreciations of you all the time."

It is also in communities that people can begin to recognize their power—both as individuals and especially as a cohesive group acting in solidarity. An old labor union song says, "Many stones can form an arch, singly none. Drops of water turn a mill, singly none" (Bones of Contention, 1998). The power of the stones or of the water is the power they have when they are joined together. Individuals can make a huge difference in the world. Many individuals acting together can often make a bigger difference. In community, people discover their collective power.

What might be our goals for our students as they learn to become classroom-community members and citizens of a broader community as well? I would propose the following:

- Students should be informed and aware of issues and problems in the world. They should approach the world with eyes wide open, noticing things that are wrong or unfair, alert to injustices and inequities.
- Students should feel a commitment to making a difference. They should have a sense that what they do matters, that they can make a difference and be willing to expend the energy and time to do so.
- Students should have the skills and strategies they need to take on problems and issues. They must have communication skills (talking to others, asking questions, listening), information-gathering skills (reading, data gathering, and ways to sort through confusing or conflicting information), conflict-resolution skills (what do we do when people don't agree or are getting angry), and skills in bringing about change (letter writing, lobbying, and advocacy).

If these are our goals for students, what is the role of teachers? What must teachers be able to do to accomplish the goal of having students who are informed, concerned, willing, and able to make a difference?

- Teachers must teach students about community and global problems in ways that are appropriate in terms of age and development, neither talking down to students nor overwhelming them with information and feelings that overpower them. Teachers can help their students become fully awake about their lives and the world. This goal implies, of course, that teachers themselves are aware of issues that surround their students in the world, constantly seeking more information and accessing multiple sources.
- Teachers must identify strategies for helping students look at big issues without feeling powerless or sunk ("I'm just one person; what can I do?" or

"Racism's been around for a long time; there's nothing I can do to change it"). Teachers can strive to counteract despair and hopelessness in their students (and themselves).

- Teachers must help students acquire the skills and attitudes they need to act powerfully and make a difference. They can teach students to have not only a strong voice but also one that can be heard. They can teach students to seek the truth but to be careful about jumping to quick or easy conclusions. They can teach students to be thoughtful and effective in building alliances, presenting their point of view well and negotiating conflicts.

It should be noted that the three teacher goals and the three student goals are directly aligned. Both sets of goals can be summarized as the following three-step model:

1. Noticing (that's something wrong)

2. Courage (to make a difference)

3. Strategies (to bring about change)

What are some of the issues that students should be alert to? And most important, what would developmentally appropriate teaching and curriculum look like for each of the following topics.

Oppressions

It is important for students to understand that, both historically and currently, not all people are treated fairly in our society (and elsewhere). Based on the age and maturity of the students, the language and examples used will vary, but teachers should be able to find ways of explaining different forms of injustice, so students can relate to and understand them. I have often found that in explaining issues to children, I must simplify them in ways that increase my own clarity and awareness. "Why does everyone make such a big deal about getting a dark tan and then discriminate against people with dark skin?" "How come some of the children at our school don't have anything for snack or lunch?" "What does the scribbling on the subway, 'Chinks Go Home,' mean, and why did someone write that?" Children's fresh ideas and questions can make us, as adults, take another look at things we may have otherwise come to take for granted.

Sexism: Why and how are girls and boys treated differently? What are some of the things that only boys are allowed to do? Only girls? What are some of the ways that we learn what is appropriate or limited for one gender or the other? What are some of the things boys wish they could do that they're not allowed to? What about girls?

Racism: What can we notice about the ways in which people of different racial backgrounds or colors are treated? What are the effects on all of us of this differential treatment? What people live in my neighborhood? Who goes to my school? Who doesn't?

Heterosexism/homophobia: How do people respond to those whose behavior doesn't mesh with traditional notions of gender and sexuality? Who gets to decide what's right for a girl or a boy to do? How do those decisions limit our options? Why are some children called "dyke" or "faggot" on the playground? Is it okay for two girls to hold hands at recess? Why do people use "That's so gay!" as a put down?

Classism: What are the ways in which differences in income and economic level show themselves in our classroom, our school, and our community? What is the relationship between educational opportunities and income level? Why can't some kids go on the field trip when it costs only $10.00? Why do people tease kids who don't have "the right" sneakers?

Religious oppression: Why are members of particular religious groups harassed or assaulted? How do issues and problems of separation of church and state affect schooling practices and attitudes? Why do we have Christmas off, but the Jewish kids have to come to school on Passover? Why did everyone jump to the conclusion that the Oklahoma bombing was the work of Arab terrorists? How has the treatment of Muslims changed since September 11, 2001, and the attack on the World Trade Center?

Handicapism/ableism: Where did we get our attitudes and beliefs about people with disabilities? How have things changed in society and schools for people with disabilities? What are some ways in which access and attitude are still a problem? Could kids in wheelchairs get around our school? When people can't talk, does that mean they can't think either?

Inequities

In addition to discriminatory and prejudicial behavior directed against specific individuals or groups, there are broader inequities in our society that students are exposed to, if not personally, then through the media.

Poverty/homelessness/hunger: Why don't some people have enough to eat? Where do children whose parents live on the street go to school? What can I do when I see someone who is poor or hungry?

Abuse: Is it okay for grownups to hit one another when they are angry? Is it okay for them to hit me? Why does my dad drink so much? What should I do when I am being touched or talked to in ways that make me uncomfortable? What should I do when I observe abuse of others?

Some might look at the above list and say, "That's too much for kids to handle. I don't want to introduce those topics in my classroom." The truth, however, is that these issues are already present in your classroom: the child who is teased for his thrift-shop jeans, the overweight boy left out of boys' games on the playground, and the Jewish child uncomfortable about the school Christmas play. Many children have daily experiences with poverty, hunger, and abuse. Even those areas that don't affect children's lives directly leak into their consciousness through television, the newspaper, and adult discussions.

The challenge is to address these issues in ways that are developmentally appropriate and relate to children's immediate lives, leaving them with an understanding not only of why these things happen but also what they can do about it at a concrete and immediate level: "What should I do when they call Jared a faggot?" "Is there any way we could celebrate the holidays so that some kids aren't left out?" "Could we figure out a way for everyone in the class to afford the final school trip?"

Not talking about abuse or hunger doesn't make the problems go away. It simply drives them into the realm of "things we don't talk about or learn about at school," leaving children confused (or misinformed) and often depressed and helpless. Teachers can take the first steps in breaking the silence and helping students to recover their voice and power.

Learning to make a difference in the world involves not just learning about oppressions and inequities but also about people who have made a difference. The historian Howard Zinn (quoted in Jones, 2005, para. 1) writes,

Human history is a history not only of cruelty, but also of compassion, sacrifice, courage, kindness.

Zinn (1994) also reminds us that

What we choose to emphasize in this complex history will determine our lives. If we see only the worst, it destroys our capacity to do something. If we remember those times and places—and there are so many—where people have behaved magnificently, this gives us the energy to act and at least the possibility of sending this spinning top of a world in a different direction.

And if we do act, in however small a way, we don't have to wait for some grand utopian future. The future is an infinite succession of presents; and to live now as we think human beings should live, in defiance of all that is bad around us, is itself a marvelous victory. (Zinn, 1994, p. 208)

Teachers can help students operationalize the idea of taking small (and then bigger) steps toward making a difference by teaching students about the following topics.

Resistance and Taking Action

Who, throughout history and now, has taken a stand against discrimination, poverty, and violence? What did they do, and what did they need to know to take action? What are the ways in which students, even very young ones, can act powerfully in the face of discrimination or injustice?

Allies

What does it mean to be an ally to someone else? If I want to be an ally to people who are in some way different from me, what do I need to know? What skills will be helpful to me when I try to stand up for other people or help them to make their lives better? What would it mean to be an *upstander* instead of a *bystander*?

Teachers can help students develop a vision for the world, and they can encourage them to make that vision big rather than small, inclusive rather than exclusive, caring rather than cruel, and hopeful rather than despairing. Schools can be places in which groups of people can work together to remember their original hopes for the world and for themselves, their dreams of a world in which there is a place for everyone to live and work together, enough food and shelter, and an abundance of love and friendship.

Having such a vision for ourselves and our world means reclaiming the often-mocked word *idealism,* not as the starry-eyed ramblings of someone out of touch with reality, but as the goal that things can be better, must be better, and that we can make it so. A button on my wall says, "I'm an unabashed idealist." All good teachers, in their hearts, believe and know that they can make a difference. To teach is to be open to new possibility; to make those possibilities broader for our students as well is the ultimate gift we can give them.

CHALLENGES TO THE VISION

What are the barriers to achieving this vision? What stands in the way of powerful teachers helping to create powerful students? Teachers often respond with reluctance and discomfort to the challenge to take on the big issues in their classroom. The following statements each give us evidence of a barrier to this kind of change-oriented teaching:

I'm not really comfortable with this issue myself; sometimes, I feel pretty confused, so how could I take it on with students?

I don't know enough about this topic myself to teach it right; I might get it all wrong.

Talking about an issue like this could really make things worse; why rock the boat?

I don't dare bring up a topic like this; I could get in trouble with parents, the administration, or other teachers.

I have so much of the mandated curriculum to cover; I simply don't have time for this.

We can think about each of these reactions in terms of our own feelings and behaviors (why might we feel this way?) and how we can overcome this obstacle to our own powerful teaching and students' important learning.

I'm not really comfortable with this issue myself; sometimes, I feel pretty confused, so how could I take it on with students?

I don't know enough about this topic myself to teach it right; I might get it all wrong.

Many of us lack confidence in our own thinking and feeling because we have had little exposure to the issue in question or because our personal responses and thinking have been systematically invalidated. We may ask ourselves, "Who am I to try to fix things? I'm not smart enough or good enough myself to make a difference. I'm only one person; this issue is a lot bigger than I am!"

Looking back at our upbringings and education can provide us insight into the origins and sources of such a response. Some of us were accorded very little respect when we were children. Although children certainly require the ongoing guidance and support of adults, many of the ways in which children are treated display a fundamental disrespect for them as people and individuals. The set of practices by which children are treated with less than full respect and dignity is sometimes called *adultism,* and because it is one of the "isms" we all experienced (we were *all* children!), it can help us understand why taking a stand and acting powerfully often feels difficult or impossible for us as adults. By understanding how some of the ways *we* were treated has affected our ability to act decisively and powerfully, we can think better about empowering our students and ourselves.

When we were young, we were often silenced. "Children should be seen and not heard." "Speak only when you are spoken to." "Because I said so, that's why." There were many occasions in which we felt strongly about something and were either silenced or told we were wrong: "That's not the way it was at all." "You'll understand when you're older." In the earlier example of Musical Chairs, the child who is pushed off a chair, excluded from the game, and cries is often told, "You're not being a good sport. It's just a game. There's nothing to cry about." But to the child, being pushed off a chair and excluded *did* matter, and it *was* a big deal. Being told how to interpret our own reality makes us distrust our instincts and feelings: "Well, I felt sad and upset, but the adults tell me this is just something to get used to—in fact, they say it's fun!" It's not surprising, then, that many of us have difficulty trusting our feelings or speaking up. The extensive campaigns of "just say no" and the difficulties we experience trying to teach children, especially girls, that they have the right to make decisions about their bodies and their lives are evidence of how many of us have been silenced, our own clear thinking discredited.

One night, when I was putting my seven-year-old daughter to sleep, she regaled me with stories and important things she had to tell me. In a burst of admiration I exclaimed, "I love listening to you—you have such important things to say." She looked at me with disbelief and skepticism, "Then how come at school, when we're talking, the teacher says, 'Is what you have to say more important than what I have to say?' And, Mama, some-times it is!"

Often, if we did notice something that confused or troubled us and asked about it, we were yelled at our told to "hush." Questions about people's differences ("Why does that man have such dark skin?" "Why does that woman walk like that?") and about inequities we noticed ("How come you let Michael mow the lawn, but I have to do the dishes?" "Why can't I go to the tennis club that Marianna belongs to?") were often not responded to with full, complete answers. As a result, we may have stopped asking or even stopped noticing the things we used to question.

When our students ask the same (or different) hard questions that we ourselves gave up asking—or gave up the hope of finding answers to—we sometimes feel embarrassed or uncomfortable. One teacher who was deeply troubled by the way students were cho-sen for the gifted program in her elementary school, said, "I'm glad they don't ask me why only some kids get to go—I wouldn't know what to say."

Silencing and invalidation, coupled with our limited exposure to some of the "hard issues" (perhaps there is no racial or ethnic diversity in my neighborhood, or I don't think I know anyone who is gay or lesbian), can make us feel like we have no right (or exper-tise) to address complex societal issues with students.

There are no easy solutions to our own feelings of inadequacy or confusion. In a wonderful children's story, *Dudley Pippin and the Principal* (Ressner, 1974), a young boy begins to cry when he is falsely accused of doing something wrong; then, he is embar-rassed about crying and exclaims, "I'm all mixed up." The principal, a wise and caring person, responds, "Of course. Why should *you* be any different from everyone else? Most people spend their whole lives trying to get unmixed up." Acknowledging how confus-ing issues of race, class, gender, and social justice are is an important step toward over-coming our sense of powerlessness. Understanding that there probably isn't perfect clarity out there shouldn't keep us from moving forward, stumbling but committed.

Certainly, as teachers, we can also take on educating ourselves about the issues around us. One teacher, upon realizing that she would have a very hard time teaching about any religion other than her own, made a systematic effort to meet and talk to people from other faith backgrounds and to find books that would make her feel better informed to deal with her students' questions. Another teacher, reflecting on all the negative things she heard about Mexicans growing up in the Southwest, decided to educate herself about Mexican culture and to study Spanish intensively.

We can also acknowledge to ourselves that if we wait to take on issues until we feel completely informed and comfortable, we may wait forever. At some point, we must "plunge," letting our students know that we ourselves are still learners as well and not positioning ourselves as the sole experts or conveyors of the truth. We can model for our students that there are many sources of information and that any single source is bound to provide a limited perspective. What a powerful example we could set for our students if we said, "We read what the textbook said about the question of illegal immigration in the United States (or slavery or changing family demographics or Christopher Columbus); where else could we look to find more information? What kinds of people or groups might have different perspectives on this topic, and how can we access their understanding and knowledge?"

> *Talking about an issue like this could really make things worse; why rock the boat?*

> *I don't dare bring up a topic like this; I could get in trouble with parents, the administration, or other teachers.*

There is little question that some of the topics already named have the potential to be controversial and contentious. There are those who fundamentally disagree about teaching values of any kind in school and those who disagree on whose or which values should be taught. When Calvin goes home and tells his father, who is watching a cowboys and Indians movie, "It didn't really happen like that," or La Marr tells her mother not to buy grapes because of the farm workers' boycott in California, there may be questions raised: "What are you teaching my child?" "Why are you making trouble? He's never asked these questions before."

Our schooling histories often didn't prepare us to be open-minded about difficult topics, nor are many of us equipped with the skills for managing disagreement and conflict. Nonetheless, becoming a citizen in a participatory democracy demands that students have the ability to engage in critical thinking and a sense of their own agency (the ability to effect change and make a difference).

As some of the examples in this chapter demonstrate, there are ways of contextualizing the teaching of challenging subject matter and keeping all stakeholders informed so as to minimize (although not eliminate) the possibility of volatile, explosive reactions. And if things do become contentious and difficult, students can benefit from watching their teachers negotiate such conflict and multiple perspectives with respect and grace. Teachers must also find places where they can talk to one another about the hard issues, so they can become more aware of their beliefs and feelings and more comfortable with discussion, disagreement, and debate.

If our goal were to teach only those things that would guarantee no criticism or dispute, the resulting curriculum would likely be both boring and inconsequential. Günter Grass says, "The job of a citizen is to keep his mouth open" (Bookrags, n.d., para. 1). How can we teach our student where, when, and how to open their mouths, so they can learn to be effective citizens of their community and their country, if we don't respond to the critical challenges of our own history and present?

> *I have so much of the mandated curriculum to cover; I simply don't have time for this.*

More than ever, now, in this era of No Child Left Behind and high-stakes testing, most teachers are overworked and overburdened. The curriculum is often established by those not in direct contact with students, and standardization has made it even more challenging to engage in culturally relevant pedagogy and responsive teaching. Some teachers report that they have had to give up teaching important content to prepare students for the deluge of testing to which they are subjected.

But it is possible to commit ourselves, as teachers, to a curriculum that makes a difference in children's lives and in the world. Sometimes, this means changing how we teach and how we approach different curricular areas; there are thousands of teachable moments related to diversity, exclusion, and multicultural education throughout the day. Aware teachers can grasp these and incorporate multiple perspectives into their ongoing routines and curriculum. When students are learning to write letters, they can write a letter to someone in a position of power about a concern they have. When learning map-reading skills, we can use maps of places in the world where there is conflict. (It is distressing how many people don't actually know where Iraq is or don't know that Egypt is in Africa.)

Some teachers have also actively resisted efforts at top-down curriculum control individually and collectively, finding ways to "teach in the cracks" as well as to protest the places and ways in which they feel their best judgments about students and teaching are compromised and impeded by external management.

REFRAMING OUR WORK

Beginning With Ourselves

- When you were a young person and were troubled or concerned about something, did you feel that adults took you seriously?
- How often, as a child, were you encouraged or supported in involving yourself in school, community, or national change initiatives?
- Do you have any early memories of thinking that what you were doing was going to make a difference?
- Do you have memories of adults you knew who were working actively to make a difference in the world?
- What issues in your community concern you? Racism? Violence? Poverty? How do you find out about these issues and inform yourself about what's happening?
- Now, as an adult, do you actively involve yourself in efforts to improve your school, community, or nation? How?

Looking at Our Classrooms and Schools

Because the original goals for students centered around three areas (knowledge and understanding of big issues, a willingness to take a stand and make a difference, and the skills necessary to do so) the following questions reflect each of these goals.

Noticing

- Do students notice practices or policies that are unfair and bring them to the attention of the teacher and their classmates?
- Do students identify stereotypes and stereotypical language in books they are reading (i.e., do they notice that in the reading book only the women do the cooking or that the pictures in the alphabet book show "I is for Indian" with a picture of a Native American with a headdress)?

- Do students identify stereotypes and inappropriate language in the media—in TV shows they watch and the movies they see? Do they notice, for example, the rampant homophobia in a movie when a man, so afraid that he had accidentally kissed another man, washes his mouth out with soap and tries to scrub his tongue? Do they recognize that many situation comedies contain racial epithets and humor directed against various ethnic communities?
- Are students able to identify jokes that are racist, sexist, or homophobic? Are they able to identify acceptable jokes to bring to class to share?
- Are students critical enough of their curriculum to notice that what their textbooks or educational videos say may not be the whole story or the same story that others might tell? Do they ask, for example, "I wonder what Native Americans think about Thanksgiving and the ways it's portrayed in the media?" or "I wonder how it feels to people who aren't Christian when all the decorations in the school and the neighborhood and the malls are for Christmas?"

Courage

- After students have noticed that something is not fair or is oppressive in any particular way, are they willing to raise the issue with the teacher? Other students? Administrators? Their parents? Other community members?
- Are students able to seek allies and supporters so that they are able to take on difficult issues?
- Do students generally appear hopeless when they notice an injustice, lamenting the situation but sure that nothing will ever change and that there's nothing they can do; or, are they able to engage in discussions about possible actions or positions they could take?
- Do students see their interests in very individual ways (what I want, what's good for me), or are they able to think about others' perspectives and situations ("If I were Muslim, that remark would really bother me," or "That movie is really offensive to people who are poor")? Can they see others' issues as their own?
- At any even higher level of awareness, are students able to understand that insults and oppression of others should be their concern (even if it's not about them!)?
- Do students see their purview as confined to their situation or classroom (what's happening in our class), or are they able to step back and take a broader view, their vision of justice encompassing their neighborhood, country, and world?

Strategies

- Are students fluent with the ways in which people throughout history have taken a stand: boycotts, petitions, letter-writing campaigns, strikes, and so on? Do they understand why each strategy is used and what the costs and benefits are of any particular way of working for change?
- Do students have the skills they need to write letters to advertisers who promote racist toys, to make polite (but powerful) phone calls to shop owners whose stores are not accessible to people who use wheelchairs, and to write a petition concerning an unfair practice at the local YMCA and seek signatures?

- Do students have repertoires for interrupting oppressive behavior in ways that are likely to be effective? Do they have ideas about what they might do or say if they see someone treating another person unfairly or if they hear someone telling a racist joke?
- Are students able to listen well to others, able to hear their stories without interrupting or becoming defensive, and are they aware that there is much to learn from even the youngest person or one perceived as less competent?

What's the Big Picture?

- What societal issues have manifestations in the school: violence, poverty, racism, homophobia, religious oppression, and the like?
- How can schools work to help students feel that they are powerful in addressing injustice locally and more globally?
- How would schools be different if they were committed to working for social justice?
- How would the world be different if schools were committed to working for social justice?
- Why does this matter?

HOW TO BEGIN

ACTIVITIES

Diversity Treasure Hunt

Chapters 3 and 4 explored ways for students to show themselves to their classmates and get to know others well. This activity can be used to deepen that knowing and to explore areas of difference that can help young people develop empathy and compassion for others as well as awareness of oppression issues.

Instruction: Give each participant a copy of the treasure hunt form and give the following directions:

1. Take your piece of paper, and walk around the room.

2. Find someone to talk to, and ask them which of the questions they can answer for you.

3. Talk to them, and write down what they say.

4. Then, answer one of the questions on their sheet for them.

5. After you have each given one another an answer, say good-bye, and find someone else to talk to.

6. You must talk to 10 different people to answer the ten questions.

7. You must complete the form by talking to one person at a time (pairs of people talking) not by having everyone gather around one person.

8. There is no prize for finishing first, and some of you probably won't get all the spaces filled in. That's fine. It's more important to listen well and remember what people tell you.

Then give students time to complete the form.

Sample Diversity Treasure Hunt

1. Find someone who has accomplished something this year.

   Write his or her name: _____. What did he or she accomplish?

2. Find someone who grew up with an older relative in his or her family. Write his or her name: _____. What did he or she learn from this experience?

3. Find someone who has a parent or a grandparent who came to this country from another country. Write his or her name: _____. What customs or traditions has he or she learned from this person?

4. Find someone who has a person with a disability in his or her immediate or extended family. Write that person's name: _____. What did he or she learn from this experience?

5. Find someone who speaks another language. Write his or her name: _____. Ask him or her to teach you how to say something in that language.

6. Find someone who can tell you a joke that isn't racist, sexist, or offensive to any ethnic group. Who is that person? _____. What joke did he or she tell you?

7. Find someone who has traveled somewhere they thought was interesting. Who is that person? _____. Where did he or she go and what's one highlight of the trip?

8. Find someone who is thinking about trying something new.

   Who is that person? _____. What would he or she like to try, and what kind of support does he or she want?

Nancy Schniedewind and Ellen Davidson (1998) call this activity a People Scavenger Hunt and suggest including questions like the following.

- Find someone who stuck up for a person being put down.
- Find someone who knows a game from another country.
- Find someone who is good at something that isn't typical of his sex (pp. 51–52)

The possibilities are endless. What is important is to include items that many students in the class will be able to respond to. It is also fine to use the Diversity Treasure Hunt activity as a way to call attention to particular students and their gifts or strengths. Some teachers develop this activity after conducting a personal inventory or interview with each student and can then focus specific questions on specific children (i.e., "Find someone who worked this summer bagging groceries?" or "Find someone who has moved to your town in the last month?" or "Find someone whose hobby is collecting pictures of Elvis"). If this option is chosen, the teacher must be sure that every child will be the answer for at least one or more questions. Care should be taken not to include items that overly emphasize material and class differences (i.e., "Find a person whose family got a new car this summer," or "Find someone who went to Disneyworld").

When it appears that many people have completed the form or you sense that it is time to move on, gather the students in the circle to debrief. Paying close attention to the process of debriefing is as important as the content of the activity itself. The teacher calls on someone (perhaps moving around the circle) and asks, "Milood, who did you find for number one?" Milood says, "I found Nikita." The teacher asks, "What did Nikita tell you?" (If it is a large group where people don't yet know one another by name and face, ask, "Where's Nikita?" and make sure that everyone recognizes who is being discussed.) After Milood has shared what Nikita said, call on the next person to respond. I generally find it works best to hear several responses to each question (i.e., the next person also tells whom he found for Question 1. If he also talked to Nikita for Question 1 or didn't find someone for Question 1, ask him to tell you who or what he found for Question 2 rather than skipping the student. Work your way around the circle, making sure that each person gets a chance to respond. About three-quarters of the way through, check with the group by asking, "Who haven't we heard about yet?" (Students may be shy and unwilling to say, "No one has talked about me yet.") Encourage other students to identify who hasn't been featured yet in one of the responses. If by the end of the go around, no one has mentioned talking to Amin or Jacinta, for example, ask, "Who talked to Amin? Which question did he answer for you, and what did he tell you?"

With upper-level elementary students or older, it can be very helpful to actually process your thinking as a teacher about this aspect of the sharing: "Why did we go around the circle and make sure that everyone spoke?" "Why was it important that we hear about every member of our class?" Help students to understand the added richness of hearing every voice in the community.

Then, talk about the content of the questions. In the version shared previously, it is possible to talk about the many different kinds of families that are represented in the classroom (Maria lives with her grandmother; Rico has a brother with cerebral palsy) and about differences in language and cultural background (Yael taught everyone how to say, "How are you?" in Hebrew, and Xiong taught people how to count to three in Chinese). Discussing where people's relatives came from can be helpful in reminding students that we are, with few exceptions, a nation of immigrants and that "real Americans" look many different ways. Asking students to share something they are proud of accomplishing can provide a wonderful occasion to illustrate that being successful (or pleased) about an accomplishment isn't a competitive activity and that we can be happy that Marquies learned to ride his two-wheeler, that Amin painted his room, and that Carolyn got to visit her big sister without comparing these to determine the best or biggest accomplishment. The discussion of Question 6 (about the jokes) can be particularly enjoyable and educational. Although students are laughing and enjoying themselves, it may be possible to talk about the ways in which jokes are often used to hurt people of different groups (Jews, blacks, people from Poland, blonds, people with AIDS, people with disabilities, and so on) and that it is possible to laugh and have a good time without it being at the expense of another person or group. This kind of consciousness-raising activity can have beneficial spin-offs throughout the year. Perhaps the teacher could have joke show-and-tell once a week, with the proviso being that the jokes fit the category described. Having students listen to jokes with new ears, alert to stereotypes and cruelty and filtering these through their new awareness can provide a powerful learning experience for individuals and the group.

Speaking Up/Speaking Out

Ouch Policy

One of the goals identified in taking a stand against injustice is noticing that something is wrong or unfair. Because many of us have led segregated lives—perhaps not a lot of connection with people who are Hispanic, Jewish, Muslim, gay or lesbian, and so on—we may not be aware of the ways in which people who are not like us in every way feel or are treated by society. One useful strategy for classroom teachers is to establish an *ouch policy* in their classrooms. Having an ouch policy means that if someone says something that hurts your feelings or pushes your buttons in some way, rather than ignoring them, bad-mouthing them to your friends, or blaming yourself for being oversensitive, you get to say, "Ouch." When, for example, someone makes an unkind remark about fat people or unconsciously repeats a racial or ethnic stereotype ("My mother really Jewed that guy down at the market yesterday"), other students can say, "Ouch." When someone has said "ouch," they are given an opportunity to tell what they felt or what they heard, not as an attack on the person who said it, but as a way of bringing the issue to awareness and raising consciousness among classmates. Using an ouch policy can be seen as an incredible teaching opportunity, and teachers must be thoughtful about modeling how to respond to others: "When you said that fat people are lazy, that really hurt my feelings because my dad is really heavy, and I hate it when people say that because he works really hard," or "When you said that stuff about people with AIDS deserving to die because they're sinners, I don't think that's true. AIDS is a contagious disease, and many people have it. I don't think we should call people names because they are sick."

Teachers who are confident about their teaching can invite students to use the ouch policy with them as well. The other day, as I was leading a game activity with a group of students, I joked with them, saying, "Come on evwebody—wets get in a circle!" A student rightfully pointed out to me that using language like that made it sound like I was making fun of people who lisp or have speech impediments. I quickly apologized and used that opportunity to acknowledge my thoughtlessness.

Oops Policy

A complementary policy states that if you say something wrong or inappropriate and recognize it, you can immediately say, "Oops!" Most of us have had that experience of saying something and—even as it was leaving our mouth—realizing that it didn't come out right or may be offensive. This practice allows students to be self-reflective about their language. Again, the teacher can also model saying "oops" as a way of emphasizing that all of us make mistakes and all of us can grown in thoughtfulness and sensitivity as a community of learners.

Speak Outs

One of the most powerful tools used in antibias work with adults is called a *Speak Out*. In a carefully structured, safe environment, people of different groups are asked to address several questions:

- What's good about being _____ (Jewish, Latina, Native American, Muslim, from a large family, adopted, and the like)?

- What's hard or challenging about being _____?
- What things do people say or do related to this characteristic of yours that really troubles or upsets you?
- What would you like from your allies, friends, and supporters?

These same questions can be adapted to the age and maturity of students in the class. There are several ways to structure such an activity. If students are comfortable with it, the teacher can form a panel of experts who are willing to share what they know with the whole group. If that kind of visibility or being singled out feels too intimidating or otherwise inappropriate, the teacher might simply ask volunteers to respond to various questions while all students remain seated in a circle. The activity can also be done anonymously, with students writing their contributions on scraps of paper, which are then read by the teacher or another student, making clear that people are reading something they didn't write.

In addition to the groups that we typically think about as being oppressed or discriminated against in society (different racial, ethnic, or religious groups), students also bring many other characteristics to the classroom that can be sources of exclusion or teasing. One group of students, for example, who lived in a low-cost housing project, shared what was good about living in the projects (lots of people to play with and easy access to their friends), what was hard (lots of noise and high crime rates), and what they didn't want to hear from others (that their parents were lazy or bad for living there or that only losers live in the projects).

In a class with considerable religious diversity, students shared what they loved and appreciated about their religions as well as what was hard. A Muslim student commented, "Stop asking me if I'm starving during Ramadan. It's our fast time, and I eat before sunrise and after sunset, and I feel fine about doing it." A Jewish student shared, "It's hard for me when everyone is making such a big deal about Christmas and asking me what I got. Chanukah isn't such a big-deal holiday for us, and it was over three weeks ago!"

It is obvious that initiating this level of deep sharing depends on the prior establishment of a tightly woven, safe community. It is unwise and unfair to ask students to reveal personal struggles and issues if there is a high likelihood that they will be teased or excluded based on their sharing. The teacher must revisit the firm guidelines (hopefully established early in the year) about respectful listening, confidentiality, and safety. This is also a perfect time to reiterate lessons on how one asks respectful questions of others: "What is the meaning of the medallion you wear around your neck?" rather than "What's that stupid thing you wear?"; "How does it feel for you when everyone else is eating hot dogs, and you're not allowed to have any?" as opposed to "Gosh, I bet not being able to eat hot dogs makes you really mad you're Muslim!"

Learning to Be Allies

What's an ally? An ally is someone who stands with or for another person. Learning to be allies is an important next step for students after they understand various oppression issues. Becoming an active ally is the *doing* component that makes real the *knowing* portion of learning about injustice and inequality.

After students have engaged in speak outs or have discussed other ways in which people of color or people from different ethnic or religious groups are discriminated against or are the subjects of prejudice, the next question is, "So, what do I do if I notice this happening?" One useful way to begin the discussion is as follows.

- Seat students in a circle, and go over some of the isms they have been studying. This might follow having read any of the books described in this chapter or after some incident has occurred in the classroom or the community.
- Ask students to think of times when they witnessed some kind of oppression. This might be someone ignoring a child, who is waiting to be served, in favor of an adult (adultism); making a racial slur about African Americans (racism); one student calling another a faggot or a lezzie (homophobia), and so on.

- Then, ask students to think about a time when they stopped or took action when they saw or heard something oppressive happening—or a time when they didn't.
- Have them share their story with a partner.
- Ask students to think and talk about the following: (1) What were the conditions or characteristics of the situation that made you feel able to do something about the oppression? (2) What were the conditions or characteristics of the situation that made it hard for you to do something? Students will likely share issues of power ("It was my teacher who said something sexist, so I didn't know what to say"), relationships ("It was someone I'm good friends with, and I knew it would be okay even if he got mad at me right then for telling him not to do that"), and knowledge ("I knew it was wrong—but I didn't know what to do or say," or "I was afraid that if I said something, I'd get in trouble or make it worse").

From there, engage students in a discussion of strategies for "interrupting" oppression, perhaps by using role-plays:

- You're on the playground, and one of your friends tells you not to invite Marcus to be in the game because he's a homo. What do you do?
- Three of you are planning what to do over the weekend, and one of your friends proposes a plan that you know the third person won't be able to afford. What do you say?
- One of the students in your reading group starts making fun of a student in a lower reading group, calling him a retard and telling him he reads baby books.
- Have students generate role-plays based on incidents that have occurred, particularly those about which they were confused.
- Generate, with students, a list of things they might say when they see an injustice being perpetrated.
- Make sure that students understand that there may very well be situations in which it is inappropriate or dangerous for them to say or do anything. Encourage them to bring such events or situations to you privately, if they want to discuss them, or to write them in their journals for possible response.

I have often found a three-step response to be important when dealing with others' oppressive comments, and this can be taught to students. (I learned this strategy from educator Beth Blue Swadener.) First, stop the behavior or the comment. Second, educate the person who is making the comment about the reality of the situation. Third, leave the person with their dignity and self-respect intact. Students might practice these skills, for example, by saying, "I know that you're a really good person and wouldn't want to hurt anyone, but I'm really uncomfortable with jokes about Indians. And it's also not true that they get everything paid for by the government and that they're all lazy and alcoholics."

Obviously, to be successful with these three steps, students must recognize the stereotype or misinformation contained in the joke or comments and be knowledgeable about the actual facts or situation. Thus, learning to interrupt oppressive behavior presents multiple teachable moments: "When Garret made that comment about AIDS being the fault of gays, I knew it was wrong, but I didn't know what to say," or "I 'm sure that Jews don't use Christian children's blood to make matzoth, but I didn't really know what matzo was made from to tell him."

The children's book *Say Something* (Moss, 2004, detailed in the book section that follows) and the children's song "I Think of a Dragon" by Nancy Schimmel (n.d.) are both excellent ways to talk about ally building.

ThinkB4YouSpeak (GLSEN, n.d.)

This campaign, coordinated by the Gay Lesbian Straight Educators Network (GLSEN), encourages students to think carefully about the negative labels and terms they are using to describe people. The Web site includes episodes from popular television shows as well as a powerful ad campaign designed to encourage students to be active allies in challenging oppressive language and behavior.

Interrupting Oppressive Jokes

One of the most age-appropriate ways to discuss issues of oppression with students relates to jokes. Encourage them to listen carefully to the jokes they hear being told (and the jokes they themselves tell) for examples of racism, sexism, homophobia, disability oppression, ageism, and so on. Whole generations of jokes (moron jokes, Polish jokes, blond jokes, and the like) are testimony to the pervasiveness of oppression passed off as humor. Unfortunately, an evening of TV watching will generally provide more than enough examples of inappropriate and oppressive language and behaviors. Set aside a time of the day (or week) for students to share jokes that aren't oppressive, both as an opportunity for fun, to increase their personal repertoire of appropriate jokes, and as a way of demonstrating that ending oppression doesn't have to leave them somber and without a sense of humor! Talk with students about how to interrupt oppressive jokes in ways that work for them, perhaps trying a humorous approach themselves, "Yikes—I don't want to hear this joke on an empty stomach," or "Quick, call the humor squad; Dave's about to tell another inappropriate joke." It is hard to state what will or will not work with individual groups of students, and different students will need to develop their own repertoires for dealing with inappropriate humor.

Curriculum

Two key components can be identified in thinking about creating classroom communities where children are able to think and act powerfully. The first is that the curriculum must be developmentally and age appropriate, drawing from children's real lives rather than imposing an outside agenda. The second is that teachers must couple teaching about the issue or the problem with some proactive response or possibility so that students do not feel overwhelmed and powerless. Each of the following examples, working from young children to older students, provides an example of pedagogy and curriculum that builds on students' real lives and experiences.

Group Activism in a Preschool

In *Anti-Bias Curriculum: Tools for Empowering Young Children* (Derman-Sparks & A. B. C. Task Force, 1989), Bill Sparks, a special education teacher, describes an ongoing project dealing with the parking space for people with physical disabilities at his school (see Box 8.1).

BOX 8.1

The project began when a parent who uses a wheelchair couldn't get into his child's classroom because there was no handicapped parking at the school. The teacher began the activity by taking the children to look at parking spaces for people with disabilities and talking about the symbol. They discussed the importance of access and then looked at their school. The students agreed to make a handicapped parking spot for their school. The students used blue paint, an *H* stencil to paint on the ground, and a handicapped parking sign. Everyone participated. When people parked inappropriately in the spot, the students suggested tickets, something they knew about, and each child dictated a few tickets. While the problem has not been completely solved, it has been greatly reduced, and the children learned a real-life lesson about advocacy (Derman-Sparks & A. B. C. Task Force, 1989, pp. 79–80).

The previous example is exciting because the situation requiring change was one easily visible and understandable by young children. It enabled them to make sense of a bigger issue (discrimination against people with disabilities) by addressing a specific, concrete manifestation in their immediate frame of reference. And rather than leaving them feeling sad or upset about what they noticed, they were able to actively participate in painting the parking lot and writing tickets. The ripples of this activity are likely to be broad—reminders to parents and other adult drivers not to park in handicapped parking spaces and an increased noticing of other places that are inaccessible and demand modification.

Preschoolers Take on Sexism

In JoAnne William's day-care center, the teachable moment arose when the students went on a field trip to visit a local fire station. In his book *The Good Preschool Teacher*, educator William Ayers (1989) describes what happened (see excerpt in Box 8.2).

BOX 8.2

All the children had sat in the truck, tried on boots and hats, and examined the sliding pole . . . As the group was preparing to leave, Caitlin said, "So, Jimmy, when are you going to get a woman firefighter around here?" Caitlin and her friends Megan and Britt, as well as several other children, had been interested all year in the news that women were becoming firefighters in New York. JoAnne had brought in pictures from newspapers and magazines of the women in training, graduating from the fire academy, joining their engine companies, fighting their first fires . . .

Jimmy's response was not encouraging. "Women?" he roared. "I hope never. We don't want any women here." The kids were shocked; Jimmy tried to explain.

"Listen, this is dangerous work and it's hard. This is not work for a woman."

Caitlin and Megan were holding hands now. "This isn't fair," said Caitlin angrily. "Yeah," Megan said. "Women can do anything" . . .

Back at school, they wrote lots of letters to the women firefighters, the station house, the fire commissioner, and the mayor. (Ayers, 1989, pp. 59–60)

The teachable moment (thinking together about discrimination and injustice, figuring out who to write to, actually writing and mailing the letters) illustrated in Box 8.2 could not have occurred if previous groundwork had not been laid. The students had already (at three, four, and five years old) been encouraged to think about the world around them, the way it was, and the way they wanted it to be.

Standing Up to Racism

Even very young children can learn to take a stand when they have the support and guidance of a concerned adult (as illustrated in Box 8.3).

BOX 8.3

In Barbara Skolnick Rothenberg's first-grade classroom at Fort River Elementary School in Amherst, Massachusetts, a concern for diversity and social justice pervades everything she does. Barbara worked with the first graders to have the arrow removed from the Pilgrim's hat (the symbol on the Massachusetts thruway signs). The students talked about how inappropriate it was to imply that the Native Americans attacked the Pilgrims. The students wrote letters to the local newspaper, the governor, and the state representatives about this issue. The turnpike sign was changed, and the first graders got real proof that they could make a difference!

Middle Schoolers Address Handicapism

While living in Cleveland, I worked with a seventh-grade social studies teacher at an integrated middle school to design a two-week minicourse designed to teach seventh graders about exceptionalities (Sapon-Shevin, 1988). The goals we decided on included (1) an understanding of the term *disability,* stressing the extent to which we all have abilities and disabilities; (2) an understanding of the ways in which society creates barriers to full integration through physical barriers and attitudes; and (3) the ability to generate, understand, and practice specific strategies for addressing and redressing some of the barriers students had identified.

The students read articles on disability oppression, viewed films, and listened to speakers with disabilities. The final two days of the project, students shared their projects, which had been drawn from one of three possible assignments (see Box 8.4).

BOX 8.4

1. Students were asked to complete an accessibility checklist for their school and for one other public building. Students were then asked to write a letter to the principal or owner detailing their findings, explaining what corrections needed to be made, and providing a rationale for these modifications.

2. Students were asked to read fairy tales that contained a character who was different (*Beauty and the Beast, The Ugly Duckling, Rumplestiltskin, The Frog Prince*) or a book with a character with a disability (*Summer of the Swans, Leo the Late Bloomer, Dummy, Peter Pan*) and then either rewrite the story from the perspective of the character who was different, or change the story (perhaps by writing a new ending) to eliminate the stereotypes of the characters with disabilities.

3. Students were asked to look for examples of disability humor; images of people with disabilities; and put-downs based on physical, emotional, or behavioral challenges in their daily lives. This involved listening to records, watching television (identifying people labeled or treated as though they had a disability); listening to conversations of friends for references to people with disabilities ("He's a real retard"); and examining television, newspaper, and magazine advertising. One student, for example, noted that people use "hearing impairment" as a way of denoting stupidity—characters who don't hear well are portrayed as being out of it, unintelligent, and the like.

After completing the lessons, students were eager to use what they had learned and to put into action plans to counter the personal and institutional discrimination they now saw around them. The letters they wrote reflected their insight into the difficulties experienced by people with disabilities.

One student detailed a long list of the ways in which the school's physical facilities were inadequate, including that the central office was up a step and therefore inaccessible to someone in a wheelchair. He asked, "What if I were expelled and my mom were in a wheelchair, and she had to come sign me back in and couldn't even get into the office?"

One student ended her letter by saying, "I think it would be much better to start making these changes one at a time, slowly, when we have time to think about them, instead of waiting 'til the last minute and having to do them all at once." Clearly, those still wrestling with implementing the Americans with Disabilities Act wish they had followed this student's advice.

Rethinking Columbus

The 500th anniversary of Columbus' arrival in America was the occasion for the publication of *Rethinking Columbus* (Bigelow, Miner, & Peterson, 1991), a virtual treasure trove of information and teaching strategies related to teaching not only about Columbus Day but also about the history of Native Americans in the United States, stereotypes, and misconceptions about Native Americans and ways to take action in the face of prejudice and discrimination. A second edition, *Rethinking Columbus: The Next 500 Years* (Bigelow & Peterson, 2003) contains new information, including a role-play that puts Columbus on trial, new poems, articles, and activities.

One of the articles, "Native Americans: What Not to Teach" by June Sark Heinrich (2003), gives direct advice:

- Don't use alphabet cards that say *A* is for apple, *B* is for ball, and *I* is for Indian (equating Native Americans with things like apples and balls doesn't teach respect).
- Don't talk about Indians as though they belong to the past; about 2 million Native Americans live in what is currently the United States, and their issues and struggles are contemporary and not simply historical.
- Don't lump all Native Americans together (there are hundreds of native groups, each with their own language, name, and culture). Don't "study the Indians." Study the Hopi, the Sioux, the Nisqually, the Apache.
- Don't expect Native Americans to look like Hollywood movie Indians, and don't expect all Native Americans to look alike any more than all Europeans look alike. (pp. 32–33)

In an article titled "Columbus and Native Issues in the Elementary Classroom," fifth-grade teacher Bob Peterson (2003) describes his antistereotype curriculum:

- Concretely explain some stereotypes and try to make analogies with children's own experiences. For example, explain that some native nations used feathers for ceremonial purposes but that many others did not. Ask students how their family dresses for special occasions and ceremonies such as weddings. Point out that it's a stereotype to think that all people of their ethnic background always dress as if they were at a wedding. Likewise, it's a stereotype to think that all Indians dress with feathers all the time.
- Explain how stereotypes are used to make Indians seem inferior or less than human. Don't limit our critiques to textbooks. Some of the most common stereotypes are in children's favorites like *Clifford's Halloween* by Norman Bridwell (1986) in which Clifford uses a feather head dress to dress up as an Indian, or Maurice Sendak's (1991) *Alligators All Around* in which the alligators are imitating Indians by wearing feather headdresses, carrying tomahawks, and smoking pipes. Also, look at stereotypes in society at large, such as in the names of sports teams or cars. Talk about the Washington Redskins or the Jeep Cherokee, or Winnebago motor homes. Ask if the children know any other cars or sports teams named after nationality groups.
- Have children read books about Columbus, talk about the ways in which books present stereotypes and distorted information, and respond to the following questions:

  o How many times did Columbus talk?
  o How many times did we get to know what he was thinking?
  o How many times did the Native people have names?
  o How many times did the Native people talk?
  o How many times did we get to know what the Native people were thinking?
  o What do you learn about Columbus' life?
  o What did you learn about Native people's lives?
  o Does the book describe the Native people's feelings?
  o Does the book describe how Columbus treated the Native people? (Peterson, 1998, pp. 36–38)

Each of Peterson's suggestions could easily be adapted to a wide range of reading levels, interest areas, and ages. The potential for weaving in history, math, language arts, and creative writing is extensive.

Teachers might want to link any of the previous activities to a close reading of *Encounter* by Jane Yolen (1996) or to the song "1492" by Nancy Schimmel (1992, and see www.cowin.com/changetheworld), which share Native American perspectives of Columbus' arrival in America. Teachers can use Columbus Day as an opportunity to present students with the idea that there are multiple perspectives to most events and that hearing from all sides is important when trying to sort out the truth. Ways in which to combat racism against Native Americans in this country in the present can also grow from the Columbus Day teaching.

SONGS

Songs can be used in several ways to help students understand the issues involved in taking a stand (Sapon-Shevin, 1994b). Several wonderful songs provide examples of students taking a stand against something that is wrong. It is also important for students to know about the history of struggles for liberation and justice that have rich musical traditions associated with them. The civil rights struggle, the efforts of workers to form unions to combat dangerous and cruel work practices, the women's movement for equal rights—all of these have given us songs that model solidarity, working together, and tackling injustice. Knowing these songs is an important part of knowing the history of our country and its struggles.

Songs About Taking a Stand

"Hey Little Ant" (Hoose & Hoose, 1998)

Preparation

Prior to playing or singing the song, put students in small groups. Ask each group to complete the following format with as many answers as they can. "If I were a _____, a _____ would feel big/small to me." After they have generated a list, ask them to extend it as follows: "If I were a _____ (from previous list), I'd want to be treated _____ (how)?
Then play or sing the song.

Hey, Little Ant	
1. Kid: Hey, little ant down in the crack Can you hear me, can you talk back See my shoe, can you see that? Well now it's gonna squish you flat	2. Ant: Please, oh please do not squish me Change your mind and let me be I'm on my way home with a crumb of pie Please, oh please don't make me die
3. Kid: Anyone knows that ants can't feel You're so tiny you don't look real I'm so big and you're so small I don't think it will hurt at all	4. Ant: But you are a giant and giant can't Know how it feels to be an ant Come down close, I think you'll see That you are very much like me

(Continued)

(Continued)

Hey, Little Ant	
5. Kid: Are you crazy? Me like you? I have a home and a family too You're just a speck that runs around No one will care if my foot comes down	6. Ant: Oh, big friend you are so wrong My nest mates need me cause I'm strong I dig our nest and feed baby ants too I must not die beneath your shoe
7. Kid: But my mom says that ants are rude They carry off our picnic food They steal our chips, our bread crumbs too It's good if I squish a crook like you	8. Ant: Hey, I'm not a crook, kid, read my lips Sometimes ants need crumbs and chips One single chip can feed my town So please don't make your shoe come down
9. Kid: But all my friends squish ants each day Squishing ants is a game we play They're looking at me, they're listening too They all say I should squish you	10. Ant: I can see you're big and strong Decide for yourself what's right and wrong If you were me and I were you What would you want me to do?
Narrator	
Should the ant get squished; should the ant go free? It's up to the kid, not up to me. We'll leave the kid with the raised up shoe. What do you think that kid should do?	

Used with permission from Phil and Hannah Hoose. Available at www.heylittleant.com

After hearing or reading the song, have small groups discuss the following:

- How would you feel if you were the ant?
- How would you feel if you were the child?
- What should the child do?

Follow-Up Activities

- Have small groups of students act out the song, using the ending they have decided on.
- Have small groups of students write what they feel the child should do.
- Have students draw a group picture of the scene in the song, including their ending (perhaps a cartoon panel).
- Have students write a group letter to the kid, telling him what they feel he should do and why.
- Have each group member adopt an identity (the ant, the ant's mother or sister, the child, the child's friends) and create a role-play in which they give their feelings about the situation.

Extend the discussion as follows:

- Have you ever felt like you were being picked on because of your size?
- Have you ever felt like you were being picked on because of some other difference?
- What are some situations in the news in which one person or one group discriminates against another because of size or another difference?
- What are some ways people can work together to take a stand when they see something wrong?

"Courage" (Blue, 1990)

Preparation

Prior to playing the song or reading the words, put students in small groups. Ask them to answer the following questions:

- Has there ever been a time when you felt like you didn't have friends or were being treated unfairly?
- What kinds of support would you want from people if you were in that situation?
- Have you ever seen someone being treated unfairly? What did you do? If you didn't do anything, what kept you from doing something (fear, didn't know what to do, scared to get in trouble, or something else)?

After hearing or reading the song, have small groups discuss the following questions:

- How did this song make you feel?
- What memories did this song bring up for you?
- Has there ever been a time when you have felt like Diane?
- What kinds of support would you want from people if you were Diane?
- (If this class has a strong sense of community and it feels safe, ask the following question.) Are there any groups of students in our school or community who get treated like Diane? How do you feel about it? What could we do about it?

Follow-Up Activities

- Have small groups of students act out the song or develop a role-play that tells the story.
- Play the song, and have small groups of students dance or do movements to the song.
- Extend the song: imagine that it's the next day, and you have invited Diane to the party. Have students assume roles (Diane, other students, the teacher, and so on) and develop the story of what happened next.
- Have students create a word and picture web around the word *courage*. "What does the word courage mean to you? What are some ways people show courage?"
- Have students discuss an issue they are faced with that involves taking a stand. Have the group formulate an action plan for taking a stand or write a group letter to a person they feel could take a stand with them.

Have students discuss the following questions:

- Would you have been able to do what the singer did (invite Diane)?
- What are some examples of people who have taken a stand for something they believe in? (Rosa Parks, Martin Luther King, Dolores Huerta, Wilma Mankiller, Dorothy Day, and so on)
- What risks do people face when they take a stand?

- Discuss the references in the song: Auschwitz, Japan, and My Lai. What happened in each of those situations? Who took a stand? Who didn't? What might keep people from taking stands? What were the results?

"Walls and Bridges" (Pirtle, 1993)

Sarah Pirtle (1994), who wrote "Walls and Bridges," describes how to use the song with students:

Prior to playing or reading the song, set up small groups of two to four students. Ask the groups to guess what the song might be about, based on the title. Each group can write down its guesses.

Three other songs that deal with the importance of speaking up and speaking your mind can also be used as part of lessons with students. The following questions are appropriate for all of the songs:

- What are the things you find it easiest to speak up about?
- What are the things you find it hard to speak up about?
- With what people are you comfortable giving your opinion? Disagreeing? Taking an unpopular or unusual position?
- When are the times you would like to say something even though you find yourself silenced (either by yourself or others)?
- What would it take for you to take a stand when you see something wrong or something that needs addressing?
- What kinds of allies would help you to take a stand?

"Speak Up" (Pirtle, 1998)

This is another powerful song about speaking up when something is wrong and learning to use your voice to challenge situations and people that are oppressive.

"What Can One Little Person Do?" (Rogers, 1999)

This song speaks to each person's ability to make a difference. It uses examples of famous people who have made a difference and talks about how even young people can change things for the better, particularly if they work together.

"Some Rights in this World" (Nigro, 1994)

This song is about every child (and every person's) right to be treated fairly and be safe. Discussion could include individual rights as well as violations of human rights that must be addressed to make a better world.

Songs of Struggle and Solidarity

Although many of these songs have become famous, they each arose from particular historical events. Students can be helped to learn history through song, studying the underlying issues that framed the event in question, and understanding the ways in which people worked together to change things.

"We Shall Overcome" (Horton, Hamilton, Carawan, & Seeger, 1964)

This song was originally a black spiritual but was frequently sung at the freedom marches led by Dr. Martin Luther King, Jr. The civil rights struggle brought about many important changes for people of color in the South and throughout the United States in the 1960s. The folk music book *Rise Up Singing* (Blood, 2005) says that this song went from being gospel to union to civil rights to antiwar in focus. What a wonderful way for people to understand the interconnectedness of struggles for freedom.

"If You Miss Me at the Back of the Bus" (Neblett, 1963)

This song commemorates the role of Rosa Parks and the Montgomery, Alabama, bus boycott. At that time, black people were required to give up their seats to white people and to ride at the rear of the bus. As part of a nonviolent change action committed to protesting this policy, seamstress Rosa Parks refused to give up her seat on the bus, sparking a successful bus boycott that cost the bus company so much in lost fares that they ended their discriminatory policy. The story is one of both personal courage and collective effort, a powerful example for students.

"I'm Gonna Sit at the Welcome Table" (Watkins, 1963)

Another turning point in civil rights' history was the boycott of the lunch counters at certain drugstores in the South. Because of the stores' policy of serving whites only, black college students throughout the South held sit-ins at lunch counters in protest. Eventually, management ended this practice, agreeing to serve people of all races. The story of the lunch-counter boycotts is an excellent teaching example about economic sanctions against discrimination. Students might be led in a discussion of their economic power, limited though it is. Where they shop, where their parents or guardians shop, and what they buy can all be used as ways of discussing economic sanctions. Students might be particularly interested in investigating boycott efforts which have been successful in bringing about change, for example the lettuce and grape boycotts in California to protest unsafe working conditions and the national Nestle boycott to protest the selling of infant formula in economically underdeveloped countries leading to massive infant deaths. With specific reference to this song, students might want to discuss what it means to sit at the welcome table and how this might be translated in their classroom or cafeteria. Are all children welcomed, or are some shunned and excluded?

"We Shall Not Be Moved" (Derived from an old spiritual)

This song was originally a spiritual but became a song of the labor union movement in the 1940s when thousands of farm workers (sharecroppers) refused to be driven off their land by the landowners for whom they worked. The song has become a standard in the union movement and has been adopted in many union struggles for better pay and safer working conditions.

"Step by Step" (Traditional Irish Melody United Mine Workers Song)

Weiss (Weiss, Prutzman, & Silber, 1986) describes this song:

> This song was a United Mine Workers' song. At first the coal miners were afraid to strike even though their wages were not enough to feed their families properly. The coal mine owners had threatened never to give them back their jobs if they went on strike. Finally, together, they called a strike. After many months, the owners, who could not run their business without the miners, gave in, raised the miners' pay and recognized their union. (p. 72)

In addition to understanding the historical significance of this song, the underlying message is a powerful one as well. No task of any importance is every accomplished immediately, without struggle, and without the efforts of many people. What issues that we are now facing in our classroom and in our world will take the collaboration the hearts, and the minds of many different people working together? What small step can each of us take to end racism, to work for justice, to end poverty, and to provide adequate housing for all?

"Study War No More" (Traditional)

This song was also a spiritual and is now a general peace song. The song speaks to individual responsibility to "laying down one's sword and shield" and to not studying war. What do children think is meant by "studying war"? How would we "study peace" instead? What personal actions can they take to lay down their swords and shields? This may have very concrete implications for schools in which guns and weapons are a problem, or it can be extended to a discussion of the other "swords" we use to hurt others (cruel remarks, taunting, and exclusion).

"May There Always Be Sunshine" (Botting, Oshanin, & Ostrovsky, 1964)

This is known as the Soviet Children's Peace Song, and it is sung widely in Russia. The song speaks to the universal and eternal hope for peace and the importance of committing to that goal. Although the Cold War is officially over, many people still harbor fear and prejudices about those in other countries, uncertain whether "they" want peace the same way (and as much) as "we" do. This song specifically focuses on the horrors of nuclear war and destruction and is a powerful statement of hope and solidarity across borders.

CHILDREN'S LITERATURE

There are many excellent children's books that can be used to address the issues related to inequities and social justice. The following represent books related to four broad themes, moving from more-general to more-specific issues.

Hard Realities (Poverty, Hunger, and Homelessness)

Unfortunately, many children have direct experience with issues of poverty and hunger. Even children from more-privileged homes are often aware, from newspapers and television or from their own observations, that there are people who are poor, living on the street, and hungry. The following books could be used as part of a unit on these topics; the goal might be to introduce children to these concerns by using children's literature and to expand this awareness to a commitment to a project or projects designed to make a difference. Although the books could be viewed as depressing, it is actually the reality that is upsetting, and teachers can help students to take proactive steps in the face of hardship and poverty rather than feeling overwhelmed or hopeless.

Fly Away Home (Bunting, 1993)

A homeless boy, Andrew, lives at the airport with his father. They move from terminal to terminal trying not to be noticed. They cooperate to try to find food and places to clean up, finding support from other homeless people in the airport, all of whom help one another (another woman watches Andrew when his father goes to work on the weekends). Andrew is given hope by seeing a bird that finds out how to escape.

   This book certainly deals with hard truths (there are homeless people, and there are children with no homes). As such, it is a difficult book. A teacher might want to follow such a book with discussions of the status of homeless people in the local community and services and people who are helping them. Students might want to generate projects for raising money; volunteering personal services; or collecting used clothing, food, and the like.

Uncle Willie and the Soup Kitchen (DiSalvo-Ryan, 1997)

A little boy goes with his Uncle Willie to the soup kitchen to feed people who are hungry. He has seen the Can Man collecting cans and an old woman sleeping on a park bench. These make him sad and scared. The boy moves from being afraid of the people and the situation to a position of great compassion and understanding. The book deeply humanizes the street people who eat at the soup kitchen, giving them names and stories. The story describes the work of the soup kitchen, how it gets donations from businesses, and so on. The boy feels good to have helped and made a difference in people's lives.

This book is a wonderful introduction to talking about poverty, homeless people, and the like. The countering of "otherness" is a striking way to talk about how we are often afraid of and distant from those whom we see as different, but that building a relationship transforms that fear. This book could be a wonderful way to initiate a project on positive and productive responses in the face of poverty, hunger, and despair. The book includes information about soup kitchens, and teachers could invite in representatives of local soup kitchens and food cupboards to talk to the class as well.

The Lady in the Box *(McGovern, 1997)*

This book tells the story of a little boy, Ben, and his sister who try to help a woman who is living in a box above a heating grate near a deli close to their home. The children bring her food and warm clothing and eventually involve their mother as well. When the owner of the deli tries to force the woman, Dorrie, to move, Ben's mother appeals to his sense of justice, and she is allowed to stay. The family also starts serving food at a food kitchen.

A Shelter in Our Car (Gunning, 2004)

After her father dies in Jamaica, Zettie and her mother come to America in search of a better life. They now live in the city in the backseat of their car while Mama tries to earn money to get an apartment. Children taunt her at school, and the book describes the indignities of having to wash in a park restroom and scavenge for food. This book is bound to occasion discussion and empathy as well as a desire to do something, and that is supported by the book's ending.

Homeless *(Wolf, 1995)*

This book, a photo essay, tells the story of Mikey, an eight-year-old who is homeless. Along with his mother, stepfather, sisters and brothers, they deal with the homeless shelters, his fifth school in a short time, food stamps, and case workers. This is an authentic look at what life is like for Mikey and his family. There is nothing maudlin about it, but there is no effort to make it sound adventurous either.

This book could start a wonderful discussion about what it's like to be homeless and why it happens. It would be particularly useful for talking about not blaming people for their life situations, particularly in these challenging economic times: "If you were homeless, how would you want to be treated?" "Are there homeless people in your community?" "Is there anything you can do to help?" Older children could be engaged in a discussion about the differences between "charity" models and those that actually empower (with dignity and respect) the people they are designed to help.

An Angel for Solomon Singer *(Rylant, 1996)*

Solomon Singer lives in a hotel for men in New York City. He is very unhappy because he can't have any of the things he loves: a balcony, a porch swing, a picture window, or a pet. He wanders the street at night dreaming of his life as a young boy in Indiana. The book explains, "Solomon Singer was lonely and had no one to love and not even a place to love, and this was hard for him." But then Solomon starts going to The Westway Cafe, where the menu reads, "where all your dreams come true." He develops a warm relationship with a waiter (named Angel), and his life brightens considerably when he begins to come to the cafe every night and finds that he hasn't lost his dreams. The book concludes, "Solomon Singer has found a place he loves and he doesn't feel lonely anymore."

This book speaks powerfully to the ability of people to find joy and connection in the most unlikely places under the most difficult of situations. Like *Uncle Willie and the Soup Kitchen* (DiSalvo-Ryan, 1997), this book puts a real face on people whose lives are difficult and on the margins. Teachers might want to lead students in a discussion of the ways in which they can reach out to those who are lonely and living on the fringes.

The Hundred Dresses *(Estes, 2004)*

This book, now a classic, tells the story of Wanda Petronski, a poor Polish girl who lives in the poor section of town and wears the same faded blue dress to school every day. The other girls tease her unmercifully, and Wanda tells them that at home she has "a hundred dresses." One of the other girls, Maddie, struggles with the situation; she is poor herself but doesn't want to risk losing favor in the eyes of Peggy and the more popular girls by standing up for Wanda. The story reaches its climax when it turns out that Wanda is an incredible artist and has drawn a hundred dresses. Unfortunately, by the time she wins the drawing contest with her skills, her father, angry and tired of the way his family is treated, has moved away, taking Wanda with him. The girls' discussion of their own roles in making Wanda feel unacceptable and uncomfortable is powerful and convincing. Maddie feels particularly bad about the chain of events and concludes,

> "If she overheard anybody picking on someone because they were funny looking or because they had strange names, she'd speak up. Even if it meant losing Peggy's friendship. She had no way of making things right with Wanda, but from now on she would never make anybody else so unhappy again." (p. 61)

This book, perfect for a read-aloud, explores issues of classism in a way that makes them accessible to even younger readers. The ways in which the other girls wrestle with their own roles in oppressing Wanda and the understanding of silencing—not wanting to interrupt teasing for fear of being teased oneself—serve as wonderful examples of the difficulties of ally making and taking a stand.

The Rag Coat *(Mills, 1991)*

Minna is a poor girl living in Appalachia. Her father used to work in the mines but became ill and died. She is unable to go to school because she has no coat to wear when it gets cold. A group of women called the Quilting Mothers gather at her house every day to sew and tell stories. They offer to make her a coat from scraps of quilting material. When her new coat is ready, Minna wears it to school proudly. But the other children tease her, and she runs to the wood to think. Her papa's words come back to her: "People only need people and nothing else." She goes back to school and tells her classmates that her coat is full of stories about everybody there. She then shares with them the story of particular scraps of fabric—one scrap was part of a little boy's baby blanket that he was wrapped in as a newborn. Another scrap is from Clyde's pants that he always wore when he went fishing with his grandpa. Her classmates apologize.

> "Minna, I sure am sorry we ever said anything bad about your coat."
>
> "I wouldn't blame you if you didn't let us touch it."
>
> "I wouldn't blame you if you didn't want to be our friend at all."
>
> "Friends share," I said, and I let them each touch their rag.

This beautiful book deals with poverty, differences, cooperation, and acceptance. Students might want to talk about making quilts for those in need, perhaps joining a group that is making quilts for babies born with AIDS or children in homeless shelters.

Following are some wonderful sources of ideas for engaging students' in projects that directly address the above issues.

The Complete Guide to Service Learning: Proven, Practical Ways to Engage Students in Civic Responsibility, Academic Curriculum and Social Action (Kaye, 2003)

A Kids' Guide to Hunger and Homelessness: How to Take Action! (Kaye, 2007)

The Kids' Guide to Social Action: How to Solve the Social Problems You Choose and Turn Creative Thinking into Positive Action (Lewis, 1998)

Having students actually do something is the best antidote to feelings of despair and hopelessness.

Illness and Death

Good Luck, Mrs. K.! *(Borden, 2002)*

All the third graders love their teacher, Mrs. Kempczinski, who teaches them sign language, talks to them about all the places she's traveled, and lets them bring their skates and Rollerblades for recess. They especially love that she tells them that, in addition to being third-grade explorers and astronauts and scientists, they are teachers as well and that she wants to learn from them. They even celebrate Worm Day.

One day, Mrs. K isn't there, and then the days stretch into weeks. It turns out that she has cancer. The students make cards and write notes. At the end of the year, Mrs. K comes back to see the class.

This is a sensitive, powerful book about children's first encounter with cancer. The teacher is lovingly portrayed, and the children are told the truth about their teacher's absence. This is an important book for talking about dealing with challenging issues and the importance of truth telling and offering support.

Always My Brother *(Reagan, 2009)*

This is the story of Becky's grieving, acceptance, and recovery from the death of her best friend and brother, John. This book can be useful in helping students understand that grieving is a process rather than a singular event and that they can play an important role in supporting classmates who have experienced such a loss. Discussions about what to say and do to someone who has experienced a death in the family can be very important to students (and teachers) who struggle with what they should do in such cases.

Always and Forever *(Durant, 2004)*

When Fox dies, Mole, Hare, and Otter are devastated. There were so many things that Fox did with and for them that they feel they can't go on. But a visit from Squirrel allows them to tell stories about who Fox was and all the things they loved about him.

> They sat together often on Mole's bend, in Hare's garden, full of Otter's pie, recalling happy times. As they laughed, they felt they could hear Fox laughing, too, as if he were still there with them. And in their hearts and their memories and their laughter, Fox *was* still there, part of their family, beloved friend and companion—always and forever.

While death may end a life, it does not end a relationship. The class could make memory books for people who have passed away, including relatives, friends, and classmates.

The Blue Roses *(Boyden, 2002)*

When Rosalie is born, Papa, her grandfather, plants a red rosebush under her bedroom window. Papa teaches her to love gardening; and when she is nine, she gets her own garden plot. Papa talks to her about what to do when plants die, digging them back into the soil to make the other plants stronger.

When Papa dies, Rosalie misses him very much, but she has a dream that helps her to see that Papa is now in a different garden and to make peace with his absence.

What Do You Know About Death and Dying? *(Sanders & Myers, 2005)*

Part of a series for older students, the book contains sections on death, dying, what happens after you die, reactions to loss, grief, and learning to cope. The book acknowledges a wide range of beliefs and customs about death and could be a useful discussion starter.

War and Violence

Many children grown up with a steady diet of books and movies that glorify war and fighting. From Saturday-morning cartoons in which conflicts are resolved violently, to a history curriculum which is taught from one war to the next, children may come to believe that violence is inevitable or even the best solution. These children's books present different glimpses of the effects and aftereffects of war, and can be a useful way to talk about the need to develop and promote nonviolent solutions to conflicts.

Silent Music: A Story of Baghdad *(Rumford, 2008)*

This picture book tells the story of a young boy, Ali, who lives in Iraq. He loves soccer, music, and dancing; but most of all, he loves calligraphy. He practices writing with his special pen and loves the way the ink looks on the page. When war begins—and continues—in his country, Ali writes words about the frightening nights of bombing. He finds it is easy to write the word for war and difficult to write the word for peace.

This is an excellent story of a boy who is very much like other boys but who is dealing with the tragic challenges of living in a war zone. Students can certainly empathize with his difficult situation and reflect on the commonalities and differences in their lives.

Half Spoon of Rice: A Survival Story of the Cambodian Genocide *(Smith, 2010)*

This book tells the story of nine-year-old Nat who is forced out of his Cambodian home when the Khmer Rouge comes into power. Before he is reunited with his family four years later, Nat experiences brutality, forced labor, and hunger; but he also makes a friend who helps sustain him.

This book spares few details about the realities of war and will require careful debriefing with students, but it will do much to disabuse students of the "glories" of war.

Faithful Elephants: A True Story of Animals, People and War *(Tsuchiya, 1997)*

This book tells the story of events at the Tokyo Zoo in 1943. The world was at war, and bombs fell daily on the city of Tokyo. The Japanese Army feared that if bombs damaged the zoo, wild animals might run free and hurt people. Therefore, they ordered the zookeepers to put all the big animals to death. Lions, tigers, leopards, bears, and big snakes were killed first. But killing the three elephants, John, Tonky, and Wanly, who were dearly loved by the crowds of visitors, was a long and painful process for the zookeepers.

This poignant story describes not only the effects of war on the animals but also on those who had to put them to death. This book is read over the radio in Japan on August 15 every year as a message of hope for continuing peace. This book provides an important reality check for students whose exposure to television violence has made them believe that after people are shot they simply get up and walk away. Although the book will no doubt sadden children, teachers can use the book to talk about small acts of peacefulness within their reach.

The Wall *(Bunting, 1992)*

This picture book is about a father and his young son who come to the Vietnam Veterans' Memorial in Washington, D.C., to find the name of the grandfather that the little boy never knew. The muted illustrations convey the sadness of the experience, and although the father says that he is also proud that his father's name is on the wall, the little boy says that he'd rather have a grandpa to play with, telling him to button his jacket because it's cold.

The book accurately describes the sadness of loss brought about by war and connects that loss to a specific child's life and story. Teachers can use this book to help students to understand the devastation of war and the importance of less-violent conflict resolution. The power of the memorial (and of the book) is the portrayal of war as an activity in which real people (with real names) die, leaving behind other real people who grieve.

Taking a Stand Against Prejudice and Discrimination

There are many excellent books that deal with different forms of prejudice or discrimination. The following books have in common an examination of the ways in which individuals or groups can take a stand against fear, misinformation, and unjust behavior in order to make things better, in whatever small or big ways are possible.

Refusing to Be Enemies

These books deal directly with the ways in which fear of the unknown or rumors about a person can keep people from connecting. They also describe the courage needed to stand up to injustice.

Rose Meets Mr. Wintergarten *(Graham, 2003)*

The Summers family moved into their new house, and all the family members got busy trying to fix up their new home. Next door lived Mr. Wintergarten; everyone on the street told stories about Mr. Wintergarten—he was mean; he had a dog like a wolf, he had a crocodile, and he ate people! The children were all terrified. But one day, Rose's ball went over the fence into Mr. Wintergarten's yard. Although the other children advise her to forget the ball, Rose gets flowers and cookies and goes to pay a visit to Mr. Wintergarten. Rose finds that there is a dog (but no wolf) and that Mr. Wintergarten is a rather sad man, eating by himself (but not eating children!). Rose's visit prompts Mr. Wintergarten to open his window, retrieve Rose's ball, and kick it back over the fence to her. Thus begins a transformation in Mr. Wintergarten's life and the life of the neighborhood. The front and rear panel illustrations tell much of the story, with Mr. Wintergarten's house transformed from a dark, gloomy, fence-enclosed, overgrown property to a light, airy house with the fence removed.

This picture book tells a powerful story of personal courage in confronting a situation that others are reluctant or unwilling to take on. At a deeper level, Mr. Wintergarten changes from a scary, isolated man who has become locked in a prison of rumor and fear to a person desperately seeking human connection and affection.

Teachers might want to explore the following questions with students: "Can you think of anyone you know who other people are afraid of and who might be looking for kindness or an entry into the community? What was there about Rose's expectations and behaviors that enabled her to cut through Mr. Wintergarten's isolation?"

Smoky Night *(Bunting, 1999)*

In this book about the riots in Los Angeles, Daniel and his mother look out of their window at the streets below. There are looters breaking windows and stealing; Daniel is scared. A fire forces them from their apartment building, and in the chaos, Daniel loses his cat, Jasmine. Mrs. Kim, a Korean storeowner, with whom Daniel and his mother don't associate, loses her cat, too. When Daniel, his mother, and Mrs. Kim end up at the same shelter for the night, both cats are returned to their owners by a firefighter who says that he found them howling underneath the stairs. "They were so scared they were holding paws," he reports. As the two cats enjoy a saucer of milk together, Mama notes, "I thought those two didn't like each other." Daniel explains, "They probably didn't know each other before. Now they do." With this bit of wisdom, the adults reach out to one another and realize that perhaps they would also like one another if they knew each other better.

This beautifully illustrated book deals thoughtfully with a child's perspective of rioting and the roots and effects of violence and prejudice. The book might occasion important discussions about how not knowing one another can lead to distance, prejudice, and—ultimately—violence. Teachers could explore the many ways we can get to know others well and the necessity of reaching beyond preliminary impressions or dislikes.

The Other Side *(Woodson, 2001)*

Clover, a black girl, and Annie, a white girl, live side by side, separated by a fence. Their parents have told each of them that they can't cross to the other side of the fence. As they grow more and more curious about one another, Clover finally approaches Annie, and they sit on the fence together. Soon, they are jumping rope together. The book ends, "'Someday somebody's going to come along and knock this old fence down,' Annie said. And I nodded. 'Yeah,' I said. 'Someday.'"

This simple picture book explores the pain and isolation caused by segregation. Neither of the girls fully understands why they are being kept apart or why they can't be friends. This book could be used from a historical context, talking about the civil rights movement and desegregation. But it could also be used to talk about fences and borders that *still* exist, keeping people apart. This could include segregation of children with disabilities, Jews and Palestinians separated by a wall, the treatment of immigrants and undocumented residents, and so on.

Ask students:

- Why do people make fences?
- What keeps people from crossing fences?
- What could you do to take down a fence in your life?

Stand for Children *(Edelman, 1998)*

This book, beautifully illustrated with quilts, was written by Marian Wright Edelman, president and founder of the Children's Defense Fund. The text describes the importance of making a commitment to protecting and nurturing every one of our nation's children. Discussion could center on how close we are to meeting this commitment and what we can do individually and collectively to move forward. The book ends with things that each person can do to make a difference.

For Every Child a Better World *(Kermit the Frog, as told to Gikow & Weiss, 1993)*

This statement by the United Nations is about what every child needs—a home, medicine, the right to go to school, peace, and so forth. Easily accessible, the book is a strong statement about what each child is entitled to. Older students could compare this book with the United Nations' Children's Rights campaigns.

Speaking Up

Say Something *(P. Moss, 2004)*

In this book, a young girl witnesses the mistreatment of her classmates—students who are teased, pushed in the hallways, and excluded at lunch and on the bus. Although she is troubled by the way the children are treated, she is somewhat self-congratulatory about her own stance, saying, "I don't do that"; "I don't say that."

Then, one day at lunch, the girl has to sit alone, and she becomes the object of painful teasing herself. After her tormentors leave, she sees that there are kids she knows sitting nearby who have witnessed her mistreatment. When she goes home and tells her brother she is angry at the kids at the other table, he says, "Why? They didn't do anything." "Right," she says. The next day, she sits next to the girl on the bus who has been excluded.

The book is a powerful starting point for a discussion about taking a stand and saying something or doing something rather than being a passive observer. Discuss the book with students, and have them practice what they might say or do when they witness mistreatment in their school or classroom.

Shiloh *(Reynolds Naylor, 1991)*

When eleven-year-old Marty Preston sees a dog being abused by his owner, he doesn't know what to do. When the dog runs away to Marty's house, the young boy struggles between listening to his parents' request to return the dog and his own conscience, which urges him to protect the endangered animal from cruelty.

This is a powerful story of a true moral dilemma, and there are no easy answers. Marty wrestles with competing ethical principles (honesty, stealing, and protecting those in danger) and finally is able to construct an "elegant" solution which saves Shiloh (the dog) and allows Marty to see the dog's master as a full (although deeply flawed) human being. Marty's powerful indignation at cruelty and injustice and the difficulty of his decisions are wonderful starting points for discussing the challenges of being an ally.

The Librarian of Basra: A True Story From Iraq *(Winter, 2005)*

When the invasion of Iraq reached the town of Basra in 2003, chief librarian Alia Muhammad Baker managed to rescue 70% of the library's collection before the library burned nine days later. This is a wonderful (true) story of heroism, collective action, and the importance of books and reading to promote peace and visions of a better future.

The Principal's New Clothes *(Calmenson, 1991)*

This is a retelling of the Emperor's New Clothes. A brave little girl tells the truth and informs the principal that he is wearing only his underwear and that his new suit is invisible. No one else had been willing to tell the truth because they were worried what others would think of them. When the truth is finally out, the children all give Mr. Bundy items of clothing so that he won't be naked.

Although the story itself is lighthearted, the message is powerful. What gets in the way of people speaking the truth? How does fear of what others will think keep us from doing the right thing? How can we support one another in truth telling?

Click, Clack, Moo: Cows That Type *(Cronin, 2000)*

Farmer Brown has a problem: his cows like to type, and all day long, he hears click, clack, moo. Worse yet, they start writing him notes making demands for better living conditions. When he refuses to give them electric blankets for the cold barn, they go on strike and tell him there will be no milk. Soon, the cows are speaking up on behalf of the hens as well. When he still refuses to meet their demands, the hens go on strike too—no eggs. Farmer Brown writes back, and there ensues a battle of wills. Duck, a neutral party, serves as the mediator, and a deal is struck—they will give up their typewriter in exchange for electric blankets. But it's not over—soon the ducks demand a diving board for the pond.

This is a fantastic book for discussing unions, strikes, civil disobedience, solidarity, and the power of numbers to make a difference.

Courage *(Waber, 2002)*

This delightfully illustrated book talks about many kinds of courage, from the "awesome kind" (trapeze stunts) to the "everyday kind" (jumping into the pool from the diving board).

Courage is nobody better pick on your little brother

Courage is being the new kid on the block and saying, flat out, "Hi, my name is Wayne. What's yours?"

Courage is the bottom of the ninth, tie score, two outs, bases loaded and your turn to bat

Courage is starting over

Courage is holding on to your dream

A wonderful way to begin a discussion of different kinds of courage, the book could inspire students to name, write about, illustrate, and honor people's courage through classroom rituals and ceremonies. Perhaps students who have been courageous in combating stereotypes or reaching out to include another child could have "Hero" badges or be otherwise recognized as a way to open more-powerful discussions of ally building and resisting oppression.

Wangari's Trees of Peace: A True Story from Africa (Winter, 2008) and
Planting the Trees of Kenya: The Story of Wangari Mathai (Nivola, 2008)

These two books tell the story of Wangari Mathai, winner of the Nobel Peace Prize for her work in Kenya. The founder of the Green Belt Movement, Mathai was deeply alarmed when she returned to Kenya after college in the United States and found the streams dry, the people malnourished, and the trees gone. These books tell the story of her courageous and important work to restore the trees and, as she said, "plant the seeds of peace."

These books offer a powerful look at the many ways one can "make peace" in the world, including protecting and nurturing the physical environment. Students might be inspired to create community gardens and plant trees in areas that have been damaged by human and environmental violence.

The Carpet Boy's Gift (Shea, 2006)

This is the story of Nadeem, who works in a rug factory in Pakistan as a bonded laborer. Trapped and unable to go to school or play, Nadeem is inspired by a former carpet boy, Iqbal Masih, to organize the children in the factory and escape their bondage.

Although the story is fictional, Iqbal Masih was a real child who worked to liberate child workers and who was shot and killed when he was only 12. Children may be inspired to explore issues of child labor and to take action to support only companies that work to make the world a better place (and to boycott or resist participation with those that don't).

Resisting Racism

White Socks Only (Coleman, 1999)

A young African American girl walks to town in Mississippi to see if it's really hot enough to fry an egg on the sidewalk. When she gets thirsty and sees a "Whites Only" water fountain, she takes off her shoes and steps up to the fountain with her clean white socks. A big white man yells at her and removes his belt to beat her. Other black folks from the church come up and drink from the fountain as well, and then the "Chicken Man" who folks say knows things "all the way from Africa" intervenes and frightens off the angry crowd. The tormentor is never seen again, and the "Whites Only" sign is removed from the water fountain forever.

This book tells a story from the time of segregation in the South and the accompanying anger and fear. This book could be linked to some of the songs described in this chapter ("Back of the Bus" and "We Shall Overcome"), and teachers might want to discuss the ways in which small acts of resistance can encourage others to act in solidarity and support.

Freedom Summer (Wiles, 2005)

This book tells the story of two friends, Joe (who is white) and John Henry (who is African American) who live in Mississippi shortly before and after the passage of the Civil Rights Act in 1964. Because John Henry has not been allowed in the public pool, they have spent many hours swimming together in the creek. After the Act is passed, they are excited to swim in the pool together, only to find that rather than integrating the pool as required, the town fills the pool with tar.

The depth of prejudice and the challenges of changing peoples' hearts and minds (even after legislation) will provoke powerful discussions among students. Teachers may want to ask what other policies or practices the students know about now that are discriminatory or unfair, and how they might respond.

Remember: The Journey to School Integration *(Morrison, 2004)*

This photographic essay with simple text tells the story of the desegregation efforts surrounding the Supreme Court ruling in *Brown v. Board of Education.* The pain, the power, and the courage of those who resisted racist attitudes and behavior is eloquently told in a way that will interest students of all ages.

Teammates *(Golenbock, 1992)*

This book tells the story of the integration of baseball through Jackie Robinson, the first African American to play on a major league baseball team. The book describes the segregation of the south (separate hotels, restaurants that refused to serve African Americans, etc.) and the abuse and humiliation that Jackie experienced even after he joined the Dodgers. But it is also the story of Pee Wee Reese, who publicly declared his support for Jackie Robinson in a dramatic display of solidarity on the field.

This is another excellent book for talking about prejudice and discrimination and the power of one person taking a stand. Teachers might want to discuss these and similar questions: "What do you think Jackie Robinson was thinking and feeling when the crowd booed and jeered at him?" "How do you think that felt to the white players?" "What was there about Pee Wee Reese that allowed him to take such a strong stand?" "What would have happened if Pee Wee Reese had gone along with those who were abusing Jackie?" "What if he had remained silent?" This is another excellent book to link to a discussion of becoming allies and developing the skills necessary to be an effective and thoughtful ally.

Let Them Play *(Raven, 2005)*

In the segregated South of 1955, all the little league teams are composed of only white players. The all-black Cannon Street YMCA All-Stars team is formed with the hope of securing a spot in the state's little league tournament. But all the white teams withdraw from the league rather than play against the black team; adult prejudices rule the day. Despite the cries of the crowd to "Let them play!" the only field time they are allowed is some warm-up practice.

Students will clearly be struck by the injustice of these events and inspired to think about ways in which segregation and racism still take their toll.

Boycott Blues: How Rosa Parks Inspired a Nation *(Pinkney, 2008)*

This book tells the story of Rosa Park's refusal to move to the back of the bus and the beginning of the Montgomery bus boycott, an important event in civil rights history. It is critical to help students understand that, contrary to many myths, Rosa Parks was not just a simple seamstress who was "tired" and decided spontaneously to refuse to move. Rather, she was carefully chosen and trained in civil disobedience at the Highlander Center, where she prepared to be a leader in the struggle against segregation and injustice.

Claudette Colvin: Twice Toward Justice *(Hoose, 2009)*

Although most students (and teachers) have heard about Rosa Parks, few know the story of Claudette Colvin, who, nine months earlier than Rosa Park's famous act of resistance, did the same thing on a bus in Montgomery, Alabama. Rather than being celebrated, however, Claudette was shunned and deemed a poor model by the black leaders of the movement. Despite her poor treatment, she went on to take another powerful stance when she challenged desegregation a year later. This book, for older readers, is full of historical artifacts, interviews, and lost history. It will occasion not only an excellent discussion about the civil rights movement and nonviolent resistance, but it can also lead to a discussion about why we know certain stories and have never been told others. It might lead students to investigate other pieces of "lost" history, for example, the role of Bayard Rustin in the movement and why his story has been minimized.

Two additional books for older readers address the struggles for racial integration and the civil rights movement.

The Watsons Go To Birmingham—1963 *(Curtis, 2000)*

This book, for older readers, tells the story of 10-year-old Kenny and his family, the Weird Watsons of Flint, Michigan. The story paints a rich portrait of this African American family as they experience the joys and challenges of daily life. Poverty, teasing, friendship, and love are explored in realistic and often-humorous detail. When the family decides to go visit Grandma in Alabama, the Watsons become part of a tragic moment in history, the bombing of a church in Birmingham in which four young girls are killed.

Perfect for reading aloud to students, this book embeds issues of racism and prejudice within the context of a warm and loving family. The book's epilogue gives a brief history of the civil rights movement and concludes,

> [There] are boys and girls and women and men who have seen that things are wrong and have not been afraid to ask, "Why can't we change this?" They are the people who believe that as long as one person is being treated unfairly, we all are. These are our heroes, and they still walk among us today. One of them may be sitting next to you as you read this, or standing in the next room making your dinner, or waiting for you to come outside and play. One of them may be you. (p. 210)

Mayfield Crossing *(Michaeux Nelson, 2002)*

The time is the 1960s, and school integration has come to the South. When the children from Mayfield Crossing, a small, integrated community get reassigned to Parkview School, which had been all white, they confront prejudice and discrimination. They are harassed, teased, accused of cheating when they do well, and not allowed to play baseball with the other children. The Mayfield Crossing children band together to challenge the Parkview children to a championship game and learn some important lessons about friendship and solidarity.

In addition to the themes of racial prejudice and discrimination, the children from Mayfield Crossing also deal with their own prejudice toward, "Old Hairy," a strange man who lives in their community. This is a wonderful book for talking about prejudice and friendship and the ways in which children can work together to address social injustice and make a difference.

In an era of growing debate about immigrants and their place in the United States, it is important to explore this topic thoughtfully with students. The growing diversity of the United States makes it crucial that students understand that with the exception of Native Americans, the United States is a nation of immigrants. Students need to understand that people came to this country willingly and unwillingly (as slaves) and that immigrants continue to face discrimination and prejudice despite the enormous contributions they have made and continue to make to all areas of our society. A curriculum developed by the aMaze project (www.amazeworks.org) identifies learning about immigration as an important curricular goal. They identify the following objectives as critical for students:

Students will

- Learn about, respect and learn from the cultures and lives of immigrants in their community.
- Understand that immigrant families enter this country for many reasons, including a search for a better life and as refugees, to escape persecution and war.
- Identify the difficulties that immigrant families might face such as prejudice, racism, language barriers, separation from loved ones, poverty and culture shock.
- Identify ways to be welcoming and supportive to newcomers at school. (aMaze, 2002–2009)

The following books can be used to meet these objectives.

Who Belongs Here? An American Story *(Knight, 1996)*

This book tells the story of a young boy from Cambodia, Nary, who flees for his life from civil war to safety in the United States. Although he is thrilled by his freedom and safety, some of his classmates call him a "chink," a "gook," and tell him to "Get back on the boat" and go back where he belongs. The book asks readers to think about what (and who) would be left in our country if everyone whose ancestors came from another place was forced to return to his or her homeland. Through the story of one young immigrant, the book also talks about the history of immigration in the United States and some of the important contributions made by past immigrants. A teacher's guide is available with many ideas for using the book as part of social studies curricula, to teach creative writing and problem solving, and to encourage an appreciation of cultural differences.

This book can be an important starting point for discussing the ways in which past immigrants have been treated and what they have contributed, and to link that discussion to the current situation. The book provides the opportunity for practicing the ally skills (discussed earlier in this chapter). Talk to students about what they would want someone to do or say if they were getting teased like Nary. Ask, "what would you need to know in order to respond effectively (and accurately) to the exclusion or teasing of immigrants?" Role-play possibilities abound in this book, and it is appropriate for students of many ages; the pictures make it accessible to young children, and the extensive text (which teachers could summarize) provides excellent information for older readers.

Molly's Pilgrim *(Cohen, 1998)*

The children in Molly's third-grade class all make fun of her imperfect English and her "old country" clothes. Molly and her family fled to the United States from Russian after the Cossacks burned down their town and their synagogue. When the children in the class are asked to make pilgrims for the Thanksgiving display, Molly's mother interprets the word *pilgrim* as someone who came to this country for religious freedom and makes a little doll dressed like she dresses, because, by this definition, she is a pilgrim! With great reluctance, Molly brings the pilgrim doll to school where the other children make fun of her. The teacher intervenes swiftly and powerfully: "Listen to me, all of you. Molly's mother is a pilgrim. She's a modern pilgrim. She came here, just like the pilgrims long ago, so she could worship God in her own way, in peace and freedom." The teacher goes on to explain that the American Thanksgiving is linked to the Jewish harvest holiday of Tabernacles (or Sukkoth) and encourages Molly to invite her mother to school. Molly is reassured. "I decided if Mrs. Stickley actually invited her, it was all right for Mama to come to school. I decided something else, too. I decided it takes all kinds of Pilgrims to make a Thanksgiving."

Lights for Gita *(Gilmore, 2000)* A Gift for
Gita *(Gilmore, 2002), and* Roses for Gita *(Gilmore, 2001)*

These three books tell stories of Gita, who has emigrated from India, as she adjusts to life in the United States, tries to make friends, and deals with her divided identity as "new American" and "Indian." These are sweet, gentle books to introduce issues of cultural identity and customs and a respect for the diversity that enriches us.

Following are excellent additional books on the immigrant experience.

Angel Child, Dragon Child *(Surat, 1989)*

This is a story about Ut, a young girl from Vietnam, who must adjust to school in the United States after she leaves her mother behind in Vietnam.

Coming to America: A Muslim Family's Story *(Wolf, 2003)*

This book is a photo essay about the experiences and challenges experienced by a Muslim family that emigrates from Egypt to New York City.

Drita, My Homegirl *(Lombard, 2006)*

The story is told in alternating chapters by Drita, a refugee from Kosovo, and Maxie, an African American child, who are in the same fourth-grade class in Brooklyn. As the girls grow to be friends, they learn about each other's stories and struggles and reach out with support and love. The book raises challenging issues about the relationship between schoolyard bullying and ethnic wars, such as the one from which Drita has escaped. Students should grow in empathy and understanding of what it's like to be a refugee, the ways in which they can support one, and the importance of learning about one another rather than assuming or reverting to stereotypes.

La Mariposa (Jimenez, 2000)

Francisco, an immigrant from Mexico and the son of migrant workers, struggles to make sense of his new school. Because his English is very limited, he is subjected to bullying and ill treatment. When he finally wins some recognition for his art, his isolation and confusion begin to abate. Discussions about the challenges of not speaking the dominant language should make students more understanding of the roles they can play in supporting new students.

The Christmas Menorahs: How a Town Fought Hate (Cohn, 2000)

Discrimination based on religious diversity, as well as the importance of community allies, is well told through this book: the true story of events that took place in Billings, Montana, in 1993. A number of incidents of anti-Semitism and racism in the community come to a head when someone throws a brick through the window of young Isaac Schnitzer's bedroom. The house is targeted because the Schnitzers are Jewish, and because of the approaching Chanukah holiday, there is a menorah in the window. Rather than remaining silent, the Schnitzers take their story to the press; and soon, many people decide to take a stand against racism and hatred. A young classmate of Isaac's makes a menorah to hang in her window (even though she isn't Jewish), and thousands of other families do the same. Isaac's mother takes him out to see all the menorahs displayed around town and tells him, "Hate can make a lot of noise. Love and courage are usually quieter. But in the end, they're the strongest." A quote on the back of the book by Keith Torney, one of the ministers from Billings, states, "I think what happened in Billings is that people found a way to do good. Never again will this town just accept bigotry and think, 'Yeah, that's the way the world works.' Kids need to hear this story."

This story is powerful because it is based on actual events. It provides wonderful examples of individual and collective courage in confronting acts of racism and hatred. The book also makes the connections between the townspeople's response in Billings and the ways in which many Danes wore yellow stars during World War II in order to support and protect their Jewish neighbors. Students might brainstorm what kinds of collective responses they might make when incidents of racism, anti-Semitism, or homophobia take place in their community.

Sami and the Time of the Troubles (Heide & Gilliland, 1995)

Ten-year-old Sami lives with his family in Beirut, the capital of Lebanon. "My name is Sami and I live in the time of the troubles. It is a time of guns and bombs. It is a time that has lasted all my life, and I am ten years old." Sami and his family live in the basement of his uncle's house. Sami remembers the better days—playing at the beach. Now, they can't go outside because of all the gunfire in the streets. They remember the "Day of the Children" long ago, when the children took to the streets to protest the fighting:

> It was a day like today, a day when everyone could be outside, a day when the guns had stopped. Without warning, children appeared in the streets. Hundreds and hundreds of children started to march. They carried banners and flags, they carried signs, and the words written on them said: Stop. Stop the fighting. The smallest children, like Amir, like me, were carried on the shoulder of their fathers. People lined the streets to see, people filled the balconies. They cheered, they laughed, they cried. It was a day to remember, the day the children marched.

The grandfather reassures Sami that they can have another children's march in the streets. "Yes," he says. "It is time. Maybe now the ones who fight will hear, maybe this time they will listen."

The book's illustrations are dark, because the children are forced to stay inside much of the time because of the fighting outside, but this is a book about eternal hopefulness in the face of hard times. The book also describes young children taking a stand against violence and fighting.

The following nonfiction books may be very helpful in talking to students about issues of race and racism.

Under Our Skin: Kids Talk About Race *(Birdseye & Birdseye, 1997)*

Six students aged 12 to 13 talk about their race, including students who are Hispanic, Arab, Asian, Caucasian, African-American, and Native American. They share how their traditions affect their daily lives, their views on racial relations in America, and their own experiences with prejudice. The students' stories are very authentic; and they describe their lives, their friends, what they do for fun, and more.

This book could be a good model for students doing their own similar digital-storytelling project—telling their own stories. The book does not avoid the subject of racism but doesn't focus on it exclusively.

What Do You Know About Racism? *(Sanders & Myers, 2000)*

This book is one in a series of "What Do You Know About" books and is a combination of text, photos, and cartoons. The book has these sections: What is racism? Different kinds of racism; Why are people racist? The effects of racism; Hidden racism; The history of racism; Racism today; Challenging racism; and What can we do?

The book contains explicit dialogs in which children are harassed or treated poorly, and there are opportunities (some taken, some not) for becoming an ally. This is an excellent book to talk about ally building.

> Racists often act in the way they do because they are allowed to get away with it. They often rely on people being afraid to challenge them. If those around them refused to accept their behavior, they might think twice about continuing. Ignoring racism only helps it to develop. Silence is no answer, because if you don't speak out against racism you will appear to be going along with it. (p. 13)

(How Do I Feel About) Dealing With Racism *(Green, 2004)*

This engaging and accessible book is similar to the one above but is written for younger children. It is also a combination of cartoons, photos, and text.

The book includes an explicit section called Stopping Racism, which has situations and questions about how other students responded. "Sometimes you will need help to deal with racism. Tell a grown-up who you trust. He or she may be able to sort things out, without anyone knowing you have told."

It's Our World Too: Young People Who Are Making a Difference: How They Do It—How You Can Too *(Hoose, 2002)*

Not only does this book offer wonderful and inspiring stories of young people who have made a difference but it also includes an entire section on Activism for Young People. The book describes how to choose a project you really care about, find others to work with, write a vision statement, keep adults from taking over, conduct research, and create a working plan. Specific "Tools for Change" are also included, including how to write a letter, use a petition to build support, use the media, ask for money and other support, conduct a boycott, lobby protest, and demonstrate. Teachers could easily use this section of the book to help student select a project that is meaningful to them and carry it through all the steps from information gathering to action.

Stories of Resistance

Two events from World War II have both been well documented in children's literature and provide rich opportunities for discussing the ways in which people have been oppressed and have resisted that oppression.

Japanese Internment Camps

Baseball Saved Us *(Mochizuki, 1993)*

The book begins with an historical note by the author:

> In 1942, while the United States was at war with Japan, the U.S. Army moved all people of Japanese descent away from the West Coast. They were sent to internment camps in the middle of American deserts up until 1945. The reason, the U.S. government said, was because it could not tell who might be loyal to Japan. None of these immigrants from Japan—or their children, who were American citizens—were ever proven to be dangerous to America during World War II. In 1988, the U.S. government admitted that what it did was wrong.

The book is about a little boy, called "Shorty," who is in a Japanese interment camp with his parents during World War II. It is depressing there, and there is little to do. His father decides that they need to build a baseball field, and against tremendous odds, they do, scrounging the materials to build bleachers and fabric to make uniforms. Surrounded by barbed wire and a guard, who stares at him from the tower, Shorty overcomes fear and insecurity in order to be a successful ball player. When he returns home after the war, he is called "Jap" as he stands at the plate but again overcomes obstacles to hit a home run.

Heroes *(Mochizuki, 1995)*

By the same author as *Baseball Saved Us* (Mochizuki, 1993), this book tells the story of a Japanese American boy during the 1960s, when the Vietnam War is raging. When the children play war, he is forced to represent the enemy because he looks like them. The boy's father and uncle fought for the U.S. Army during World War II, and he is desperate to use this fact to alter his status, but they tell him, "You kids should be playing something else besides war." Discussions might include prejudice, misunderstanding, the plight of the "outsider," as well as the realities of war—which are not playful at all.

The Bracelet *(Uchida, 1996)*

Emi and her family are sent to Japanese internment camps even though they have done nothing wrong and are loyal Americans. The day before they leave, Emi's best friend, Laurie, comes over to give her a going away present, a heart bracelet. Emi vows to wear it forever to remember her friend Laurie. When they arrive at the camps, they find that they are forced to live in a horse stall at the old racetrack. Emi realizes that she has lost her bracelet, and she is devastated. Her mother helps remind her that we carry the memories of people in our hearts. The mother says,

> You know, Emi, you don't need a bracelet to remember Laurie anymore than we need a photo to remember Pap or our home or all the friends and things we loved and left behind. Those are things we carry in our hearts and take with us no matter where we are sent.

Journey to Topaz *(Uchida, 2004) and* Journey Home *(Uchida, 1992)*

These two books for older readers tell the story of Yuki and her Japanese American family who are forced from their home in California and imprisoned in a U.S. concentration camp called Topaz. The first book tells the story of Yuki's experiences in the camp. The second books begins with her family's release from the camp, when, penniless and with no where to go, they try to rebuild their lives in a world still marked by prejudice and discrimination against them as Japanese Americans.

The above three books can be part of a thematic unit on prejudice and discrimination or part of the study of World War II. Unfortunately, many Americans are unaware of this portion of U.S. history because its shameful nature has kept it from being taught. It is important for students to know that prejudice is not just something that happens "out there" (as in the holocaust), but something which has happened (and continues to happen) in our own backyards. Vigilance and awareness are important precursors to becoming an ally, and the United State's apology (although belated) is an excellent example of trying to right past wrongs.

Sadako and the Thousand Paper Cranes *(Coerr, 2004) and* Sadako *(Coerr, 1997)*

Author Eleanor Coerr has written two books about Sadako, a young Japanese schoolgirl who contracts leukemia as a result of the Hiroshima bombing—the first for older readers and the second a picture book for young readers—tell the same story: a Japanese legend says that if a sick person folds a thousand paper cranes, she will become well again. After Sadako folds 644 and realizes that she won't be able to finish, her classmates fold the remaining 356 cranes, and they are buried with her. A statue of Sadako stands in the Hiroshima Peace Park in Japan, and children visit the statue and leave paper cranes in honor of Sadako and the quest for world peace.

Elizabeth Senger, Sara Platte, and Julie Van Zandt (1997) describe the integrated thematic unit they constructed using *Sadako and the Thousand Paper Cranes* (Coerr, 2004). Working with two classes of fourth graders, they incorporated math, science, social studies, and writing into a unit that stretched the students and the teachers in many exciting directions. The students learned to fold paper cranes, studied Japan, and wrote and illustrated their own books. The science segment on Japan incorporated information about landforms, rocks, and volcanoes. The students connected the events in the book to a local tragedy in their community in which Yoshi Hattori, a foreign-exchange student from Japan, was shot and killed when we was mistaken for an intruder while on his way to a Halloween party, and the students decided they wanted to fold a thousand cranes to send in Hattori's honor to the Peace Memorial in Japan. The book and their projects enabled them to learn the social and cooperative skills of working together and problem solving; create a beautiful object of art; and think, talk, and take action about the intended and unintended consequences of violence.

Mieko and the Fifth Treasure *(Coerr, 2003)*

Mieko is a talented young calligrapher. According to Japanese tradition, she has the four treasures for painting pictures—the brush, the ink stick, the ink stone, and the rice paper—but she also has the fifth treasure: beauty in her heart. But when the bomb is dropped on Nagasaki, Mieko's village is destroyed, and her hand is badly hurt. She is sent to live on her grandparents' farm and goes to a new school. The children there are cruel and tease her about her scarred hand. Mieko has no friends and fears she will never be able to paint again because she has lost the fifth treasure forever. A growing friendship with another young girl, Yoshi, however, becomes important for Mieko, and that friendship brings beauty and joy back into her heart, including her ability to paint again.

The book develops themes of friendship and support while also sharing many aspects of Japanese culture and tradition. Teachers might want to discuss the other children's cruel teasing as well as the ways in which Mieko develops inner strength and courage to confront her painful past and difficult current situation.

Under the Blood-Red Sun *(Salisbury, 2005)*

This book for older readers tells the story of Tomi, who is of Japanese descent and born in Hawaii. His grandfather and parents were born in Japan and came to American to escape poverty. When Pearl Harbor is attacked by the Japanese and the United States declared war on Japan, life become very difficult. Tomi's father and grandfather are arrested, and Tomi must help his mother and sister to survive.

This historical fiction recounts a very difficult period in American history, full of fear, prejudice, and tensions among people of different racial and cultural groups. This book could be linked to the study of World War II and used to discuss the ways in which misjudgments and fear can lead to hatred and violence.

The Holocaust

Because the events of the Holocaust are so terrifying, it is important that teaching about this event includes not only the details of the horror but also the numerous examples of people of all religious and ethnic backgrounds who resisted and fought against such genocide. It is also important for students to know that Jews were not the only group targeted by the Nazis, but that the disabled, the elderly, trade unionists, Catholics, Gypsies, and homosexuals were also imprisoned and killed. The importance of being a strong ally and standing up to oppression cannot be overemphasized.

Historians of the holocaust often talk about categorizing people into four categories: perpetrators, bystanders, resistors, and victims. It is important when studying any kind of oppression to balance an understanding of the oppression with real-life examples of those who resisted and took a stand. To do otherwise is to leave children sunk in injustice and despair. Positive examples of people who took a stand can allow students to conceptualize personal and collective courage and relate it to actual events.

The Number on My Grandfather's Arm (Adler, 1987)

A little girl who has a warm relationship with her grandfather notices the numbers tattooed on his arm. With some reluctance, he tells her the story of Hitler's reign of terror and the concentration camps. After he tells her the story, the little girl responds, "You shouldn't be ashamed to let people see your number. You didn't do anything wrong. It's the Nazis who should be ashamed" (p. 22).

This is a tender, yet honest story about the horrors of the Holocaust, in language appropriate for young children. The book provides a good jumping-off place for discussing an infamous period of history and leading into stories of those who resisted the Nazis and helped Jews and others to stay safe.

Terrible Things: An Allegory of the Holocaust (Bunting, 1989)

This picture book uses the metaphor of a forest that is being terrorized by "terrible things" that first come for the birds. The other animals are grateful that they aren't in danger, and, predictably, by the time the magnitude of the horror is obvious, there aren't enough animals left to resist. Drawing on the powerful quote by Pastor Martin Niemoller ("First they came for the communists/But I wasn't a communist, so I didn't say anything . . ."), the book makes the dangers of "not speaking up" very obvious. The book asks students to think about what horrible things might have been averted if everyone had stood together at the very beginning.

The Little Boy Star: An Allegory of the Holocaust (Hausfater, 2001)

This is another allegorical tale in which a young Jewish boy is given a star to wear. Although he is at first proud of the decoration, he finds that the star overshadows him so that no one sees him, but only the star. As the boy watches the other star wearers be led away in the night, we share his confusion and fear.

This book could be excellent for discussing the dangers of labels and, particularly, of singular labels that consume the person and reduce them to one characteristic. Talking about the importance of "people-first" language could fit here nicely: the differences between "Joshua is Jewish" and "Joshua the Jew," or "Caitlin uses hearing aids" and "Caitlin, the deaf girl."

The Butterfly (Polacco, 2009)

This true story is about a little French girl, Monique, who finds out that her family has been harboring a Jewish family (including a little girl her age) from the Nazis. The Jewish family is forced to flee, and, ultimately, only the little girl survives.

There is no attempt to minimize the brutality of the Nazis, but the discussion of the "Righteous Gentiles" who hid Jewish families can be used to discuss the horror of prejudice and the courage of those who risked their lives to rescue those in danger.

Erika's Story (Vander Zee, 2003)

This book for upper elementary students narrates the true story of Erika, who was thrown from a train as an infant as her parents were being taken to a concentration camp. A German woman, at great risk, raised Erika to adulthood, when she married and had children of her own. The detailed illustrations provide much to discuss and provide another story of someone rescuing and saving the life of a person in grave danger.

Four Perfect Pebbles: A Holocaust Story (Perl & Blumenthal Lazan, 1999)

Another book for older readers, the story traces the complex and harrowing journey of Marion Blumenthal and her family as they flee Germany. First, they go to a refugee camp in Holland, but their planned relocation to the United States doesn't happen when the Germans invade Holland. The families end up in a concentration camp, Bergen Belsen, and although they survive the war, her father dies shortly thereafter.

Older students may be interested in the extensive details of the war and the ways in which families attempted to survive. Parallels to the struggles and journeys of other immigrant families could create an excellent connection to what it's like to be displaced and relocated, whether voluntarily or involuntarily.

The Yellow Star: The Legend of King Christian X of Denmark (Deedy, 2000)

This book tells the story of the Danish king who wore a yellow star and encouraged all the Danes to do so when Jews were forced to wear yellow stars as part of Nazi persecution. The book is a powerful example of resistance and solidarity, and there are many entrees for discussing what it means to be an ally and to stand up for and with other people.

The book concludes with some facts about the history of Denmark during World War II, including the fact that, among the Nazi-occupied countries, only Denmark rescued the overwhelming majority of its Jews. The author asks,

> And what if we could follow that example today against violations of human rights? What if the good and strong people of the world stood shoulder to shoulder, crowding the streets and filling the squares, saying, "You cannot do this injustice to our sisters and brothers, or you must do it to us as well."

What if?

The Lily Cupboard: A Story of the Holocaust (Oppenheim, 1995)

During World War II, a young Jewish girl, Miriam, is sent away from the city to live in the country with a non-Jewish family. When the soldiers come, she hides behind the wall, in the secret lily cupboard. The story provides wonderful examples of being an ally to oppressed people and the many ways in which people can be brave and kind. Miriam's friendship with Nello, a young boy her age who is the child of the family that takes her into hiding, is authentic and honest.

Number the Stars (Lowry, 1998)

This book for older readers tells the story of Ellen Rosen, who must move in with her friend Annemarie Johansen when the persecution of the Jews begins in Copenhagen during World War II. Annemarie goes on a dangerous mission to save the life of her friend, demonstrating personal courage and a refusal to yield to persecution and hatred.

Passage to Freedom: The Sugihara Story (*Mochizuki*, 2003)

The year is 1940, and Hiroki Sugihara is the five-year-old son of the Japanese consul to Lithuania. Jews fleeing the Nazis in Poland ask Sugihara to write them visas to escape the Nazis. The Japanese government tells him not to, but he does anyway, writing thousands of visas and saving the lives of many people.

This book is an excellent example of people standing up as allies to an oppressed group. At great personal cost and risk, many "righteous gentiles" helped Jews to escape Nazi persecution. It is important for students to know that, even under the worst oppressive conditions, there have always been people who have resisted violence, hatred, and prejudice.

Seeking Sanctuary: The Underground Railroad

The story of the Underground Railroad is one of people taking active steps to resist slavery and racism and to work together to free enslaved African Americans and help them to relocate north. It is important for students to understand the many people of different backgrounds (racial and religious) who worked for the abolition of slavery.

Sweet Clara and the Freedom Quilt (*Hopkinson*, 1995)

Clara, a 12-year-old slave, works as a seamstress in the Big House. Slowly, she learns about the Underground Railroad and how some slaves are trying to escape north to freedom. The thing that they desperately need is a map. Using the information she gathers from different sources, she uses scrap materials to sew a patchwork quilt that is a map to freedom. When the quilt is complete, she leaves it behind for others to use, and makes her way north via the Underground Railroad to retrieve her mother (whom she was separated from) and go on with her toward Canada.

This true story models resourcefulness and creative problem solving in the face of danger. Connecting the ancient craft of quilting to the story of the Underground Railroad could easily provide a starting point for quilting and map projects as well as further study of the travesty of slavery and the bravery of those who escaped and helped others. The book could serve as great introduction to a quilt project that is more than decorative. What could it be, and to whom could it be given?

Under the Quilt of Night (*Hopkinson*, 2005)

This is another story of a young slave girl who leads her loved ones away from the slave master as they travel along the Underground Railroad. By the same author and illustrator of *Sweet Clara and the Freedom Quilt* (Hopkinson, 1995), this is another powerful narrative of courage and transformation. The fear is palpable as those who pursue the escaping slaves are pictured in hot pursuit. The author connects the "quilt of night" with the quilts with blue squares, which indicated safe homes.

Another opportunity to discuss the role of allies in the struggle for freedom (those who helped provide safe passage and hiding places), possibilities for extension again include quilt making and an exploration of quilting symbolism.

Barefoot: Escape on the Underground Railroad (*Edwards*, 1999)

This picture book describes a young boy's flight from slavery on the Underground Railroad. He is aided by the animals, who help the "barefoot" escape from the "heavy boots." The story is told as a touching description of trust and interdependence, with many examples of helping others.

Aunt Harriet's Underground Railroad in the Sky (*Ringold*, 1995)

Cassie Louise Lightfoot, an eight-year-old African American girl, soars above the rooftops in New York City where she meets Harriet Tubman. Harriet Tubman transports her and her brother, BeBe, back to the time of the slave plantations.

This richly illustrated picture book includes factual information about the Underground Railroad as well as maps of the journey undertaken by the escaping slaves.

Minty: A Story of Young Harriet Tubman *(Schroeder, 1996)*

This is a story of Harriet Tubman as a young child, whose nickname was Minty. Students will be fascinated by the story of what Harriet Tubman was like as a girl, before her historic role in the Underground Railroad. The book makes it clear that Minty's spunky personality, sometimes considered a problem, was what allowed her to play such a courageous role in helping slaves escape slavery.

Allen Jay and the Underground Railroad *(Brill, 1993)*

In this true story, an 11-year-old boy, Allen Jay, whose family's farm is a stop on the Underground Railroad, helps a runaway slave reach freedom, putting himself at great jeopardy in the process. The book includes a brief history of the role of Quakers in the Underground Railroad, and it provides a wonderful example of a young child taking a risk in order to do something he believes is right.

Nettie's Trip South *(Turner, 1995)*

Young Nettie takes a trip to the south in 1859, where she sees a slave auction. She is horrified about what slaves' lives are like and returns to the North committed to changing things. This book is based on the actual diary of the author's grandmother, who became a confirmed abolitionist because of what she saw on her "trip south."

This book is a powerful testament to the ways in which learning about injustice can help people to become powerful and take a stand. The book could easily be linked to an historical examination of people who have made a difference and what inspired or motivated them. Students could be asked to identify issues and concerns about which they would like to learn more and to formulate action agendas based on what they learned.

LINKS TO THE CURRICULUM

This chapter has been filled with examples of curriculum connections in the areas of music, art, literature, social studies, and language arts. In addition to integrating issues of social justice into all aspects of classroom practice and curriculum, teachers can also encourage students to become critical consumers of the curriculum itself. Teacher Bob Peterson encouraged his students to take a thoughtful look at a computer encyclopedia program (Peterson, 1994). He asked them to look up famous people and note how much was written about each and what the information was. Among those people the students looked for were Thomas Edison, Sojourner Truth, Abraham Lincoln, Langston Hughes, Roberto Clemente, Felisa Rincon de Gautir, Ida B. Wells, Delores Huerta, Wilma Mankiller, George Washington, Malcolm X, Sitting Bull, and General Custer. Students found that some of the "famous people" their teacher asked them to look for weren't even listed! Students were encouraged to explore ideas such as (1) who decides who is famous and worthy of space? (2) what gender are the famous people included in the database? and (3) what racial or ethnic backgrounds are represented? The students worked to develop a chart showing the average entry, in inches, of selected famous people, by race and gender on the CD-ROM Encyclopedia. Note: See Box 8.5 for another example.

Encarta (the online encyclopedia that Peterson used) is no longer available, but *Wikipedia* has become a tool often referenced by students. I have asked students to look up moments in history, conflicts, and controversies both in *Wikipedia* and on the World

BOX 8.5

In Jose Cadillo's sixth-grade class at Fort River Elementary School in Amherst, Massachusetts, a teachable moment arose when the students discussed how the post office decides whom commemorative stamps should honor. The students became part of a letter-writing campaign urging the U.S. Postal Service to issue a commemorative stamp to honor James Armistead Lafayette, a former slave who served the Marquis de Lafayettte and General George Washington as an espionage agent during the siege of Yorktown in 1781. This project involved studying local history and lead to discussions of voice, power, and homelessness, when the students discovered that people who were homeless couldn't sign petitions!

Wide Web. Students were asked, for example, to pick an event (e.g., the bombing of Hiroshima, Columbus Day, Thanksgiving, Japanese internment in the United States) and talk about what multiple perspectives they might hope to find. Then, they looked up the event and noted what was said and what seemed missing. The students realized that the missing part was harder, since we often don't notice things that are missing—they are simply that, missing. They were encouraged to brainstorm where else they might find more information.

Students were asked to explore the implications of what they found, conflicts and contradictions between perspectives, and holes in the information. They were fascinated, for example, by the differences in what they had learned about Helen Keller and the broader information about her life and passions. They saw that what the U.S. State Department had to say about the island of Vieques was very different from what a Puerto Rican Web site said. They compared various versions of the events of September 11, 2001, and analyzed voice and perspective.

In a similar activity on the gaps in our knowledge, I gave each student a copy of the Syracuse Cultural Workers' Calendar (available from http://syracuseculturalworkers .com/products/calendars). This is a calendar, published yearly, that contains many important dates and information related to labor union history; Hispanic, Native American, and African American history; holidays from many different religious traditions; dates related to gay and lesbian history; women's history; civil rights struggles; and so on. Students were asked to find at least 10 events on the calendar that they were unfamiliar with and then try to find information on these events on the Internet. After some individual and group exploration, the class reunited to discuss (1) which events were easy to find information about, (2) which events or dates were difficult to find out about, and (3) what patterns of visibility/invisibility and information/silence emerged. The discussion concluded with different groups of students assigned to find out about different events or issues and report back to the class.

Final Thoughts

First Steps for New Beginnings

Building classroom communities, teaching students to work together, changing the world—what an impressive (and overwhelming) set of tasks. Where can we begin? We can begin by doing the same things for ourselves as teachers that we try to do for our students: establishing a strong community, developing a solid and reliable support system, setting reasonable goals, and celebrating each achievement no matter how (seemingly) small. We can also give ourselves permission to breathe deeply, relax . . . and then dig in for the long haul! We can continually remind ourselves that small steps do count and that even small, seemingly insignificant changes in our classroom practice can make big differences in children's lives. We can be patient with ourselves. Nothing important is ever achieved easily or quickly. But persistence and determination have seen many major accomplishments through!

Each chapter in this book (excluding Chapter 1) includes a section titled "Reframing Our Work." By working through the questions in each chapter together, teachers can involve themselves in their own self-study as well as outlining next steps for professional development and school improvement. The following questions might also be useful for teachers hoping to reinvent their classrooms and their teaching lives:

Think about yourself as a teacher. What kinds of support do you have? What kinds of help would you like? Who can you choose to be your partner, coconspirator, ally, and friend? Some teachers have found it useful to identify a learning partner with whom they meet on a regular basis. You might decide, for example, to have coffee after school every two weeks, at which time you

- celebrate what's gone well so far;
- laugh, cry, or bemoan the things that didn't work;
- receive appreciation, suggestions, and acknowledgement from your partner; and
- share your next steps in building community and working for change.

Setting goals and receiving appreciation and support is just as important for teachers as it is for students. Actually, there is a clear relationship between the level of support and connectedness *teachers* feel with their ability to provide that kind of support for students. Teachers working in isolation can accomplish great things—but usually at great personal cost and with a high rate of burnout. It makes sense to work with others. Despite recent efforts to put teachers in competition with one another through merit-pay schemes and other attempts at motivation, teachers can resist those strategies and remind all involved that collaboration is what will make a difference in children's lives.

Teachers may have to overcome the same reluctance to ask for support and elicit positive feedback that students sometimes experience. Working with a learning partner who has agreed to support you can help you overcome any shyness about sharing, "Guess what went so great yesterday!" or "I'm really not sure I can work with this little boy—he makes me feel so incompetent and frustrated!"

Think about the whole school community, not just your own classroom. Starting small makes sense—thinking big has additional pay offs! Brainstorm with other teachers to come up with ideas for making the school community feel warm and welcoming for all teachers and for all students.

Some possible teacher ideas (see Box 9.1 for an example):

- *Birthday List:* Compile a list of all faculty and staff birthdays. Put up a sign-up sheet in the teachers' lounge where two people can sign up to bake or bring cakes or cookies for a certain month. On the first day of each month, celebrate all of the birthdays for that month.
- *Party Wagon:* Have people bring in leftover balloons, paper cups, napkins, hats, streamers, and other party favors. If a teacher is having a bad day, send the party wagon to his room to cheer that teacher up!
- *Community Building:* Start your own faculty meetings with a community builder. Try some of the ideas in this book (New and Goods, Diversity Treasure Hunt, Secrets About Me, Two Truths and a Lie), or make up your own. Spend time getting to know other faculty and staff. Remember that time spent building community among teachers is never wasted time! When the hard parts come up (conflicts over shared resources or scheduling), the positive seeds of community, which have been sown, will help teachers get over the rough spots better.
- *Base Groups:* Organize teachers into staff "base groups" (like in cooperative learning). Begin every faculty meeting with a chance for base groups to meet and discuss their week, items on the agenda, concerns, and so forth. These groups can do community-building activities and also share ideas and solve real problems at school.
- *Shared Teaching/Team Teaching:* Try trading teaching with another teacher. Volunteer to do a special lesson or something about your own hobbies, background, or cultural knowledge with another group of students. Establish a list in the teachers' lounge where teachers can volunteer their lesson or services to other teachers (an extension of the Help Wanted/Help Offered idea).
- *Community Lounge:* Turn the teachers' lounge into a supportive community. Post favorite quotes, poems, or articles on the wall. Invite other teachers to come to your classroom to see the diorama your students just built, the bulletin board you're proud of, or the cave you just built out of milk cartons.
- *Staff Socials:* Hold staff-social activities and retreats; let staff have fun and get to know one another away from the pressures of school. In one school, monthly potlucks bring people together for good food and good fun.

Here are some possible additional schoolwide ideas:

- Announce all student, staff, and faculty birthdays every morning. Real community is built when a third grader, a kindergartner, a lunchroom aide, and the vice principal find out they share a birthday.
- Reclaim the concept of all-school assemblies (if space is available) or all-school sing-alongs. Make a schoolwide songbook and encourage teachers to learn the songs and teach them to their classrooms. Invite parents to the assemblies.

- Assign every student in the school to an adult who agrees to be their special friend or mentor. Every adult in the school plays this role: custodians, cafeteria workers, bus drivers, secretaries—everyone. Have the student and adult agree to check in with each other once a week just to see how things are going.
- Establish an internal mail-delivery system. Students in different classes can write to one another and then mail carriers can deliver the mail to the mailboxes set up outside each room. Encourage students to write notes of appreciation to teachers and other adults who have been kind to them. Everyone loves getting mail.
- Establish cross-grade peer-tutoring programs and special projects. In one school, the first graders and fourth graders always went on field trips together. The older students were responsible for younger students and learned to explain what they were seeing and experiencing to younger students. Rather than just walking by exhibits at the science museum, the older students were faced with younger students asking, "Why does that work?"
- Share good news about what's going on in your classrooms and school in any way and as often as you can. Encourage everyone in the school to think seriously about how the school is represented and viewed and increase the "good publicity." (See Box 9.3 on page 242.)

BOX 9.1

When Sid Morrison was the principal of P. S. # 84 in New York City, he organized the lunch program so that the meal was served "family style," with children sitting at tables together, sharing in serving and cleanup responsibilities. Another school organized interest tables at lunch, where students from all grade levels and classes could meet and talk about football, dinosaurs, dealing with little brothers, or other student-generated topics.

Think about ways of making parents part of the classroom and school community. Think beyond asking them to chaperone trips or bring in snacks. Consider asking parents to come in to share family stories or information about their culture or lives with the class (see Box 9.2).

BOX 9.2

First-grade teacher Kim Rombach organized evenings she called "Families Learning Together" in her classroom. She set up six learning centers in the classrooms and divided participants into groups that mixed families up—parents were with their own children, but they were also with other parents and children. Within the context of math, science, and technology, families explored math games that involved and needed each participant to play, did science discovery lessons, and explored the classroom Web site. In the language arts centers, families listened to literature on tape, read stories, and wrote letters to other family members or friends. The groups rotated through the centers, enjoyed refreshments, and got to know one another.

Kim also established a Community Puppet Theater through which families worked cooperatively to make puppets, wrote a show that was based on a scenario suggested by class members, and then performed the puppet show for other families. Families worked in pairs to write their puppet show and practiced performing it ahead of time. One little boy, discussing his family with another family, said, "This brings out the good in my dad."

BOX 9.3

At the Muscota New School in New York City, teachers and students developed a school newsletter. Originally designed as a calendar of upcoming events and notes from the director about points of interest and practice in the school, the newsletter evolved to become an important vehicle for community sharing and communication, a representation of everyone's voice and ideas. When a child created a drawing or a story that she was particularly proud of, she would ask, "Can I put this in the newsletter?" Former director, Leslie Alexander, says that such requests were always granted. "Children held themselves to a particularly high standard, and when they felt they had reached it, it was time to make a submission." The newsletter also included a column called "Quotes of the Week," and whenever anyone heard something particularly clever, cute, or poignant, they would say, "That's a quotable quote." The newsletter was always translated into Spanish, so the readership was an inclusive group as well.

Think inclusively about inclusive schools. Inclusive school communities are caring and effective. All members feel that they belong and can make contributions. Transforming schools into inclusive communities involves rethinking taken-for-granted ideas about how schools are organized, how children are grouped, how adult resources are utilized, and what constitutes appropriate or essential education.

An inclusive school is one in which all members of the school community think proactively and thoughtfully about all types of diversity, both the diversities represented in the school itself and those not immediately present. It is critical that students in an all-white school learn about challenging racism and that all students learn about religious diversity, even if the school is fairly religiously homogeneous. We must look beyond what occurs in individual classrooms and include an analysis and critique of what goes on in the school as a whole. Thinking about the following questions may help us to think more inclusively.

Diversity: What are some possible goals for schoolwide recognition and celebration of differences? How can peer support be built for all children? What would be some key indices that the school is dealing well with diversity issues in general? What would a visitor to the school discern about the values and beliefs about diversity held by teachers and administrators? What if we published a Diversity and Inclusion Index for each school rather than just reporting students' results on standardized tests?

Curriculum and Instruction: What is considered critical curriculum for all students, and how is this decided? How can special services be provided to students without isolating them from the general population of students? How can the resources and skills of the gifted teacher or the learning disabilities teacher be used in a way that supports inclusion and respect for all students' diversity?

Cocurricular Activities: What are some ways of organizing school recreational and physical education activities so that they are more inclusive of children with all levels of ability? Are there ways of structuring musical, theater, and art activities so that a wider range of students can participate and still maintain the high quality of performance? Can't there be a place for everyone in the choir?

School Environment: What can be done in the cafeteria, at recess, and on the playground so that all students feel safe and secure? What roles could adults play to increase positive social interactions and make sure that all students have friends? How do we take a strong stand against bullying and ill treatment by students (and teachers as well)?

School Policies and Planning: Have all the people who will be affected by this decision been involved to the maximum extent possible? What values does this decision communicate to the people in the school and the general community? Does this decision model respect for diversity and individual differences? Will this decision bring people closer together or push them farther apart?

As usual, there are many more questions than there are answers, but we must remind ourselves of the importance of asking hard questions, especially those to which we *don't* know the answers. A poster in my office reads, "The measure of our success is not whether we still have problems, but whether we have the same problems we had a year ago."

Recently, I found myself needing to change planes in an airport that was in the midst of remodeling. The tram had not yet been built, so the walk between terminals was very long and felt endless. Dragging two suitcases, I was feeling cheerless and tired. Then, as I looked up, I saw a yellow sticky note on the wall in the long passageway. It read, "Think not about the length of the tunnel but how the walk will build your strength." It was as though someone knew just what I needed to see at that moment.

It is easy to feel overwhelmed or discouraged when we think about all that needs changing, in schools and in society. When we are disconnected from others, we can feel particularly alone and ineffective. Working together, however, we gather strength and energy and enthusiasm from one another. Teachers can and do make a difference. You need and deserve the same love and support you give your students. Let us continue working together to make a world that's right for—and includes—everyone.

References

Many of the sources in this list are excellent children's books. These are marked with icons showing the reading level of the book: 📖 for primary, ◢ for intermediate, and ▤ for advanced.

📖 Adler, D. (1987). *The number on my grandfather's arm.* New York: UAHC.

Allen, L. (2001). Courage is the letting go. On *Women's work* [CD]. Bellingham, WA: October Rose Productions.

aMaze. (2002–2009). *Families all matter curriculum guide.* Minneapolis, MN: Author. Available from http://www.amazeworks.org/programs/fam/cg.html

📖 Andreae, G., & Parker-Rees, G. (2001). *Giraffes can't dance.* New York: Orchard Books.

Applebaum, P. (1999, June 28). [Review of the book *Because we can change the world: A practical guide to building cooperative, inclusive classroom communities*]. Retrieved March 28, 2010, from http://www.amazon.com/Because-Can-Change-World-Cooperative/product-reviews/0205174892

Armstrong, T. (1994). *Multiple intelligences: Seven ways to approach curriculum.* Retrieved March 26, 2010, from http://www.thomasarmstrong.com/articles/7_ways.htm

Arnold, A. (1972). *Children's games.* New York: World.

Au, W., Bigelow, B., & Karp, S. (Eds.). (2007). *Rethinking our classrooms: Teaching for equity and justice, Vol. 1* (2nd ed.). Milwaukee, WI: Rethinking Schools.

Ayers, W. (1989). *The good preschool teacher: Six teachers reflect on their lives.* New York: Teachers College Press.

Banks, J. A. (2003a). Educating global citizens in a diverse world. *New horizons for learning.* Retrieved March 24, 2010, from http://www.newhorizons.org/strategies/multicultural/banks2.htm

Banks, J. A. (2003b). Introduction: Democratic citizenship education in multicultural societies. In James A. Banks (Ed.), *Diversity and citizenship education: Global perspectives.* San Francisco: Jossey-Bass.

📖 Bateman, T. (2004). *The bully blockers club.* Morton Grove, IL: Albert Whitman.

Battistich, V., Schaps, E., & Wilson, N. (2004). Effects of an elementary school intervention on students' connectedness to school and social adjustment during middle school. *The Journal of Primary Prevention, 24*(3), 243–262.

📖 Beckwith, K. (2005). *Playing war.* Gardiner, ME: Tilbury House.

Bigelow, B., Miner, B., & Peterson, B. (1991). *Rethinking Columbus.* Milwaukee, WI: Rethinking Schools.

Bigelow, B., & Peterson, B. (1998). *Rethinking Columbus: The next 500 years.* Milwaukee, WI: Rethinking Schools.

Bigelow, B., & Peterson, B. (2003). *Rethinking globalization: Teaching for justice in an unjust world.* Milwaukee, WI: Rethinking Schools.

◢ Birdseye, D. H., & Birdseye, T. (1997). *Under our skin: Kids talk about race.* New York: Holiday House.

Blood, P. (2005). Rise up singing: The group singing songbook. Bethlehem, PA: Sing out!

Blos, J. W. (1987). *Old Henry.* New York: William Morrow.

Blue, B. (1990). Courage. On *Starting small.* Harrisonville, NH: Black Socks Press. Available from http://www.bobblue.org/pages/prod_descrip/StartingSmall1.html

Bones of Contention. (1998). Step by step. On *Power* [Audio cassette]. Never Surrender Records/ICEM. Available from Labor Heritage Foundation, 815 16th St. N.W., Room 301, Washington, DC 20006.

Bookrags. (n.d.). Encyclopedia *of world biography on Günter Grass.* Retrieved April 1, 2010, from http://www.bookrags.com/biography/gunter-grass/

Borden, L. (2002). *Good luck, Mrs. K!* New York: Aladdin Books.

Botting, T., Oshanin, L., & Ostrovsky, A. (1964). May there always be sunshine [Recorded by P. Allard, E. Allard, and M. Allard-Madaus]. On *Raise the Children* [CD]. Worcester, MA: 80-Z Music, Inc. (2002) Lyrics and mp3 sample available at http://www.peterandellen.com/lyrics/always_sun.htm

Bowles, N. E., & Rosenthal, M. (Eds.). (2001). *Cootie shots: Theatrical inoculations against bigotry for kids, parents, and teachers.* New York: Theater Communications Group.

Boyd, L. (1990). *Sam is my half brother.* New York: Viking.

Boyden, L. (2002). *The blue roses.* New York: Lee & Low Books.

Bregoli, J. (2004). *The goat lady.* Gardiner, ME: Tilbury House.

Bridwell, N. (1986). *Clifford's Halloween.* New York: Cartwheel.

Brill, M. T. (1993). *Allen Jay and the underground railroad.* Minneapolis, MN: Carolrhoda Books.

Browne, A. (1991). *Willy and Hugh.* New York: Alfred A. Knopf.

Broyles, A. (2000). *Shy mama's Halloween.* Gardiner, ME: Tilbury House.

Bunting, E. (1989). *Terrible things: An allegory of the Holocaust.* New York: Jewish Publication Society of America.

Bunting, E. (1992). *The wall.* New York: The Trumpet Club.

Bunting, E. (1993). *Fly away home.* New York: Clarion Books.

Bunting, E. (1999). *Smoky night.* New York: Harcourt.

Bunting, E. (2001). *Jin Woo.* New York: Clarion Books.

Bynum, J. (2006). *Nutmeg and Barley: A budding friendship.* Cambridge, MA: Candlewick Press.

Calmenson, S. (1990). *Wanted: Warm, furry friend.* New York: Macmillan.

Calmenson, S. (1991). *The principal's new clothes.* New York: Scholastic.

Campbell Ernst, L. (1992). *Sam Johnson and the blue ribbon quilt.* New York: Mulberry Books.

Cannon, J. (1993). *Stellaluna.* New York: Scholastic.

Carlson, N. (1985). *Making the team.* Minneapolis, MN: Carolrhoda Books.

Carlson, N. (1988). *I like me.* New York: Viking Kestrel.

Carlson, N. (2004). *There's a big, beautiful world out there!* New York: Puffin Books.

Carson, J. (1992). *You hold me and I'll hold you.* New York: Orchard Books.

Caseley, J. (1987). *Apple pie and onions.* New York: Greenwillow Books.

Caseley, J. (2002). *On the town: A community adventure.* New York: Greenwillow Books.

Choi, Y. (2001). *The name jar.* New York: Dell Dragonfly Books.

Choldenko, G. (2007). *Louder, Lili.* New York: Penguin Books.

Clements, A. (1997). *Big Al.* New York: Scholastic.

Clements, A. (2001). *Jake Drake, bully buster.* New York: Simon and Schuster.

Cocca-Leffler, M. (2002). *Bravery soup.* Morton Grove, IL: Whitman Books.

Cocca-Leffler, M. (2007). *Jack's talent.* New York: Farrar, Straus and Giroux.

Coerr, E. (1997). *Sadako.* New York: The Putman and Grosset Group.

Coerr, E. (2003). *Mieko and the fifth treasure.* New York: Bantam.

Coerr, E. (2004). *Sadako and the thousand cranes.* New York: Dell.

Cohen, B. (1998). *Molly's pilgrim.* New York: Lothrop, Lee and Shepard Books.

Cohn, J. (2000). *The Christmas menorahs: How a town fought hate.* Morton Grove, IL: Albert Whitman.

Cole, J. (2005). *Graduate teacher program.* Retrieved March 24, 2010, from http://www.colorado.edu/gtp/training/publications/tutor/wisev6n1.htm

Coleman, E. (1999). *White socks only.* Morton Grove, IL: Albert Whitman.

Combs, B. (2001a). *A, B, C: A family alphabet book.* Ambler, PA: Two Lives.

Combs, B. (2001b). *1,2,3: A family counting book.* Ambler, PA: Two Lives.

Costanza, C. (2002). *A perfect name.* New York: Dial Books for Young Readers.

Coulman, V. (2003). *Sink or swim.* Montreal, Quebec, Canada: Lobster Press.

Couric, K. (2000). *Brand new kid.* New York: Doubleday.

Couric, K. (2004). *Blue ribbon day.* New York: Doubleday.

Cowen-Fletcher, J. (1996). *Mama zooms.* New York: Scholastic.

Criswell, P. K. (2009). *Stand up for yourself and your friends: Dealing with bullies and bossiness and finding a better way.* Middleton, WI: American Girl.

Cronin, D. (2000). *Click, clack, moo: Cows that type.* New York: Simon and Schuster.

Cummings. (1991). *Tattlin' Madeline.* Edmonds, WA: Teaching.

Curtis, C. P. (2000). *The Watsons go to Birmingham—1963.* New York: Bantam Books.

Cuyler, M. (2007). *Kindness is cooler, Mrs. Ruler.* New York: Simon and Schuster.

Davis, S. (2003). *Schools where everyone belongs: Practical strategies for reducing bullying.* Wayne, ME: Stop Bullying Now.

deHaan, L., & Nijland, S. (2000). *King and king.* Berkeley, CA: Tricycle Press.

Delaney, N. (1976). *Two strikes four eyes.* Boston: Houghton Mifflin.

Delton, J. (1974). *Two good friends.* New York: Crown.

dePaola, T. (1973). *Nana upstairs and nana downstairs.* New York: G. P. Putnam's Sons.

dePaola, T. (1980). *Oliver Button is a sissy.* New York: Harcourt Brace Jovanovich.

dePaola T. (2006). *Now one foot, now the other.* New York: G. P. Putnam's Sons.

Deedy, C. A. (2000). *The yellow star: The legend of King Christina X of Denmark.* Atlanta, GA: Peachtree.

Derman-Sparks, L., & A. B. C. Task Force. (1989). *Anti-bias curriculum: Tools for empowering young children.* Washington, DC: National Association for the Education of Young Children.

DiSalvo-Ryan, D. A. (1997). *Uncle Willie and the soup kitchen.* New York: Morrow Junior Books.

Donkin, P. (2007). Kindness is everywhere. On *A hop, skip, and a jump* [CD]. Albany, NY: A Gentle Wind.

Dooley, N. (1991). *Everybody cooks rice.* New York: Scholastic.

Dragonwagon, C. (1987). *Diana, maybe.* New York: Macmillan.

Durant, A. (2004). *Always and forever.* New York: Harcourt Children's Books.

Edelman, M. W. (1998). *Stand for children.* New York: Hyperion Books.

Edwards, P. D. (1999). *Barefoot: Escape on the underground railroad.* New York: HarperCollins.

Estes, E. (2004). *The hundred dresses.* New York: Harcourt.

Everett, B. (1995). *Mean soup.* New York: Voyager Books.

Farrell, J. (1999). *It's just a game.* Honesdale, PA: Boyds Mills Press.

Fierstein, H. (2002). *The sissy duckling.* New York: Simon and Schuster.

Finkelhor, D., Turner, H., Ormrod, S. H., & Kracke, K. (2009). *Children's exposure to violence: A comprehensive national survey.* Retrieved October 2009, from the U.S. Department of Justice, Office of Juvenile Justice and Delinquency Prevention, http://www.ojp.usdoj.gov.

Fox, D., & Beane, A. L. (2009). *Good-bye bully machine.* Minneapolis, MN: Free Spirit.

Gantos, J. (1998). *Joey Pizga swallowed the key.* New York: Farrar, Straus and Giroux.

Gardner, H. (1999). *Intelligence reframed: Multiple intelligences for the 21st century.* New York: Basic Books.

Gaskins, P. F. (1999). *What are you? Voices of mixed-race young people.* New York: Henry Holt.

Gibbs, J. (2001). *Reaching all by creating Tribes learning communities.* Windsor, CA: Center Source Systems, LLC.

Gikow, L., & Weiss, E. (1993). *For every child a better world.* New York: United Nations.

Gilmore, R. (2000). *Lights for Gita.* Gardiner, ME: Tilbury House.

Gilmore, R. (2001). *Roses for Gita.* Gardiner, ME: Tilbury House.

Gilmore, R. (2002). *A gift for Gita.* Gardiner, ME: Tilbury House.

GLSEN. (n.d.). ThinkB4YouSpeak. *GLSEN.* Retrieved March 27, 2010, from http://www.thinkb4youspeak.com/

Golenbock, P. (1992). *Teammates.* New York: Harcourt.

Graham, B. (2003). *Rose meets Mr. Wintergarten.* Cambridge, MA: Candlewick Press.

Grant, B. (1974). Together we can move mountains. On *Working people gonna rise* (P-1024) [CD]. Brooklyn, NY: Paredon. Lyrics and recording available at http://www.bevgrant.com/workingpeople.html

Greenberg, S., Vaughan, R., & Connier, L. (lyrics and music). (2004). When I get mad [Recorded by Two of a Kind]. On *Family Album* [CD]. Cheltenham, PA: Magillacutty Music. (2007) Lyrics available at http://www.twoofakind.com/ShowLyrics.asp?id=96

Green, J. (2004). *Dealing with racism (How do I feel about).* Mankato, MN: Stargazer Books.

Gunning, M. (2004). *A shelter in our car.* San Francisco: Children's Book Press.

Habib, D. (Writer), & Desgres, R. (Ed.). (2009). *Including Samuel* [DVD]. Durham, NH: Institute on Disability at the University of New Hampshire, & Northampton, MA: Pinehurst Pictures and Sound. Available from http://www.includingsamuel.com.

Hallinan, P. K. (2006). *A Rainbow of friends.* Nashville, TN: Ideals Children's Books.

Harrison, M. (1976). *For the fun of it: Selected cooperative games for children and adults.* Philadelphia: Nonviolence and Children/Friends Peace Committee.

Harshman, M. (1995). *The storm.* New York: Cobblehill Books.

Hatkoff, I., Hatkoff, C., & Kahumbu, P. (2006). *Owen & Mzee: The story of a remarkable friendship.* New York: Scholastic.

Hatkoff, I., Hatkoff, C., & Kahumbu, P. (2007). *Owen & Mzee: The language of friendship.* New York: Scholastic.

Hausfater, R. (2001). *The little boy star: An allegory of the Holocaust.* New York: Milk and Cookies Press.

Hausherr, R. (1997). *Celebrating families.* New York: Scholastic.

Havill, J. (1989). *Jamaica tag-along.* Boston: Houghton Mifflin.

Havill, J. (1993). *Jamaica and Brianna.* Boston: Houghton Mifflin.

Hehir, T. (2002). Eliminating ableism in education. *Harvard Educational Review, 72*(1), 1–32.

Heide, F. P., & Gilliland, J. H. (1995). *Sami and the time of the troubles.* New York: Clarion Books.

Heine, H. (1997). *Friends.* New York: Simon and Schuster.

Heitler-Klevans, J., & Heitler-Klevans, D. (2009). "Pitfalls" [Performed by Two of a Kind; commissioned by Peacemakers: The New Generation]. Lyrics, sheet music, and mp3 available at http://www.twoofakind.com/ShowLyrics.asp?id=130

Heinrich, J. S. (2003). Native Americans: What not to teach. In B. Bigelow & B. Peterson (Eds.), *Rethinking Columbus: The next 500 years* (pp. 32–33). Milwaukee, WI: Rethinking Schools.

Henkes, K. (1988). *Chester's way.* New York: Greenwillow Books.

Henkes, K. (1991). *Chrystanthemum.* New York: Greenwillow Books.

Hess, D. (1994). *Wilson sat alone.* New York: Simon and Schuster.

Hoffman, M. (1991). *Amazing grace.* New York: Dial Books for Young Readers.

Holmberg, B. R. (2008). *A day with dad.* Cambridge, MA: Candlewick Press.

hooks, b. (2004). *Skin again.* New York: Hyperion Books.

Hoose, P. (2002). *It's our world too: Young people who are making a difference: How they do it—How you can too.* New York: Little, Brown.

Hoose, P. (2009). *Claudette Colvin: Twice toward justice.* New York: Farrar, Straus and Giroux.

Hoose, P., & Hoose, H. (1998). Hey, little ant. On *Hey, little ant* [CD]. Available from http://www.heylittleant.com/songs.html.

Hoover, J. H., & Oliver, R. L. (1996). *The bullying prevention handbook: A guide of principals, teachers and counselors.* Bloomington, IN: National Educational Service.

Hopkinson, D. (1995). *Sweet Clara and the freedom quilt.* New York: Alfred A. Knopf.

Hopkinson, D. (2005). *Under the quilt of night.* New York: Aladdin.

Horton, Z., Hamilton, F., Carawan, G., & Seeger, P. (musical & lyrics adaptations). (1964). We shall overcome [traditional; Recorded by P. Seeger]. On *If I had a hammer: Songs of Hope & Struggle* [CD; Catalogue #SFW40096]. Washington, DC: Smithsonian Folkways Recordings. (1998) Recording available at http://www.folkways.si.edu/albumdetails.aspx?itemid=2419

Howe, J. (1998). *Pinky and Rex.* New York: Atheneum.

Howe, J. (1999). *Horace and Morris but mostly Dolores.* New York: Simon and Schuster.

Howe, J. (2003). *The misfits.* New York: Simon and Schuster.

Hunt, J. M. (1961). *Intelligence and experience.* New York: Ronald Press.

Hunter, T. (n.d.). *Mrs. Squires.* Unpublished manuscript.

Igus, T. (1996). *Two Mrs. Gibsons.* San Francisco: Children's Book Press.

Jimenez, F. (2000). *La mariposa.* New York: Houghton and Mifflin.

Johnson, C. (1981). Love Grows One by One. On *Might as well make it love* [CD]. Grand Rapids, MI: Carol Johnson Music. Lyrics and recording available at http://www.songsforteaching.com/caroljohnson/lovegrowsonebyone.htm

Johnson, D. W., & Johnson, R. T. (1989). *Cooperation and competition: Theory and research.* Edina, MN: Interaction Book.

Jones, B. (2005). *Marx in Soho: A play on history.* Retrieved April 1, 2010, from http://www.marxinsoho.com/

Kandel, B. (1997). *Trevor's story: Growing up biracial.* Minneapolis, MN: Lerner.

Kasza, K. (1996). *Wolf's chicken stew.* New York: G.P. Putnam's Sons.

Kaufman, G., Raphale, L., & Espeland, P. (1999). *Stick up for yourself: Every kid's guide to personal power and positive self-esteem.* Minneapolis, MN: Free Spirit.

Kaye, C. B. (2003). *The complete guide to service learning: Proven practical ways to engage students in civic responsibility, academic curriculum, and social action.* Minneapolis, MN: Free Spirit.

Kaye, C. B. (2007). *A kid's guide to hunger and homelessness: How to take action!* Minneapolis, MN: Free Spirit.

Keller, L. (2007). *Do unto otters: A book about manners.* New York: Scholastic.

Ketteman, H. (2000). *Armadillo tattletale.* New York: Scholastic.

Kinney, J. (2007). *Diary of a wimpy kid: A novel in cartoons.* New York: Amulet Books.

Kluth, P. (2005). *Differentiating instruction: 5 easy strategies for inclusive classrooms.* Retrieved March 24, 2010, from http://www.paulakluth.com/articles/diffstrategies.html

Knight, M. B. (1996). *Who belongs here? An American story.* Gardiner, ME: Tilbury House.

Kohn, A. (1986). *No contest: The case against competition.* Boston: Houghton and Mifflin.

Kohn, A. (1993). *Punished by rewards: The trouble with gold stars, incentive plans, A's, praise and other bribes.* New York: Houghton Mifflin.

Kreidler, W. J. (1984). *Creative conflict resolution: More than 200 activities for keeping peace in the classroom K–6.* Tucson, AZ: Good Year Books.

Krishnaswami, U. (2006). *Bringing Asha home.* New York: Lee and Low Books.

Lantieri, L. (1995). Waging peace in our schools: Beginning with the children. *Phi Delta Kappan, 76*(5), 386–388.

Lantieri, L, & Goleman, D. (2008). *Building emotional intelligences: Techniques to cultivate inner strength in children.* Boulder, CO: Sounds True.

Levin, E. (1995). *I hate English!* New York: Scholastic.

Lewis, B. A. (1998). *The kids' guide to social action: How to solve the social problems you choose and turn creative thinking into positive action.* Minneapolis, MN: Free Spirit.

Lombard, J. (2006). *Drita, my homegirl.* New York: Puffin Books.

Lord, C. (2008). *Rules.* New York: Scholastic.

Lowry, L. (1998). *Number the stars.* New York: Random House.

Lowry, L. (2002). *The giver.* New York: Random House.

Lowry, L. (2006). *Gathering blue.* New York: Random House.

Ludwig, T. (2005). *My secret bully.* Berkeley, CA: Ten Speed Press.

Ludwig, T. (2006). *Just kidding.* Berkeley, CA: Tricycle Press.

Ludwig, T. (2008). *Trouble talk.* Berkeley, CA: Tricycle Press.

Maguire, A. (1995). *We're all special.* Santa Monica, CA: Portunus.

Martin, A. (1992). *Rachel Parker, kindergarten show-off.* New York: Holiday House.

Massachusetts Advocacy Center. (1990). *Locked in/locked out: Tracking and placement practices in Boston public schools.* Boston: author.

McCain, B. (2001). *Nobody knew what to do: A story about bullying.* Morton Grove, IL: Albert Whitman.

McCully, E. A. (1992). *Mirette on the high wire.* New York: Scholastic.

McGovern, A. (1997). *The lady in the box.* Madiston, CT: Turtle Books.

McKee, D. (2001). *Tusk, tusk.* London: Red Fox Books.

Merrifield, M. (1990). *Come sit by me.* Toronto, Ontario, Canada: Women's Press.

Michaeux Nelson, V. (2002). *Mayfield crossing.* New York: Putnam Juvenile.

Millman, I. (2002). *Moses goes to a concert.* New York: Farrar, Straus and Giroux.

Mills, L. (1991). *The rag coat.* Boston: Little, Brown and Company.

Mochizuki, K. (1993). *Baseball saved us.* New York: Lee and Low Books.

Mochizuki, K. (1995). *Heroes.* New York: Lee & Low Books.

Mochizuki, K. (2003). *Passage to freedom: The Sugihara story.* New York: Lee and Low Books.

Morris, A. (1989). *Bread, bread, bread.* New York: Scholastic.

Morrison, T. (2004). *Remember: The journey to school integration.* Boston: Houghton Mifflin.

Moss, M. (1995). *Regina's big mistake.* Boston: Houghton Mifflin.

Moss, M. (1998). *Amelia's bully survival guide.* New York: Simon and Schuster.

Moss, P. (2004). *Say something.* Gardiner, ME: Tilbury House.

Moss, P., & Tardiff, D. D. (2007). *Our friendship rules.* Gardiner, ME: Tilbury House.

Most, B. (2003). *The cow that went oink.* New York: Scholastic.

Munson, D. (2000). *Enemy pie.* San Francisco: Chronicle Books.

Myers, C., & Bersani, H., Jr. (2008/2009). Ten quick ways to analyze children's books for ableism. *Rethinking Schools Online, 23*(2). Retrieved March 24, 2010, from http://www.rethinkingschools.org/archive/23_02/ten232.shtml

National Council of Social Studies. (2002). *National standards for social studies teachers* (Rev. ed., Vol. 1). Silver Spring, Retrieved March 26, 2010, from http://downloads.ncss.org/NCSSTeacherStandardsVol1-rev2004.pdf

National Council of Social Studies. (n.d.). *Expectations of excellence: Curriculum standards for social studies.* Retrieved March 24, 2010, from http://www.socialstudies.org/standards

National Council of Teachers of English. (1998–2010). *NCTE/IRA standards for teaching the English language arts.* Retrieved March 24, 2010, from http://www.ncte.org/standards

Neblett, C. (1963). If you miss me at the back of the bus [Recorded by P. Seeger]. On *For kids and just plain folks* [CD]. New York: Sony BMG Music Entertainment. (1998)

Neubecker, R. (2006). *Courage of the blue boy.* Berkley, CA: Tricycle Press.

Nigro, J. (1987). Walk a mile [Recorded by Vitamin L]. On *Walk a mile.* Janimation Music BMI. (1989). Lyrics available at http://www.vitaminl.org/lyrics/walkamile.php?lyrics=walk

Nigro, J. (1994). Some right in this world [Recorded by Two of a Kind]. On *So many ways to be smart* [CD]. Cheltenham, PA: Magillacutty Music. (2005) Lyrics and audio recording available at http://www.twoofakind.com/ShowLyrics.asp?id=75

Nivola, C. A. (2008). *Planting the trees of Kenya: The story of Wangari Maathai.* New York: Farrar, Straus and Giroux.

Oakes, J. (1985). *Keeping track.* New Haven, CT: Yale University Press.

Oakes, J. (2005). *Keeping track: How schools structure inequality* (2nd ed.). New Haven, CT: Yale University Press.

O'Leary, M. (1981). Most valuable player [Recorded by Two of a Kind]. On *Patchwork Planet* [CD]. Cheltenham, PA: Magillacutty Music. (2002). Lyrics and mp3 available at http://www.twoofakind.com/ShowLyrics.asp?id=68

Oppenheim, S. L. (1995). *The Lily cupboard: A story of the Holocaust.* New York: HarperCollins.

Orlick, T. (1978). *The cooperative sports and games book: Challenge without competition.* New York: Pantheon Books.

Osterman, K. E. (2000). Students' need for belonging in the school community. *Review of Educational Research, 70,* 323–367.

Otey, M. (1990). *Daddy has a pair of striped shorts.* New York: Farrar, Straus and Giroux.

Oyler, C. (2001). Democratic classrooms and accessible instruction. *Democracy and Education, 14,* 28–31.

Page, N. (1995). *Sing and shine on! The teacher's guide to multicultural song leading.* Portsmouth, NH: Heinemann.

Paley, V. (1992). *You can't say you can't play.* Cambridge, MA: Harvard University Press.

Parnell, P., & Richardson, J. (2005). *And Tango makes three.* New York: Simon and Schuster.

Parr, T. (2001). *It's okay to be different.* New York: Little Brown Books for Young Readers.

Parr, T. (2003). *The family book.* New York: Little Brown Books for Young Readers.

Parr, T. (2009). *The peace book.* New York: Little Brown Books for Young Readers.

Passen, L. (1991). *Fat, fat Rose Marie.* New York: Henry Holt.

Pearpoint, J., Forest, M., & O'Brien, J. (1996). MAP's, circles of friends, and PATH: Powerful tools to help build caring communities. In S. Stainback & W. Stainback (Eds.), *Inclusion: A guide for educators* (pp. 67–86). Baltimore: Paul H. Brookes.

Pearson, E. (2002). *Ordinary Mary's extraordinary deed.* Layton, UT: Gibbs Smith.

Pelham, R. (1982). Under one sky. On *Under one sky* [CD]. Albany, NY: A Gentle Wind.

Pellegrini, N. (1991). *Families are different* New York: Scholastic.

Perl, L., & Blumenthal Lazan, M. (1999). *Four perfect pebbles: A Holocaust story.* New York: Avon Books.

Perry, W., & Smith, G. (1992). What part of no [Recorded by Lorrie Morgan]. On *Watch me* [CD]. Nashville, TN: BNA Records.

Peterson, B. (1991). Helping children critique Columbus books. In B. Bigelow, B. Miner, & B. Peterson (Eds.), *Rethinking Columbus.* Milwaukee, WI: Rethinking Schools.

Peterson, B. (1994). Bias and CD-ROM encyclopedias: How a fifth grade class integrated math and social studies to analyze bias. *Rethinking Schools, 9*(1), 6–7.

Peterson, B. (2003). Columbus and Native American issues in the elementary classroom. In B. Bigelow, & P. Peterson (Eds.), *Rethinking Columbus : The next 500 years.* Milwaukee, WI: Rethinking Schools.

Petrillo, G. (2009). *Keep your ear on the ball.* Gardiner, ME: Tilbury House.

Philbrick, R. (2001). *Freak the mighty.* New York: Scholastic.

Pinkney, A. D. (2008). *Boycott blues: How Rosa Parks inspired a nation.* New York: Greenwillow Books.

Pinkwater, D. M. (1977). *The big orange splot.* New York: Scholastic.

Pirtle, S. (1986). Here's a hand. On *Two hands hold the earth* [CD]. Albany, NY: A Gentle Wind.

Pirtle, S. (1994). Using music to raise issues of racism, bias, and mistreatment. *Cooperative Learning, 14*(2), 46–47.

Pirtle, S. (1998). Sing about us. On *Liking up!* [Book and CD]. Cambridge, MA: Educators for Social Responsibility & Pap/Dis edition.

Pittar, G. (2004). *Milly, Molly and different dads.* Oxford, UK: Tula.

Platt, K. (1977). *Hey, dummy.* Radnor, PA: Chilton.

Pochocki, E. (2006). *The mushroom man.* Gardiner, ME: Tilbury.

Polacco, P. (1992). *Mrs. Katz and Tush.* New York: Bantam.

Polacco, P. (2009). *The butterfly.* New York: Puffin Books.

Polland, B. (2000). *We can work it out: Conflict resolution for children.* Berkeley, CA: Tricycle Press.

Prutzman, P., Burger, M. L., Bodenhamer, G., & Stern, L. (1988). *The friendly classroom for a small planet: Children's creative response to conflict programs.* Wayne, NJ: Avery.

Ransom, J. F. (2005). *Don't squeal unless it's a big deal: A tale of tattletales.* New York: American Psychological Association.

Raposo, J., Stone, J., & Hart, B. (Writers). (1969). One of these things. On *Sesame Street: 40 Years of Sunny Days* [bonus DVD with *Sesame Street: A Celebration—40 Years of Life on the Street*, Har/DVD edition: Gikow, L. A., Author]. New York: Black Dog & Leventhal Publishers (2009). Available from www.amazon.com.

Raven, M. T. (2005). *Let them play.* Chelsea, MI: Sleeping Bear Press.

Reagan, J. (2009). *Always my brother.* Gardiner, ME: Tilbury House.

Ressner, P. (1974). Dudley Pippin and the principal. In C. Hart, L. C. Pogrebin, M. Rodgers, & M. Thomas (Eds.), *Free to be you and me* (pp. 52–53). New York: Bantam Books.

[Review of the book *Because we can change the world: A practical guide to building cooperative, inclusive classroom communities*]. (2000, March 12). Retrieved March 28, 2010, from http://www.amazon.com/Because-Can-Change-World-Cooperative/product-reviews/0205174892

Reynolds Naylor, P. (1991). *Shiloh.* New York: Simon & Schuster.

Ringold, F. (1995). *Aunt Harriet's underground railroad in the sky.* New York: Crown.

Romain, T. (1997). *Bullies are a pain in the brain.* Minneapolis, MN: Free Spirit.

Rumford, J. (2008). *Silent music: A story of Baghdad.* New York: Roaring Book Press.

Rylant, C. (1996). *An angel for Solomon Singer.* New York: Orchard Book.

Salidor, S. (2005). I've got peace in my fingers. On *Come and make a circle 2* [CD]. Chicago: Author.

Salisbury, C. L., Evans, I. M., & Palombaro, M. M. (1997). Collaborative problem-solving to promote the inclusion of young children with significant disabilities in primary grades. *Exceptional Children, 63,* 195–209.

Salisbury, G. (2005). *Under the blood-red sun.* New York: Bantam.

Saltzberg, B. (2003). *Crazy hair day.* Boston: Walker Books.

Sanders, P., & Myers, S. (1996). *What do you know about bullying.* Markham, Ontario, Canada: Fitzhenry and Whiteside.

Sanders, P., & Myers, S. (2000). *What do you know about racism?* London: Franklin Watts. [P/I/A]

Sapon-Shevin, M. (1982a). Mentally retarded characters in children's literature. *Children's Literature in Education, 13*(1), 19–31.

Sapon-Shevin, M. (1982b). You can't judge kids by their covers. *The Advocate, 11*(2), 80–90.

Sapon-Shevin, M. (1986). Teaching cooperation. In G. Cartledge & J. F. Milburn (Eds.), *Teaching social skills to children: Innovative approaches* (2nd ed., pp. 270–302). New York: Pergamon Press.

Sapon-Shevin, M. (1988). A minicourse for junior high students. *Social Education, 52*(4), 272–275.

Sapon-Shevin, M. (1990). Student support through cooperative learning. In W. Stainback, & S. Stainback (Eds.), *Support networks for inclusive schooling: Interdependent integrated education* (pp. 65–79). Baltimore: Paul H. Brookes.

Sapon-Shevin, M. (1994a). *Playing favorites: Gifted education and the disruption of community.* Albany: State University of New York Press.

Sapon-Shevin, M. (1994b). Using songs cooperatively to help students take a stand. *Cooperative Learning, 14*(2), 44–45.

Sapon-Shevin, M. (1996a). Full inclusion as disclosing tablet: Revealing the flaws in our present system. *Theory into Practice, 35*(1), 35–41.

Sapon-Shevin, M. (1996b). Ability differences in the classroom: Teaching and learning in inclusive classrooms. In D. Byrnes & G. Kiger (Eds.), *Common bond: Anti-bias teaching in a diverse society,* (2nd ed., pp. 35–47). Wheaton, MD: Association for Childhood Education International.

Sapon-Shevin, M. (1996c). Celebrating diversity, creating community: Curriculum that honors and builds on differences. In S. Stainback & W. Stainback (Eds.), *Inclusion: A guide for educators* (pp. 255–270). Baltimore: Paul H. Brookes.

Sapon-Shevin, M. (2007). *Widening the circle: The power of inclusive classrooms.* Boston: Beacon Press.

Sapon-Shevin, M., Ayres, B. J., & Duncan, J. (1994). Cooperative learning and inclusion. In J. S. Thousand, R. A. Villa, & A. I. Nevin (Eds.), *Creativity and collaborative learning: A practical guide to empowering students and teachers* (pp. 45–58). Baltimore: Paul H. Brookes.

Sapon-Shevin, M. & Breyer, R. (2004). *And nobody said anything: Uncomfortable conversations about diversity* [DVD]. Syracuse, NY: Syracuse University.

Sapon-Shevin, M., Dobbelaere, A., Corrigan, C. R., Goodman, K., & Mastin, M. C. (1998). Promoting inclusive behavior in inclusive classrooms: "You can't say you can't play." In L. H. Meyer, H. S. Park, M. Grenot-Scheyer, I. S. Schwartz, & B. Harry (Eds.), *Making friends: The influences of culture and development* (pp. 105–132). Baltimore: Paul H. Brookes.

Sapon-Shevin, M., & Schniedewind, N. (1989/1990). Selling cooperative learning without selling it short. *Educational Leadership, 47*(4), 63–65.

Sapon-Shevin, M., & Schniedewind, N. (1990). Cooperative learning as empowering pedagogy. In C. Sleeter (Ed.), *Empowerment through multicultural education* (pp. 159–178). New York: SUNY Press.

Sapon-Shevin, M., & Schniedewind, N. (1993). If cooperative learning is the answer, what are the questions? *Journal of Education, 174*(2), 11–37.

Sapon-Shevin, M., & Smith, C. J. (2004). *EndRacism/EndInjustice: Challenging oppression, building allies.* Available through Syracuse University, New York, Center for the Support of Teaching and Learning (CSTL).

📖 Savageau, C. (2006). *Muskrat will be swimming.* Gardiner, ME: Tilbury House.

📖 Schiff, N. (1973). *Some things you just can't do by yourself.* Berkeley, CA: New Seed Press.

Schimmel, N. (lyrics) & Fjell, J. (music). (n.d.) "I think of a dragon." Sheet music and recording available at http://www.sisterschoice.com/moresongs.html

Schniedewind, N., & Davidson, E. (1987). *Cooperative learning, cooperative lives.* New York: Harcourt Religion.

Schniedewind, N., & Davidson, E. (1998). *Open minds to equality: A sourcebook for learning activities to affirm diversity and promote equity* (2nd ed.). Needham Heights, MA: Allyn and Bacon.

Schniedewind, N., & Davidson, E. (2006). *Open minds to equality: A sourcebook of learning activities to affirm diversity and promote equity* (3rd ed.). Milwaukee, WI: Rethinking Schools.

Schniedewind, N., & Sapon-Shevin, M. (1998). Professional development for socially conscious cooperative learning. In C. M. Brody & N. Davidson (Eds.), *Professional development and cooperative learning: Issues and approaches* (pp. 203–219). Albany, NY: SUNY Press.

📖 Schreck, K. H. (2006). *Lucy's family tree.* Gardiner, ME: Tilbury House.

📖 Schuman, C. (2003). *Jenny is scared! When sad things happen in the world.* Washington, DC: Magination Press.

Schrock, J. W. (2008). *Give a goat.* Gardiner, ME: Tilbury House.

Schroeder, A. (1996). *Minty: A story of young Harriet Tubman.* New York: Dial Books.

Scieszka, J. (1996). *The true story of the 3 little pigs.* New York: Viking Kestrel.

Scott, E. (2000). *Friends!* New York: Atheneum Books for Young Readers.

Sendak, M. (1991). *Alligators all around.* New York HarperCollins.

Senger, E. S., Platte, S. B., & Van Zandt, J. (1997, March). Mathematical meaning in context. *Teaching Children Mathematics, 3,* 362–366.

Seuss, Dr. (1984). *The butter battle book.* New York: Random House.

Shanker, A. (1994, fall). A full circle? Inclusion: A 1994 view. *The Circle.* Atlanta, GA: Governor's Council on Developmental Disabilities.

Shea, P. D. (2006). *The carpet boy's gift.* Gardiner, ME: Tilbury House.

Skutch, R. (1995). *Who's in a family?* Berkeley, CA: Tricycle Press.

Smith, I. (2010). *Half spoon of rice: A survival story of the Cambodian genocide.* Manhattan Beach, CA: East West Discovery Press.

Southern Poverty Law Center. (n.d.). Mix it up. *Teaching tolerance.* Montgomery, AL: Author. Retrieved March 26, 2010, from http://www.tolerance.org/mix-it-up.

Stallings, M. A. (1993, May). When Peter came to Mrs. Stalling's class. *NEA Today, 22.*

Stallings, M. A. (1994, December). *Educating Peter.* A presentation at the Association for Persons with Severe Handicaps Conference, Alliance for Action, Atlanta, GA.

Staub, D. (1998). *Delicate threads: Friendships between children with and without disabilities.* Bethesda, MD: Woodbine House.

Steig, W. (2009). *Amos and Boris.* New York: Farrar, Straus and Giroux.

Streibel, B. (1977). *Conflict resolution in children's literature.* Madison, WI: Center for Conflict Resolution.

Stuve-Bodeen, S. (1998). *We'll paint the octopus red.* Bethesda, MD: Woodbine House.

Stuve-Bodeen, S. (2005). *The best worst brother.* Bethesda, MD: Woodbine House.

Surat, M. M. (1989). *Angel child, dragon child.* New York: Carnival Press.

Suvanjieff, I., & Engle, D. G. (2008). *Peace jam: A billion simple acts of peace.* New York: Puffin Books.

Tate, J. (n.d.). *Voices from a kindergarten table.* Unpublished manuscript.

Tatum, B. (1997). *"Why are all the Black kids sitting together in the cafeteria?" A psychologist explains the development of racial identity.* New York: Basic Books.

Tomlinson, C. (2003). *Fulfilling the promise of the differentiated classrooms: Strategies and tools for responsive teaching.* Alexandria, VA: Association for Supervision and Curriculum Development.

Thousand, J. S., Villa, R. A., & Nevin, A. I. (Eds.). (1994). *Creativity and collaborative learning: A practical guide to empowering students and teachers.* Baltimore: Paul H. Brookes.

Tsuchiya, Y. (1997). *Faithful elephants: A true story of animals, people and the war.* New York: Trumpet Books.

Trivizas, E. (2004). *The three little wolves and the big bad pig.* New York: Scholastic.

Turner, A. (1995). *Nettie's trip south.* New York: Macmillan.

Tyler, M. (2005). *The skin you live in.* Chicago: Chicago Children's Museum.

Uchida, Y. (1992). *Journey home.* New York: Macmillan.

Uchida, Y. (1996). *The bracelet.* New York: Philomel Books.

Uchida, Y. (2004). *Journey to topaz.* New York: Athenaeum.

Uhlberg, M. (2010). *Dad, Jackie and me.* Atlanta, GA: Peachtree Press.

Vander Zee. R. (2003). *Erika's story.* North Mankato, MN: Creative Editions.

Van der Klift, E., & Kunc, N. (1994). Beyond benevolence: Friendship and the politics of help. In J. S. Thousand, R. A. Villa, & A. I. Nevin (Eds.), *Creativity and collaborative learning: A practical guide to empowering students and teachers* (pp. 391–401). Baltimore: Paul H. Brookes.

Verdick, E. (2004). *Words are not for hurting.* Minneapolis, MN: Free Spirit.

Villa, R. A., & Thousand, J. S. (1986). Students collaboration: An essential for curriculum delivery in the 21st century. In S. Stainback & W. Stainback (Eds.), *Inclusion: A guide for educators* (pp. 171–192). Baltimore: Paul H. Brookes.

Viorst, J. (2009). *Alexander and the terrible, horrible, no good, very bad day.* New York: Atheneum Books.

Waber, B. (2000). *Ira sleeps over.* Boston: Houghton Mifflin.

Waber, B. (2002). *Courage.* New York: Walter Lorraine Books.

Wade, R. (2007). *Social studies for social justice: Teaching strategies for the elementary classroom.* New York: Teachers College Press.

Watkins, H. (1963). I'm gonna sit at the welcome table [traditional]. On *Sing for freedom: The story of the civil rights movement through its songs* [CD, Catalogue #SFW40032]. Washington, DC: Smithsonian Folk ways Recordings. (1990) Recording available at http://www.folkways.si.edu/albumdetails.aspx?itemid=2061

Weinstein. M., & Goodman, J. (1980). *Play fair: Everybody's guide to noncompetitive play.* San Luis Obispo, CA: Impact.

Weiss, E., Prutzman, P., & Silber, N. (1986). *Children's songs for a friendly planet: Kindergarten through grade 6.* Burnsville, NC: World Around Songs.

Wiggins, G., & McTighe, J. (2005). *Understanding by design.* Alexandria, VA: Association for Supervision and Curriculum Development.

Wiles, D. (2005). *Freedom summer.* New York: Aladdin.

Winter, J. (2005). *The librarian of Basra: A true story from Iraq.* New York: Harcourt.

Winter, J. (2008). *Wangari's trees of peace: A true story from Africa.* New York: Harcourt.

Wolf, B. (1995). *Homeless.* New York: Orchard Books.

Wolf, B. (2003). *Coming to America: A Muslim family's story.* New York: Lee & Low Books.

Woodson, J. (2001). *The other side.* New York: G.P. Putnam's Sons.

YogaBeez. (2007). *Yogakids.* Retrieved March 26, 2010, from http://www.yogabeez.com/yogakids.html

Yolen, J. (1996). *The encounter.* San Anselmo, CA: Sandpiper.

Zimmer, T. V. (2007). *Reaching for sun.* New York: Bloomsbury Books.

Zinn, H. (1994). *You can't be neutral on a moving train: A personal history of our times.* Boston: Beacon.

Index

CORWIN

A SAGE Company

The Corwin logo—a raven striding across an open book—represents the union of courage and learning. Corwin is committed to improving education for all learners by publishing books and other professional development resources for those serving the field of PreK–12 education. By providing practical, hands-on materials, Corwin continues to carry out the promise of its motto: **"Helping Educators Do Their Work Better."**